D1168215

JOAN BAUER

JOAN BAUER

ALLEEN PACE NILSEN

TEEN READS: STUDENT COMPANIONS TO YOUNG ADULT LITERATURE

GREENWOOD PRESS
WESTPORT, CONNECTICUT • LONDON

Library of Congress Cataloging-in-Publication Data

Nilsen, Alleen Pace.
  Joan Bauer / Alleen Pace Nilsen.
    p. cm. — (Teen reads: student companions to young adult literature)
  Includes bibliographical references (p.) and index.
  ISBN 978-0-313-33550-1 (alk. paper)
  1. Bauer, Joan, 1951—Criticism and interpretation. 2. Young adult fiction,
American—History and criticism. 3. Women and literature—United
States—History—21st century. 4. Youth—Books and reading—United
States—History—21st century. I. Title.
  PS3552.A83615Z76 2007
  813'.54—dc22
  [B]   2007008191

British Library Cataloguing in Publication Data is available.

Library of Congress Catalog Card Number: 2007008191
ISBN-13: 978-0-313-33550-1
ISBN-10: 0-313-33550-8
ISSN: 1553-5096

First published in 2007

Greenwood Press, 88 Post Road West, Westport, CT 06881
An imprint of Greenwood Publishing Group, Inc.
www.greenwood.com

Printed in the United States of America

The paper used in this book complies with the
Permanent Paper Standard issued by the National
Information Standards Organization (Z39.48–1984).

10 9 8 7 6 5 4 3 2 1

To my grandchildren—Taryn, Britton, Kami, Erich, David, Lauren, Michael, Jenna, Avery, Jim, and Luke—who remind me of some of my favorite Joan Bauer characters

CONTENTS

Series Foreword

When young readers first find a book they love, the result is magical. A whole new universe opens up to them with possibilities as limitless as their own young imaginations. Finding a favorite author brings with it a powerful curiosity about that author as person and a thirst for more books from him or her. The Teen Reads series brings to young readers just the information they need to satisfy their curiosity and slake their thirst. Chapters about the authors' lives reveal to the young reader that this person was once young, too, with all the trials and tribulations of young people today. Sometimes, young readers will be surprised to find that their favorite author had a very difficult journey in life, and the admiration they hold for that author will grow even more with one wonderful benefit: the realization that challenges create the people we become and adversity does not equal failure in life.

We have chosen six of the most popular and accomplished authors who write for young adults: Joan Bauer, Sharon Creech, Chris Crutcher, Walter Dean Myers, Gary Paulsen, and Tamora Pierce. These six authors represent a priceless wealth of life experience, distilled through an author's heart and soul and poured out onto the page in stories of adventure, challenge, love, hardship and triumph, some set in the Old West, some on another planet, and some right here and now. Each book in the Teen Reads series will delight young readers with connections between their favorite authors books and the events in their lives that lead them to this vocation in life and sometimes even to the specific settings, characters, and events in their stories.

For each important novel or series of novels, readers will find synopses of the setting, characters, plots, themes, and literary techniques along with interesting information that sheds light on how and why the author chose to write these books as they did. Using this series will help young readers to make connections with themselves, the world, and other books as they dig deeper in investigating their favorite authors and the books they have written. In addition, each book in this series will help to answer the foremost question on very reader's mind who is lucky enough to find joy in the work of a particular writer: "What else did this author write?"

James B. Blasingame

PREFACE

I fantasize about a classroom in which everyone reads a Joan Bauer book, and toward the end of the two weeks that are devoted to the project, I get to peek into their classroom and see small groups getting ready to share their reading experiences. In one corner are students who read *Rules of the Road* because they are excited about getting their learner's permits; they are making YIELD, MERGE LEFT, and CAUTION signs to use as props when they explain some of the things they've learned about driving. Other students with restaurant experience are practicing a skit inspired by *Hope Was Here,* while another group is putting together a PowerPoint presentation showing that such American-looking shoes as NBA athletic sneakers, Sesame Street light-up shoes for kids, and Cherokee work boots are actually made in China. They are pulling in various Web sites to illustrate the kinds of big business complications they learned about in *Best Foot Forward.* Two students who read *Thwonk* are preparing a demonstration on the principles of fine arts photography that A. J. McCreary taught them, while four outdoorsy types who read *Backwater* are preparing a wilderness survival lesson, and those who read *Stand Tall* are looking at Web sites and reading news accounts to compare the flood that ran through Tree's house in the midwestern town of Ripley to the Hurricane Katrina floods that destroyed people's homes in New Orleans. Two boys and a girl who read *Sticks* are trying to replicate Mickey and Arlen's science fair project connecting mathematics principles to the game of pool, and two other students are devising the kind of quiz that Ellie took in *Squashed* to measure the potential for building a better relationship with her father.

One of the secrets to the success of this kind of classroom reading experience is that students have something to say about which book they choose to read. And here is where my book on Joan Bauer enters the picture. I've written it as a reference tool to help young readers decide which of Bauer's books they want to read. And once they've made their choices, then I hope that what I have written about the novel or the short story will help them to get more from their reading.

Schools are sometimes criticized for teaching only one kind of reading—the kind where students pick up a book and beginning on page one read every word until they get to the last word on the last page. I don't want teenagers to feel that they have to do this with my book. I want them to read the introductory material, and then to skim and to be selective in choosing the chapters they read. As soon as they feel well acquainted with Joan Bauer and her writing, I want them to set aside my book and go and read Bauer's short stories and her novels. In the preface to some of the Lemony Snicket books, Daniel Handler advises readers to go and find something to read that is more cheerful than his *Series of Unfortunate Events*; however, he is only kidding, while I am dead serious. I will consider my book a failure if a high school student reads this book *instead of* reading Joan Bauer's books.

But judging from the variety of students in my young adult literature classes at Arizona State University, there are readers who will benefit from reading this entire book. These include teachers and librarians who want to know Bauer's work so well that they can introduce the most appropriate titles to individual readers. They will also benefit from knowing Joan Bauer as a touchstone example of a contemporary writer who creates not only likable characters, but also provides her readers with something extra. A second audience for careful reading is the growing body of creative writers who, thanks to a youth-oriented society and the big-business aspects of today's publishing and entertainment worlds, are increasingly thinking about writing books for teenagers. Writers, both beginners and professionals, can learn a lot from Joan Bauer's success, especially her treatment of serious subjects in ways that make readers smile and sometimes laugh out loud. One of her most interesting techniques is the manner in which she builds the tone and the style of her stories by creating metaphors related to the subject of her books, as with the dozens of tree-related allusions in *Stand Tall* and the food-related allusions in *Hope Was Here*.

A cliché that has been fashionable ever since readers and critics rejected the didactic books written for young people during the 1800s and the early 1900s is that young people do not want to learn things from their leisure-time reading. The facts are not quite so simple. Of course they do not want to be pounded with obvious moral messages, but Bauer has proven that they very much want to learn about more aspects of life than they can personally experience. America is a work-oriented society in which people are defined by the jobs they perform. Bauer shows that it is not so much the job one holds as how one performs it. She writes about teenagers who have a passion for what they do above and beyond going to school. With Hope it is food service, with Jenna it is selling shoes, with Ellie it is growing prizewinning pumpkins, with Arlen it is becoming a world-class pool player, with A. J. it is fine arts photography, and with Ivy it is mastering the art of interviewing people and writing their histories.

I have discussed both the short stories and the novels that Bauer has written for young readers between 1992, when she won the Delacorte Press Prize for her first young adult novel (*Squashed*), and the end of 2006. Chapter 1 is an introduction to Bauer through an interview, and chapter 2 is loosely organized around Bauer's favorite literary techniques, which means that the stories are not mentioned in any particular order. Chapters 3 through 10 are arranged according to the publication dates of Bauer's novels. I introduce each of these chapters by tying the subject matter of the book into Bauer's own life, followed by an introduction of the characters and the setting and a discussion about the plot, the themes, and the literary techniques.

For purposes of illustration, in the chapters treating the novels, I chose to focus on different literary techniques with each of the books. As of the beginning of 2007, this is a complete collection of Bauer's fiction for young readers, but because she is an active writer, there will undoubtedly be more books, articles, and stories in future years. Concepts that I hope readers will acquire from reading not only my book on Joan Bauer but also the other books in this series include:

- Criticism is not always negative.
- There is more to literary criticism than saying "I like it!" or "I don't like it."
- The purpose of literary criticism is to help readers get more from their experience with a book.

- Reading reviews is an efficient way for readers to help themselves decide which books will be the most rewarding for them to read.
- Good authors, regardless of the age of their protagonists, make use of sophisticated literary techniques.
- Young people's experiences are worthy of being depicted in powerful books, which might inspire more young people to write their own stories and more people of all ages to respect and enjoy such stories.

In closing, I need to thank the English Department at Arizona State University for supporting my interest in young adult literature, namely our department chair, Neal Lester, my colleague James Blasingame, our secretarial assistants, Bonnie Rigmaiden and Erika L. Watt, and student workers Elizabeth Dern and Greg Rambo. I also need to thank my daughter, Nikki Wickman, and her sons, Jim and Luke, for inspiring me with their insights about Bauer's writing.

Alleen Pace Nilsen
Tempe, Arizona
February 2007

CHAPTER ONE

AN INTERVIEW WITH JOAN BAUER

AS JOAN BAUER WRITES on her Web site, she has "always believed in comic entrances," and when she was born on July 12, 1951, and the nurse put her in her mother's arms, she had a severe case of hiccups and "no discernible forehead." However the hiccups soon went away and so did her caved-in forehead, although not as quickly as did the hiccups.

Bauer grew up in River Forest, Illinois, and as early as first grade knew that she wanted a career in which she could make people laugh. This was not an easy concept to get across when adults asked her what she wanted to be. Nevertheless, she kept her dream and relied on the fact that her mother was one of those high school English teachers with a "great comic sense," while her grandmother, "Nana" had been a professional storyteller. Nana never said, "Now I'm going to tell you a funny story." Instead, she would just tell a story, and the humor would flow naturally because of her personality and how she and her characters saw the world. She showed Bauer "the difference between derisive humor, which hurts others, and laughter that comes from the heart." She was a keen observer of people and showed Bauer how to look beyond surface appearances if she really wanted to understand people.

Bauer's first book was published in 1992 when *Squashed* won the Delacorte Prize for a First Young Adult Novel. Since then, she has written eight other books as well as short stories and several articles and essays. *Hope Was Here* received a Newbery Honor Medal, and *Rules of the Road* was chosen as one of the top young adult books of the last twenty-five years by the American Library Association. Her books, which are listed on p. 155, regularly win statewide contests in which readers vote for their favorite book. They also appear on best book lists compiled by various committees of the American Library Association, the National

Council of Teachers of English, and the International Reading Association, as well as by publishers and the editors of newspapers and magazines.

Bauer made the statements printed here through an e-mail interview conducted in September of 2006, except for the statement on humor, which she had sent me earlier for the 2001 edition of *Literature for Today's Young Adults*. I had almost finished writing this book when I learned that on February 3, 2007, Bauer was going to be a featured speaker at the Brigham Young University mid-winter symposium on books for young readers in Provo, Utah. I contacted the symposium chair and asked if I could share a meal with Bauer or squeeze in a brief interview. He did better than that. Since my husband, Don L. F. Nilsen, and I would be flying to Salt Lake City and then driving to Provo, he said we could meet Bauer at the Salt Lake City airport on Friday morning and then drive her back to the airport on Sunday. During her visit, I could be her host and introduce her at the general session as well as at three question-and-answer sessions, and also help during the autograph session. This meant that for two-and-a-half days, I shadowed Bauer and was privileged to see how she treats formal audiences, small groups, and individuals.

My job during the autographing was to move people along, so I opened the books to the signing page (the one with the author's name on it) and enforced the previously established "five-book-only" rule—mostly by shifting someone's sixth book to the person behind them. Being accustomed to bookstore sales, I discouraged a girl who brought only her diary for a signature, but Bauer happily signed the diary and added a personal note.

I made people write their names and any short message they wanted on sticky notes. As the afternoon wore on, I began to sound less than cheerful, even telling people if they wanted her to write a message in five books, they had to write it on five sticky notes. We had sort of a bad-cop, good-cop routine, with her cheerfulness never waning. She was a genius at copying what was on the sticky notes and signing her name, all the while smiling and maintaining eye contact and making sure she pronounced everyone's name correctly. We were the last of the three speakers to finish autographing. I was too busy to count so I don't know whether it was because more people were in Bauer's line, or whether she took longer with each person, but I do know that everyone in line went away smiling and looking fondly at what she had written.

I had begun the *Squashed* chapter with the statement that Bauer is not a patient person. I told this to Bauer and said the afternoon had convinced me that I should probably go back and change that lead-in, but she laughingly told me to leave it. She is not patient in waiting for publishers' decisions or for reviews to come out, but meeting people who have read—or plan to read—one of her books is a genuine pleasure because she feels a connection.

She is a people person, which she had already proven in the question-and-answer sessions each attended by thirty to forty people. Three times as the room was filling, she walked around and personally greeted several people, often using their names. When I asked what magic was afoot, she explained that she had taught a one-week writing workshop at the university a few summers ago and she remembered some of the people. She even asked one young woman how she was coming along with the novel that the two of them had worked on.

I had sent Bauer a draft of this book so that she could use it for airplane reading on the way to the symposium. She did not argue with my basic observations, but kindly corrected little mistakes, as when I said Jenna's grandmother had her tailor shop on Clark Avenue (it was Clark Street) in Chicago, and that after September 11, 2001, her daughter was going to the University of Chicago as a freshman (she was a sophomore). Over the three days, I took notes on comments she made both in her speeches and to individuals. I think this made for a better book thanks to the BYU organizers, Chris Crowe and Rachel Wadham, who kindly shared their guest of honor. Comments from Bauer that are not otherwise identified come from these three days or from comments that she sent by e-mail after she arrived home.

Other interviews, as well as a biography, comments on each of her books, and five articles that Bauer has written are available on her Web site, http://www.joanbauer.com. It is an unusually fine Web site probably because it is managed with love by her husband, Evan. Besides identifying him as her "squash partner" on the dedication page of her first book, Bauer explains that he is a computer scientist working with some of the biggest banks in New York. If the family had not been in Connecticut

Joan Bauer. Photograph by Evan Bauer.

packing their household goods in preparation for moving to Brooklyn on September 12, 2001, Evan would have been at work in Windows on the World, located in Tower One of the World Trade Center on the day the terrorists attacked. People he worked with died that day.

ON BEING IN A BOOK LIKE THIS

It's such an honor. After I read a draft of the book, I told Alleen Nilsen, "You taught me so much about my writing and writing in general!" I got such a kick out of reading the assessment of how my made-up stories follow "the rules" and how some of my hidden secrets (like what I name certain characters) can be seen in a broader light.

As I read this critical assessment of the narratives, the characters' challenges, the themes, the humor, I couldn't help but remember how in each of the novels, there was a point in the writing process where I felt hopelessly blocked. I arm-wrestled words. I told characters to stop being difficult. I gave up. But not for long. Ultimately, I let the characters tell me the story.

That's always the breakthrough moment.

Then I could understand Ellie's complicated relationship with her father in *Squashed*. I found the bandwidth to comprehend the irritable cupid in *Thwonk*. I learned to think like a ten-year-old boy in *Sticks* after following my husband around, pleading, "I need to know everything you remember about being ten." I could face down the dark memories of my dad's alcoholism in *Rules of the Road* and then find the humor in the story. I saw that Ivy's passion for history wasn't just internal, but a quest in *Backwater*. I could cook with all the ingredients I'd laid out in *Hope Was Here*—comfort food, politics, cancer, and the search to belong—and actually make a stew. I found the courage to write about wars on the battlefield and in our minds and hearts in *Stand Tall* while living in New York City after 9-11. I understood the depth of my characters from earlier books as with Jenna and Mrs. Gladstone in *Rules of the Road* and I knew they had the sole to stomp on new shoe evil in *Best Foot Forward*.

What is it like to be in a book like this? For me, it's the joy of remembering. The exhilaration of when *Squashed* first came out; the first time I ever spoke to a group (I spoke too fast and clung to the podium); the first time I got a letter from a student announcing: *Dear Mrs. Bauer, I want to congratulate you on your success as an authoress. This means you have become homework.* To become homework; to be an assembly at a middle school; to have a student grab my hand and say, "*I couldn't put your book down. I read it at breakfast, on the bus, and all through math and biology!*" These are the special rewards of this business. I carry them with me in the deep places of my heart.

ON MY OWN TEEN READING

As a teenager, I was a reader. I breathed in words even though I had no exposure to what today we call young adult literature. My mother was a high school English teacher, my grandmother was a storyteller—what a set-up for a budding writer. I found such truth in fiction—in many ways, it helped me make sense of the world around me. I was a teenager in the sixties, that decade of drugs, social change, the Vietnam War, and the Beatles. I remember where I was when JFK was shot (seventh grade math class); I remember weeping when Martin Luther King Jr. and Bobby Kennedy were assassinated. I was looking for stories that explained the madness, expressed the rage, and helped me feel safe. So my reading was rich and varied. I was reading lots of plays including *Who's Afraid of Virginia Woolf?, Tea House of the August Moon,* and several plays by Thornton Wilder. I was fascinated with dialogue and was studying the *Dick Van Dyke Show* because I thought the writing was just so superior. I wanted to be a comedy writer back then, so Bill Cosby's material was important to me. *The Smothers Brothers Show—That Was the Week That Was*, and the satirical songs of Tom Lehr—that's where I was at back then. I remember getting very involved with Joseph Conrad's books, *Lord Jim*, et cetera, as well as *The Great Gatsby* and some of Hemingway's books. It feels awfully dark now, but I simply adored Salinger's short stories—among them, *A Perfect Day for Bananafish*.

I was into short, sharp writing: the poetry of Bob Dylan's songs—I'd just read those lyrics—and I loved Phil Ochs as another poet songwriter. I was a Robert Frost fan: "The woods are lovely, dark and deep, but I have promises to keep, and miles to go before I sleep, and miles to go before I sleep." I think of that line so often these days. I was reading the newspaper a great deal and because I lived in Chicago I was a huge Mike Royko fan. We had quite a library in my house—I can remember reading and rereading a book, *Mr. Jones Meet the Master*, about the Reverend Peter Marshall. I also remember reading C. S. Lewis's *The Screwtape Letters*, Jack London's *Call of the Wild*, Jean Kerr's funny comic essays (I loved her stuff!), Max Schulman's funny novels, and a well-worn copy of Leo Rostens' *The Americanization of Hyman Kaplan*. I also appreciated Robert Benchley's and E. B. White's stunning essays. My favorite novel was *To Kill a Mockingbird*.

ON HAVING ONE OF MY BOOKS MADE INTO A FILM

I studied screenwriting with single-minded focus, and even though I never got as far as to have a screenplay made into a movie, I learned a great deal about the process. When I'm writing, I can see the story play out visually in my mind. I can hear the characters talking. I will often read the dialog I'm writing out loud to get the proper flow of the conversation. I would love to see any number of my books as movies, but if I had to choose, I'd pick *Hope Was Here*. I think it's a visual book with the crazy restaurant scenes and the fish-out-of-water theme of big city girl Hope coming to teeny Mulhoney, the land of lactose. I think the struggle for honor in politics is a theme we'll always be dealing with in this country and beyond. And we could finally see (although not taste) Addie's food!

ON HOOKING READERS WITH HUMOR

I like the word *hook*. It floods my mind with images. Captain Hook reaching to snatch a lost boy. When my daughter was a teenager, her wall was covered in hooks of various sizes upon which she hung mysterious treasures. I think of boxing where a *short hook* is delivered with a circular motion, the *hook check* in ice hockey which knocks the puck away from an opponent, the *hook-up* of our technological age that connects different parts to one another forming a system, or, as Webster's calls it, "a state of cooperation or alliance often between antagonistic elements."

Using humor as a hook incorporates all of these approaches. Humor reaches out and grabs us; it is a tool upon which to hang other things; it can define character, develop plot, be quick, sharp, and deliver its message with lightning clarity.... Laughter builds bridges between people. It can connect different people, seemingly unconnectable, to universal truths.

We would do well to heed the words of William Zinsser: "What I want to do is to make people laugh so that they'll see things clearly." When Woody Allen quips that his mother's two passions are God and carpeting, we understand instantly. We know people like that; perhaps we're like that. His statement rings so clearly that it is forever etched in our minds—like a remarkable photograph that captures an image or feeling. Every writer, every humorist, strives to find those defining words that say it all.

Humor teaches us about ourselves in non-threatening ways. Take obsession—a subject, sadly, in which I excel. I am passionately obsessive about my work—writing fuels me and it never, ever stays just in my office. It oozes out everywhere and touches all that I do. Depending on the occasion, this can either be wonderfully charming or bleakly inappropriate. When it is the latter, being able to laugh at myself very often saves the day. One of my favorite Bible verses is the one from Genesis: "The Lord has made me to laugh so that all who hear me will laugh with me."

Mark Twain said the secret ingredient in humor isn't joy, but pain. Humor often squeezes laughter from painful experiences. Does that mean we're laughing at the pain? Not at all. It means we've snatched hope from the midst of difficulty. And hope is humor's most sacred gift.

ON FAVORITE SCENES

I have lots of favorite scenes in my books and with the notable exception of the one in *Squashed,* they each required several drafts. The pumpkin weigh-in in *Squashed* is my favorite—when Cyril Pool's despicable pumpkin, Big Daddy, has, shall we say, a cosmic comeuppance. I had written an entirely different second half to the book and a good friend read it and told me I had to change it. At first I didn't think I could, but then the atmosphere seemed to change in my office and I was off like a racehorse (or a pumpkin rolling downhill) and I wrote, feeling Ellie's overcoming nature leading me on. I was laughing and whooping and totally satisfied. Okay, that's all I'm going to say. You have to read it.

Other most loved scenes are:

- The moment in *Thwonk* when the cupid comes alive. I really hope you like that scene because I killed myself getting it right. I had so much trouble with the cupid initially that I almost took him out of the story, but my daughter Jean saved him from literary extinction.
- The part in *Hope Was Here* when G. T. announces he is running for mayor and how crazy things get at the diner after that.
- The scene in *Stand Tall* when Tree, his grandfather, and the Trash King are at the Vietnam Vets Memorial. I lived in Alexandria, Virginia, years ago and would go to that memorial so often— it helped me deal with that war in profound ways.
- *Rules of the Road* has one of my all-time favorite characters— Harry Bender, the world's greatest shoe salesman. I had such fun writing the scene when Jenna first meets him at the bigger than life, three-story Dallas Gladstone's Shoe store "with a huge white spiral staircase that wrapped around the largest plastic foot in the universe."

ON FANTASY AS A GENRE

I enjoy writing fantasy and feel it opens up a funny and freeing approach to my storytelling. I don't think I will ever move completely away from realistic fiction, but I do have several fantasy ideas I'd like to try out. It's a different experience writing fantasy—I don't feel like I have the restrictions that I do in realistic fiction. Although, I hasten to add that *Thwonk* was a difficult book to write—I almost gave up on the cupid, but that was because I was trying too hard to explain him. The gift of fantasy is that we enter into the world, we suspend disbelief. *Thwonk* is still one of my favorite books. I think humor and fantasy are compatible because humor is really about letting the absurd break into your perspective. So, watch this space. Hopefully more fantasy will be forthcoming.

ON DEVISING TITLES

Titles are such complicated things. Sometimes I just know—like *Squashed* and *Rules of the Road,* but others, like *Hope Was Here* and *Stand Tall* were hard to figure out. Those two had numerous titles. *Hope* was actually called *Welcome Stairways* after the diner, and at the final hour we changed the title *and* the cover art. I was breathing into a brown paper bag from the stress. A title just has to be right. I don't like really long titles, so I try to keep them short and sweet. I suppose *Joan Bauer's First Novel, Joan Bauer's Second Novel,* et cetera, wouldn't quite work.

ON CREATING CHARACTER NAMES

Names are so important to me. Maybe it's because I always thought my life would be more exciting if my name ended in a vowel, like *Bianca.* I never liked Joan until I got older. My mom told me what it meant, too (gift of God), and I wrestled with all that pressure. I've always been interested in what names mean and I picked A. J. (Allison Jean) McCreary's name based on the fact that *Allison* means one who deserves to be loved. That is a big part of A. J.'s journey in *Thwonk.*

ON MY OWN EDUCATION

My education is a complicated story. I had a very hard time as a young person. By sophomore year in high school, my emotions dive-bombed and so did my grades. The best thing I had going was a waitress job—oh, I loved that! But the rest of my life back then felt like one long, interminable ache until what was happening around me, inside me, and in my family became too much. I dropped out of high school, continued waitressing, and left home when I was seventeen. I worked in numerous waitress and office jobs and got my first big break at the *Chicago Tribune* in the classified advertising department after I came in second (I swear) in *The Chicago Tribune Magazine*'s Fruit and Vegetable Poetry contest. I wrote about lima beans, which I hated, but that bilious bean got me into sales and advertising where I worked for a decade.

I honed my writing, taking many college writing and screenwriting courses. But I want to emphasize that the pain and incompleteness of high school followed me for years. Don't think, *Well, Joan Bauer dropped out of school and was successful—so can I.* Listen to me—I understand that sometimes emotional strain and depression can make it seem impossible to learn or to keep going. But don't give up—*never* give up. There are so many ways to learn, so many people out there who can help you. I've got a different way of looking at life now that I'm so much older. Harry Bender, one of my favorite characters, said it to Jenna in *Rules of the Road:* "If you set your mind and heart toward a healthy way of living and thinking, you'll find a way to climb out of the biggest pit life throws your way." I believe that with all my heart because I've done it—not alone, but with God's astonishing grace.

ON GETTING IDEAS FROM PEOPLE I TALK TO

Many years ago I spoke at a very tough high school in California. It was a challenging audience—four hundred ninth graders who had English as a second language. I wasn't doing too well because I hadn't realized the language barrier between us and I'd prepared a talk that wasn't right for that group. Boy, I was drowning, and then I just stepped out there and we started putting a character together from thin air and kids were talking about these awful situations they were in with uncles in jail and parents so messed up. I started telling them about my dad and what it was like growing up with an alcoholic, and lots of them knew what that was like. Then a really tough-looking guy in the back said to me, "You've got to write that story." I told him I wasn't sure I was ready. "You've got to do it," he said. So I did. It was *Rules of the Road.*

ON WHAT I'VE LEARNED AS A WRITER

I've always wanted to be asked what's the biggest lesson I've learned as a writer. And my answer is that in creating my characters, I've learned in such a deep way about the gray areas in life. It's easy sometimes to live in a black and white world of good and evil, right and wrong. I do think there are plenty of issues that *are* that clear, but people are complex—we all have good and bad in us; we all respond to life differently and for vastly different reasons, we all have broken parts. Do we keep them to ourselves or use them to connect with others? Sometimes a character is on a personal quest, sometimes trying to right a wrong, sometimes there's an answer he or she needs about life to be fulfilled, sometimes a person is angry and afraid to show it, is hurt and can't tell anyone. When I create characters I think about their whole lives—their strengths, weaknesses, challenges, family structures, dreams—and that has given me a new understanding of human nature, forgiveness, and mercy. I think what ultimately draws people together isn't the great times in life, but the hard times. I would prefer to sit with someone who has been made wise through suffering, than someone who has had an easy road. I try to write about people like that. When I can find the warmth of humor in their lives, I feel pretty close to heaven.

ON DEVELOPING A LOVE OF WRITING

When I was in school, I wrote all the time—short stories, essays, poetry, songs, greeting cards. I had a few poems published in my high school literary journal and once won a prize. I was on fire with the love of writing. Over the years, sometimes that fire has gone out. It's usually when I'm too busy or too stressed to remember that I love what I'm doing. Deadline pressure can kill the flame, too. Wanting more to happen than is realistic always drops me in a sinkhole. How does a writer hold on to what's important? That's a question I've been asking for years. It's a question that I consider when students tell me they've written a book. I'm impressed by that achievement because I didn't write a book until I was in my thirties. But what worries me is the question that often follows: How do I get my book published? I struggle with my answer because I don't want to discourage anyone, but I also know that with some notable exceptions, books by middle school and high school authors don't get published. I'm afraid that our success-oriented culture is causing some young people to miss the joy of learning to love writing by focusing too much on publishing as the ultimate goal.

And all of that brings me to this: To be a writer of any age, you have to love words. So play with them, toss them around, jiggle them, and see what they can do. Be a crazy kind of reader, too, the kind who gets so excited about a certain sentence that you just have to read it out loud to someone. Think about stories—why they work and why they don't. Take risks with your writing. Know your characters until they seem real—actually they have to be real (almost) because there's a point in the process where they will begin talking to you, so learn to listen and talk back, too. Develop your style and your voice. An artist paints with a brush, you paint with words. Don't be discouraged by criticism. Editing is key to the writing process. Listen to it. Be challenged by it. Revision is your friend. Keep practicing—it's like playing scales on the piano, like batting balls over the net in tennis, like rehearsing lines for a play—the better you get at writing, the more fun it is. And do you know what can ruin it? When you begin to think that the most important thing is being published. It's not. *But I have to get published!* I know. Being published is great, but don't make it a too-early goal. You'll lose the joy of dancing with words.

Keep dancing.

CHAPTER TWO

BAUER'S WRITING STYLE AS ILLUSTRATED THROUGH HER SHORT STORIES

ARTOONISTS SAY that they have only seven seconds to grab the attention of the typical newspaper reader. While the authors of novels or short stories may have a little more time than that—maybe as much as thirty seconds—authors know that when potential readers pick up something to read, they look first at the cover and perhaps the first couple of pages. In the time it takes to do this, they need to find at least a hint, if not a promise, of a problem to be solved or a conflict to be settled.

Bauer feels apprehensive when she finally lets go of a manuscript. She gets the same feeling as the first time she gave her daughter the keys to the car or let her go to the mall alone. But she knows that a book is her baby and if she never lets go, it cannot make its way in the world. Nevertheless when the first printed copy arrives in the mail, she is always amazed at how small it looks. She laughs at herself for having the feeling that after all the work she has put into it, it should look maybe not as big as the *Oxford English Dictionary* but at least as big as a desk dictionary.

She does not have the same expectations for her short stories and so when these books arrive she looks at them happily and enjoys reading the other stories in the collections to see how they compare to her own. She likes the immediate feedback and the excitement of writing short pieces, but she finds it harder to develop characterization. The stories have to be based on plot, but she is happy with how much readers get to know about the family in "Hardware." Also, with short stories she gets a chance to experiment with new styles and ideas.

When she wrote "Blocked," she was literally blocked and could not seem to move forward, but when her on-screen characters begin

A relatively new genre for teenagers is books of short stories written around a chosen theme, by authors of contemporary young adult fiction. Joan Bauer is often invited to contribute stories to such collections as shown here: (Top row) *Dear Author, Letters of Hope* (Philomel, 2007), *Dreams and Visions* (Tom Doherty, 2006), *From One Experience to Another* (Tom Doherty, 1997). (Bottom row) *911: The Book of Help* (Cricket Books, 2002), *What Are You Afraid Of? Stories about Phobias* (Candlewick, 2006), and *Necessary Noise: Stories about Our Families as They Really Are* (HarperCollins, 2003). Photograph by A. P. Nilsen.

criticizing her and she is sure such a thing cannot be happening, she explodes in exasperation, "You guys are just …" She struggles for the right words. "You're just a *first draft!*" This sentence freed Bauer to write the rest of the story.

For most of her short stories, Bauer has created one- or two-word titles that hint at multiple meanings, while also foreshadowing the coming events. For example, in "Smoke," Annie and her former boyfriend, Julian, are summer interns at MCK Advertising Agency. On her first day at work, Annie is not at all pleased to learn that she has been tricked into contributing her best efforts to a campaign encouraging teenagers to buy cigarettes. The title, "Smoke," triggers thoughts relating not only to cigarettes but to such phrases as *smoke and mirrors*, *where's there's smoke, there's fire*, and *going up in smoke*, all of which are appropriate to a story about the tobacco business and the sneaky ways that advertisers try to seduce young people into smoking.

After Annie, the narrator, figures out that the brainstorming session in which she had offered her best ideas was part of a sly campaign to attract teenagers to smoking, she feels manipulated and resentful. One reason is that a favorite uncle has recently died from emphysema. She heads down the hall to talk to Rupert Sack, the boss. When she accuses him of being less than honest, he does not exactly *sack* her, but she quits anyway. He had offered her a big bonus, along with a warning that everything they had discussed that day was "strictly confidential." As Annie walks toward his office, she feels like "Dorothy going to see the Wizard of Oz. Except I've got no Tin Man, no Lion, no Scarecrow, and no magic slippers" (48).

This is an especially appropriate allusion because cultural critics point to the *Wizard of Oz* as a pioneering icon for modern-day commercialism where dreams instead of real products are marketed. Mr. Sack is very surprised that Annie does not take the bonus. She tries to explain to him:

> "I couldn't sleep if I took the money. I'm like the princess and the pea. I'd know it was there somewhere."
> "The princess and the pea is a fairy tale, Annie. The money is real."

Annie realizes the truth of what he says; nevertheless, she gets up and leaves. She meets her former boyfriend (they had applied for the internships back when they were "a couple"), who is also packing up the few belongings he had brought to the first day at work. They are relieved that they have the same ethical values, and the story ends with them going to look for a lawyer to help them figure out whether they are bound to the employee confidentiality agreement if they have not accepted any money.

The title of "Clean Sweep" comes from baseball and describes a five-game series in which one team wins every game. If the home team has already won four of the games, fans are likely to show up carrying brooms as a way of encouraging their players to put forth the extra effort to accomplish a clean sweep.

In Bauer's story, "Clean Sweep" is the name of the housecleaning business run by Katie's mom with help from hardworking Katie and her not-so-hardworking little brother, Benjamin. Katie's mother frightens potential customers with scary enlargements of dust mites and clinches her sales pitch with comments such as, "People just don't understand what important things can be hiding in the dust." By the end of the story, Katie comes away with a different interpretation after she helps an elderly neighbor reconcile with her sister because of a book they find while cleaning out the woman's attic.

As Katie explains, she is "a specialist in cleaning rooms of kids who have just gone off to college. It takes nerves of steel," which she has (153). In contrast, her younger brother Benjamin does not have Katie's strength, at least not according to Katie, who is the narrator:

> To begin with, he's allergic to dust—bad news when the family business is dedicated to eliminating it. To end with, he's a devoted underachiever, in stark contrast to myself. And Benjamin knows how to get out of work—he could give seminars on this. He gets the perfect look of abject pain over his face, says he's not feeling too well, he's sorry, he doesn't want to be a *burden*. He talks about the pain moving across his back, down his leg, and into his ankle. Then he gets dizzy and has to sit down; lying down comes moments later after his face gets a little pale (I don't know how he does this) and his hand touches his forehead which, I swear, has small drops of sweat on it. Then he'll try to get up and help, but by this time, you feel like such a snake that a sick person is going to get sicker because of your insensitive demands that you say, no, you rest, I'll do it. (153)

Bauer's title "Extra Virgin" isn't nearly as sexy as it sounds; it is the standard way of identifying the first batch of olive oil pressed from a vat of olives. The purpose of the phrase in the story is to provide a way for Beth and Cal, who are eating at an Italian restaurant, to joke about how Beth's ideas about sexuality differ from the popular culture images that seem to surround the couple.

The story begins as a person-against-person plot with Beth "holding out" against Cal's desire to have sex, but really it is more of a person-against-society story. The crux is that Beth has vowed to be a virgin until she's "sort of ... married ... I mean definitely ... married ... in years to come" (22). However, careful readers will recognize that Bauer is illustrating a societal problem as much as an individual problem in a scene showing Cal and Beth walking from the ice cream shop, where Beth works, to a nearby coffee bar. They proceed "past a poster of a model in underwear flagging down a taxi. Past a big sign that read JUST DO IT. Past a movie theater placard with a man and woman kissing passionately underneath the grabber headline THEY COULDN'T SAY NO TO THE FIRE THAT RAGED WITHIN THEM" (16).

Coming face-to-face with these stimuli that contradict Beth's vow of chastity is only one of the ironies in the story. Another one that Beth *feels* in a more literal sense is the fact that when it gets really hot, everyone wants to buy ice cream. The more times the door to the store is opened the more likely it is that the ice cream will melt, and so on hot days the manager turns the freezer temperature down. This means that Beth has to work harder to scoop out the ice cream. By the end of her evening shifts, her wrist, and sometimes her whole arm, is in pain.

The hesitation in the manner that Beth explains her vow to stay a virgin until she marries leaves "Extra Virgin" with something close to an open ending. In reality, nearly all books written for teenage readers have open endings because good authors bring their characters only a few tiny steps on the road to growing up. The implication is that there's always more to come.

The story "Pancakes" has a perfectly plain word as its title, but Bauer puts a narrative hook in the first line by having Jill, the protagonist/narrator, explain:

> The last thing I wanted to see taped to my bathroom mirror at five-thirty in the morning was a newspaper article entitled "Are You a Perfectionist?" But there it was, courtesy of my mother, Ms. Subtlety herself. I was instantly irritated because Allen Feinman had accused me of perfectionism when he broke up with me last month. The term he used was "rabid perfectionism," which I felt was a bit much. (132)

As Jill goes on to tell about her "selfless offer" to alphabetize Allen's CD collection, complete "with a color-coded cross-reference guide by

subject, title, and artist" (134), readers begin empathizing with the boyfriend and wondering why Jill doesn't understand his point.

"Pancakes" is an example of a person-against-self plot because over
the course of the story Jill comes to a realization about her personality
and her attitudes and is forced to make changes based on the circumstances.
Internal growth happens deep inside a person's mind or heart, which means
that authors have to be clever in figuring out some external way to reveal this
growth, especially in a short story where there is less space for character
development.

Bauer uses rising action to show readers how Jill comes to a realization that the world, including her part in it, cannot always be perfect.
Bauer, who worked for a year at an IHOP (International House of Pancakes) restaurant, says she still breaks out in sweat if she goes into a pancake restaurant on a Saturday or Sunday morning, which is when ninety
percent of all pancakes are sold. In the story, Jill was hired as a result of
convincing the owner that she has "a system for everything." However,
she has to rethink her claim on a busy Sunday morning when the other
two waitresses fail to show up. Jill, in her usual conscientious fashion,
arrives two hours early so that she can put everything in order. Usually
the owner manages the cashier, but his wife occasionally makes him take
a weekend off, and this is one of those weekends. Even so, Jill has the
cook and the busboy, and she expects Shirl and Lucy, the other two waitresses, to arrive soon. However, Lucy phones in to say her baby is sick,
and Shirl gets stuck on the freeway behind a tractor-trailer that jackknifed
and covered the freeway with cans of Coca-Cola. In spite of Jill's best
efforts, things begin slipping and take a full slide when a bus filled with
"MICHIGAN WOMEN FOR A CLEANER ENVIRONMENT" pulls
into the parking lot. One of them is a real wit as she laughingly comes
through the door and asks for "a table for sixty-six."

Jill sweetly tells them to sit anywhere and proceeds to inform people
that she's the only waitress so things will be slow, and really they are welcome to go someplace else. Nobody leaves, and she describes the situation as follows:

> I was falling down a dark, disorderly tunnel. There was no end in
> sight. Coffee grounds were in my eyebrows, my hands smelled

like used tea bags. I was exhausted, syrup encrusted, I'd had to go to the bathroom for three hours. People were going to get their own coffee—the ultimate defeat for any waitress. (146)

Just as she is thinking, or perhaps hoping, that she will be dead by noon, in walks her old boyfriend, Allen Feinman, and his mother and father. "Can I help, Jill?" he asks, already rolling up his sleeves. She puts him on the register, while his mother makes coffee, and his dad goes back outside to sit in the car and read the newspaper. Jill's admission that she needs help and that she receives it make up the climax of the story. The denouement comes a few hours later when the mess on the freeway has cleared up, Shirl has made it into work, and the crowd has thinned. Jill and Allen can at last sit down at the back table and eat pancakes. She looks up and sees the busboy "speed-pouring boysenberry syrup," not at all in the way she taught him, but somehow it doesn't matter: "It was good enough," and that, she happily realizes, is fine (147).

Jill is a dynamic character, meaning that because of what happens over the course of the story she changes her thinking and, in at least a small way, her personality. Her old boyfriend, Allen, is a static character, meaning that he stays pretty much the same throughout the story. In realistic short stories about young people, it is common to have dynamic main characters, while the background or supporting characters are more likely to be static because authors do not have the space that it takes to develop more than one or two characters who undergo believable changes.

Another example of a story in which the main character undergoes a personality change is "The Truth about Sharks." To understand the story, readers need to be familiar with the advice that if you are in the ocean being attacked by a shark, you should not try swimming away. Instead, as the last line of the story says, "if one comes barreling at you, the best thing to do is hit it in the nose" (47). The story is mainly a person-against-person plot, but in the preface, Bauer makes it clear that it is also person-against-self because her reason for writing the story was to come to terms with her experience of being wrongly accused of shoplifting when she was nineteen. For decades she has regretted that she did not stand up for herself and demand an apology from the store.

Through having written the story, Bauer can at least feel a little better about the event. Today it seems a little exaggerated, but incidents like this must have happened to cause high-end stores to change their practices. Most security people no longer wear uniforms, and they work in pairs and communicate electronically so that suspected shoplifters are followed and then arrested when they step through an outside door or make a handoff to an accomplice.

Beth is the protagonist who begins the story in conflict with her "morning person" mother, who comes into Beth's bedroom to announce that it is 10:30 AM and time to start the day (32). The first task on Beth's list is finding something to wear to Uncle Al's birthday party so that she won't look dowdy in comparison to her cousin Bianca. After her mother says she can have the car until 1:00, Beth drives to the new store on Route 1 in Norwalk. It is huge, with five stories, and as she enters she notices a stocky, stern security guard picking her teeth. Her tag reads: MADGE P. GROTON, SECURITY GUARD. In Beth's mind, this tag later comes to read "Security SHARK" and then "Security NEANDERTHAL" and finally "Security WITCH."

The two get to know each other because the woman is keeping an eye on Beth, who, while trying on pants, sees a sales rack and without taking off the store's pants walks over to see if there isn't something better. She had been visiting with a clerk and had left her purse, her coat, and her other pants in the dressing room, but when Ms. Groton grabs her arm, she won't listen to Beth or check out her story about her purse and her own clothes being in the dressing room. Instead, she insists that "that's not the way we play the game" (36). She pulls Beth's hands behind her back and forces her onto the elevator and then past waiting customers (including a nosy neighbor of Uncle Al's) and into a windowless "security" room where she demands that Beth take off the pants. Beth replies, "No, Ma'am. Not until I get my pants back" (38). Ms. Groton pushes some buttons on her phone and says, "I've got one. Send a car."

This is probably where Bauer's old "true" story ends and the new "fictional" story begins. In the imagined account, Beth is able to explain the situation to the arresting officer, even though she is in the backseat of the car and they are driving toward the station to file the arrest papers. He makes a U-turn and together they go into the store. The officer's last name is the brave-sounding *Brennerman* as compared with the more guttural-sounding *Groton*. Together they go upstairs and check with the original sales clerk, who says she wondered where Beth went and why she left her coat, her purse, and her own pants in the changing room. The sales clerk had set them aside, and when she hands them over, Officer Brennerman takes Beth's purse and pulls out Tums, dental floss, breath mints, hairbrushes, Kleenexes, Milk Duds, a giant panda key ring, sunglasses, and four lipsticks. He then asks, "You got a wallet in here?" (42). Beth reaches deep down and pulls it out. He checks her driver's license and sees that she has seventy-five dollars and dismisses the shoplifting charge.

Beth goes back into the dressing room and changes into her own grungy sweatpants and starts for home. But then she begins thinking about her embarrassment, and even though she knows her mother will be mad about not having the car at the promised time, Beth turns around and goes back to see the store manager and demand an apology. After some blustering about getting a lawyer, she obtains both an apology and a large gift certificate. And best of all, Ms. Groton gets transferred to another store.

A short story based on a much more recent event is "Children of War," which Bauer wrote for a 2002 book entitled *911: The Book of Help.* On September 11, the Bauers' daughter, Jean, was supposed to fly to the University of Chicago, where she was enrolling for her sophomore year. Because all the planes were grounded, Bauer and her husband drove Jean to Chicago. When strangers at rest areas along the way saw their license plates, they would ask about the city and what they saw. Verbalizing the experience for strangers so soon after being in New York at the time of the tragedy inspired a great deal of thinking, and, consequently, a couple of months later, when Bauer was invited to contribute to the book, she had something to say.

She wrote a story through the voice of Liza, a girl living in Brooklyn and in the process of applying for college. Liza had just finished her admissions essay when the tragedy occurs. She had "worked on it so hard, bled over every adjective," but "now it seemed small and unimportant" (42). She had written about falling out of a boat when she was whitewater rafting. At the time it seemed like a life-changing moment, but now she is embarrassed that she ever thought it was important. "So change it," advises her friend Hanrahan (44).

This is easier said than done. Liza is so devastated by the experience that "Thanksgiving came and went" and "Christmas tried to come," but she is in a funk and not even sure that she wants to go to college and become a teacher (45). What's the use?

Her friend, whose name is Jewish, argues with her and tells her that she is just buying into the terrorists' game if she allows them to rule her life and keep her from going to college and becoming a teacher. When she accuses him of trying to make her mad, he smiles and says, "Your face is red and you're screaming." Finally, he takes her down to the Promenade where they can look over at the empty space that used to be the towers. He puts a pad of paper in her hands and says, "Write it ... write your essay. I dare you" (45).

Liza's thinking takes a step forward, and she starts to write about the whole experience. Her concluding paragraph follows:

> I am a New Yorker. I smelled the smoke, saw the ash from the towers, felt the fear settle over my shoulders, had the nightmares, lit the candles, went to the funerals. I wish to God that none of it had ever happened and I thank God that I was here when it did. I've been changed forever—that much I know. And because of that, I want to teach. I want to teach because I want to learn and understand. I believe we have a choice in this world, we, the children of war. We can learn from the hate, we can learn how to stop it, or we can learn to hate even more. (47)

Bauer uses concrete, visible events or items, such as Liza's admissions essay, to symbolize the more important resolutions, which are harder to see because they occur inside her characters' minds. These kinds of internal plots are sometimes referred to as themes because they are more abstract than plots yet are larger than morals and more convincing than "messages." They develop from an author's philosophy of life and from the story that is being told. On the "Stories Connect Us" page of her Web site, Bauer shares her most common theme by asking readers if they have ever seen a baby chicken peck its way out of an eggshell.

The process is grim. The chick is wet, ugly, and totally stressed. It emits this pitiful cheep that makes me want to pick it up and dry it off. It's got eggshell stuck to its body. It's trying to shake the shell off and not keel over. I want an 800 number to call where there's a chicken therapist who can talk the bird through this ordeal. But I don't move. I watch. I know that baby chick is getting strong through the fight.

   And that's what happens to us a bit. These sad, unfair, frightening, discouraging, impossibly hard things come at us—if we let them, if we keep working to peck our way out, they can help to make us stronger.

With this metaphor, Bauer is describing a theme about characters growing and becoming stronger that underlies most of her fiction. Part of the idea is for her protagonists to develop an internal locus of control, which means that rather than asking themselves, "What is going to happen to me?" they ask themselves, "What am I going to do?"

Moving a story away from a person-against-person to a person-against-self plot allows Bauer's characters to define their own well-being rather than to focus on what other people think or say about them. One of Bauer's favorite quotes, which she uses both in her book *Stand Tall* and in her short story "A Letter from the Fringe," is Eleanor Roosevelt's saying that "No one can make you feel inferior without your consent."

Bauer works with this idea when exploring relationships between "mean" kids or "bullies," and the majority of students who each day hope to get by without some kind of confrontation. Bauer worked with this idea long before the tragedy at Columbine High School, but in "A Letter from the Fringe," Dana writes a letter to the ICIs, the "In-Crowd Individuals." She tries to tell them what life is like from the other end of the school cafeteria, that is, from an outsider perspective. She never actually sends the letter, except for a copy she puts in a birthday card for her friend Sally, who has suffered from being one of the ICIs' victims. Dana asks: "What really drives the whole thing. Is it hate? Is it power? Are you afraid if you get too close to me and my friends that some of our uncoolness might rub off on you? I think what could really happen is that learning tolerance could make us happier, freer people" (190).

Bauer is skilled at using figurative language to draw attention to specific points or to amuse her readers and give them a break from especially somber parts of her stories. One kind of language usage (similes, metaphors, symbols, parodies, allegories, allusions, playing with names, etc.) deals with the meanings or the semantics of words, while the other kind (alliteration, assonance, rhyme, rhythm, puns, etc.) relates to the sounds or the phonology of words. When Dana introduces the principal plot problem in "A Letter from the Fringe," she uses both alliteration and rhyme by explaining that "*Get the Geeks* is a popular bonding ritual among the jock flock at Bronley High" (182). She uses more alliteration and rhyme a few lines later when Dana tells Booker, who is giving Sal a hard time about eating a cookie, to get lost. His response is "Sneer. Snort. 'Now how can I get lost in school?'" (182).

Bauer uses repetition for emphasis in the line: "You can never be too athletic, too popular, too gorgeous, or too rich, but you can be too smart and too nerdy" (188). She relies on semantics (the meanings of words) when some of the characters fight back through language play. When Dana is snubbed by her lab partner in biology, she makes herself feel better by explaining that the girl is "stricken with *affluenza,* a condition that afflicts certain segments of the excruciatingly rich" (186). Another character, who "used to skip school after getting hassled," decides to go on the offensive by walking up to a group of popular kids and while breathing "like a degenerate" hissing:

> "I'm a *bibliophile.*" A bibliophile is a person who loves books, but not many people know that. He'll approach a group of cheerleaders and announce, "You know, girls, I'm *bipedal* ... " That means he has two feet, but those cheerleaders scatter like squirrels. "I'm a *thespian,*" he'll say lustfully. This means he's an actor, but you know how it is with some words. If they sound bad, people don't always wait around for the vocab lesson. (185)

Jewel Lardner, a "zany artist with pink-striped hair," who "long ago stopped caring about being in, out, or in between," says they all need to get cell phones.

That way, if any of us sees big trouble coming, we can warn the others. If a jock on the prowl comes close to me, I whip out my phone and start shouting into it, "Are you kidding me? He's got *what* kind of disease? Is it catching?" People don't come near you when you're talking disease. (184)

Bauer's style and her flip and often funny tone have undoubtedly been influenced by the years that she spent working in advertising, where she learned the value of succinctness. She also realizes that pages and pages of small type all set to look exactly the same can be intimidating. To achieve variety and to leave white space on some of her pages, she uses different fonts and techniques. Her story "Blocked" is a good example. Chloe is co-editor of her school's first-ever fantasy anthology, which is about to go to press. Space is being saved for Chloe's story to come first; however, she is suffering from a major case of writer's block. She bemoans her fate and looks frantically for help in figuring out her plot.

She gives herself motivational talks and makes lists showing how she is arguing with herself. She uses both quotation marks and italics and sometimes all-capital letters as she experiments with writing dialogue, for example:

CREATURE WITH FOURTEEN EYES: So Adriana, we meet
again.

ADRIANA: Guess so.

The "lameness" of this dialogue causes the readers, along with Chloe, to suspect that she has lost her touch. But finally Chloe's characters come alive on her computer screen and tell her what the story needs. The result is both an amusing story and a pleasure to read, at least partly because of the inviting format.

"Thin" is narrated by a girl named Deenie, who is suffering from an eating disorder. It is part of a collection of stories about phobias and fears. Although Deenie keeps insisting that she is perfectly normal, readers see that there is more to her problem than she imagines. Deenie begins starving herself after her father leaves home and moves in with a woman who is both younger and thinner than her mother. Deenie oversimplifies the matter and concludes that the reason for the family breakup is that her father wanted someone "thin." It is true that Deenie's mother has gained forty pounds, but Deenie does not stop to figure out that her mother gained this weight after the breakup. The difference between Deenie's and her mother's attitudes is a big part of the story.

Bauer gives an especially good description of the kind of denial that Deenie practices when in the school cafeteria Deenie is eating a salad with no dressing (her first meal of the day) and she chokes. Her throat closes up and she has "a full-out panic attack." She has to sit with her head between her knees as her friends give first-aid advice:

> "Breath deep, Deenie."
> "Let yourself relax."
> "Let your body go limp."
> "Breath into this paper bag." (47)

Usually it is Deenie giving herself advice, but it is isn't as sensible as what her friends are saying. Deenie says such things as, *"Think, Deenie, how very much you want to have flat abs and a perfect body. ... Think how that will change your life"* (50).

Bauer has stated that with short stories, as compared to novels, she limits the setting and the time. "Thin" is an illustration of this in that Bauer does not continue the story long enough to let readers know whether Deenie gets cured, but she does have Deenie come to the realization that something is wrong and she needs to ask for help.

In most of her stories, Bauer uses a lighthearted and humorous tone, which is the characteristic most often pointed out by people who recommend her books. It's not that she tells jokes; instead, she has her characters make succinct observations. For example, in her short story "Hardware," when she is introducing Cali's family, she writes, "Big Mel was Aunt Phil's half brother." Then as an afterthought, she adds, "Most relationships in Cali's family were explained by fractions" (6).

"Hardware" is an exploration of the downside of what happens to a mom-and-pop hardware store when it has to compete with a big chain store that moves into the neighborhood. Bauer focuses attention on the importance of names to people when she writes that Aunt Phil was given "a hard name for a girl" because the character's father wanted her "to remember that life is hard" (8). And indeed it is when a Waldo Super

Store (which surely must remind readers of Wal-Mart) establishes itself right across the street from the store that Phil's father had built in hopes of providing his family with a living for generations to come. Bauer lightens up the family argument over what to do by playing with the difference between literal and metaphorical meanings. When Aunt Phil says, "'My father built this store; his *soul* is between the floorboards.' Lewis, who had been spitting on the floor, stopped" (7).

The "victims" end up doing something, but the story is left open-ended so that readers do not know if their solution will really work, but at least all of the characters have hope, except for Cali's uncle, Big Mel, who gives up early and moves to Boise.

The family sets up a small kiosk thirty feet from the main entrance to the "big box" store. They advertise on the Internet and get lots of free publicity by having a one-month countdown to their grand opening. They promote the slogan "WE'VE GOT WHAT THEY DON'T HAVE," which is personalized advice and assistance, along with free home delivery. On opening day, Aunt Phil "has her balloons out just like Waldo's had had" (19). The manager of Waldo's comes out and shakes Aunt Phil's hand, and she gives away "David and Goliath" T-shirts to the first thirty customers. She releases two pigeons (she couldn't afford the doves that Waldo had released), and when the birds catch the wind and send "a stream of pigeon droppings on the giant Waldo head," the newspaper photographer gets a photo—and so, at least for a while, it's a new day in the hardware business (20).

In summary, authors have their own writing styles just like people have their own personalities. It does not mean that all their books will be the same, but it does mean that they are likely to have certain similarities. Below are some of the characteristics present in Bauer's short stories, which will most likely also be present in her novels.

- Youthful protagonists: Some of her characters are as young as twelve or thirteen, although most are in high school with a few entering college.
- Important adults: As in "Hardware," where readers get to know the whole family, Bauer includes multiple generations in her stories. In her novels where she has more space for character

development, several of her youthful protagonists are strongly influenced by grandparents—either real or "adopted."

- Self-against-self plots: While Bauer's plots include both protagonists and antagonists, the main theme in most of her stories is that the young protagonists are fighting against one of their own tendencies that they want or need to change.
- A light touch: Bauer makes readers giggle—or at least smile—with her succinct and on-target observations and with her language play.
- Clever dialogue: Probably because Bauer did her first serious writing for screenplays, she likes to have her characters talk to each other.
- Solid character development: Even with minor characters, Bauer finds succinct ways to trigger readers' minds to fill in the details by thinking of someone they know who resembles the character. With her major characters, she uses a range of techniques including telling readers what they say, what they look like, what they do, what others say to or about them, and even what they think.
- White space on the pages: Bauer reproduces lists, signs, business cards, notes, illustrations, and whatever she can think of to break up the monotony of pages and pages of densely packed type.
- Explorations of work: Readers usually come away having learned trade secrets of some kind, whether from the world of a big city advertising firm, an ice cream shop or a pancake house, or such family-owned businesses as a hardware store and a cleaning service.
- Revealing names: The names Bauer chooses often serve for more than identification. They foreshadow events and hint at the role characters play or at their personality quirks.

For complete bibliographic information on these short stories see p. 155.

CHAPTER THREE

SQUASHED

OAN BAUER SAYS that she is not a patient person. On her Web site, she writes that when she is forced to wait for something, she begins to worry and fret and then to eat chocolate. It is probably because she knows so much about being impatient that she wrote so effectively about Ellie's struggle to be patient as she tries to grow the biggest pumpkin in the state of Iowa. Once the growing is done, Ellie is even more impatient as she waits for the day of judgment. To ease the stress, she bakes a batch of triple chocolate fudge bars and eats thirteen of them. She reorganizes the baking pans in the kitchen; she talks to her best friend for an hour about what age women start "going to pot"; she counts the tiles on both her and her grandmother's bathroom walls for a total of 587; she uses up two hours writing a get-well card to Wes, the boy she has a crush on; and then she dusts off two books about General Patton that she needs for her midterm paper but can't bring herself to start reading (138).

Ironically, Bauer's book about impatience gave her a lesson in developing her own patience. *Squashed* is the first novel she wrote, and, as most authors will verify, editors at major publishing houses receive so many manuscripts that they seldom read, much less publish, books from unknown authors. In order to get an editor to read *Squashed*, Bauer submitted her manuscript to the Delacorte Press contest for first-time authors, which was being judged by the editors. Nine months went by between the time she submitted her manuscript and the time she was announced as the winner. Students who have written what they thought was a wonderful essay, and then had a teacher who was slow about grading and returning it, probably have some empathy for how long Bauer had to wait to hear back from the contest judges.

When the book won the prize, it was praised for its fresh voice and for its originality. Authors have written many books about teenagers winning athletic competitions, scholarships, places on Olympic teams, beauty contests, spelling bees, and talent shows, but no one had written a book about a teenager growing a giant pumpkin. Yet, the book is not a fantasy; Bauer took the idea directly from a daily newspaper, where she saw a photo of a huge pumpkin and began wondering what on earth a grower had to do to come up with such a result. At the time, Bauer knew nothing about growing pumpkins, but she knew a lot about having a dream and being fiercely determined to accomplish something. She also knew how to conduct research and talk to people to learn what real growers go through. In her books, Bauer likes to strike a balance between writing about things she has to research and about places and jobs she already knows, such as restaurants and food service. The fun and the excitement, she says, lies in learning new things. If you have lived the emotions, you can research and find the facts for your story. That's what keeps writers fresh.

Main Characters

Ellie Morgan is the sixteen-year-old narrator of *Squashed*. She inherited her love for growing things from her mother, who was killed in an automobile accident when Ellie was eight. Ellie has won the junior division of Iowa's biggest pumpkin-growing contest twice, but this year she is entering the adult division. She wants desperately to win, because if she loses she will have to start all over, and it won't be nearly as impressive if she does not win in her first year of eligibility. Ellie's wry wit and humorous—often sarcastic—observations provide much of the originality that makes *Squashed* fun to read.

Ellie's father grew up on his parents' nearby farm, but he turned his back on farming and provides for himself and Ellie as a motivational speaker. He sells tape recordings of his encouraging speeches and tries to get Ellie to buy into the kind of self-confidence he promotes. He wants Ellie to make lists and prioritize her goals, but she resists because, as she finally gets him to understand, she needs to find her own way.

Cyril Pool is an obnoxious thirty-five-year-old bachelor who lives with his aunt. For the past four years, he has won the prize for the biggest pumpkin at the festival. Because his behavior is so childlike and offensive, readers feel free to join in and applaud Ellie when she ridicules him and his pumpkin, which he has named BIG DADDY. Ellie hates it when he addresses her as "Missy," but that's what he calls all females under seventy because he is bad at names. Actually, Ellie thinks he is "bad at life in general" (18).

Nana is Ellie's grandmother on her father's side of the family. She is the one who supports and encourages Ellie and helps her understand why her father turned his back on farming. Nana explains that Ellie's father likes to be in control, and with farming there are so many forces of nature that farmers can never predict what they can produce. Throughout the book, Nana tries to get Ellie to look past the competition with Cyril and to see that the important thing is how all of the pumpkins that Ellie has grown over the last eight years have contributed to her own growth.

Richard is Ellie's cousin and a nearby neighbor. He is a year younger than Ellie and serves as a sounding board for her. He is almost as obsessed with playing baseball as Ellie is with growing a giant pumpkin. In February, when it is too cold to play ball, Richard ties his right hand behind his back in hopes of developing his left arm because switch-hitters are much more valuable. Mostly, he ends up owing his mother his February allowance because he has the job of drying the dishes and she charges him a breakage fee for whatever he drops. He doesn't mind, because when he plays for the Chicago Cubs he's sure his commercial endorsements will more than make up for the loss.

Wes is a new boy in town who used to live in Gaithersville, where he was the agriculture club president. Luckily, the Gaithersville kids haven't gotten around to formally electing a new president, and so when he goes to spy on Cyril he can honestly introduce himself as the president of the high school agriculture club who has come to interview him about his plans for BIG DADDY. Ellie is immediately attracted to Wes, not just because he has the soul of a grower (he wins prizes for his corn), but also because he has beautiful gray eyes. His aunt once won a pumpkin-growing contest, and he advises Ellie to follow his aunt's method and to talk to her pumpkin. At least she has given it a name (Max) so she has a place to start, but she is still skeptical. He

I took this picture of Joan Bauer in 1994 when we were both attending the International Society for Humor Studies conference at Ithaca College. At the time, Bauer's only published book was *Squashed*. What made her happy about the conference was that her daughter, who loved reading Paul Zindel's books, was finally convinced that her mother was a real writer because she was speaking on the same panel as Mr. Zindel, shown to the right of Joan. Photograph by A. P. Nilsen.

gives her a demonstration, which is only the first of his surprising and supportive acts on behalf of Ellie and Max.

SETTING

Of course, a story written about growing a giant pumpkin would have to be set in a fertile part of the country, hence Bauer's choice of Iowa. She also needed to place the story in a small enough town that the people would have community spirit and would take pride in their annual Harvest Festival. Rock River and the Harvest Festival are most likely fictional composites, rather than actual places. On my road map of Iowa, I could find no town named Rock River, although I found a Rock Rapids and a Rock Valley, plus several places whose names start with *Rock* across the border in Illinois, the state where Joan Bauer grew up.

When Bauer first started writing *Squashed*, she says she was not thinking of writing a novel for teenagers, but of doing for rural Iowa what Garrison Keillor does for rural Minnesota in his humorous stories set in Lake Wobegon, "where all the women are strong and all the men are good-looking and all the children are above average." Keillor's slogan has the same level of exaggeration that Bauer puts in some of her statements. For example, Ellie says about her cousin Richard that his "baseball usually showed up before he did, indoors or out" (2). He would throw it and then run to retrieve it. When Ellie sits outside listening to her secret booster solution of two parts Orange Crush and one part buttermilk gurgling into Max's stem, her fantasies fit right in with the kinds of daydreams that Garrison Keillor creates for his Lake Wobegon residents. Ellie imagines herself "acing the blue ribbon from Cyril Pool's grungy hands," and then standing proudly as Mrs. McKenna pins the blue ribbon on her. She will bow and wave and say to the press, "It was nothing, really," then she will look ever so humble as her classmates carry her across Founders' Square (2).

Bauer trained to write screenplays, but she much prefers to write novels, where she can have more control. However, one advantage to writing screenplays is that writers do not have to spell out all the details of their settings. They can simply write, "CUT TO. ..." This would have saved Bauer some trouble in *Squashed* because according to the plot she has to figure out a way for Ellie and her father to live close enough to town to be part of the community, but far enough out that Ellie will have room to grow her pumpkin. And since Ellie's father hates farming, it would not have made sense for them to live on a real farm, yet they need to be fairly close to Nana's farm and to her cousin Richard's house so that Ellie can easily relate to both of these characters, who, in the absence of a mother and brothers and sisters, are Ellie's closest confidantes. Also, to increase the tension in the plot, Ellie needs to be close enough to Cyril Pool's farm so that she will be constantly irritated by him when she passes by and sees the ornate sign his aunt painted: "POOL'S PUMPKIN PATCH, HOME OF THE WHOPPER" (17). The sign makes Ellie want to puke because Cyril has no respect for giant pumpkins. Ellie thinks they are majestic, while Cyril treats them as "cutesy."

Weather conditions are also part of the setting that contribute to the story and add tension. Ellie has to cover Max with heavy plastic and dig drainage ditches when it rains, put blankets over him when there's a cold snap, and, just before the opening of the festival, stand with Wes and her dad holding up a tarp to protect Max from getting bruised by a storm of hailstones.

PLOT

For the past two years, Ellie has won the junior division of the annual pumpkin-growing contest at the Rock River Harvest Festival, but now that she is sixteen and eligible to compete in the adult division, she has no intention of letting Cyril Pool grab the blue ribbon yet again. By mid-August, her pumpkin Max is estimated to weigh more than four hundred pounds. While there is no way to actually weigh him until the vine is cut and he is lifted onto a truck and taken into town for the official weigh-in, she has a chart provided by the World Pumpkin Federation that gives fairly accurate estimates of how much a healthy pumpkin will weigh based on its outside measurements. Chapter 2 begins with Ellie experiencing disgust that "some jerk" at the board of education has decided to start school in August, which is a high-maintenance month for Max. When it's raining she anxiously waits for the rain to stop for fear there will be so much water that he might rot, or his leaves might fall off, or he might develop a fungus. When there's a dry spell she worries and waits for rain to come, and when she waters Max she waits for the water to absorb so that she can check to see if it has gone deep enough to reach his roots. And once her pumpkin has reached what she considers its ideal weight and its skin has darkened just a little, she still has to wait for the opening of the festival and the cutting of Max's vine (it's like cutting a baby's umbilical cord) and then the loading of Max onto a truck for his ride to the all-important weigh-in.

Ellie's father refuses to let her start school late. He thinks that "spending night and day with a squash is not healthy ... or fulfilling" (7). Ellie tries to cope with tending Max while also concentrating on school, but she can't keep from relating everything to her immediate goals of losing twenty pounds and winning the pumpkin-growing contest. The losing weight part takes precedence in chapter 4 because she is getting ready for the annual festival party given by Mrs. McKenna for the town's young people. Ellie is especially eager to look good because she wants to make an impression on Wes, the new boy who has moved to town and happens to be a cousin to her best friend.

Chapters 7, 8, and 9 are among the most exciting because pumpkin thieves have started their annual mischief. In the middle of the night, they drive their pickup trucks onto people's land, cut the pumpkins, and take them to Des Moines, where they sell them for more than $1.00 a pound to designers of fall displays. Last year, a pumpkin suspected to have been stolen from Rock River was put in a grand display at a funeral home. Ellie's cousin Richard brings Spider, a dog who is in trouble at his own house for making too much noise, to Ellie's house to serve as a watchdog. Only after certain adjustments are made does Ellie's father let him stay.

People are beginning to take notice of Ellie and her pumpkin. Justin, the editor of the school newspaper, comes out to her house with Ralphie, the school photographer, to do a story for the paper. Ellie has never much liked Ralphie, but she is impressed that he once sold a photo of newly born pigs to a national magazine. During the visit, he is supercooperative about taking pictures that show only Ellie's best side. He is also interested in everything around Max; he even makes friends with Spider by pulling out a piece of beef jerky, an act that Ellie later wishes she had paid more attention to.

It is big news when, thanks to help from Ellie—which she gives with mixed feelings since it was Cyril's pumpkin that was being stalked—a dramatic arrest of pumpkin thieves is made. Pumpkin growers more or less relax, but as shown by another attempted robbery at Ellie's house, the feeling of security is premature. When the school newspaper editor comes back from spending the weekend at his grandmother's house, he is horrified to find out his own photographer was arrested in Ellie's pumpkin patch. He stays up all night taping a photocopied "late-breaking news addition" under the story about Ellie. He's embarrassed that it looks amateurish and aesthetically lousy, "but at least Rock River High would have the hard news he had promised to deliver when he took his journalistic oath" (130).

Partly because of all the publicity given to the arrests, Ellie's story travels from the school paper to the town paper, and on Sunday morning Nana is first in line at Robertson's Newsstand to buy twenty-two copies and a Baby Ruth. She has Ellie autograph the papers before she sends them off to friends and relatives. It is appropriate that Ellie's grandmother is so proud because she is the one who took Ellie to see Walt Disney's *Cinderella*, which Ellie credits with inspiring her love for giant pumpkins. Ellie wonders if anyone else noticed that the Fairy Godmother changed a pumpkin into a chariot before she worried about Cinderella's clothes (7–8).

Along with the support that Nana gives Ellie, she dispenses lots of advice, which in effect changes the plot of the book. It begins with Ellie focusing only on beating Cyril, but all through the book Nana tries to get Ellie to focus beyond Cyril. Early on, she tells Ellie, "One of the saddest things in life is to take something that gives you joy and let it get ruined." When Ellie protests that she's not to blame, "It's Cyril Pool. He's ... ," Nana interrupts and says, "Ellie, as long as you're watching Cyril you're going to miss the point" (27). This isn't an easy concept for Ellie to understand, but Nana keeps trying by explaining that "growing's not something you do, it's something you are" (98). No one's life is fulfilled just by winning a contest. There are always challenges, especially for farmers who have to deal with nature, which is like holding onto a slippery pig. Nana says that she could never get this idea across to Ellie's father, which is probably why he turned away from farming.

Keeping Nana's advice in mind, Ellie tries to concentrate on things besides the contest, but the whole town seems to be interested only in the outcome of the Harvest Festival pumpkin contest. As she explains, "A cloud had fallen on Rock River and divided the town. The nice folks were on my side, the cranky ones went with Cyril" (166). As the contest gets closer, even Ellie's father begins to show his support. When Ellie tells him she does not feel worthy of all the attention, he tells her she is the toughest person he knows and that, if anybody deserves to win, it is her.

By the time of the giant pumpkin weigh-in, Ellie has come to terms with the other issues in her life. Because of her new celebrity status, her teachers are giving her a break on her schoolwork. And although Ellie hasn't lost twenty pounds, she lost enough weight to fit into her favorite pants for the Harvest Festival party. And luckily the seam does not split until after the party when she is outside all by herself and squats down to check on Max.

Ellie and her father rediscover some of the things they have always enjoyed together, such as eating her homemade, coconut ice cream while discussing the stars in the sky. She can now count on her new friend, Wes, to either cheer her on to victory or console her in defeat. With help from her friends, she has saved Max from both freezing weather and pumpkin thieves. And, she can continue to count on the love and support of Nana. Although it's hard not to keep looking over at Cyril and BIG DADDY, most of the time at the Harvest Festival she concentrates not so much on the size and heart of pumpkins as on the heartfelt support and friendship that she feels all around her. And for sheer entertainment value, the climax to the contest beats anything the town has ever seen or is likely to see in the future. It will be remembered and talked about for years.

THEMES

Bauer develops two major themes in *Squashed*. The first one has already been mentioned as part of the plot. It is the idea that doing something really unusual and grand is what life is all about. Winning a contest may add a little fun and excitement, but the contest itself is not as important as the actions leading up to it and the skills, the feelings, and the attitudes that develop as a result of the contest.

The second theme that Bauer develops is the commonality of conflicts between parents and their children or, more generally, between adults and teenagers. Nearly every young adult novel contains elements of this theme because parents and teenagers are facing challenges that accompany a changed relationship once teenagers are old enough to drive, have jobs outside of school, and choose their own friends. It isn't Ellie's fault that she and her dad are so different—that he is six feet four inches tall and looks like Abraham Lincoln, while she is both more rounded and more grounded. As a motivational speaker, her father "guarantees" to help people make their lives "more interesting, productive, and self-sustaining." This makes overweight Ellie feel that her father views her as walking evidence of his failure. When she isn't focusing on her weight, Ellie thinks "what bugs Dad most about me is that I love something he's always resented" (11).

Ellie's dad says that "A life without goals is a life without direction" (4). He encourages Ellie to write down her goals, but she argues that she isn't likely to forget her dreams of growing the biggest pumpkin in Iowa and losing twenty pounds. She has succeeded in the latter goal several times, but the pounds keep coming back. A contributing factor is that she cooks dinner for her dad, and often for her cousin Richard, who mostly gets TV dinners at home. Ellie is a wonderful cook, especially with desserts, and it's through her cooking that she tries to reach her father.

When Ellie reads an article in *Seventeen* magazine about kids getting along better with their parents, she consults Richard about how she can get her father to respect her. His opinion is that "people respect people that are either like them or people they want to be like" (9). She responds with "so?" and he advises her that it's a lost cause. She needs to be her own person, and to have a *good* relationship with her father (she already has *a* relationship) she would have to change everything about herself. Fortunately, Richard is wrong, and when Ellie and her dad visit her mother's grave just before it's time to cut Max from his vine, Ellie feels closer to her father than she ever has. And when she pulls back from joining him in repeating one of the slogans that he uses with his customers, he accepts her explanation.

What makes *Squashed* refreshing is that Bauer is able to treat these conflicts with both humor and respect. While readers are reminded of their own conflicts with parents and other adults, they are also encouraged because once you've smiled at something it doesn't seem quite so frightening, and the happy ending with Ellie and her father leaves readers with hope.

In *Squashed,* parent/child conflicts are not restricted to Ellie and her father. It is obvious that Richard and his mother are a good team, yet they don't always agree. The same can be said for Ellie and her schoolteachers, especially Miss Moritz, the history teacher who sends a note home to Ellie's dad saying that Ellie isn't working to full capacity and that she seems to tie everything she does to pumpkins. Ellie's dad writes back that he's getting used to it. An important difference is that underneath these three conflicts, there is really a sense of love and respect, while the conflict between Ellie and Cyril is different because Ellie's contempt for Cyril is justified by his actions.

The previous year, when Cyril became the "four-time Weigh-In champ" and beat Ellie by 91.3 pounds, he complained so loudly that the whole world could hear that he was disappointed that the town "couldn't find him a more formidable opponent." This is Ellie's paraphrase. Cyril didn't really say *formidable* because he doesn't "use words more than six letters long" (19). He is the only farmer in the area so pretentious as to name his farm. He lives with his aunt—Ellie is sure he will never marry, which is "just as well for future generations" (17).

Early in the book when Ellie and Richard take the long way to school so they can get a glimpse of BIG DADDY, Cyril rises to his full five feet four inches, smacks down his oily hair, and "with his eyes on fire" says, "I call that a *champeen* pumpkin, Missy. Better'n anything you've ever seen." Ellie fakes casualness and tells Cyril that it could make a real nice jack-o'-lantern for some child, and then, in what even Ellie recognizes as childish behavior, she grabs Richard and they run off "like little kids who had just rung some old codger's doorbell for the fifteenth time" (18).

It speaks well for Ellie's growth that by the end of the book she is much too sophisticated for this kind of behavior.

LITERARY TECHNIQUES

Joan Bauer does a good job of drawing readers into the emotional lives of her characters. Readers who have never grown anything, much less given a thought to the growing of giant pumpkins, nevertheless feel nervous for Ellie as she awaits the outcome of the contest. Readers empathize with her, when in one way she wins and in another way she loses, because they know that the compromised dream is a part of life. Readers, along with practically the whole town, cheer when the mayor describes Ellie as "a rising Rock River star." They also agree with the *Chicago Tribune* reporter who interviews Ellie for forty-seven minutes and then writes that she is "the most determined teenager" she has ever met (189).

Bauer has fun with her writing. Even before readers get into the story, they might notice that she dedicates the book to "Evan, my squash partner." Evan is her husband, and whether or not they play the game of squash, the dedication is funny because of the visual images it inspires, including the fast-moving sport that is far removed from the idea of majesty that Ellie thinks is appropriate for giant pumpkins.

Judging from the twenty-eight readers, mostly young people, who by fall of 2006 had contributed reviews to Amazon.com, what they appreciate most in *Squashed* is Bauer's ability to tell a serious and believable story while at the same time making them smile. Here are excerpts from what some of them wrote:

- ◆ Ellie went through some challenging times, but it was just plain fun to read.
- ◆ Who knew a book about pumpkins could be so ingenious?

- What a fantastic book! Funny, touching, interesting.
- I found myself laughing every few minutes even though I've read the book about six times.
- I laughed out loud at Ellie's cynical remarks, including when she looks outside and sees "Old Abe" (that's what she calls her father) playing Handel's *Messiah* and giving Max one of his inspirational talks.
- Unfortunately I did not choose *Squashed* for my required reading book in class (woe is me!), but still I enjoyed rewarding myself with *Squashed* every time I finished a few chapters in the book I had chosen [but didn't like].
- It is proof that you can't judge a book by its cover. I groaned when our teacher said we had to read it, but I loved it so much I bought my own copy.

Along more serious lines, a reviewer praised the "gentle evolution" of Ellie's confidence, while another said she liked the way the "characters grew along with the pumpkin." A male teenager wrote that he made his mom read *Squashed* (she liked it too) because even though the party scene was written from Ellie's viewpoint, it was so well presented that he felt embarrassed for Ellie: "All of her feelings were mine." He identified so closely that he said he had to constantly look away from the book, something that rarely happens when he's reading, unless the book is so horrible that he wants to fling it against a wall. This wasn't at all the case with *Squashed.* He loved feeling so much empathy for the characters.

Bauer shows how every part of Ellie's life is influenced by her obsession with Max. When the new history teacher, Miss Moritz, assigns Ellie's class to study Winston Churchill and ponder all the dilemmas he faced during World War II and then to write an essay on one of them, Ellie thinks about the dilemma with which she can most identify. She writes on Churchill's eating habits. She works on it while sitting outside with her stomach growling as Max sucks up one of her secret booster solutions through a wick running from a steel dish to a carefully created slit in Max's vine. Her ponderings on Churchill, "a highly motivated individual and world leader who only thought great thoughts and reached his full potential," are interrupted by her father's appearance at the back door. As she sighs and gathers up her papers, she defensively explains that she was doing her homework. "With a vegetable in the dirt?" he asks. She corrects him by explaining she is with "an award-winning squash in the moonlight," and wonders why he can't see the same things in Max that she does (29).

Ellie labels her essay "Churchill's Dilemma: The Weight of World War II." Miss Moritz gives Ellie a C minus. Ellie figures this is a typical reaction from "a sneaky, skinny person like Miss Moritz," but Richard is more philosophical and says it is because Miss Moritz is a new teacher, and new teachers can't help themselves, "having been filled with all that poop in college." Students simply have to "wait them out" until their enthusiasm dies (31).

CHAPTER FOUR

THWONK

*T*HWONK IS DIFFERENT FROM BAUER'S OTHER NOVELS in that it contains a fantasy element. It was one of her hardest books to write, but now it is one of her favorites because of the way it shows how humor is about letting the absurd break into your everyday perspectives.

The book's title comes from the noise that is made when Jonathan shoots one of his tiny arrows. Jonathan is a magical creature temporarily inhabiting the somewhat bedraggled, stuffed body of a six-inch cupid doll. But other than Jonathan, who is as much of a surprise to the characters as he is to Bauer's regular readers, *Thwonk* is as realistic and as believable as Bauer's other books, which treat the challenges of growing up with humor and originality.

Jonathan pays an off-and-on, one-week "visitation" to seventeen-year-old Allison Jean (commonly known as A. J.) McCreary. She has to promise not to tell anyone about him, at least not until she is mature enough to understand the situation. This means that neither her parents nor her friends, not even the boy that Jonathan shoots with his arrows—A. J. insisted on it—knows what's going on. Much of the fun for readers comes from the fact that they know more than the characters do, and quite often, more than A. J. does, even though she is the one telling the story of how in the week preceding the King of Hearts Valentine's dance, the most handsome boy in school suddenly thinks he is in love with her.

As Bauer did in *Hope Was Here,* when Aunt Addie and Hope move to the Welcome Stairways diner in Wisconsin, she shares some of what she knows about good food and its preparation and marketing. A. J.'s mother is a partner in a high-quality gourmet shop, where A. J. frequently works. However, A. J. considers her work at the gourmet shop, which is a fancy bakery and catering service, as just something she does to help her mother. What she really wants to do in life is to become a world-class photographer. She has already won several prizes and is presently the leading photographer at her high school even though she does not "do normal." Her father has taught her to look for "decisive" moments and to create photos that "drip with emotion."

When A. J. was still in early elementary school, her father decided that he could not make a living as a fine arts photographer or filmmaker, so he joined an advertising agency in New York City and A. J.'s family moved from Chicago to live in a Connecticut suburb. The family move from Chicago to Connecticut was probably inspired by Bauer's own life because she grew up in Chicago and worked there during her twenties. Then, when she met and married Evan Bauer, they moved to Connecticut, and he commuted to his job in New York City.

MAIN CHARACTERS

A. J. McCreary is unusually ambitious and wants desperately to become a famous photographer. She has even named her black-and-white fuzz ball of a keeshond Alfred Stieglitz, after the great black-and-white photographer from the turn of the century. A. J. has a vivid imagination and a flair for the dramatic. For example, when she catches a glimpse of the mother of the boy she has a crush on, she smiles as she thinks about how the two of them will soon be spending holidays together and what a model daughter-in-law she will be: "caring, hospitable, impervious to stinging criticism." She will keep her judgmental thoughts to herself and won't even make them get rid of the pig statue on the front lawn that makes a perfectly fine house look like it might be a petting zoo (73–74).

A. J.'s mom is a wonderful chef and, according to A. J., "businessperson of the century." When it comes to food, she is a perfectionist. She had a fairly successful catering business in Chicago, which is why eight years ago she resisted the idea of moving to Crestport, Connecticut. But after being in town for a few months, she walks into Hal Blitzer's gourmet shop and tells him that the women of Crestport are bored. She could increase his business exponentially by giving lessons on out-of-the-ordinary cooking and entertaining. Within a few years, she becomes a full partner in Blitzer's greatly expanded business, which is now named The Emotional Gourmet. An example of her thoughtfulness is the bouquet of yellow roses she keeps by the cash register. When customers come in to pick up their orders for a special event, she hands them a yellow rose along with her best wishes.

A. J.'s dad wanted to be a fine arts photographer, but when he discovered that he could not make a living by taking the photos he wanted, he stored his equipment, his partly finished short films, and hundreds of negatives and prints in a closet. He donned a suit and put his creative energies into commercial advertising. Even though he passed his love of photography on to A. J. and taught her everything she knows about taking and developing pictures, he resists A. J.'s plans to go to art school because he does not want her to suffer the same kind of professional disappointments that he went through. Other than this one disagreement, which they tiptoe around, they have a warm and loving relationship.

Peter Terris is the most gorgeous boy A. J. has ever seen. When the book opens, she has secretly been taking pictures of him during the last five months, ever since she accidentally tripped over his "flawless foot" when she was walking through the student center on her way to English lit. She would have just forgotten about the incident except that she was especially vulnerable because her last boyfriend, who went off to college, hadn't telephoned as he said he would, and she happened to look up into Peter's "ice-green eyes" and observe that "they were positively riveting" (6). She is so swept off her feet that she does not even consider that he is captain of the varsity soccer team, that he already has an excruciatingly beautiful girlfriend, and that she knows nothing about what he thinks or what he likes to do. Readers learn little more about him except that he does things with vigor.

Jonathan is a little hard to explain because he is a magical creature temporarily disguised as a cupid doll complete with a quiver of arrows and a tiny bow. When he falls off a delivery truck right in front of A. J.'s car, she jumps out and picks him up thinking that maybe she can use him in the photo she has agreed to supply for the front page of the special Valentine's issue of the *Oracle,* her high school's newspaper. As A. J. later learns, Jonathan's sudden appearance is no accident. He was sent to her because he failed with his last assigned visitation to a teenager. When A. J. demands to know what planet he's from, he shakes his head in disbelief and says, "You must rid your mind of the dowdy American notion that anything you don't understand comes from outer space" (47).

Trish is A. J.'s best girlfriend. Readers get to know A. J.'s innermost thoughts because of what A. J. shares with Trish. They've been best friends for seven years, ever since they got stuck in the same seat on a stalled carnival ride. Even then, Trish was a sympathetic listener and a comfort. Now, she is so noble that when A. J. gets ditched at the Valentine's dance by her "true love," Trish pretends her foot is hurting and makes her date go over and ask A. J. to dance. Especially after the fiasco with her new boyfriend, A. J. values Trish's friendship as a precious relationship "mired in history" (103).

SETTING

The town of Crestport, Connecticut, serves mostly as a backdrop setting for *Thwonk*. However, its location within commuting distance of New York City is part of the plot related to A. J.'s dad and his career switch from freelance photography and filmmaking to working in commercial advertising. The fact that the people are generally affluent relates to Mrs. McCleary's success at The Emotional Gourmet.

Ever since her mother started her business, A. J. has been coming to the shop after school, first sitting quietly behind the scenes doing her homework, but later working in the store or helping with tasks ranging from bagging people's orders to rinsing lettuce for three hundred salads. Readers get a glimpse into the town and the mother-daughter relationship when A. J. writes about how she and her mother always work into the late afternoon on Saturdays getting orders ready for Saturday night parties. The hardest part for A. J. is kissing up to the most demanding customers. As she sardonically observes, "It takes big lips to succeed in this business" (24). Another one of her observations is that rich people never carry money with them. When she tells Mrs. T. Alexander Worthington, who just ordered a dozen of her mom's famous sautéed cashew buns, that the cost is twelve dollars, Mrs. Worthington bristles, "I have an account, dear!" A. J. writes in the account book, "Old Bat! Twelve bucks," which makes her ever-observant mother slam the book shut.

The time of year is a more important part of the setting. The story, except for the denouement, takes place during the week before

Valentine's Day, which as most people agree comes at the absolute low point of the year. Everybody's bored with cold weather and dirty snow; spring break is a long way off, and winter coats are starting to look grubby. Even though the students at A. J.'s school are fairly well-off, still they are surprised when A. J.'s date brings her to the King of Hearts Valentine's Day Dance in a limousine. Previous trendsetters have hired limousines for the prom, but never for the King of Hearts Dance.

PLOT

At first glance, readers might think that the conflict in the story is going to be between A. J. and her father, or between A. J. and Jonathan (the magical doll), or between A. J. and Peter Terris (the handsome hunk), but really the conflict is that of A. J. against herself. She is a dynamic character who over the course of the book changes her thinking and her values. At the beginning, she is sure that all she needs is to be loved by Peter Terris. At the end, she still wants a boyfriend, but her thoughts about the situation are considerably different.

In plots of this kind, in which most of the action takes place inside the main character's mind, authors have to find ways to let readers get to know and come to like their main character. Only when readers have feelings for a character will they care whether or not the character develops insights or undergoes a change of heart.

Whether or not A. J. can develop a more realistic outlook on matters of love and life is the real problem of the book, but the story begins with one dilemma that is easier to illustrate. A. J. is fretting over the fact that the King of Hearts Valentine's Day Dance is only eight days away. Even though it is a girl-ask-boy event, she does not have anyone she can ask. She missed the Let's-Keep-the-Magic-Forever Prom, last year's Homecoming Howl, and, for three years running, the King of Hearts Dance. She is now a senior and is obsessing over her lack of a date because she won't have another chance. Besides, the dance is often a kind of trial run for the prom. Couples who have a good time at the Valentine's dance often go to the prom together.

Because nearly all readers can see from the beginning that the way A. J. goes about getting Peter Terris to ask her—even though she is supposed to be the one doing the asking—to the dance is not the basis for a long-lasting romance, the plot is more episodic than one of continually rising action. Bauer tells the story through the following episodes.

Episode One: Home Alone

On a weekend when her parents are out of town, A. J. has to slam on her brakes to keep from literally running into (or over) Jonathan, who suddenly appears on the road looking "like a Pillsbury Doughboy dressed up for Valentine's Day" (40). She brings the doll home to her photography studio, thinking she can use it as a prop for the cover shot she has promised the editor of the school newspaper. However, at midnight, the whining and barking of Stieglitz prompts her to look into her studio, where she is shocked to find "*the cupid!*" standing there looking at her with fiery black eyes, little rosy cheeks, and "*breathing!*" (45). After the initial shock of learning that the cupid, whose name is Jonathan, has been "assigned" the mission of helping her in order to rectify a previous "failed" assignment, A. J. is amused by Jonathan's ability to flutter around like a butterfly (seen and heard only by her and Stieglitz) and by his dinky bow and tiny satchel of poisoned arrows, which he claims will allow him to bring the truth to people.

Episode Two: Making a Deal with Jonathan

Jonathan tells her that he can help her in one of three ways: academically, professionally or romantically. Jonathan shows his academic abilities by helping her ace a test in art history for which she had forgotten to study. Then he demonstrates his photographic genius by finding the perfect subject for her to photograph for the Valentine's edition of the school paper. He takes her to the beach where, to the left of an embankment, a big, craggy rock juts out toward the sea. It has been painted with a huge graffiti message:

> DONNA LOVES ~~STEVE~~
> ~~GARY~~
> ~~DEREK~~
> ~~NATHANIEL~~
> DONNA IS CONFUSED (60)

A. J. is ecstatic because with the crossed-out names it is "love in the age of angst ... perfect Valentine funk" (61). Jonathan even coaches her on how to capture the best light. Later in her studio when he continues giving advice on how to best develop the film, she dismisses him by saying she doesn't really want advice from a miniature Ansel Adams. He holds his tongue, even when his advice turns out to be right. In spite of this proof that Jonathan can really help her academically and professionally, A. J. stubbornly insists that he help her romantically. She wants him to shoot Peter Terris with an arrow so he will fall in love with her. Jonathan is not at all enthusiastic about A. J.'s choice of his talents nor of the boy he is supposed to "get" for her. He argues that "infatuation cannot be sustained indefinitely.... Love that embraces the entire person is a monumental gift that takes time to grow!" (73). A. J. is nevertheless insistent and even drives Jonathan to Peter's house and sits out front while Jonathan goes in to do the deed.

Episode Three: A Seven-Day Romance

Because of his breathtaking girlfriend, his self-interest, and his hard heart, even after being shot directly in the heart Peter takes some time to come to the realization that he simply cannot live without A. J. Jonathan's arrow finally takes effect on Sunday night while Peter is eating meatloaf. He phones A. J. and shows up at her house at the same time that her parents are returning from their trip. He suffers a brief relapse, but the next morning he is there in his Jeep with the offer of a hot blueberry muffin for breakfast and a ride to school. A. J. is mesmerized at the new lifestyle that Peter's love brings her. He can hardly bear to be apart from A. J. He walks her to every class, showers her with presents, and buys a full page ad in the school newspaper to declare how much he loves her. The popular people who have ignored A. J. for years suddenly see her as someone special with an outstanding gift for taking photographs. She is invited to put together an exhibit for the student center, and of course the happy couple makes plans to go to the Valentine's dance, where Peter will undoubtedly be crowned the King of Hearts.

Episode Four: A Change of Heart

After a few days of this constant attention, A. J. resents her loss of freedom. She is miserable because Peter is acting like a robot and has lost interest in his schoolwork and even in sports. His beautiful ice-green eyes have grown dull and listless, "clouded with cupid manipulation" (143).

When she begs him to curb his enthusiasm because it embarrasses her, he does not try to understand her feelings, nor does he have any interest in her aspirations as a photographer. She desperately tries to locate Jonathan in order to beg his forgiveness and ask him to return Peter to his former self. Unfortunately, Jonathan has mysteriously disappeared from her life. A. J. reaches the end of her rope at the Valentine's dance when she and Peter line up with the other contestants for the King of Hearts announcement and A. J. suddenly realizes that she is not a legitimate member of this group of popular students, nor does she want to be. Her mind sizzles with the idea that she is there by trickery, *"Fake! Fake!"* (179). At last, Jonathan comes back into view, and after much begging and manipulation by A. J., he shoots Peter with a counterbalancing arrow that changes him back into the self-absorbed "world-class chump" he always was (191).

Episode Five: The Denouement

Peter returns to his former girlfriend, Julia, and A. J. returns to her photography, getting many great shots at the dance—ones with which even her father is impressed. It has only been a week, but as spring comes to Benjamin High School and to the town of Crestport, A. J. has changed. She has a new status and a more mature outlook on people and life. Everyone knows who she is, and since the best boy in school fell madly in love with her, people continue to be curious about her. A. J. begins seeing people for who they really are and begins choosing her (boy)friends a little more carefully. And although she has to say good-bye to Jonathan (he leaves the cupid doll behind), she has learned a great deal from him. She is alive to things she had never seen before. Her senses are heightened so that she laughs and cries more. Through her camera she watches life and studies it, "from a new plane ... hungry for truth" (209). And even without Jonathan's academic help, she is so successful in her schoolwork and in her photography that in the same week she gets admitted to two excellent arts colleges: NYU and the Rhode Island Institute of Design. She complains:

> "Isn't that just like the educational system, to throw in a multiple choice test when they think you're not looking?" But for once A. J. felt ready. (213)

THEMES

As with many fantasies, *Thwonk* allows readers to walk through a kind of mirror and then look back and see the real world through a different lens. Quick and easy ways to state some of the themes that Bauer explores in *Thwonk* include the following:

- ◆ Be careful what you wish for.
- ◆ There can be too much of a good thing.
- ◆ People are human, that is, no one is perfect.

The trouble with such clichés is that they are like those tricky little rules in English grammar that have to be learned over and over again because the situations are never exactly the same. When Peter suffers a temporary release from the power of Jonathan's arrow and runs back home from his initial visit to A. J.'s house, she remembers Mrs. Pilson, her Sunday school teacher, telling the story of King Solomon and how when God asked Solomon what he wanted, he replied, "Wisdom." Billy Haggamon piped up to say he would have chosen to own the Lionel Train Company, and Mrs. Pilson implied that this is why God would not be giving Billy such a choice. A. J. moans: "*I* had had a choice. A rich, magical life-changing choice. And I had gone the way of Billy Haggamon. I had blown it" (104).

But then the phone rings, and it is Peter calling to apologize for running out like he did on his first visit. Will she please forgive him? A. J. not only forgives him, she forgets all about King Solomon versus Billy Haggamon, and she curls into a happy ball on her futon and looks forward to the next morning when Peter has promised to come by in his Jeep and give her a ride to school.

Another example of a theme is the old cliché: "You can lead a horse to water, but you can't make him drink." This is a description of what A. J. does to Peter. The magic arrow makes him go through the outside motions of being in love with A. J., but it could not make him understand or empathize with her. Nor could it make A. J. relate to Peter's interests or enable her to have a real conversation with him.

Although A. J. lives to regret her foolishness and also to feel sorry for keeping things secret from Trish, she is not sorry to have had the experience of living in what she calls "the Big Time." Having Peter Terris totally in love with her was like "tooling down a busy road in a brand-new Ferrari" (116). Everyone looks, and everyone is jealous, but the best part is that when it is all over, A. J. has a new kind of confidence and a new set of acquaintances. She has grown into her name of *Allison,* which Bauer said she chose because of its meaning of "one who deserves to be loved."

LITERARY TECHNIQUES

Because *Thwonk* starts out as a realistic book and then turns into a fantasy, Bauer relies more on the literary techniques of foreshadowing and the inclusion of motifs related to magical creatures than in her other books. While foreshadowing does not give away the plot, hints or clues are dropped that prepare readers to suspend their disbelief. An early example occurs when A. J. shares the fact that her parents are worried about how quickly she falls in love. This is accompanied by her complaint about how within the last year she has lost four boyfriends whose dream potential turned "into Swiss cheese" (8). Two of the boys went back to their previous girlfriends, one went off to college, and one insulted her true love, namely photography. The one who insulted her love for photography was probably Todd Kovitch, who felt "ripped" when she brought her camera to the prom and appeared less interested in him than in taking advantage of the photo ops provided by "a boundless supply of photogenic bozos who could be counted on to do something base" (10).

When A. J.'s mother sees how she has fallen for Peter, she tries to warn her that maybe she should slow down, but A. J. rejects her advice by saying she doesn't want to talk about it. Her mother responds, "I know you don't ... but we need to talk about it" (109). She points out that A. J.'s infatuation with Peter is very similar to what happened with Robbie Oldsberg, Scott Zimmerman, and Don Lucetti. She doesn't want A. J. to jump into another relationship without thinking about it. She advises A. J. that she will never find the kind of perfection she is looking for because it just isn't "out there" (109).

Instead of trying to understand the point her mother is making, A. J. takes off on how funny it is for her mother to speak against perfection, when she is the one who slaves for hours to "perfect her Candied Claret

Pears that guests … consume in eleven minutes flat" (109). In another observation on A. J.'s impatience, when she complains to Mr. Zeid, the art history teacher, that she can't get her photos to show the pain she is feeling, he tells her that even such a genius as Michelangelo took years to figure out how to communicate his feelings when he painted the Sistine Chapel. When looked at together, these incidents give readers insight into A. J.'s flair for exaggeration and dramatization, which, in turn, allows readers to be amused rather than alarmed at A. J.'s current and future experiences with her "painful" love life.

Foreshadowing serves a different purpose when A. J.'s parents are getting ready to go away for the weekend and A. J. keeps asking, *"What could possibly happen in forty-eight hours?"* (18). The fact that A. J. and her mother have "been back and forth for weeks" about this matter helps readers predict that something unusual is going to happen between the time A. J.'s parents leave on Friday night and when they arrive back home on Sunday night. Of course, there is no way readers could have guessed that A. J. would pick up a cupid doll that would come to life, but that is the fun of foreshadowing. It inspires a sense of anticipation while still providing opportunities for surprises.

Motifs are small incidents, items, or events that are repeated from story to story so that they have become almost symbolic. While magic is set outside of the regular physical laws of the world, imagined magical creatures are nevertheless created by humans and so reflect common human dreams and desires. Over the centuries, certain beliefs about "magic" have coalesced into motifs, several of which Bauer uses in relation to her creation and characterization of Jonathan. Because most readers have had previous experience with the concepts, authors can rely on their readers' knowledge of the basics while they spend their time adding interesting new details.

- *Magical creatures are small.* A. J.'s first happy idea was that Jonathan would be her own tiny pet that she could carry around in a pocket. However, he put a quick stop to that by explaining that he was not a toy, but was on a serious assignment. Readers soon forget how small he is because of the unusual things he can accomplish.

- *Animals are more sensitive to magic than are people.* Stieglitz, A. J.'s dog, gives the first clues that something is not quite right. After A. J. tosses the cupid into her studio and tries to go to bed, Stieglitz won't stay in the bathroom as usual but shakes "in uncurbed neurosis," then whines pathetically at A. J.'s feet and begins running in circles and pawing at the door (42–43).
- *Midnight is a magical time.* Probably the best-known example of this motif is in the Cinderella story where the poor girl has to get home from the ball before midnight, which is sometimes called "the witching hour," when her finery is scheduled to turn into rags. In A. J.'s case, Stieglitz pounces on A. J. and gets her out of bed so that just as "the clock struck midnight (only figuratively—it was digital)" she and Stieglitz find themselves at the door to her studio where "a weirdness" is winding its way into the night. The whole thing is "creepy, crawly," as the wind picks up and Stieglitz howls like a wolf (44).
- *Magical creatures are psychic.* If this were not the case, the magical beings in old folktales would not be able to figure out who among all the young people of the world deserve their help as opposed to characters who are just plain greedy or selfish. One of the first things that A. J. learns about Jonathan is that he can read her thoughts, and when she asks him to stop he explains that it is not within his power to disconnect, but then he adds, "Confusion when addressed, can bring forth clarity" (54).
- *Magic has to be paid for.* The clichés about there being "no such thing as a free lunch" and "if something sounds too good to be true, it probably is" have come from hundreds of cautionary tales in which characters are tricked into giving away their souls, or their birthright, or their firstborn child in exchange for some immediate but relatively trivial reward. We know that A. J. has heard her fair share of such stories because when Jonathan finally convinces her that he really is magical and has come to "assist" her, she asks him about the catch. He assures her there is no catch, but she's skeptical.
- *Magicians have their own sets of rules.* These restrictions, which usually include trust and honesty, are often what is demanded as

"payment" by both the magician and the recipient. There would be little excitement in the plot of a story if magicians could simply wave a wand or shoot an arrow and thereby solve all the world's problems. On page 52, Jonathan informs A. J. of "the laws governing the Visitation." These include the fact that only A. J. and her "dog, of course," can see Jonathan; the two of them must "press on" because they have much to accomplish in a limited amount of time; A. J. must tell no one about Jonathan; and A. J. must believe him when he says that he has come to help her, not harm her.

- *Three is a magical number*. People's reverence for the number three extends from such serious realms as the Holy Trinity in Christianity to such favorite folktales as "The Three Bears," "The Three Little Pigs," and "The Three Billy Goats Gruff." Magical creatures usually offer people three wishes. As a variation on this theme, Jonathan offers A. J. the choice of helping her in one of three areas. He proves his academic prowess when he helps her ace a test and his professional powers when he leads her to the perfect subject to photograph for the Valentine's edition of the newspaper. As she later admits, she foolishly ignored these demonstrations, and even without proof of his abilities in romance, asked him to help her nab Peter Terris as a boyfriend.

- *Things must be done right*. The idea in the popular 1993 film *Groundhog Day*, starring Bill Murray, is that because Murray's character, a TV weatherman, muffed his reporting assignment (for one thing, he got caught in a blizzard that he failed to predict) and refuses to recognize truths about himself, he must keep reliving February 2nd in Punxsutawney, Pennsylvania, until he gets it right. This is the situation facing Jonathan. He had been assigned to help a teenager, apparently someone with romantic dreams much like A. J.'s, and there's tension throughout the story as A. J. tries to get him to tell her what went wrong.

- *Only the original magician can "correct" or redo a charm*. This is a necessary restriction seen throughout the fantasy genre. Stories would lose their integrity if there were no restraints on one magician "topping" another one. This is why when A. J. comes to the realization that her "romance" with Peter is all wrong, she does not go looking for a new cupid, but frantically searches for Jonathan. It is in keeping with his independent spirit that he comes on his own schedule, but still he arrives at the Valentine's dance when A. J. needs him most. He even brings along her camera so that A. J. can return to being a star photographer once Peter goes back to his old girlfriend. By this time, readers, along with A. J., have developed such a trust in Jonathan that they do not question how such a tiny creature could fly in carrying A. J.'s heavy camera, which she uses to trick Peter into standing still long enough for Jonathan to get a good aim as he shoots a counterbalancing arrow into Peter's heart.

CHAPTER FIVE

STICKS

O N HER WEB SITE, JOAN BAUER SAYS that she learned to play pool as a young teenager and was instantly smitten with the "womb-like atmosphere of the pool hall." Outside it could be any season, any temperature, and any weather, but inside there are people playing pool and taking it seriously. Players can come in any size, shape, or age, and they can be from any race or cultural background; all that is necessary is for them to take the time to watch good players and to hone their skills.

The game has rhythm so that the best players move like dancers, and just by listening you can tell who the good players are. Bauer likes the fact that pool is basically simple—players just aim and shoot—but at a deeper level, players also use complex strategies to own and defend their tables. The game has a physical and a mental side, and to demonstrate this point Bauer devised the plot of *Sticks* to show two good friends working together. Mickey Vernon has the physical dexterity, while his best friend Arlen Pepper has the intellectual talent. Mickey and Arlen help Bauer share her fondness for pool with both a new generation of players and readers whose only chance to learn about pool might be through her book.

Main Characters

Mickey Vernon is ten years old and tall for his age, "five-four to be exact," which puts him even with his grandmother, Poppy, who is the owner and manager of Vernon's Pool Hall. Mickey has been waiting for his tenth birthday because that's when kids are eligible to compete in the annual youth tournament sponsored by his family's business. Mickey knows that it sounds pretty impossible for him as a ten-year-old to beat a teenager, but he has beaten lots of older kids. His father, who died when Mickey was a baby, was a nationally ranked player, and so Mickey thinks he was born with pool in his blood (4).

Arlen Pepper is a very bright but at the same time very forgetful ten-year-old. He is close to being a genius in mathematics, but he often can't remember where he's left his jacket or his book bag. He and Mickey are such good friends that, except on rainy days, Mickey walks the eight blocks to school with Arlen because the bus fumes make Arlen carsick. Arlen owns a pet pig named Mangler, and between the two of them they provide readers with smiles and maybe even laughs.

Francine is Arlen's cousin. After school, Arlen stays at her house until his parents get home. She is the same age as Mickey and Arlen, but she goes to the Catholic school instead of the public school. Mickey and Arlen like her because she is as ambitious and dedicated as they are. She wants to be the first teenage magician to perform in Las Vegas, while Arlen wants to become a famous mathematician, and Mickey wants to be the nine-ball champion of the world.

Buck Pender is a thirteen-year-old bully and a cheat. Besides looking like he "eats cement for breakfast," Buck takes every opportunity to let Mickey know that he plans to win the championship (61). He "smiles ugly" and calls Mickey "*Vernon*" in a tone that makes Mickey feel like he doesn't deserve the name (19).

Poppy is Mickey's grandmother, who, for much longer than Mickey has been alive, has managed Vernon's Pool Hall, which she and her late husband built forty years ago in the town of Cruckston, New Jersey. On Wednesday nights she teaches pool at the senior center because she thinks older Americans would be better off if they played more pool than bingo.

Mickey's mom, Ruthie, teaches in a preschool, but she is just about to earn her college diploma and a teaching certificate so that she can teach kids who won't be as likely to smear her clothes with food. She was widowed at age twenty-seven, when Mickey was eight months old. When her husband died from cancer, the people in Cruckston were so supportive and kind that she decided to stay and live with her husband's mother on top of the pool hall rather than move to Florida where her own mother lives.

Mickey's dad, Charlie, died from cancer, but he is important to the story because he was such a good pool player that by the age of twelve he was beating adults on the professional nine-ball circuit. In one of the videos Mickey has seen, his dad played nearly three hundred balls without missing. Mickey proudly claims to have "everything about him memorized good," including the fact that his hair was jet black, he had brown eyes, and blue was his favorite color (5).

Big Earl Reed is the day manager of the pool hall. His great-great-grand-father was a slave in Mississippi, and his father died when he was only two. Mickey says this gives them something in common and is one of the reasons that they are friends even though Mickey is only ten and Big Earl is fifty-three. Earl uses Baby Gal, a guitar that he got in New Orleans, to play the blues. He played a sad song about good men dying young at Charlie Vernon's funeral. Sometimes Mickey asks him to play it for him (28).

Camille is Mickey's sixteen-year-old sister. When the book opens, she is involved in designing and sewing costumes for the high school play. This is her chance "to show the world her talent," but she's afraid she'll mess up. Mickey tries to console her by saying what people say to him about pool, "there's always another game." Her feelings are hurt because this "isn't a stupid pool game," it's her *life* (26).

Joseph Alvarez is an old friend of Mickey's father who disappeared from Cruckston almost immediately after Mickey's dad died from cancer. He has now come back to town in his own shiny, green Peterbilt rig. He and his brother saved enough money from working in Alaska to establish a long-distance trucking firm with its headquarters in Cruckston.

Setting

Mickey Vernon has grown up in the family home on top of the pool hall in Cruckston, New Jersey. Mickey thinks it's a cool place to live, especially when he gets to have his tenth birthday party on the fenced-in roof. Mickey and four friends have to use flashlights to climb up the creaky stairs leading from the passageway out of the back of Mickey's closet. From the top, they see the whole layout of the abandoned paper mill, the neon sign on LOANS WHILE U WAIT, and six blocks away the New Jersey Turnpike with its constant string of moving lights. Even though it rains and the boys have to sleep in a tent, it is the best birthday Mickey can remember.

The fact that the freeway is close by is crucial to the plot because that is the only way that Joseph Alvarez could have chosen Cruckston as the headquarters for his trucking company. The first night that Joseph comes to dinner, he says he remembers the dining table. Grandma Poppy is amused because of all the special scratches and nicks that are on it, and if anyone is interested she will be glad to tell the history of each one.

Bauer is clever in the way she uses the names of characters and places to communicate extra information almost on a subconscious level. Readers get the idea that at least for Mickey's sister, Camille, living in *Cruckston,* New Jersey, is her personal *cross to bear.* This is highlighted by the difference between the name of *Cruckston* and the exotic places from which Joseph Alvarez sends postcards:

Ottawa.
Winnipeg.
Moose Jaw.
Medicine Hat. (114)

And later they arrive from Thunder Bay and Toronto (121). Joseph's last name of *Alvarez* also conveys that he has a different background than Mickey's family.

Readers can hardly blame Camille for preferring a nice, new house in the suburbs to Flax Street with its old, gray buildings and boarded-up stores intermixed with small shops. Two years ago, Mr. Shankiss came to town and promised to build a fancy restaurant that would revitalize Flax Street. But after he dug a huge, dangerous hole in the ground, he ran out of money and moved away. He is referred to as "the quitter" and is the most hated man in Cruckston.

Mickey does not want to be like him; he would rather be like Mrs. Cassetti, who runs the bakery and has a worn-out sign and the same old wedding cake in the window, or like Mr. Kopchnik, who runs the fix-it shop and when the weather is good sits outside listening to opera and taking apart a blender or a vacuum cleaner or whatever someone has brought in. On lucky days when Mickey passes Cut Rate Gas and Groceries, Mr. Gatto sticks his head out the window and tosses him a Tootsie Roll. As Mickey's mom tells Camille and Vernon, they aren't living above the pool hall just to keep alive the memory of their father. Instead, she has chosen to stay in Cruckston because she wants to be someplace where every day they will see people practicing the values that she holds dear: "loyalty, hard work, love, determination" (126).

Vernon's has twenty-four Brunswick tables, plus a small one for children that both Mickey and his dad learned to play on. By now, Mickey has won and lost on all twenty-four tables. The pool hall serves as almost a community center for a town that has seen better times. Poppy makes sure that pool remains "big stuff" in Cruckston. She offers special deals, including free lessons on Saturdays for kids and their families, and for a year after the paper mill closed she invited unemployed workers and their families to play for free every Wednesday afternoon. The mayor presented her with a plaque praising Vernon's for being "an anchor for the town." Poppy keeps it on a shelf where people can see it, right "next to her Pepto Bismol" (3).

Part of the story is set in the Grover Cleveland Elementary School, which Bauer makes more interesting than most schools. When Mickey's class starts studying the Revolutionary War, the history teacher brings in a tub of water and a plastic boat filled with Lipton tea bags and lets the students reenact the Boston Tea Party. Their room is covered with maps and drawings, and as they get further into the war, students draw names of real soldiers. They each get to choose one of the Revolutionary War battles for their soldier to fight in. After the battle, they imagine themselves in the place of the soldier and write a letter home to his family.

PLOT

The plot of *Sticks* is relatively simple. For as long as Mickey can remember, he has been playing pool, and now that he has passed the minimum age requirement, he feels that he *must* win the junior tournament. Part of his reasoning is the fact that his father was on his way to becoming a national champion when he died and so Mickey figures that it is up to him to carry on the family legacy. Mickey plans to be nationally known, but for now all he can think about is beating thirteen-year-old Buck Pender, a talented player but also a bully and a cheat. Mickey spends hours practicing, and he is happy to take tips from the regulars in the pool hall but is nevertheless surprised when a bearded stranger—a magnificent player—wearing cowboy boots offers the advice: "I'd watch that focus of yours son. ... You're missing more shots than you need to" (8).

The stranger turns out to be Joseph Alvarez, an old friend of Mickey's father. Readers, along with Mickey, gradually learn that Mickey's dad taught Joseph how to play. This fact contributes to Mickey's feeling that Joseph has miraculously appeared to get him ready for the tournament. Mickey's mother is not so sure about this "miracle," and warns Mickey that if he depends on Joseph he stands the chance of being disappointed.

Mickey's major problem is that while he is practicing, he spends almost as much time and energy peeking over at whatever table his nemesis, Buck, is playing on. Arlen lectures Mickey on the powers of positive thinking by asking him if he thinks mathematicians start their work thinking they can't finish a problem. In response, Mickey walks over to one of the tournament posters that Big Earl is putting up. He hopefully touches the YOU in "WE'RE LOOKING FOR THE BEST AND THAT COULD BE YOU!" But then he is distracted by the arrogant way that Buck walks out the door. Big Earl touches his shoulder and says:

> "World's full of Bucks, Mickey V."
> "One's too many."
> "First one just helps get you ready for the others."
> "Yeah ..." (61)

Much of the time while Bauer was writing *Sticks,* she was in pain. She had carpal tunnel syndrome, which occurs when the nerves that run through a person's wrist are being pinched or compressed. When this happens, people lose their fine motor control because the nerves are not registering what the skin is feeling. The person's hands are weakened and they hurt. The condition can usually be corrected through surgery, but still recovery time is needed. Bauer wanted to make use of all the experience she was having with pain. Maybe she thought that if she wrote about it, it would go away. First, she gave Poppy arthritis, and then she got the idea of Mickey hurting his hand and having to play through the pain or else miss his chance of winning the tournament at age ten.

A month before the tournament, Mickey and Buck are practicing on nearby tables, and, as usual, they are watching each other through sideways glances. Mickey is anxious because Joseph Alvarez is on a long delivery and Mickey worries that maybe he isn't coming back. Buck sneers, "Where's the cowboy, *Vernon?*" Mickey's friends tell him to ignore

Buck, but then Buck walks over and plants himself in front of Mickey and repeats, "I said, where's that stupid cowman of yours, *Vernon?*" (115).

Buck challenges Mickey to a game. Joseph has warned Mickey not to play Buck before the tournament, but as Mickey says while accepting Buck's challenge, it's like everything Joseph Alvarez taught him "went down the sewer" (116). Mickey loses the first two games, while Buck keeps needling him. Mickey pushes Buck away from him, and they begin hitting each other and actually fighting and rolling on the floor. Buck pushes Mickey off, and Mickey lands hard on his hand. Someone runs upstairs and gets Mickey's mom, and she and Big Earl put Mickey into her old Chevy and rush to the hospital.

His hand is not broken, but it's badly hurt. Mickey wants to blame the whole thing on Buck, but he knows that it would not have happened if he had followed everyone's advice and been thinking about his own game rather than about Buck. Now he has to decide whether to play through the pain or miss his chance of winning the tournament. Most people think he should just wait for next year. Arlen uses his calculator to show Mickey that he shouldn't be depressed. Figuring that the average male lives to be about seventy-three, he explains to Mickey that so far he has lived out only one-eighth of his life, "meaning you have about sixty-three years left to make good." When Mickey only sniffs in response, Arlen punches more buttons on his calculator and reports that if Mickey lived to be one hundred, this three-week setback would only be "six one hundredths of a percent, which is basically nothing in the whole sphere of the universe" (131).

Mickey refuses to be comforted. Poppy, probably because she is accustomed to working through her arthritis pain, encourages Mickey to keep practicing. His mom says he definitely cannot play if there is any danger that he will cause permanent injury to his hand. Three weeks after the injury and one week before the tournament, they go back to the doctor, who had originally said to give it three weeks. Mickey is hopeful because the swelling is gone and he can make a fist, but he has to admit that it hurts when the doctor bends his hand up. Finally, the doctor says something about Mickey Mantle playing baseball with unceasing pain for nineteen seasons and decides that "Mickey Vernon can play this week" (146). Nevertheless, she makes him promise to stop and use ice and put the brace back on if it hurts too much. As he and his mom get up to leave, the doctor asks him just how good he is. Mickey says he's "okay," but his mom says, "He's awesome!" (146).

THEMES

Sticks is a book about many kinds of friendship. There is the bittersweet friendship that Mickey's mom and Joseph Alvarez have; the respectful friendship that the downtown business people feel for Mickey, who they've watched grow up; the trusting friendship between Poppy and Big Earl as they run Vernon's Pool Hall; and the many incidental friendships that are part of the Vernon family's daily lives. However, the fullest example of what it means to be friends is the relationship between Mickey, Arlen, and Francine. Bauer published *Sticks* two years before the first Harry Potter book came out, but this three-way friendship is in many ways similar to the one between Harry, Ron, and Hermione. The relationship between Mickey and the bully, Buck Pender, along with Buck's two cronies named Freddie Castle and Pike Lorey is also similar to the one between Harry Potter and Draco Malfoy and his cronies, Crabbe and Goyle.

When the book opens, Mickey is in a practice match against Buck. Arlen is standing nearby eating Raisinets and passing secret codes to Mickey. He coughs twice and taps his Red Sox cap to tell Mickey that he should go for a bank shot, he shakes his Raisinets box to say "good shot," and he tugs his earlobe when he thinks Mickey is about to make a mistake. When Arlen, who is a gifted mathematician, first brought up the idea of relating geometry to pool, Mickey thought he was crazy, but since Arlen has been in gifted math since first grade, Mickey decides to listen in hopes of "getting the inside track" (6).

Arlen explains that whatever angle Mickey uses to hit the ball, it will bounce off the edge at exactly the same angle. This is just the first of many lessons that Arlen gives to Mickey about such matters as Isaac Newton's Laws of Motion "as they work on a pool table," how "every action has an equal and opposite reaction," and how great pool players picture "vectors" in their heads (177–80).

Mickey, Arlen, and Francine, Arlen's cousin, have been best friends since at least first grade. While they are equally ambitious, their goals are different, which is a good thing because they can use their complementary interests and skills to help each other, as when Arlen uses his math abilities to help Mickey, and Mickey uses his common sense to help Arlen remember—at least some of the time—to pick up his book bag, to take his jacket home, and to go back for whatever else he has accidentally left behind. When Francine is making a list for her parents of reasons why she must have a rabbit for her magic show, Mickey helps out by suggesting that she tell them that without a rabbit she will be unfulfilled. Arlen nods and suggests that she can tell them her creativity will dry up. Later, when the letter fails to move Francine's parents and she declares that she will no longer speak to her father, Arlen provides a reality check by using his calculator to show Francine just how many days and nights she is going to have to bite her tongue.

After Mickey composes a letter to Joseph, he reads it to Francine over the phone to see if he should include the sentence: "I'm pretty sure my dad would have wanted me to learn from you." Francine approves and tells Mickey that it has just the right touch and will probably get through to Joseph even if he "is a criminal" (59). Francine adds a light tone to the story because while Arlen and Mickey usually agree on things, she chimes in with a different viewpoint. For example, when Mickey is waiting eagerly for Joseph Alvarez to come back in his big Peterbilt rig, Francine warns Mickey that he better wear a bulletproof vest and be ready to call 911 "if Joseph does anything fishy" (72).

When Arlen and Mickey are launching into a big-time math project to figure out scientifically how many jelly beans are in the guessing tank at Pearlman's World of Fashion, Francine, who goes to Catholic school and plans to be a nun, touches her silver cross necklace and announces that Sister Immaculata has told her that God knows everything. She hints that maybe the boys should pray about it, but since Arlen and Mickey are convinced that God isn't going to tell them, they keep working on counting and measuring. Francine "pops the rubber band on her braces, grabs her mountain bike, … and heads out," because she can't be involved in anything dishonest. The sign, she points out, says they are supposed to "guess" (62).

While Francine will have nothing to do with the "scheme" to win the jelly bean contest, she is not above spying and reporting on Mickey and Arlen's competition for the science fair. She is also happy to bring them news about Buck, who since he was expelled from the Grover Cleveland Elementary School has attended the Catholic school. Mickey sits down hard on the day that Francine brings the news that Buck won the Good Citizen Award of the Week, but then she explains he won the prize for bringing in the most cans of food for the hunger drive. When Sister Immaculata notices Theresa Raster's initials on twelve cans of Chunky Soup, Buck has to give back the award and apologize at the class assembly, where students had to be lip-readers to understand what Buck was saying.

Arlen is scrupulously fair in sharing honors with Mickey both in the jelly bean "guessing" game and at the science fair, where they are full partners in creating their project. Arlen lectures and Mickey demonstrates connections between geometry and pool. However, Arlen is not so generous with more casual friends, as shown on the day that he figures out how to use his and Mickey's money plus that of Petie Pencastle, Matt Fitz, and Jeremy Dozier to get a better bargain than if they each paid forty-five cents for a bag of M&M's. Arlen explains the math while he heads past the "BEST BETS OF THE WEEK" sign to the regular candy aisle and picks up a one-pound bag. After taking out a handful for his management fee, he divides the pound into equal piles and Petie and Jeremy are "silenced by genius" (75).

Arlen has a pet pig named Mangler. When he and Mickey take Mangler out for walks, people gather around and watch, thanks partly to Mickey's admiring comments. As people look admiringly at Mangler, Arlen begins a lecture on how humans have misunderstood pigs and forced them to live in slop even though they are highly intelligent. Arlen holds a raisin above Mangler's head so that he dances for it. This demonstration is more fun at home when Arlen has Mangler dance to Beethoven's Fifth, but the crowd applauds anyway because they don't know what they are missing.

The friendship between Mickey's mom and Joseph Alvarez is not so clear. Joseph was the best friend of Mickey's dad, and when he died Mickey's mom expected Joseph to be nearby and to lend a hand to the family as Charlie had asked. Joseph was not good at communicating, and in dealing with his own grief he went off to Alaska, where he and his brother earned enough money to buy their trucks and eventually come back and establish the headquarters for their long-distance trucking enterprise close to Cruckston. He had been thinking about the Vernons the whole time, but Mickey's mom had no way of knowing this. When he reappears after nearly ten years of silence, she is cautious for herself, but especially for Mickey. She does not want him to develop a close relationship with Joseph and then to be hurt if Joseph disappears for another ten years.

The friendship that runs throughout the adult community is expressed through the graduation party that Poppy—and nearly the whole town—throws for Mickey's mom when she earns her teaching certificate. Mickey and his friends blow up one hundred balloons that they hang from ribbons all over the pool hall. Francine, who vowed to never speak to her father again when he refused to let her have a rabbit for her magic tricks, has acquired a dove that flies out of her magic hat. Poppy hires Francine to be the entertainment, and Joseph Alvarez brings buckets of Texas barbecue—the best anyone has ever tasted. Mickey's sister, Camille, kisses her boyfriend over by the Coke machine and Arlen gets a picture of the big event. Mickey's mom cries and thanks everyone for giving the party and for having it in the pool hall, where she's learned so much. Mickey adds his own opinion that some people just learn the rules, "But when the game's in your blood, you learn what's inside of you" (182).

A secondary theme in the novel is similar to the one that Bauer explores in *Squashed,* when Ellie's grandmother tries to get her to focus on her own giant pumpkin and to quit worrying about her competitor, the obnoxious Cyril Pool. In *Sticks,* Joseph Alvarez uses the Spanish word *ganas* as he tries to explain to Mickey the importance of focusing on his own long-term dream rather than on wasting his emotions and energy on distractions that are only temporary. Joseph compares his dream of owning a truck to his grandfather's dream of owning a cattle ranch and to Mickey's dream of becoming a champion.

Joseph uses the Spanish word *pundonor* when he talks to Mickey about "something you've got to do—a point of honor" (38). He also tells Mickey about *ganas.* While the two of them are getting acquainted in his truck during a stop at a red light, Joseph asks Mickey if he knew what Joseph found in Alaska. Mickey expects it to be something like gold and is surprised when Joseph says, *"ganas!"* He explains that it is a Spanish word meaning something like "desire," but even stronger. It is something you have to have if you are going to make your dreams come true (85). Significantly, this relates to the big question in the story of whether Joseph Alvarez has changed from a decade ago when he left Cruckston with no explanation.

LITERARY TECHNIQUES

As usual, Bauer shares interesting facts that readers might never have heard about without her book. In connection to pool, readers learn that in nine ball it does not matter what happens to the other balls. Whoever gets the nine ball in with a legal shot wins because "the nine ball is king" (1). The best player in a hall is called the *"head stick"*; pool players applaud by pounding their sticks on the floor; and winners chalk their sticks light, while losers chalk them hard. A good practice is to set quarters against the rail of a pool table and then try to hit them so they will dance across the table, and pool halls are not likely to have the kinds of snack bars that bowling alleys have because getting Cheese Whiz on the tables ruins the felt.

In different realms, readers learn that pigs are very intelligent and that Abraham Lincoln had a pet pig. They also learn that cumulonimbus clouds (the ones with flat bottoms and puffy tops) are likely to bring showers, and that Grover Cleveland was born in New Jersey and was both the twenty-second and the twenty-fourth president of the United States.

Bauer finds ways that are both efficient and amusing to describe new concepts. For example, when Arlen first explains to Mickey that pool is based on geometry and shows Mickey how the angle of incidence (the direction of the pool stick) is going to determine the angle of reflection (the direction the ball will travel), Arlen sits back as satisfied as if he had "just invented chocolate" (7). Near the end of the book, when Mickey manages a wonderful shot he lifts his stick into the air and thinks about how his hand is killing him but how great he feels at the same time.

Bauer has more opportunities in *Sticks* than in some of her other books to fit in extra white space on the pages. She includes a couple of drawings that Arlen makes to explain connections between geometry and pool. Near the end of the book, she reprints the posters that Arlen and Mickey make for their science fair project demonstrating relationships between geometry and playing pool. She also reprints Joseph's business card and various signs from the pool hall, including one on page 9 in which Poppy outlines the rules of her establishment. Players are "out" if they spit or swear, and if they want to make trouble they are not to come in. She signs it with her authoritative name and title: Edwina P. Vernon, Proprietress.

A more humorous sign on page 16 illustrates Arlen's sense of humor along with his optimism and his willingness to exaggerate. He puts the sign up to warn people to stay away from his tree house, which might never get finished. Arlen's parents run a construction company and they have promised to build him a tree house, which they work on for one hour every Saturday, but if Arlen forgets something—even one thing during the week—they cancel their promised work time.

BEWARE
ATTACK PIG ON PREMISES
ENTER AT YOUR OWN RISK
THIS MEANS YOU
I'M NOT KIDDING.

CHAPTER SIX

RULES OF THE ROAD

B AUER HAS SAID THAT *Rules of the Road* was her quickest, although
not necessarily her easiest, book to write. One reason is that it
contains so many of the emotions and experiences that have
played out repeatedly in her mind as she has sought to come to terms
with her adolescent years. These include having a father whose alcoholism kept him from playing the role of a good parent, and also experiencing a dearly loved grandmother's mind and memories melt away much
like they did with the grandmother in *Rules of the Road*.

However, Bauer is quick to add that *Rules of the Road* is not an autobiography. If she had tried to write her own story exactly as it happened,
she thinks she would have gotten so bogged down with her emotions that
she could not have finished the book. Also, she would not have felt free
to invent the wonderful characters of Mrs. Gladstone and Harry Bender
or come up with the idea of Jenna serving as Mrs. Gladstone's driver for
the trip from Chicago to Dallas.

Bauer created Harry Bender, the Great Mahatma of the shoe world,
for a movie script that she was trying to write. She gave up on writing
movie scripts when she had such a bad automobile accident that she
could not write full-time or keep up with the kind of strict schedule that
screenwriting requires. Plus, during her recovery she was in physical
pain, and she began looking for things to make herself smile, both as a
way to keep her mind off the pain and as a way to better her writing
skills. She was so successful in developing a humorous "voice" (her first
attempt at this was in *Squashed*) that even in a relatively serious book
such as *Rules of the Road* she uses humor to counterbalance some of the
sad parts.

The book's title comes from Jenna's summer job when she is hired to
drive Mrs. Gladstone, the owner and manager of the Gladstone Shoe
Company from Chicago to Dallas, Texas, where she will attend the

annual stockholders' meeting. Along the way, she will stop and visit several of her shoe stores.

Main Characters

Jenna Boller, a junior in high school, is a five-foot-eleven-inch "shoe professional." She has worked at Gladstone Shoes for more than a year, and she loves coming to work after school and on Saturdays because she feels successful. Besides making money, she likes the fact that customers look to her for help and advice. Her grandmother always told her that people need something in life "they do pretty well." Jenna's something is selling shoes (6).

Mrs. Madeline Gladstone is the "supremely aged" president of the Gladstone Shoe Company, which has 176 outlets in 37 states. Jenna says that even though, or maybe because, Mrs. Gladstone is short, she has a powerful persona. She reminds Jenna of those little yippy dogs who make their presence known by barking at everything. When Jenna accidentally says something about Mrs. Gladstone being rich, she good-naturedly explains the difference between "rich" and "Texas rich." Mrs. Gladstone is "somewhere in between" (51).

Jenna's grandmother was "best friend" to Jenna all through her difficult childhood, but now she has Alzheimer's and sits lonely and scared in the Shady Oaks Nursing Home. Her role in the story is revealed mostly through Jenna's memories and through Jenna's concern for her grandmother when she is away and misses her weekly visits.

Jenna's dad is an alcoholic—not the recovering kind. Jenna's parents divorced when Jenna was eight and her sister, Faith, was four. He stays away for years at a time and then suddenly appears and wants to connect. Jenna has fond memories of their on-again, off-again relationship from when she was young. She holds out hope of helping him, but is always disappointed. As she explains to her mother, the whole family gets crazy when "Dad comes back in town" (39).

Harry Bender is the manager of Gladstone's premier store in Dallas, Texas. A few days before the stockholders' meeting, he is killed by a drunk driver. After the funeral, when Mrs. Gladstone is anxiously wondering what she should do, she asks Jenna what she thinks Harry would be doing if he were alive. Jenna lightens the sadness by checking her watch and when she sees that it is 4:30 on a Wednesday afternoon, she tells Mrs. Gladstone that he would be selling shoes, "doing his level best to make you rich" right up until closing time (166).

Elden Gladstone is Mrs. Gladstone's son and the villain of the story. He wants to squeeze his mother out of the company that she and her late husband founded some fifty years ago. He has cancelled the training courses for new employees and has gone behind his mother's back to negotiate a partnership with Ken Woldman, owner of the Shoe Warehouse, which prides itself on quantity rather than quality.

Jenna's single mom works as an emergency room nurse and has chosen the night shift so she can earn more money. She is a wonderfully sensible mother who is determined to give her two daughters what they need to make their lives successful.

Faith is Jenna's incredibly beautiful fourteen-year-old sister. In spite of her name, Jenna has little faith that her sister can take over the kind of family responsibilities that Jenna has carried. When Jenna gets home from her trip she is genuinely surprised at how well Faith did, while Faith is also surprised to discover that over the years Jenna has been protecting her from their father rather than hogging his attention.

Opal is Jenna's friend and serves mostly as a sounding board and as someone who expresses contrary opinions, like when she tries to convince Jenna to stay home for the summer. Opal warns Jenna that Mrs. Gladstone is "a bona fide Hansel and Gretel–eating witch!" who will drive Jenna over the edge, so she will have to spend all the money she earns on psychiatric care (39).

Murray Castlebaum is the manager of the Chicago shoe store where Jenna has been working since her sophomore year. She wonders if he has X-ray vision because of the way he can see the insides of shoes and tell whether they are cheap knockoffs or the real thing.

Alice Lovett is a longtime friend of Mrs. Gladstone, with a matching age and fiery temperament. Alice joins Jenna and Mrs. Gladstone for the last half of the trip, and because she used to be a shoe model and a hairdresser she has good fashion sense. She is like a fairy godmother to Jenna and styles her hair and gives her tips on clothing so that Jenna comes home feeling not quite as beautiful as Faith, but at least pretty.

SETTING

Mrs. Gladstone has homes in both Chicago, Illinois, and Dallas, Texas. At the beginning of the book, she is in Chicago, but she needs to get to Dallas, which is home to the company headquarters. The story is contemporary and is set during the summer so that Jenna is free from school and can concentrate on driving Mrs. Gladstone from her Chicago home to her Dallas home. On the dedication page, Bauer thanks Betsy Barker for teaching her about Texas, which is what adds a sense of grandeur to Jenna's story. The first clue that Jenna is excited about Mrs. Gladstone's job offer is when she wistfully tells her mother that she's never been to Texas. Bauer puts across the point that the trip for Jenna is more than just an ordinary summer vacation when on the morning that they are to leave from Mrs. Gladstone's elegant brownstone house, Jenna whispers to her mother that after depositing Jenna and her luggage, her mother should slip away because this is a grown-up job for which Jenna is getting paid. She does not want her mother waiting around like parents wait for the bus to leave when kids go off to summer camp.

Even though Mrs. Gladstone's Cadillac is always moving, it is still a part of the setting because it represents the responsibility that has been given to Jenna. And being locked in a car with one other person (two when Alice, a friend of Mrs. Gladstone's, joins them) for long days on the road provides the time for Jenna and Mrs. Gladstone to get to know each other. As Jenna good-naturedly points out, it is fairly unusual for one of today's teenagers to have listened to so much retro music that she can recognize the subtle differences between Duke Ellington's and Count Basie's piano playing. Also, the challenges of driving the oversize car and competing for places on the freeway as she merges into traffic provide Jenna with inspiration and time to ponder the similarities and the differences between merging traffic and merging companies.

When they finally get to Dallas, Harry Bender's oversized shoe store serves as a symbol of Texas for Jenna. It has three floors and a white spiral staircase that winds around "the largest plastic shoe in the universe" (127). Harry is such a good salesman that when Jenna and Mrs. Gladstone come in, he does not interrupt what he is doing and as a result they get to watch him work his magic. He is wearing a large Stetson hat and

Tony Lama snakeskin cowboy boots, hand-stitched, with the red Texas star that is part of the Gladstone insignia. He is telling his customer that the shoes he is lacing up have traction and will hug the road. The customer immediately understands the connection to a tire, and Harry goes one step further by saying that the shoes will go to places that tires only dream of. By the time Harry finishes his spiel, the laughing man likes the shoes so much that he doesn't want them boxed up; he'll wear them right out of the store (127–28).

After the trip, when Jenna is back home and has used her money to buy her own little red car, she keeps her promise to her grandmother and takes her on a picnic. Her grandmother probably does not understand what Jenna says, but it is nevertheless good for Jenna to talk about her summer adventure. She concludes by saying that she has never been anywhere that changed her more. Texas makes people think about things in a big way.

PLOT

When the book opens, Jenna has been working for a year at one of the Gladstone shoe stores in suburban Chicago. She is in a back room daydreaming about buying her own car so she can explore all of Illinois and then Wisconsin, when she hears a familiar voice: *"Where's my Jenna girl?"* She freezes at the sound of her father's drunken voice and then looks for a place to hide or a back door. Her boss, Murray, is trying to get her father to leave, but he firmly announces that he has come to see his daughter. Murray tells him that Jenna has gone, but her father isn't convinced, and with his words slurring together he says that he hasn't seen her in a very long time. Jenna comes out of the back room, thinking to herself, "Two years and seven months, to be exact. But who's counting?" (8–9).

Jenna takes her father outside—luckily he is not a mean drunk—and finally gets him settled in a taxi heading for an address he has written on the inside of a matchbook. When she gets back to the store, she is embarrassed that Mrs. Gladstone witnessed the whole event. She apologizes and says she will understand if Mrs. Gladstone does not want her to work at the store anymore, but Mrs. Gladstone responds with "what manure!" and Jenna assumes she hasn't been fired (14).

As it turns out, Mrs. Gladstone has been watching how well Jenna works for several days, and instead of thinking less of Jenna because of her father's behavior, she is impressed with the way Jenna manages the event. She telephones Jenna at home and invites her to be her driver and assistant on a six-week summer trip from Chicago to the corporate offices in Dallas. She does not want to fly because she needs to stop and see how things are going at the Gladstone shoe stores between Illinois and Texas. Jenna has had her driver's license for only six months, and her mother does not think Jenna is experienced enough as a driver to commit to six weeks alone on the road with a seventy-three-year-old woman. Jenna is almost relieved to tell Mrs. Gladstone that her mother will not let her accept the job because she has been looking forward to a leisurely summer, hanging out with her friend Opal and selling shoes; plus, she feels obligated to keep up her weekly visits to her grandmother (4).

But Mrs. Gladstone persists and offers Jenna double her regular salary, plus she will pay all the travel expenses and provide Jenna with spending money. She also hints at "an additional bonus" upon their *safe* return to Chicago (35). Jenna's eyes brighten at this point because she has been saving money to buy her own car. She dreams of a sporty, red car with bucket seats and a sunroof. Meanwhile, Jenna's father keeps telephoning the house and alternately begging or demanding to come and talk to Jenna. His insistence and Jenna's fear of a repeat visit to Jenna's workplace make Jenna and her mother rethink Mrs. Gladstone's offer, and the result is that Jenna becomes Mrs. Gladstone's official driver and all-around assistant. After a few days Jenna feels comfortable enough to ask why she was chosen, and Mrs. Gladstone says it is because Jenna reminds her of herself when she was seventeen.

As they drive along, Jenna learns that at the meeting in Dallas, Mrs. Gladstone is scheduled to hand the business over to her son, Elden. She is not looking forward to retirement, and she does not like the changes her son is proposing because Elden plans to become partners with a discount shoe chain. Mrs. Gladstone strongly believes that when companies start cutting quality both the company and the customers lose out (68).

Mrs. Gladstone is especially angry at Elden when she talks to her longtime friend, Alice Lovett, and when she is surrounded by her best and most loyal store managers, including Harry Bender. He is the manager of the company's flagship store in Dallas, and according to other Gladstone employees, "the world's greatest shoe salesman" (77). At other times, Mrs. Gladstone feels like giving up because she is so dismayed at her son's behavior and also because she has arthritic pain in her hip, which is going to be replaced as soon as she and Jenna make it back to Chicago. When Mrs. Gladstone is at an especially low point, Jenna dares to offer an opinion. She says she does not know about saving companies, but she knows that with families everyone has to come together and talk honestly to each other because "there's power in truth," and the truth needs to come out "where it can get some fresh air" (84).

Alice joins Mrs. Gladstone and Jenna in Springfield, Illinois, and rides along with them to Dallas, where Jenna finally gets to meet the legendary Harry Bender. Jenna is overwhelmed both by Texas and by Harry Bender. Indeed, getting to know Harry Bender is one of the highlights of Jenna's trip, but it is also the saddest part because tragedy strikes when Harry is killed by a drunk driver. Jenna is nevertheless grateful for the happy memory. It helps her get through the week after his death, which includes the meeting of the stockholders and a very open confrontation with Elden.

When Jenna and Mrs. Gladstone arrive home to Chicago at last, Jenna is surprised at how much responsibility her sister, Faith, has taken on. She is also surprised that her mom has gotten both a raise and a new boyfriend. Jenna writes that the raise doesn't take getting used to, but the boyfriend does, even though her mom assures her that they are taking things "*very, very* slow" (187). After this first surprise, Jenna is amused at herself for expecting her mom and Faith to be exactly the same when she got back because she had certainly changed. In fact, they had all been on journeys even though Jenna was the only one who had actually traveled.

THEMES

Near the very beginning when Jenna is selling shoes, readers get introduced to the major theme of the book which is that Jenna is troubled by not having a father she can depend on. In a telling scene on a spring Saturday, she observes the relationship between a father and his daughter. She suspects that he is a weekend dad because she overhears him asking his daughter what she's doing in school this week, and in a tired voice, she says she already told him last week. The man keeps checking his watch and, sure enough, buys the little girl all the shoes she tries on—cowboy boots, ballet slippers, and patent leather dress shoes. While he's getting out his Visa card to pay, he tells her that he has to take her back a little early. When she looks disappointed, Jenna gives her an understanding smile and a balloon and thinks to herself that at least this dad comes around (3).

Bauer shows that she is writing not just about Jenna's father but about the disease of alcoholism by bringing in several characters who are alcoholics. Of course the main one is Jenna's dad, but there is also Harry Bender, who proudly shares the fact that he hasn't taken a drink in twenty-three years and takes phone calls at the store to counsel other alcoholics. Then there is the drunk driver responsible for the automobile accident that kills Harry Bender, plus the troubled young people at Al-Anon, where family members meet to learn how to deal with the problems of someone else's addiction.

Although Joan Bauer has made it clear that *Rules of the Road* is not her autobiography, the explanation that Jenna offers her little sister about her father having "a disease … that keeps him from being the person he could be" (17) sounds like something Bauer has said many times to herself as well as to other people. When Jenna offers to take Faith with her to Al-Anon and her mother tells her that it isn't necessary because Faith does not have the same memories since she was younger when the parents divorced, it also sounds like an example of rationalization that Bauer has heard more than once. Although Jenna has a full life with many more aspects to it than her father's alcoholism, it is the alcoholism that casts a pall over everything else. At the end of chapter 2 when Jenna talks about her grandmother developing Alzheimer's, she says that if she were God she would wipe out all the diseases in the world that begin with A: "AIDS, Alcoholism, Alzheimer's …" (24). Later in chapter 5, Jenna enters the kitchen to see her mother, who is an emergency room nurse, "steeling" herself like she does at the hospital when rough cases come in. Jenna's dad is on the phone saying he is coming over to see Jenna. Jenna's mom answers, *"Not when you're drunk!"* and then reminds him that he has two daughters and has not made his child support payments in months (41).

Even on the trip, Jenna keeps being reminded of her father's alcoholism. Mrs. Gladstone tells her to feel free to use hotel phones to call home, but Jenna mostly sends postcards. She still doesn't feel comfortable talking on the telephone because when she was a child her father would force her to answer the phone and tell angry callers that he wasn't home. When she and Mrs. Gladstone stay in a Springfield, Illinois, hotel that is filled with salespeople for the Markoy Electronics annual meeting, she observes them pouring margaritas into fishbowl-size glasses and remembers when her father was in a Latin American drinking phase and would make margaritas at home. He would sing "*la la la la la la la bamba*" in a high voice while squeezing lime and putting salt around the glass before pouring the ice and the liquor combination into the blender. He was so exact when he made drinks that he reminded Jenna of a pharmacist with one difference being that by the end of the evening he would be lying on the floor while carefully measuring his concoctions.

In contrast to Jenna's memories of her father, Mrs. Gladstone reminisces about her father, who as a preacher centered three of his best sermons on the making of shoes. In one that she shares with Jenna, she tells how he said that as shoes take people through their journey of life, they get muddy and scratched, but good owners keep them clean, dry, and polished. Then he compared God to a master cobbler, who stretches leather over a wooden form, fastening it down with nails, then stitching everything together to make "something special" (63). The point of his sermon was to urge his listeners to think about the miracle of creation—how much more complicated it is than making a shoe—or maybe he wanted them to expand on the idea that people need taking care of even more than shoes do. Mrs. Gladstone confesses to wondering when she was a child why in the world her father was fixated on shoes. She never figures out the answer, but as she muses about the matter she concludes that it really made her think about selling shoes in a different way. Jenna doesn't say anything, but wonders to herself why she had to be given "a father who was a drunk" (64).

That night, because there aren't enough available hotel rooms, Jenna has to curl up on the hotel's rollaway bed, which is too short. This reminds her of how she used to try to help her drunken father fit his six-foot-four-inch frame on the living room couch. She resents that as the oldest child she was the one her parents "practiced on," but then she drifts off into happier memories. Her dad was a salesman, and he used to take Jenna out to watch other salespeople practice their trade. The worst they ever saw was a man who sold washers and dryers. He would "slap the machines" and announce that he had lowered the price so much that he would be hung when his manager found out. One customer offered to "get the rope" (65).

In contrast they once watched a woman selling Singer sewing machines. She obviously liked to sew and liked her product so it was more like she was sharing something special with a friend than like she was trying to push people into buying something they did not want. When they would come home from these excursions, Jenna's dad would let her practice selling whatever they had just seen and, except when she was pitching something like swampland in Florida, he would always buy, but then he would feel the need to celebrate what a good salesperson she was becoming by having a few drinks. In thinking back, she realized that he really was a good father up until the alcohol got him (65).

As the book progresses and Jenna has more time to think about how she has been affected by her father's alcoholism, she begins to realize that in ways it has taught her lessons that she can apply to other aspects of life. Jenna makes a comparison between the way her father treats her and the way Mrs. Gladstone's son is treating his mother through what he is doing to the Gladstone shoe company. She decides that neither her dad nor Mrs. Gladstone's son are causing pain on purpose. They just don't stop to think that the people they are hurting need their love so much that they end up lying to themselves and actually contributing to the person's power to hurt (68).

One of the reasons that Bauer brings Harry Bender into the story is to show contrasting approaches to alcoholism. While Jenna's father always insists that he is "handling it," Harry cheerfully acknowledges, even to total strangers, that he has a problem with alcohol. Jenna watches him tell a customer that shoes can turn a life around. Twenty-three years ago, he confesses, when he was drunk and so broke that he was wearing bedroom slippers, a priest took pity on him and gave him a pair of soft leather tie-ons.

> "I figured then and there that God was telling me to straighten up and sell shoes or join the priesthood."
> "I see the shoes won," the man said, chuckling. (128)

Nearly one hundred pages later, after Harry Bender has been killed and Jenna attends his funeral along with many of the people he had helped in Alcoholics Anonymous, Jenna cries not just for Harry and his wife, but "for all the places in life where dreams die and people get ripped from this earth … for unfairness and pain and loss and death that comes in so many forms." She knew she was also crying for her grandmother, whose old self had died, and for people with problems so big they couldn't even see them, but most of all she was crying for herself and Faith and for the father they both needed but who just couldn't make it (158).

Later, when Jenna is trying to get Mrs. Gladstone to fight for the good of the company at the stockholders' meeting, Jenna explains that she knows what it is to be tossed aside by someone you love. It made Jenna think that she was not worthy because she just kept being a "good sport," hoping that her dad would change. She felt powerless, as though she "didn't have a right to be angry and say no" (167). When Mrs. Gladstone asks Jenna if she thinks it would have changed things if Jenna had spoken up to her dad, Jenna says that it might not have made a difference with her dad, but "speaking the truth would have changed me." Jenna figures out that she had always been afraid to let her dad know how she felt for fear that he would hate her. She just kept on trying to be perfect to "make up for the fact that he had all these problems" (167).

By the end of the book and with the summer's experiences behind her, Jenna is able to take a stand with her father. She even stops him, at least temporarily, from driving drunk. This wasn't easy, either for her, her father, or her mother, but at least she knows that for a little while her father won't be causing traffic accidents and killing or harming someone as innocent as Harry Bender. In the long run, probably the best thing that Jenna got from her summer was the realization that people don't have to be defined by their problems. What makes the difference is not so much the problems but how people stand up and face them.

While this is an important insight, Bauer is honest enough to show her readers that life's problems may get easier to handle but they do not totally disappear. Jenna is still left cleaning up after her dad. They later meet to talk at the rookery of the Lincoln Park Zoo, where Jenna hopes to make peace after she reports him for driving drunk. However, the conversation does not go as she had hoped, and her dad disgustedly throws a whole bag of bread into the pond that he brought to feed the ducks. After he leaves, Jenna finds a stick and fishes it out. Then she tells the ducks "it's okay," and tears up the bread and tosses the little pieces into the water. She has one piece left when a baby duck waddles out, unsure. She tells the duckling to "go for it," and make her "proud." When she tosses the last little piece in his direction, he dives in, races past the others, and gobbles it up: "Daring Duck Beats Odds to Win. Another true survivor. Like me" (200).

LITERARY TECHNIQUES

As with all of her books, Bauer leaves readers with information they probably did not have before reading the book. In *Rules of the Road,* they learn from Jenna's sales training lessons (the ones that Elden cancels to save money) that in an average lifetime, a person does enough walking to circle the globe four times (115,000 miles). They also learn that the human foot contains twenty-six bones and thirty-three joints, plus ninety muscles and more than one hundred ligaments (59).

Driving is another area where Bauer shares helpful information. Wisely, Mrs. Gladstone provides Jenna with some early practice by having her come over and drive her back and forth to work for several days before they set out on the real trip. She gives crisp hints and firm directions, all from the backseat, but these aren't as surprising as the lessons that Jenna's mother gives her. She is an emergency room nurse and is well acquainted with what can happen on highways so she takes Jenna out in their Honda onto the Kennedy Expressway during rush hour and gives Jenna her own idea of a refresher course in driver's ed. She gives her facts about how much space to leave between her car and other cars, she gives wrong directions and then leaves it to Jenna to find her way home, and for a surprise while they are filling up with gas, she pretends to have a heart attack to give Jenna practice in laying a gravely ill person flat onto the backseat while remaining calm enough to telephone for help. Instead of calling for help, Jenna has to explain to the "woman in the Plymouth Voyager not to call 911" because her mother is a real kidder (40).

Humor scholars ranging from Plato and Aristotle to Thomas Hobbes and Sigmund Freud to James Thurber and E. B. White have noted that when examined from a distance, expressions of hostility or feelings of superiority are one of the things that make people smile. Bauer takes advantage of this when she has Jenna vent her feelings toward other drivers. Jenna is surprised to observe that even teenagers raise their fists (or make other "filthy gestures") to her when she is simply obeying the law by stopping at yellow lights before they change to red. She concludes that to drive you have to become a trusting person because "you're on the road with potential dangers everywhere and like an idiot you keep moving forward" (29).

Bauer's wordplay includes making puns based on *soul* to refer to a person's spirit or inner feelings and *sole* taken from the Latin *solea* ("sandal") or *solum* ("base, ground, or soil"), which refers either to the bottom of a shoe or to a species of fish that is so flat that it resembles the soles of shoes. Even before Jenna goes on the trip with Mrs. Gladstone, which is when she finds out that Elden is trying to push his mother out of her job as president, Jenna's boss tells her that Elden doesn't "have a shoe person's heart." His major interest "is money, not sole" (57). Then when they get to Texas to the biggest and best shoe store in the world, Jenna gets to meet the legendary Harry Bender, who is called "the Great Mahatma," which in Hindi means "Great Soul," but in the shoe business means "Great Sole" (79). Near the end, when Mrs. Gladstone makes a deal with Ken Woldman to stay on the board of directors and be in charge of quality control, Elden is both disappointed and angry. But because the "whole world," or at least all the people at the shareholders' meeting, is watching, he forces himself to give a "half-smile" as he slumps "soleless" in his chair (184). In another example of Bauer's wordplay, readers are not surprised when Jenna gets home from her summer trip and buys herself a red car because Bauer foreshadowed it. On Jenna's first day of being Mrs. Gladstone's driver, she had sighed, "someday," when a hot red Mustang convertible whizzed by her and she noticed the license plate: "ITSORED" (61).

A humor technique that Bauer uses to keep her characters from becoming overly self-satisfied is to step in and take them down a notch. For example, on the trip to Texas Jenna goes into one of the new outlet stores as a "shoe spy." When she sees a harried mother trying to buy shoes for five children, she lends a hand and gets each one fitted with something that they like and that will wear well. Then the cashier makes a spur-of-the-moment decision to let the mother use her twenty-percent-off coupon on only two out of her five purchases, and Jenna steps in and demands to see "in-print" where it says the coupon is limited to only two pairs of shoes. She even uses a passing policeman to threaten the cashier. When the grateful mother asks her who she is, it comes out almost like the old line from *The Lone Ranger*: "Who is that masked man?" Jenna smiles mysteriously, puts on her "extra-cool driver sunglasses," and after giving the woman "a tough-guy salute," walks "down the street whistling, just missing a mound of dog poop" (75).

Another way that Bauer amuses her readers is to play with character names. While Jenna was on the trip, her mother got both a pay raise and a new boyfriend. Jenna said it was easy to get used to the pay raise but not so easy to get used to the boyfriend. Probably just for fun, Bauer gave the boyfriend the name of Evan, which is the name of her husband. Readers can remember, perhaps only subconsciously, that Harry Bender is a recovering alcoholic because the slang phrase for excessive drinking is *going on a bender*. It is surprising that Harry didn't make such jokes about his name because he was always on the lookout for ways to make people smile. For example, when Jenna telephones for advice about how to keep Elden from harassing his mother as he tries to get her to agree to something she does not want, Harry tells Jenna to smile but to stay firm and explain that Mrs. Gladstone's hip is hurting too much for her to see anyone. Jenna is doubtful, but Harry insists she can do it. He ends his little pep talk by telling her that all she needs to remember is not to go "punching a man who's chewing tobacco" (95).

Jenna thinks this might be a good bumper sticker, but she's not sure what it has to do with selling shoes. However, she does not have long to think about the matter because at breakfast Elden comes pushing his way into the hotel restaurant. He is talking on a cell phone while at the same time snarling at a waitress that he is looking for his mother. Fortunately, Alice and Mrs. Gladstone are having their breakfast upstairs, courtesy of room service. Jenna introduces herself to Elden and says she will deliver whatever he has to say to Mrs. Gladstone. Only in her mind does she add "you ungrateful slimeball" to the end of her polite statements. And when he stomps off in a "stinking cloud of deceit," she thinks to herself: "Evil Retreats in the Presence of Goodness" and "What a snake" (98).

Jenna is glad that she and Alice have gotten a wheelchair for Mrs. Gladstone, even though she resents this sign of weakness. Nevertheless, the next time Elden appears to harass his mother, the wheelchair allows Jenna to push Mrs. Gladstone into a ladies restroom—what Jenna describes as a "vermin-free zone" (106). Jenna keeps in her mind this image of Elden as vermin, and when she works her way onto the platform at the shareholders' meeting to make a speech in favor of keeping Mrs. Gladstone involved in the management of the company, she hears Elden behind her making "rodent noises" (181).

CHAPTER SEVEN

BACKWATER

O N THE DEDICATION PAGE TO BACKWATER, Joan Bauer thanks her daughter, Jean, who is a graduate student in history, for helping her with historical knowledge and also for sharing family stories "with humor and grace." Bauer also thanks her husband, Evan, who besides programming computers, is a "wilderness guide extraordinaire." She gives him credit for taking her up and down several of the same Adirondack Mountains that figure prominently in the plot of *Backwater*. We assume they hiked under better weather conditions than does the heroine of *Backwater*, who finds herself at the top of a mountain during a terrible storm on New Year's Eve.

These two loves of Bauer's life—her daughter and her husband—played a crucial role in one of the first articles that Bauer managed to sell after she left her job in advertising so that she could be both a stay-at-home mother and a writer. This humorous article appeared in a magazine for parents and was about the first hike that she and Evan took with Jean when she had just learned to walk. Jean wanted to explore so many things along the way that all in all they took almost as many steps backward and sideways as forward. It is fun to think about this early family experience developing over twenty years to culminate in such a good book as *Backwater*.

MAIN CHARACTERS

Ivy Breedlove is the sixteen-year-old storyteller. She is a quiet, introspective girl who thinks she might like to be a historian, even though everyone in the family expects all Breedloves to become lawyers. Bauer says she based her personality on that of her daughter, Jean.

Egan Breedlove is Ivy's cousin and confidante. Ivy helps him stay on the honor roll, and he returns the favor by lending her a helping hand and also by providing her with occasional reality checks when she needs

them. Maybe Bauer chose his name as a subtle way of comparing his
good sense to that of her husband, Evan.

Daniel Breedlove is Ivy's father and one of the several Breedlove lawyers
gathered for the annual holiday. Since Ivy's mother died when Ivy was
six, Daniel (or Dan) has been a single parent and thinks it is his duty
to demonstrate firmness and strength as he prepares Ivy to join the
family profession.

Great Aunt Tib is nearing her eightieth birthday and has recently lost
her sight. When Ivy's mother died a decade ago, Aunt Tib moved in to
become a substitute mother for Ivy. She used to teach history and was
writing a book about the Breedlove family but after becoming blind she
handed the job over to Ivy. She remains Ivy's strongest supporter.

Uncle Archie is Dan's older brother. Readers learn that he was a gifted
child who naturally warmed to all the dinnertime discussions of law
conducted by Dan and Archie's father. Dan had a hard time keeping
up and developed his harsh and unbending personality as a result.

Aunt Josephine is Dan and Archie's younger sister. As a child she was
quiet and would hide under the table during the high-powered dinnertime discussions. She was so different from the rest of the family that
she left about the time that Ivy's mother died. Ivy is intrigued by the
veiled references she picks up to this mysterious woman who, judging
from her high school yearbook pictures, looks a lot like Ivy.

Aunt Fiona is the most assertive of the women in the family. Although
she is not a lawyer, she has a cable TV show aimed at making housewives feel better about their jobs by saving time.

Mountain Mama is a capable and quirky mountain guide who agrees to
take Ivy to the top of one of the nearby mountains, where Aunt Josephine has built her own little community of one person and several
animals.

Jack Lowden is a "medium-sized male, about eighteen, with a few
days growth of beard. . . . He had brown eyes that crackled with intelligence, . . . an eclipsing smile, . . . and dark curly hair" (70). He is
training to be a forest ranger but is doing make-up work during the holidays because he made a major mistake during the search-and-rescue
part of his training; however, later in the story he earns an A plus for
his help in rescuing Ivy and Aunt Jo.

SETTING

The story takes place in upstate New York mostly during the two weeks of Christmas vacation when the extended Breedlove family gathers in the old family home to "argue away the holidays" (3). This is a couple of hundred miles away from where Ivy lives and goes to school. The distance is a nuisance when Ivy gets a boyfriend in the area, but it allows the story to be more exciting than it would have been had it been set in Ivy's high school. High schools are pretty much the same, but few readers have climbed to the top of a mountain like the one where Aunt Josephine built her A-frame cabin and the various other buildings for her birds. While schools usually serve only as backdrop settings, the setting in *Backwater* is integral because the Adirondack Mountains and the weather conditions are as important to the plot of the story as are the characters.

PLOT

The title of *Backwater* comes from the beginning of a sermon preached by one of the Breedlove ancestors: "Brothers and sisters, are you *stuck* in the backwater of sin?" (28). The original meaning of "an isolated or backward place or condition" is now used by family members to describe anyone they do not understand, namely Ivy's Aunt Josephine. They all feel hurt that she has, in effect, rejected them by leaving.

Ivy's present concern—actually her obsession—is to get the family history finished within the next sixty-three days so that it will be ready for distribution by the time the family gathers again to celebrate Great Aunt Tib's eightieth birthday. Ivy feels she cannot complete the task unless she talks with Aunt Josephine, but finding her aunt proves to be something of a challenge and the search is only the beginning.

The book opens with Ivy out in the family cemetery making a rubbing of the message on her great-great-great-great-grandfather's gravestone where he expresses his heartfelt desire that all of his sons become lawyers. Ivy's father interprets *sons* to mean "descendants" and constantly argues with Ivy over her desire to be a historian rather than an attorney. By the time Ivy's father was sixteen, he had read everything available about all of the U.S. colleges of law and had acquired such a love for the law that he feels he could "defend it to the death," never taking no for an answer. Ivy says to herself that what he learned was how "to bill by the hour" (9). The argument over whether Ivy must aspire to become a lawyer or be free to choose her own career is the surface plot of the story, but actually the conflict runs deeper by asking the kinds of questions that many young people wonder about:

- I feel so different from my family; could I be adopted?
- How much like my parents am I?
- They are two different people; how can I be like both of them?
- What if I don't want to be like either of them?

In trying to convince her father that not all of the successful Breedloves have been lawyers, Ivy tells him about Mercy Breedlove, who, at the time of the Women's Suffrage Movement, wore a dress day in and day out that she embroidered with quotations from Susan B. Anthony—and this was "long before antiperspirant" (10). She tells him about the fifteen-year-old twins Iza and Baldwin Breedlove, who during the Depression quit school and worked at eleven part-time jobs to support their family. When that wasn't enough they trained the family dog to do tricks and help them beg on the street. She also tells him about Vesta Breedlove, who arrived on the Mayflower with two birds and a husband—the husband died at sea, but the birds made it. Although Vesta mourned her husband, she said the birds were better company, and she and the birds lived happily ever after. Ivy's father tells her that she has nothing in common with someone like that. To emphasize his point, he shouts that "Breedloves do not emulate disturbed people!" (10). This was the second angriest Ivy had ever seen him. The first was when she backed her father's Lexus into the rhododendron bushes terminally scratching the paint.

Ivy knows that, except for Aunt Tib, the family does not approve of her ambition to complete the family history. They think it's a job for an adult, and they act as if all adults have been sprayed "with instant insight" (6). Ivy did not "inherit" her interest in history exclusively from Aunt Tib. In the big, old house she has found many history books that belonged to her mother. Since her mother did not keep a diary and no one saved letters that she wrote, Ivy looks through the books to see if she can learn something about her mother. In one book about women, her mother had made a note: "This is my family tree" (11). Because Ivy's mother was adopted and knew nothing of her birth parents, Ivy surmises that she used the history books to imagine a past for herself. When Ivy reads these books, she feels her mother's spirit "pushing through the pages." Deep down, Ivy also wonders if perhaps her mother shared Ivy's feelings of being out of place in such an outspoken family.

Early in the book, Aunt Fiona, whose claim to fame is running a cable TV show in which she helps stressed-out housewives believe that time can be their friend, plays the part of a literary foil. The term comes from a jewelry technique where craftsmen use a thin layer of gold foil placed behind a jewel to make it shine brighter. Aunt Fiona comes to the reunion prepared to "do" the family history by making a quickie video tape. Her attitudes and comments serve as a foil to make Great Aunt Tib's support and Ivy's desire to do a thorough job look all the brighter.

For her video, Aunt Fiona passes out little cards telling people what to say. Then in fifty-seven minutes she interviews six Breedloves, talking to each one for six and a half minutes, which she will edit down to even shorter segments. She is determined to keep the video succinct because somewhere she heard that the human mind can concentrate on a video for no longer than forty-seven minutes. As Aunt Fiona pans the camera past a painting, a handmade quilt embroidered with the names and birth-dates of twelve Breedlove children, and large copper pots engraved with every part of Comfort Breedlove's journey, Ivy asks Aunt Fiona if she is going to tell the stories behind these artifacts. Her response is, "We want sounds and images, Ivy. There's no time for stories" (14). Ivy thinks to herself but doesn't say, "*Sometimes saving time doesn't matter!*" (15). As Aunt Fiona is interviewing Egan and interrupts him to ask if he's aware that the video cam is running, Ivy thinks that Aunt Fiona's cable TV tactics are as inappropriate to the job of getting to the heart of a family as a plastic knife would be for a surgeon performing heart surgery.

In the second part of the book, Ivy goes with a mountain guide (called Mountain Mama) to find Aunt Josephine so that her story can be included. Mountain Mama decides to leave Ivy with her aunt so that they can get to know each other as "family." She will come back for Ivy in two days, but a terrible storm comes and a huge tree falls on the roof of Aunt Josephine's cabin. The roof caves in, breaking Josephine's upper leg, and it is left to Ivy to rescue her aunt before she dies either from the freezing temperature or from internal bleeding.

Near the end of the book, when the rest of the family is treating Ivy with great respect because of what she went through on the mountain with Aunt Josephine, Fiona finally gives a token blessing to the idea of Ivy's written history, but she can't refrain from one last bit of advice in which she reminds Ivy that humans have limited attention spans. Egan puts his hand over Ivy's mouth to keep her from screaming.

THEMES

Backwater is built around one of the oldest themes in the world, which is that of a young person, an "innocent," embarking on a journey or a quest and coming home to new respect after having gained wisdom and understanding. Before Ivy even thinks about going up the mountain to find Aunt Josephine, she experiences one aspect of such stories that involves a young person being given mysterious clues by an elderly witch or a gremlin. Ivy is outside pondering the eccentricities of her extended family when she hears a rasping cough and turns to see ninety-three-year-old Mrs. Englebert, who lives in the house next to the Breedloves, sticking her face out from behind the holly bush and mumbling, "She's alive you know." Mrs. Englebert suffers from dementia, but as Ivy knows, she has moments of clarity, and this may be one of them. As she points to the birdbath, Mrs. Englebert says something to the effect that the Commies have "the bird girl" up "in the woods." Then she confides that she saw the "the bird girl"—who, by now, Ivy realizes is Aunt Josephine—come and sit in the graveyard (29). Mrs. Englebert's closing words are "you look just like her." Ivy eventually figures out that Aunt Josephine is the one who placed the mysterious Christmas wreaths on the graves belonging to the parents of Aunt Josephine, Uncle Archie, and Ivy's father.

With the moderately enthusiastic help of her cousin Egan, Ivy sets out to find a tax record or an address for her missing aunt. They do even better by finding Mountain Mama, a wilderness guide who takes a liking to Ivy and says she will take her up the mountain "at cost" if she can include Ivy's story in a book she is writing. Mountain Mama plays the role of the older, wiser helper, sort of like the Fairy Godmother in old folktales or Merlin in the King Arthur stories or Gandalf in J. R. R. Tolkien's *Lord of the Rings*. She even recognizes that Ivy is on a quest, and when Ivy says, "I hadn't thought about it that way," Mountain Mama tells her that some people turn down their chance to go on a quest while others give up before completing the task. However, she assures Ivy that she's making a good decision because "mountains bring clarity" if you take them *"one mountain at a time,"* which is the title of the book she is writing (46).

While Ivy is arguing with herself as to whether she really wants to find Aunt Josephine, Egan senses that she has a deeper fear than just the physical hardships, and he asks her if she's afraid that she is like Josephine. *"No!"* Ivy shouts, but deep down she realizes that this is exactly what she is afraid of since she knows that she is not like the rest of the family (49). At five o'clock on Saturday morning, Ivy, now resolved to find her aunt, lugs her bag downstairs and says goodbye to Aunt Tib before her dad drives her over to Mountain Mama's place. She thinks to herself about how ancient teenage warriors had to "prove themselves in the wilderness before they could become full members of the tribe and receive the mantel of manhood" (57). Then she quickly adds, "Make that *personhood.*"

The journey in classic stories serves as a metaphor for people's lives, which is why it is the foundation of so many of the world's great epics, including Homer's *The Iliad* and *The Odyssey,* John Bunyan's *Pilgrim's Progress,* Jonathan Swift's *Gulliver's Travels,* and such Old Testament stories as Adam and Eve being banished from the Garden of Eden and Joseph being sold by his brothers to the slave traders traveling to Egypt.

To illustrate how *Backwater* is a modern version of this old theme, the qualities of "The Journey" as outlined by folklorist Joseph Campbell in his book *A Hero with a Thousand Faces* are listed below along with supporting evidence from Bauer's story. It is not that Bauer looked at Campbell's, or someone else's, description before writing her story; instead, the theme is so natural that many stories about the experiences of young people fit into this pattern. Readers could write a description much like the one below for several of Bauer's books, even ones in which the protagonist does not take a literal journey.

1. *The story begins with a young person (an innocent) who has been shown to be special and worthy.*

Readers learn right away that Ivy is a "special" young person. How many other teenagers would be out on a cold, snowy day during Christmas vacation making gravestone rubbings? On page 2, readers learn that she wants to be different from her family; she does not want to follow the expected path of being a lawyer. Later, readers learn that she's smart when her cousin Egan agrees to help her because he is indebted to her for keeping him on the honor roll. However, although she is smart, she is also "innocent." She knows very little about her deceased mother and she has heard only occasional, mysterious references to Aunt Josephine.

2. *The young person embarks on a journey or is lured or carried away not knowing what lies ahead.*

Because Ivy knows little or nothing about mountain climbing, especially in the winter, she seeks professional help from Mountain Mama. While concentrating on getting to the top of the mountain, she gives little thought to how she is going to talk to Aunt Josephine or to what exactly she wants to find out. She draws on everything she has ever learned about conducting interviews, but still she feels unsure and awkward in her first couple of days.

3. *The traveler meets a shadow presence, a foe, or a complication of some kind that must be overcome if the journey is to continue.*

Ivy's first complication is getting her father's permission for the trip, which, thanks to help from Aunt Tib, she manages. Her second complication is the physical challenge of carrying her forty-pound backpack and keeping up with Mountain Mama in the freezing temperatures. Ivy faces absolute terror when they have to traverse an ice-covered ledge and leap over a small crevasse, but she manages. While they are climbing, Ivy concentrates only on getting to the top, but once they arrive at Aunt Josephine's, she faces the third challenge, which is communicating with Aunt Josephine, who says so little that Ivy and Mountain Mama come up with the idea that it might be best if Mountain Mama—because she is an outsider to the family—leaves and comes back in two days to bring Ivy down the mountain and back home.

4. *Once beyond the threshold, the traveler journeys through a world of unfamiliar yet strangely intimate forces.*

A tradition of quest stories is that wisdom is acquired in a high place, which fits with Ivy being in Aunt Jo's cabin at the top of the mountain. Ivy is shocked at how silent her aunt is even after Mountain Mama has gone. Ivy notes how much time passes (the longest stretch is ninety-seven minutes) without anyone speaking. She is surprised that this bothers her because all her life in her loud and talkative family she has longed for a little peace and quiet, but now in the long silences her heart races, and her forehead pounds; too much quiet leaves "too much time to think" (129). Nevertheless, Ivy closes her eyes and listens to "the quiet," the fire sputtering, and the wind moving through the trees. Eventually, Aunt Jo begins to talk. She tells Ivy that Aunt Tib had shown her how to really listen to people, which was a valuable skill in "a family of big talkers." She explains the difference between passive and active listening as she tells Ivy to look at people's faces, hear their voices, see their eyes and their body language, "put your biases aside and the things you want to say next and just let them talk" (131). As they warm up to each other, she also shows Ivy a statue she carved of Ivy's father when he was a boy happily going off with a fishing pole. And what's most important to Ivy is that eventually she talks about Ivy's mother. Ivy was six when her mother died, and she tells Jo that she can't remember much about the funeral, but she remembers a dream she had afterwards about birds coming and flying in honor of her mother. Jo smiles happily and tells Ivy that it wasn't a dream. The day after the funeral, Jo had taken Ivy to a preserve where they had fed the birds and built a little rock monument to her mother's memory. When they share this old "togetherness," something intimate and powerful moves between Ivy and Aunt Jo (138).

> 5. *The traveler meets severe obstacles and tribulations. A gallant fight on the part of the young hero proves his or her worthiness and brings help from unexpected (often supernatural) sources.*

A terrible storm comes that night and makes Ivy grateful that she is in Aunt Jo's cozy cabin. They talk warmly and openly for four hours before falling asleep. But in the early morning, Ivy is jolted awake by the sound of a huge crash, followed by howling wind and a howling wolf. A tree has crashed through the roof of the cabin, and although it has missed Ivy, it fell on, or very near, Aunt Jo. Ivy grabs a flashlight and runs to Jo, who is on her side and moaning with pain. Ivy gets Jo onto the sled and drags her from under the gaping hole to be closer to the stove. Jo's upper leg has been broken and already ugly purple bumps on her skin show that she is bleeding internally. On top of this bad situation, Ivy hears some terrible creaking and realizes that the whole cabin is caving in. They escape just in time to avoid being crushed, but both Aunt Jo and the survival manual that Ivy manages to find say that they have to get immediate professional help for the hemorrhaging. It is barely dawn when Ivy starts on her true test of dragging the sled down the mountain and cutting across the partially frozen lake to get to the ranger's station. The "mythical" or unexpected help comes from Malachi, Aunt Jo's wolf, who encourages Ivy and provides companionship as Aunt Josephine fades in and out of consciousness. Ivy is horrified to hear the cracking sound of ice under them. She stops dead still and begins to call for help, even though she's sure there is no one to hear her. But to her surprise and joy, she hears Mountain Mama calling out to her and also Jack Lowden, the ranger-in-training. Jack tells her that wolves have the ability to pick out solid ice—she is to follow Malachi.

6. *In the course of the conflict, the young person usually must make a sacrifice as when in J. R. R. Tolkien's* Lord of the Rings, *Frodo becomes so emotionally attached to the ring that he cannot take it off his finger and so he must let Gollum take his finger along with the ring.*

With encouragement from both Jack and Mountain Mama, and genuine help from Malachi, Ivy manages to get to the other side of the lake. However, this is not the end of the ordeal because they are still a few miles from the ranger station. Jack pulls the sled carrying Aunt Josephine while Ivy runs behind on trails so steep that she could never have managed them ordinarily without the adrenalin provided by the emergency. Finally, they arrive at the ranger station, and as rangers' hands lift Aunt Jo from the sled and take her in by their fire, Ivy hears herself screaming, "*Is she all right? ... Is she going to be all right?*" (162).

The next thing she knows she hears the sound of a motor, probably a helicopter or maybe a snowmobile, and she feels herself being moved. Someone is rubbing her hands and someone else is asking if she can hear them. Ivy is in a hospital being treated for exhaustion and exposure. While doctors and nurses work with her, she falls asleep and does not wake up until the next morning when she faces her gray-faced father, along with Jack and Mountain Mama standing near the bed. A nurse is taking her blood pressure and saying it was a miracle that she made it.

7. *What is actually gained is wisdom, illumination, emotional freedom, and an expansion of consciousness, but for the sake of the story these abstractions are illustrated through something concrete, such as winning a desirable marriage partner or obtaining a position of trust.*

The next day when the night nurse allows Ivy to get out of bed long enough to walk Mountain Mama to the elevator, Ivy slips on her knee-length L.L. Bean arctic parka to cover her inadequate hospital gown. She looks down at her NO YIELD button and thanks Mountain Mama. She tells her that she learned more in the past week than in any other week of her life. Mountain Mama in her typical immodest fashion agrees.

The concrete reward that Ivy gets is Jack Lowden as a boyfriend. In the relatively short time they had spent together when they first met on the mountain, Ivy becomes so enchanted with him that she gives him three of her Hershey bars with almonds, which leaves her only seventeen to last four more days. But near the end of the book, when Jack walks into Aunt Tib's birthday party, Ivy thinks to herself, "If there was ever a reason to cross an icy ledge in the middle of winter, that reason was standing there in the hallway looking up at the balloons" (181).

8. *The young person emerges from the kingdom of dread and is acknowledged by family and the public with a new degree of respect and responsibility as appropriate to one who has successfully traversed the route from Innocent to Hero.*

So many Breedloves come rushing to the hospital that the nurses have to keep shushing them and explaining that there are other patients besides Ivy and Aunt Josephine. Even Uncle Archie hugs Ivy and tells her that if she had not been there, Aunt Josephine would have died. Several weeks later, when Ivy is distributing the one-hundred-and-eighty-page Breedlove history that she and Aunt Tib produced, her father, who has always avoided mentioning his deceased wife, tells Ivy that he is proud of her—both for himself and for her mother.

To keep the whole thing from becoming overly sentimental, Bauer shows Egan reacting more skeptically. When Ivy returns to school after Christmas break, she feels a little disappointed that her schoolmates have no idea what she has gone through. She tries explaining this to Egan, but he teases her with the observation that except for a severe case of chapped lips, she looks "exactly the same" (175).

LITERARY TECHNIQUES

Before Bauer started writing young adult fiction, she studied how to write scripts for movies. This is probably one of the reasons that instead of establishing her settings through long descriptive paragraphs, she helps readers imagine the settings through what the characters say and what they do. Some of the most inviting pages in her books are filled with white space and sprinkled with quotation marks to indicate dialogue and italics to indicate inner thoughts. An especially good example of how she creates drama that readers imagine themselves experiencing is the scene on pages 154 and 155 when Ivy is trying to pull the sled carrying her injured Aunt Josephine across the frozen lake to the rangers' station. Ivy hears cracking sounds and immediately stops because "given the choice of where to die," she knows she would rather be on frozen land than on partially frozen water. Readers, even if they have never pondered the question, are probably in agreement with Ivy.

Another of Bauer's strengths as a writer are her succinct and creative descriptions, as when Ivy asks herself how she "got dumped in this ampli-fied family" (4), when she observes that in the context of Aunt Fiona's videotape "sound bites are to history what condensed books are to litera-ture" (18), and when at Aunt Tib's birthday party she notes that "his-torians and hermits aren't used to applause" (181).

Bauer is also skilled in creating names for her characters. Ivy's mother was an orphan, which means that the focus in this family story can be on the Breedloves, whose surname is old-fashioned but at the same time sort of edgy and suggestive. Nicknames tell almost more than the names people were born with because they are usually given to peo-ple when they are old enough to have displayed the kind of person they will become. Ivy's grandfather was known as William Washington "Iron Will" Breedlove. The name William has the old English meaning of "reso-lute protector," so his nickname of "Iron Will" reinforces the name he was given by implying that he is doubly strong willed.

Another ancestor was given the name of Winsted Attila Breedlove. In the early 1900s, he was "the most feared professor at Harvard Law

School" (3). Students probably made jokes about him being as mean as Attila the Hun, who in the 400s was known as "the scourge of God." Other Breedlove names are not so fearsome, but they definitely fit with early American history: Mercy, Comfort, Eliza, Uncle Clarence, Iza and Baldwin, and Vesta with her two beloved birds: Florence and Luther.

The name that Bauer chose for Jack Lowden is memorable because it is so close to that of Jack London, another adventurous young man who is famous for writing about cold and snowy mountain storms. The only other boyfriend that Ivy mentions is a boy named Claude. He can hardly compare to Jack Lowden, especially because he did not have sense enough to stay around even when Ivy used an old family recipe and made him rum cake with candied walnuts.

Formula fiction is defined as stories with no surprises and no new information. Bauer keeps her books from being formula fiction because in each one she includes information about a skill or an activity of interest to young people. In *Backwater,* readers learn several things about mountain survival including the dangers of falling asleep for someone who is injured and near freezing. And thanks to the survival manual in Aunt Jo's cabin and the feeble instructions from the injured woman herself, Ivy understands how necessary it is to get immediate professional help for a person with internal bleeding. And because of Jack being on the opposite side of the ice-covered lake and shouting out directions, Ivy immediately comprehends the crucial fact that by crawling instead of walking her weight will be spread into fourths instead of all bearing down on the same place as she pulls the sled across the ice. Ivy also learns several things about relating to a wolf and about training birds from Aunt Jo. And closer to everyday life, readers learn what goes into conducting successful interviews and into the "ethics" of historical research. They also learn that even when Ivy follows all of her own rules, she doesn't always feel successful. It is not easy to build a sense of trust and understanding or to get to know a person well enough to ask appropriate questions. Just making a list of what readers learn from *Backwater* is an oversimplification because the benefit of learning concrete facts in a novel rather than in a "how-to" manual is that a well-written novel presents the information inside a believable context that reveals both the emotional and the practical information. Also, a good writer can take the time to develop details and alternative ideas that would be out of place in an informative "how-to" manual.

CHAPTER EIGHT

HOPE WAS HERE

O NE OF JOAN BAUER'S early career goals was to be a comedian. She gave up on that, but she still loves to make people laugh both in her stories and in her actions. When Bauer was in high school, she worked as a waitress and developed skills that, she says, stay with a person, just like riding a bicycle. She proved this one year at a formal dinner given for English teachers at their national convention. Her publisher was treating the teachers to dinner so that they would have a chance to get to know one of their most successful authors. Bauer provided the funniest moment of the evening when instead of sitting at her table of eight and conversing politely over dessert, she jumped up and bussed the table. She proved to the astonished guests and the restaurant staff that she was every bit as skilled as the title character in *Hope Was Here*, who on her first day in the Welcome Stairways diner shows a skeptical, older waitress that she can "deliver the goods" by layering four dinner plates on her outstretched arm and carrying in her left hand six coffee cups with saucers, "piled on two by two" (37).

Besides loving to make people smile, Bauer loves words. She says that she grew up loving words, "drinking them in." As a child, she would pore through *Bartlett's Quotations* and would read *Roget's Thesaurus*. The first thing she would do each month when the family's *Reader's Digest* came was to read the jokes and then turn to the Word Power section and learn a new word. She took Latin in high school, where she learned the historical bases for many words she already knew. Learning those bases helped her to tie words together and to realize that words have stories and "parents," sort of like characters in books. One of her favorite discoveries was that *anger* is related to *strangle*; they both come from the Latin word *angare*. She likes reading the definitions in good dictionaries because they help her "pull more meat" out of words. In an article entitled "Words," she observed that it is easy to say out loud that something

Bauer is at her best in *Hope Was Here*. She creates dozens of metaphors and allusions, many based on some aspect of food service. From *Hope Was Here* by Joan Bauer. Used by permission of G. P. Putnam's Sons, A Division of Penguin Young Readers Group, A Member of Penguin Group (USA) Inc., 345 Hudson Street, New York, NY 10014.

speaks the truth, but when she understands that truth is *fidelity, constancy, sincerity in action, character,* and *utterance,* the word suddenly "takes on more muscle."

In the same article, Bauer talked about how she believes that everyone should have favorite words like they have favorite colors and favorite flavors. Her three favorite words are *hope, brouhaha,* and *salubrious.* She likes *salubrious* because "it sounds thick, rich, and high caloric." She likes *brouhaha* because it is fun to say and it makes people smile even though in a real brouhaha "it's a safe bet that no one is smiling." But judging from Bauer's writings, *hope* is her true favorite and she has worked it into several of her stories. In *Hope Was Here*, which is probably Bauer's best-known book because it was selected as a Newbery Award finalist in 2001, she lets her protagonist change her name from Tulip, a name she despises, to Hope because "hope is just about the best thing a person can have" (7).

MAIN CHARACTERS

Hope Yancey is the sixteen-year-old narrator who over three years changes from a resentful girl to a confident young woman looking forward to her first year of college. She prides herself on being an exceptionally good waitress because food service is the family business.

Aunt Addie has raised Hope since the time she was in a hospital incubator with tubes sticking out of her two-and-a-half-pound body. Addie takes as much pride in her cooking as Hope does in her waitressing. They have lived in three different time zones because the kind of independent, mid-level restaurants that hire Aunt Addie often change ownership and close for renovations so that Addie and Hope have to move to new locales.

Deena is Hope's birth mother, who according to Aunt Addie did not lose her parenting instincts—she simply never had them. Deena is Addie's younger sister. Hope describes her as a "pen parent" because she sends mimeographed Christmas letters to Addie and Hope. She has visited Hope three times, and over the course of the book comes once more.

G. T. Stoop is the owner and manager of the Welcome Stairways diner in Wisconsin. He was raised as a Quaker and is surprisingly strong and at the same time gentle. When he is diagnosed with leukemia, he sends out a call for restaurant help, which results in Addie and Hope moving to work for him in Mulhoney, Wisconsin.

Gleason Beal is important in the story only through his absence. He was Addie's dishonest business partner in the Blue Box diner in Brooklyn. When he skipped town, he took not only the night waitress with him, but also the restaurant's bank account and Hope and Addie's dream of owning their own restaurant.

Braverman is the short-order cook at the Welcome Stairways diner who becomes Hope's boyfriend. When Deena comes for an awkward and unpleasant visit, Braverman hands Hope a red, sponge clown nose that helps to turn "discouragement into hope" (142). He is a couple of years older than Hope and plays a key role in helping her begin to refer to Wisconsin teenagers as *we* rather than *they* and in managing G. T.'s political campaign.

A. B. Hall is the pastor of the Gospel of Grace (GOG) Evangelical Center in Mulhoney. He is a good friend of G. T.'s and comes through with just what is needed whether it is convincing the election board that the only "right" thing to do is to give the petition carriers a few more hours to check the addresses that are said to be "wrong" on G. T.'s petitions, providing hot chocolate and doughnuts to the teenagers circling city hall in the middle of a cold December night, or presiding over G. T.'s inauguration as mayor and, a year and a half later, over his funeral.

SETTING

As Hope explains about the Blue Box diner in Brooklyn, when the furnace died and the roof started leaking, "we were toast" (3). She and Aunt Addie find themselves pulling a U-Haul trailer to a new job without even seeing the restaurant or meeting the owner. They are moving a month before Hope finishes her sophomore year in high school, partly because they are desperate and partly because their new boss, G. T. Stoop, needs someone immediately. As an extra incentive, he says they can live in one of the two apartments on top of the restaurant. When Addie and Hope get to Mulhoney, Wisconsin, (what Hope calls "cow-country") just before Memorial Day, they pull into the parking lot of their new home and spend a few minutes watching the people who are leaving the restaurant and getting in their cars. Two men with toothpicks in their mouths are not communicating at all. They are followed by a woman and a teenage boy who are talking, but without enthusiasm. Addie says that customers who have just enjoyed a good meal would be happier and more animated. She opens the car door and marches toward the diner, telling Hope that they are like missionaries coming to a new place and saying, "Lord in heaven, I've got my work cut out for me here" (16).

Bauer uses settings to create contrasting images, such as when Hope thinks about how different Wisconsin and the Welcome Stairways customers are from the restaurant and the customers they had in Brooklyn. Once Hope gets unpacked, she looks at the empty cardboard boxes and thinks of them as "symbols of starting over" (57). She's happy about her new room with its light-yellow walls, a blue rug, and her bed sitting crisscross between the windows, but she doesn't feel that she fits as well as the furniture does. She wonders if, or when, the magic will hit and make her feel at home. In Brooklyn, she remembers, it hit when she met Miriam at soccer practice and Miriam picked a ladybug from her shin guard and handed it to Hope. In Pensacola it hit when she got a waitressing job, and in Atlanta it hit when she stopped fighting.

Bauer uses the fact that there are two apartments above the restaurant, with Addie and Hope living in one of them while G. T. lives in the other, to reveal something about Addie's character. G T. and Addie become more than friends, and when G. T. makes a dinner date with Addie—one not at their own diner—Addie insists on meeting him in the parking lot. Apparently, it doesn't seem right to Addie to go out with a man who would just holler from across the hall that he was ready.

Time, as well as place, is part of the setting, and Bauer has Addie and Hope leave Brooklyn toward the end of May, which is symbolically a time of new beginnings when farmers sow their crops, trees grow new leaves, and flowers and animals come out of winter hibernation. A few months later when another new beginning is needed, Bauer makes it happen at sunrise. The teenagers of Mulhoney discover that more than 120 voters listed on the official books claim that they neither registered nor voted. The election was held in November, and it is now the third week in December, when Wisconsin is "a vast frozen tundra" (166). Such weather makes it all the more impressive that 297 frozen teenagers dressed like Eskimos hold a mind-numbingly cold candlelight vigil outside the town hall where they sing "We Shall Overcome." Their screaming taunts turn into ice crystals the minute they leave their mouths (166), but that doesn't stop the crowd from embracing the spirit of the season and shouting at the dishonest mayor, "Time to go! Ho, ho, ho!" (167). Dawn is breaking across the sky when a spokesperson appears to read a statement from Mayor Millstone saying that he is resigning "because of the dissension of certain factions," but he prays that the town will continue in the great tradition he has set (167). Braverman shouts back that they might change a few things, and Pastor Hall shows up with seven GOG members to serve hot chocolate and doughnuts and to compare the way the teenagers are shouting down the walls of Mulhoney's town hall to the way that Joshua shouted down the walls of Jericho in the Bible.

PLOT

Addie and Hope have their first day of work on Memorial Day, and they are surprised when at the town's celebration G. T. announces that he has decided to run for mayor. He explains that since he now has leukemia he can't stand at the short-order grill for ten hours a day so he is looking for "more of a desk job" (31). G. T. is only joking about why he has decided to run. The real reason is that the disease has taught him that it is important to do the right thing, no matter what happens. After he makes a surprisingly effective campaign speech documenting several kinds of corruption in Mayor Millstone's administration and in Sheriff Greeb's department, he walks off the stage and tells Addie that he is glad she has come to run things so he can make a fool of himself in politics. Addie gives a slight nod, and Hope in her cynical way wonders whether Addie is agreeing that she can "run things" or that "G. T. is being a fool" (35).

While the book begins with the immediate challenge of Addie and Hope settling into their new home and new jobs and Hope into a new school, Hope also has some long-standing challenges. As she explains, she knows about survival. She was born prematurely and kept gasping for air like she couldn't "get the hang of breathing" (5). The doctors didn't think she would make it because she was too tiny to suck a bottle. Deena named her daughter Tulip, and then "went off to live her own life" (5). Hope hated being named Tulip, and with Addie's help officially changes her name on her twelfth birthday.

Readers learn how much Hope resents her mother leaving her when Hope hangs a pair of boxing gloves on the back of the door of her new Wisconsin bedroom. Hope explains that she brought them along just to remind herself that she had finished fighting. She had learned to box when she was eleven. Addie had a policeman friend, Mickey Kazdan, who boxed and would take Hope with him to the ring. She didn't fight opponents, but she learned how to do quick jabs, to protect her face, and to dance lightly around an opponent. She would work on the punching bag until she was exhausted, but one day "a chord deep down" inside connected to fury, and she began hitting the bag harder and harder with "jabs and rights and left hooks." Tears were streaming down her face, and Mickey Kazdan told people to stand back and let her "punch it out …

until it's all gone." He later told Hope that she was saying, "You shouldn't have done it! You shouldn't have!" Hope doesn't remember this, but when she finally fell in a heap on the floor and the "rage was out," she realized that she had been hitting and punching and crying at the unfairness of Deena so casually abandoning a tiny baby who, with tubes up her nose, was struggling for survival.

Aunt Addie had arranged for Hope to go to the boxing gym because when the two of them were moving to a new job in Atlanta, Hope had screamed at Addie that she wasn't going, that Addie couldn't make her. There is still a dent in the side of Addie's car from Hope picking up a big rock and swinging it at the car. After she did this, she ran away to her friend Lyla's house, where they hid in the attic and ate Fritos and drank root beer. But Hope soon began to worry that maybe Addie would leave her, just like Deena left her. In a panic, Hope ran the two blocks home. Addie saw her coming, and as she put the last of the boxes into the U-Haul, she told Hope that she wouldn't have gone without her, which was something Hope "wanted to believe more than anything" (12). They both sat down on the curb, and Addie then told Hope that she is not sure that Hope will understand, but that Addie needs Hope as much as Hope needs Addie. She suggests that Hope write it down and keep it in her pocket so she doesn't forget. When Hope says she'll remember, Addie only half-jokingly threatens a later test. Then as she looks at her dented car, she hugs Hope and tells her they'll have to find something else for her to hit.

Because Hope has more or less come to terms with the fact that Deena isn't likely to change, she pins her dreams on finding her father, a man that Deena claims not to remember. Hope fantasizes about running a personal ad, but she writes it only in one of her scrapbooks: "*Transitional teen seeks whereabouts of true father. No questions asked. No leads too small*" (58). At the back of that scrapbook is her collection of magazine pictures of men who look like they would be good fathers. She doesn't go for guys wearing strange clothes or with spiked hair. Mostly the men are wearing business suits and smiling because steadfastness is the trait she's looking for, so, unsurprisingly, many of the pictures come from life insurances ads where fathers are holding on to kids and looking as if they will never leave them (59).

One reason that Hope has kept eleven scrapbooks about the significant people, places, and food in her life is to keep from forgetting that she and Addie have a history, even though they move around. But a more important reason is that she has a feeling that her dad's out there searching for her. When he bursts through the door and tells her how he's spent a fortune on detectives who've been looking all over the world for her, she's not going to sit there like a dumb cluck when he asks what she's been doing. She's going to yank out her eleven scrapbooks and share her experiences and innermost thoughts on her life in three different time zones (9).

Hope carries this dream to Wisconsin when newspaper reporters come to cover the election. Some people, like Addie, refuse interviews, but Hope never does because deep down inside she is thinking that maybe her father will see one of the TV interviews and recognize her face, her name, or "*something*" and will "jump into his Jaguar sedan and drive fast, but not recklessly" to find her (129). This portrayal is enough to make readers smile but not laugh at how much Hope is bothered by being a near orphan.

THEMES

Hope Was Here is a journey story in which the moves that Hope and Aunt Addie make are visible ways of demonstrating the less visible changes that take place inside Hope's mind. When Aunt Addie and Hope leave Brooklyn for Wisconsin and Aunt Addie says, "On to greener pastures!" (5), she is making both a literal and a metaphorical statement. As she describes each move, Bauer finds ways to encourage readers to examine the theme of what it means to be hopeful. One of the ways she does this is by having Hope choose her own name. This was a twelfth birthday gift from Aunt Addie, who knew how much Hope hated the name Tulip. Hope chose from a book of names that included meanings; nevertheless, during the month before they make the change official, Addie makes Hope carry her new name written on a three-by-five card to be sure that she feels up to having a name that people will associate with being cheerful and positive. People will expect more from someone named Hope than they will from girls named Patty, Lisa, or Danielle. Hope goes on to develop her own set of expectations related to her name. For example, during the election campaign in Wisconsin when one of the boys makes a Voter Reality sheet where he asks the CQ "Critical Questions" about each voter, the four boxes are labeled:

YES
NO
MAYBE
ABANDON HOPE.

Hope doesn't like her name being used like that (92).

When Hope worked at the Blue Box diner in Brooklyn, she invented the Keep Hoping Sandwich, which people ordered like mad. Hope decides its popularity is based on the fact that its name makes it "a sandwich for our time" (3). As a pick-me-up for Hope, Aunt Addie reintroduces the sandwich in Wisconsin, where it proves to be as popular as it was in Brooklyn. On the first night in the new apartment in Wisconsin, Hope gets out her dictionary and writes out her favorite definition of her name on a three-by-five card because she is not sure she remembers just what Hope means—"*to cherish a desire with expectation of fulfillment*" (21). Later that night when she still can't sleep, she fantasizes about talking to her father—the man she knows she will meet someday. She tells him how hard it is for her to fit into new places and to stay hopeful. She suspects that she made a mistake with her name and should have chosen one that didn't carry so much responsibility: "Susan, maybe" or "Lucy" (59). At 3:14 AM she is still awake and worried, so she goes to her *Roget's Thesaurus* and looks up the word *thief* and lists all the words that describe what Gleason Beal is: a robber, a stealer, a purloiner (she especially likes this one), a larcenist, a pilferer, a poacher, and a swindler. Then she flips to the "H" section and lists the meanings of Hope: belief, credence, faith, trust, confidence, and assurance (60).

Near the middle of the book, when G. T. has proposed to Aunt Addie and Hope returns to her scrapbooks to look at all the imaginary fathers whose pictures she has cut out over the years, hope flutters "in the room like a butterfly getting ready to light" (158). A few pages later, after all the reporters have left town thinking that there's no story because Mayor Millstone has been re-elected, Hope feels like everything "hopeful" is dead. However, her depression is only the darkness before the dawn because she happens to mention the election to one of her customers who had sworn he would never vote. Hope saw his name, along with that of his wife, listed on the public record as having registered and voted. His adamant denial that they voted is the key to uncovering what had actually been a fraudulent election. Hope's optimistic spirit returns, and she decides that despite everything that Gleason Beal stole from her and Aunt Addie, she is not going to let him also steal her name and what it means to her.

The title of the book comes from a little going-away ritual that Hope invented for herself. When she and Addie would leave a place, Hope would write her autograph in half-inch letters—"HOPE WAS HERE"—in some inconspicuous but "significant" place. Even if no one ever saw the message, Hope wanted to envision it documenting that she had been there and had made a difference. At the end of the book, the day before Hope leaves for college, she takes out her blue marker and under the counter of the Welcome Stairways diner by the honey jar and the bowl of lemon wedges that her mother had advised keeping close by, she writes in small letters: "HOPE WAS HERE." It feels different from the other times because this time she knows she is coming back now that Wisconsin and the Welcome Stairways diner are really home.

A second major theme that Bauer develops is the value of honest labor. For example, when Hope lists the "magic" moments that made her feel at home in other cities, she includes getting promoted from bus girl to waitress in Pensacola and inventing the Keep Hoping sandwich in Brooklyn. Several of the townspeople who come forward to sign G. T.'s petition mention how over the years he had given work to a family member who needed it. Braverman is especially loyal to G. T. because when his father abandoned their family, G. T. took Braverman under his wing and taught him to cook. And even at the end of the book when Hope suffers from bouts of grief, she pulls herself together and takes another order because "the sad heart needs work to do" (183).

LITERARY TECHNIQUES

Bauer's skill in creating vivid mental pictures in just a paragraph or even a couple of sentences probably goes back to her experience in writing scripts for movies. For example, it is easy to envision a movie scene based on the description of how Hope, on her fourteenth birthday, was promoted from busing to waitressing at the Rainbow Diner in Pensacola, Florida. It was during the lunch hour rush when Bambi Barnes, who had accidentally spilled navy bean soup on a man, who in restaurant lingo was "one taco short of a combo platter," stood crying by the decaf urn (1). The manager's screaming at her to stop just made her cry all the harder. When she tore up her order book and flung the pieces in the air like confetti, she got fired and Hope got promoted.

Another scene right out of a movie occurs on Hope's first day at Welcome Stairways. Lou Ellen, one of the waitresses, trips over a man's leg and lets "a nacho plate with meat, beans, and guacamole go sailing." In her frustration and irritation about Hope getting a job just because she is related to the new cook, she asks Hope if she's ever waitressed before. Then she thrusts an order pad at Hope and tells her to take the counter so she can see what Hope is made of. Hope looks at the twelve hungry people already seated and thinks to herself, "Even when you're not in school, life is a test" (36).

Since food service is the subject of *Hope Was Here,* Bauer fills the book with allusions to food. Hope takes "to waitressing like a hungry trucker tackles a T-bone" (2), and when Hope thoughtlessly says something about life and death in front of G. T., he assures her that she doesn't have to mince her words—"The only thing we mince around here is garlic" (25). Practically the only motherly advice that Deena offers to Hope is her observation that men tip better when they are not with their girlfriends, and that it's a good idea to keep honey and lemon slices where they are easily available. Hope explains her relationship to Aunt Addie by saying that Addie never promised her an easy life, but she did promise good food. Hope keeps her personal history by saving menus from the restaurants where they have worked, and she judges the sophistication of new acquaintances by asking if they've eaten sushi. Near the end of the book when G. T. has proven to the people of Mulhoney that his running for mayor was more than the frivolous wish of a dying man, he explains that politics isn't about power, control, or manipulation: "It's about serving up your very best." Hope loves "the fact that it took a short-order cook to get it right" (176).

Another of Bauer's literary techniques is to make multiple uses of the names she creates for her characters. Of course she doesn't do as much with the names of minor characters as she does with Hope's name, but she gives many of the townspeople names with extra meanings that help readers remember who is who. Miss *Pittypat*, for example, is the teacher and organizer of the town's "Dancing Darlings," while Mr. *Sage* is the high school political science teacher who is wise enough to encourage his students to get involved in the election. Deputy Sheriff Brenda *Babcock* has a name that sounds like she's got her gun—or whatever else it will take—ready to get the job done when she is appointed first to be the acting sheriff and then the acting mayor. Her job includes proving the guilt of the *Carbingers*—"five boys, each one worse than the next" (83). While their family name may remind some readers that they are "harbingers" or "bringers" of bad news, other readers might be reminded of carbine rifles because these boys really are dangerous. Mayor *Eli Millstone*'s last name hints at how he is a millstone weighing down the town, while Sheriff L. *Greebs*'s last name is just one letter off from "greed." The waitress at Welcome Stairways who is calm and welcoming to Hope is named *Flo*, while the short-order cook who becomes Hope's boyfriend goes by the noble-sounding surname of *Braverman*.

Only near the end of the book when G. T. is installed as mayor, do readers learn that his Quaker parents had named him *Gabriel Thomas*. In the Old Testament, Gabriel is the "Messenger of God" and one of only three angels mentioned by name. In the New Testament, Thomas, commonly called "Doubting Thomas," was one of Jesus' most loyal apostles. He was the one who refused to believe that Jesus had been resurrected from the tomb until he saw him in the flesh. During the election campaign, some of Eli Millstone's supporters try to point out that G. T.'s family name of *Stoop* sounds a lot like "stupid," but a more optimistic view is that the allusion is to the double-sided "stoop" (an old-fashioned word related to *steep* and *step*) that provides the entrance to the Welcome Stairways diner. The double-sided stairway in front of the diner was copied after the houses of early Quakers in Massachusetts who considered such stairs to be symbols of faith and hospitality. They reminded the owners that guests were to be welcomed from whichever way they came (13).

One of the most moving scenes in the book occurs following G. T. and Aunt Addie's marriage when G. T. asks Hope if he can adopt her. After Hope shows him the scrapbooks of her life, which all along she had been keeping for G. T. but "just didn't know it," he walks over to the two little trees that were a wedding present and are now sitting in the corner under the special light trying to get a good start before spring when he will plant them in the backyard. He takes out his Swiss army knife and cuts a little branch from one of the trees and slices off a bit of the other tree. Then he tells Hope to get the twine from over on the table and some scissors and tape. While she holds the little branch to the cut spot on the other tree, he tapes it on and then ties it with twine and sets both trees back under the growing light. He explains to her that the process is called "grafting," and that's what is going to happen to them. Even though they did not start from the same tree, they are going to grow together. Hope thinks there wasn't "a better thing a father could have done." Over the next few weeks she watches, waters, and mists the tree because she loves thinking about the symbolism, but at the same time she worries that something might go wrong and then she'd "be stuck with a metaphor that couldn't go the distance" (173).

In conclusion, Bauer told Elizabeth Koehler-Pentacoff in an interview that *Hope Was Here* was her hardest book to write, but "it's nice to know that your problem children can go out into the world and make you proud." What made it hard was that the political speeches kept slowing down the action and the humor wasn't coming through. Her editor, Nancy Paulsen, showed her how to strip away layers and layers and cut the political speeches. In the end, she managed to show what her characters believed in by what they did rather than by what they said.

CHAPTER NINE

STAND TALL

W HEN JOAN BAUER CONTRIBUTED an "Author's Perspective" to a teacher's journal, she wrote about the importance of words in her life. As an illustration she related how just before Gambit, her beloved keeshond dog (the same breed the protagonist has in *Thwonk*), was put to sleep, she carried him outside to the front lawn where she laid him on a soft blanket and talked to him for an hour telling him how much she was going to miss him and how much he had meant to her and her family. She wasn't sure Gambit understood, but somehow she felt the "need to say the words to him" (45).

Bauer transferred this experience and her feelings to a scene in *Stand Tall* when the family's aging dog is unable to get up. The family suspects that the dog has had a stroke, and so they make an appointment to take the dog to their veterinarian. The doctor tells them that they are probably correct in their diagnosis, and he offers to administer a shot that will stop the dog's heart. But first, he asks if they want to have a few minutes to talk to the dog. They say yes, even though not one of them has the least idea of how to say goodbye to a dog that has been in their family so long. But then the doctor's cat comes sneaking into the room and the dog opens one eye, gives a little bark and then a real bark. He shakes his head, stretches his front paws, struggles to stand up, and successfully faces down the doctor's cat.

At this point, Bauer enters the story as the narrator and lets readers know that this isn't going to be one of those stories where an old dog dies in its owners' arms. With encouragement from the doctor, the family lifts the dog off the table. He walks shakily forward, banishes the cat, turns around, and comes back to the grieving family. The doctor tells them that it is their decision, and although he can't promise anything, if they want they are welcome to take the dog home because it looks like he's "got some life in him yet" (137). This is a relatively small incident in *Stand*

Tall, but it is one of the most memorable in the life of the twelve-year-old protagonist, who during his seventh-grade year at the Eleanor Roosevelt Middle School has more than his share of challenges.

Another aspect of the story that comes from Bauer's own thinking and experience is the lingering influence of the Vietnam War. Bauer was a teenager during the years that the United States was engaged in that war, and people of her generation were the most vociferous protestors. Over the years, Bauer has thought a lot about the war and the veterans who came home with various kinds of injuries that changed their lives. The grandfather in the story is one of those veterans, and at the beginning of the book he is undergoing surgery to have the lower part of his leg amputated because, rather than healing over the years, his damaged leg has deteriorated.

Main Characters

Tree is the twelve-year-old protagonist who, of course, was not named Tree by his parents, but this is what he has been called ever since first grade when he sat on a stool and his classmates stood around him for the class photo. By the seventh grade, he is already six feet three and one-half inches tall, but this year his worries about being "too tall" are almost eclipsed by the shadow of his parents' divorce.

Tree's parents, who insist that their recent divorce is friendly, share custody of Tree, and so every other week he stays at his mother's new house. In between, she wants him and his two brothers, who are away at college, to keep in touch through heymom.com. Tree's dad manages a sports store but has little interest or ability in managing the details of running a household, such as getting a Christmas tree or thinking ahead to dinner—even when he has invited company.

Tree's brothers, Curtis and Larry, have athletic scholarships to different colleges. Tree misses them, even though when they are home he feels like a misfit because he doesn't share in the love they and their father have for athletics. Their talent makes him feel all the worse about letting down the well-meaning people who regularly express their surprise that he does not even want to become a great basketball player.

Grandpa Leo lives with Tree and his father, and because he is loved and respected by both parents and by Tree, he can be a go-between and a comfort to Tree. He is a Vietnam veteran and a skilled electrician and handyman, but what is more important to the story is his empathy for other people and his ability to help Tree see the lighter side of some of the problems that the two of them face.

Sophie is in eighth grade and a newcomer to the school attended by Tree and his buddies, Sully and Eli. Sophie is "different" from most girls in school; for one thing, she has a motto: "Speak your mind and ride a fast horse." Over the course of the book, Tree and Sophie become good friends.

SETTING

The story is contemporary and takes readers through most of Tree's seventh-grade year at the Eleanor Roosevelt Middle School, which is located in a midwestern city named Ripley. Much of the excitement in the book takes place in early spring, when the river that runs through town overflows its banks and floods the houses in Tree's neighborhood. Parts of the city, including the apartment house where Sophie lives and the small house where Tree's mother now lives, were not damaged in the flood.

The town of Ripley is small enough to have some of the qualities of a rural town, but large enough to have a good-sized hospital, where Grandpa Leo has his leg amputated. It also has a YMCA where, thanks to an overly ambitious basketball coach, Tree has to take dance lessons. There is also a fairly large park with an impressive oak tree. The ending of the book is set in this park when the townspeople come together in thankfulness and hope after the flood. Two smaller parts of the setting that are described so well that readers can easily visualize them are Grandpa Leo's hospital room and Tree's house after the flood.

PLOT

Stand Tall includes elements of all four of the basic plots: person against society, person against person, person against nature, and person against self. Although these plot elements are often discussed as separate entities, skilled authors do not create them one at a time. Stories are stronger when the elements are intermingled in such a way that the plot is more than a summary of the individual strands.

Person against Society

One of the happier parts of the book is Tree's friendship with Sophie, but this story line starts out with Sophie in conflict with the popular girls at school. She is in eighth grade and a newcomer who is "different." When girls in a school clique are making fun of her, Sophie challenges them by pointing out that she is a person just like they are. The girls are not any better than Sophie, who explains that she is not crawling with bugs nor does she have green slime running down her neck (50). Tree catches Sophie's eye and asks if she wants to sit with them. His friends, Sully and Eli, look shocked because they are seventh-graders, and seventh-grade boys do not sit with eighth-grade girls.

Sophie declines by shaking her head, but Tree surprises himself by saying, "We're not crawling with bugs or have purple slime running down our necks." Sophie half-smiles and says, "It was green, the slime I mentioned." Tree nods his head in the direction of one of his friends and tells Sophie that he "has green slime on his neck, but he's done eating" (51). After this convincing argument, Sophie hesitantly sits down, and in the seven minutes remaining of the lunch period she tells them practically her whole life story. This begins a friendship that, as the book progresses, means more and more to Tree.

Person against Person

The person-against-person plot is best illustrated through two sets of divorced parents. Readers do not get to know Sophie as well as they know Tree; nevertheless, what Sophie says about her parents' divorce helps Tree—as well as readers—gain insights into the complications of divorce.

Tree goes on the city bus with Sophie to take a Christmas present to her dad at the muffler shop where he works. The visit is so awkward and strained that Tree comes away thinking, "Sophie's mother was right. She deserved a better father" (77). Sophie must have read Tree's mind because she begins defending her father by telling Tree that he is an excellent mechanic. When his shop had a contest last year, he took out a muffler three minutes faster than anyone else. Later she explains that her dad doesn't know how to love people and that's what drove her mother crazy. After the divorce, Sophie's mother sends her to a therapist because she fears that Sophie has hidden anger. Sophie explains to Tree that her anger isn't hidden; it's right "here on the surface" (78).

On the day that Tree's Grandpa Leo gets home from the hospital, Tree's mother has been invited to come over for dinner. When Tree's dad tells him that she will be arriving in thirty minutes, they both look around in despair because there's no food either on the stove or in the oven. They send out for pizza, and while the dinner starts out "okay," things go steadily downhill. To make room for the pizza they have to move a can of motor oil off the table, and when Tree's dad asks his mom if she wants sausage or veggie, she is insulted because he has already forgotten that she never eats sausage. "Right," says Tree's dad as he puts a huge piece of veggie pizza on a paper plate and adds a plop of salad with too much dressing. Then he makes himself a pizza sandwich by slapping two pieces of sausage pizza together facedown and taking a huge bite. Tree shudders to himself because he knows that's one of the things his mom hates.

Person against Nature

Nature comes into the story through both health and weather problems. Grandpa Leo's leg that was damaged years ago in Vietnam is being amputated; Bradley, the family dog, is dying from old age; and Mother Nature sends a flood through the town of Ripley and through Tree's home. Luckily, the flood was not as severe as the one in New Orleans caused by Hurricane Katrina, but still it was bad enough to force Tree's family and all their neighbors to leave their homes and take shelter in Tree's school. When they come home after a few days in the shelter, they find the basement of their house filled with five feet of muddy water with dirty clothes, half-filled paint cans, basketballs, and footballs floating on top. On the first floor, the watermarks were three feet high on the walls while the floors were littered with broken lamps, an overturned couch and stereo, soaked boxes of food, broken dishes, and soggy books and magazines. Even though they had all been given white masks by the public health department, the smell was terrible. Tree leans against the dining room wall and starts to cry, but Grandpa steadies himself and says, "I know what you're thinking. ... I bet you're thinking this whole house will have to be torn down."

That was exactly what Tree was thinking, but Grandpa is much more optimistic as he starts looking at the clues left by the flood. He tells Tree that anything above the high-water line is perfectly fine. This includes the mirrors and the hanging lights and the whole second floor. To check out the first floor, Leo puts an arm on Tree's shoulder and kicks a hole in the wallboard. He sticks his hand in through the insulation and feels that the plumbing is still solid. "I'll have to rewire where it got wet," he says, "but we haven't lost the farm. Not by a long shot" (157).

When they start to work, Grandpa Leo gives clear explanations and then sets out to do as much of the work as he can. The city has provided everyone with their own dumpster because the first job is to drag out all the wet and ruined carpets, furniture, clothing, and other debris. When Grandpa Leo tells Tree to think of something positive, the only thing that comes to mind is that he hasn't thrown up yet (159).

By the time Tree's two older brothers get home to help—they can stay for only seventy-two hours—the basement has been pumped out, and Grandpa gives them big rubber gloves and puts them to work washing the cement walls with Clorox because the floodwaters had been partly sewage and are therefore infectious. The boys go to work prying off the Sheetrock, pulling out the wet and rotting insulation, and carrying it to the dumpster. They have to be careful not to cut through the wires that carry the electricity or break the pipes that provide the plumbing. Because Tree has had a head start on this, for once he gets the satisfaction of demonstrating to his brothers how to do something. Grandpa Leo probably planned it this way because he has a strong sense of understanding and empathy for other people's emotions. After the flood, while everyone is still in the school gymnasium waiting to get back to their homes, Grandpa Leo and his friend, The Trash King, fix up a big sign and get it hoisted to the roof of Temple Beth Israel where it is fully lit up for everyone to see as they leave the shelter and make their way back to their mostly ruined houses:

> WELCOME HOME, FOLKS
> WE'RE GOING TO MAKE IT. (155)

Grandpa Leo wanted people to feel good about returning home, because he still smarts from the unenthusiastic welcome that people gave to the soldiers coming back from Vietnam.

Person against Self

The major point of the story is whether Tree can come to accept his parents' divorce and turn his focus to other aspects of his life. Grandpa Leo helps Tree accomplish this. Because both of Tree's parents feel mutual love and respect for Leo, he can serve as a go-between for Tree and his bickering mother and father. On the day that Tree helps his mother move to her new house, he comes back and finds a full load of her clothes still in the dryer. He takes them out and starts carrying them up the stairs, but he's suddenly overcome with sadness and drops the clothes and runs into his bedroom crying. Grandpa Leo knocks on his door, asking Tree if he's okay. When Tree responds affirmatively, Leo says, "Convince me." Tree lets him in and tells him about finding his mother's clothes. Leo sympathizes and says he would have cried, too. Then he limps over and sits on the bed with Tree and explains that it is the unexpected things "that just rip the scab off." He goes on to explain that when people are quarreling and doing something as difficult as moving, they "do all kinds of things they wouldn't normally do." He sits with Tree and helps him fold the clothes as if each piece "had cost a fortune." Then he tells Tree to call his mother and let her know that she left a load of laundry (72). He compares the divorce to a war in which everyone has lost a piece of themselves. Things have blown up and left empty places where "something important used to be." Tree realizes that this is how he feels about his parents' divorce, and this is how Grandpa Leo feels about the leg he is losing. Leo goes on to explain that empty places "don't get filled in right away." People have to look "straight on" into the empty places and see what's still standing. His advice is to "concentrate on what you've got as much as you can" (73).

THEMES

One of the themes that Bauer likes to work with is the idea that humor is important to people's well-being. She incorporates humor into virtually everything she writes, but in *Stand Tall* she has a character speak openly about the matter. When Tree and Sophie come back from their less-than-successful visit to deliver a Christmas present to Sophie's dad, they climb on the city bus and Tree bumps his head. Sophie laughingly tells him that he needs a bus with a sunroof. Tree doesn't think this is funny, but Sophie elbows him and says, "You've gotta laugh. If you don't you'll cry" (77–78).

More often Bauer shows, rather than talks about, the power of humor as when she explains that Tree has always felt like a misfit in his family because he is nonathletic in an athletic family. His father likes sports so much that he runs a sporting goods store, and his two brothers both have athletic scholarships to different colleges. When at basketball practice a short classmate makes an easy basket and smirks at Tree, Tree tries hard because he really wants to make a basket, but then he realizes that even more than that "he wants to go home" (26).

The appropriately named Coach Glummer is sure that anyone as tall as Tree will sooner or later turn into a "natural" basketball player. However, Coach Glummer is so single-minded that he also thinks Eleanor Roosevelt, in whose honor the middle school had been named, had "untapped basketball potential." Since it is too late to recruit her for his team, he does the next best thing and has the PTA make an inspirational plaque with her words on it: "No one can make you feel inferior without your consent" (24).

Almost as funny as the thought of Eleanor Roosevelt playing on a middle school basketball team is the image of Tree trying in vain to do remedial house-training with Bradley, his elderly dog. Tree gives Bradley some serious lectures supplemented by hand-drawn illustrations with big Xs on the places that are "*no-poop*" zones (98). Tree's teaching method is even less successful than that of Sheila, Coach Glummer's cousin, who is in charge of the ballroom dancing lessons at the YMCA. She convinces Coach Glummer that his team will be much smoother once they've learned such secrets as

> right foot forward,
> left foot matches,
> right moves back
> and left detaches. (66)

Coach Glummer agrees and sends the team to Sheila's dance class at the YMCA. Tree probably would not have survived if not for his friendship with Sophie. And even with the "understanding" Sophie, they had to dance cheek-to-chest instead of cheek-to-cheek and he had to hold Sophie's elbow instead of Sophie's hand.

All through the book, Grandpa Leo somehow manages to bring smiles out of pain. Once when Grandpa Leo and Tree are sorting their own laundry, Leo is disappointed to discover that he is holding five of his own unmatched socks, but then he suddenly realizes that having only one foot means that he doesn't have to match up his socks. They both laugh, and Tree thinks to himself that he has to love a man who can teach people to laugh at such sad things.

When Tree visits during Leo's recuperation from the surgery, they don't just sit and stare around the room. They work out in the physical therapy room where Tree serves as a leaning post because "if there was ever a reason to be a too-tall seventh-grader, it was so you could help your grandpa get walking again" (16). They also eat the submarine sandwiches and barbecue potato chips that Tree brings, and then they work at Grandpa's trade. He is a master electrician, and he keeps a trunk of tools and "stuff" from his workshop under his bed. On the night that Tree and Leo create the world's ugliest lamp, complete with a little rubber tarantula hanging from the side and a motor that rotates the lamp so that the tarantula's shadow crawls around the room, Belle, the night nurse, says it is "disgusting," which makes Tree proud because that is exactly what they were aiming for. Belle also reminds Leo that he isn't supposed to have tools in the room, but Leo, at his most persuasive, explains that he is saving her grief. If he didn't have something to tinker with, he might be so bored that he would start taking "the hospital apart piece by piece." One of the other patients laughingly points to the peeling paint and the broken TV and says, "Someone already beat you to it," which makes Tree all the more eager to get his grandpa home (18).

When transportation delays caused by the bad weather keep Leo's prosthetic leg from arriving on time, Leo complains that his leg is getting to see the country and here he is confined to the hospital. When it finally arrives, Leo works with it for so long that his physical therapist cautions, "Easy does it. This isn't a race." When she removes it from his stump, Leo sits there holding it on his lap. She suggests that he set it down, but he responds, "No way. We're bonding" (107).

One of Grandpa Leo's biggest strengths is his optimism. When the day arrives for Grandpa to come home, Tree, his dad, and his two brothers race out to the VA hospital in the van from the sporting goods store. Unfortunately, the step is so high that Leo can't get in. Curtis and Larry try to lift him, but they crack his head on the door, and he complains that he's going to need more surgery and he's not even home yet. Finally, Tree kneels down as a living stepstool, which becomes more than a metaphor when Curtis steps on Tree's right hand and Larry steps on his left hand. Tree shrieks, and Grandpa Leo hollers that they have to "grab hold of the first rule" of electricity, which is that to get something going people need both a negative and a positive charge. "We've got the negative; we're going to find the positive if it kills us" (47).

Grandpa Leo's goal is to get strong enough to walk on his artificial leg in the Memorial Day parade. He makes it—at least halfway. Tree marches on one side holding the flag, while Leo's best friend, The Trash King, marches on the other side. A Jeep follows behind. Before the half-way mark, Leo has to slow down, but he still insists on walking. Mona Arnold, his physical therapist, comes out from the crowd and walks beside him saying, "Enough of this, Leo. I want you to ride," but Leo wants to keep pushing, "just like Vietnam." Finally she convinces him that he already went farther than anyone expected him to go, and that, no, she isn't losing faith in him—she's losing patience. The Jeep stops and Leo hoists himself in. And in his typical way of turning bad moments into good moments, Leo takes off his fake leg and waves it over his head to the smiling cheers of the crowd (178–79).

LITERARY TECHNIQUES

Critics often praise Bauer for her craftsmanship. With very few words she can draw vivid word pictures as when Tree sums up the first Christmas after his parents' divorce: "You learn the flexibility of the human spirit when you have two different Christmas experiences in less than twenty-four hours" (90). In a more positive example, when his two older brothers come home from college to work for three days on making their flooded home livable again, Bauer describes the companionship they felt as "one of those moments you want to cover with plastic to keep safe" (174).

One reviewer quoted on the Amazon.com Web site compared the way that Bauer thinks about words and then blends them together to the way that artists choose their paints and then blend them to create master-pieces. Bauer's skill is especially apparent in the way that she uses related metaphors to create allegories, which are extended comparisons that readers can appreciate on both literal and metaphoric levels. When all of the allusions are thought about collectively, they serve to communicate some fairly complex ideas. And because readers incorporate their own ideas and experiences as they interpret literary allusions, they won't all come away with the exact same idea. In this way, allegories make for interesting group discussions.

A good example is Bauer's allusion to the phantom pain that people feel after they have lost an arm or a leg. With amputations, the nerves leading to the lost limb are still in place, and so they communicate some of the same feelings to the person's brain that they were communicating when the arm or the leg was whole. Grandpa Leo shares this strange experience with Tree. People who have not had a limb amputated cannot understand exactly how this feels, but still the idea is fascinating. As Tree thinks about what his grandfather is going through and then what he is going through with his parents' divorce, he sees some similarities. When he looks at his favorite photo of his mother and father laughing together on a beach, he gets a stab of "phantom pain" and thinks if there were memorial walls for lost marriages, he would post this picture of a happy marriage, which is no longer there.

Tree's older brothers, Curtis and Larry, were more prepared for their parents' divorce than was Tree. The brothers are off at college, and so they are not at home to see all the uncomfortable, or actually painful, moments that Tree witnesses. In a metaphor that ties in with the plot, Tree tells his brothers that when their parents decided to divorce, it was like floodwater bursting through a dam that Tree had expected would hold (167). After the real flood arrives, and Tree and his dad and Grandpa Leo have no place to stay when the shelter closes, the three of them go over to spend the night at his mom's new house. It was such a terrible evening that Tree gives up all hope that his parents will ever get back together. The next night it is just Tree and Grandpa who sleep at his mom's while his dad stays at a motel. But as Tree gradually realizes, it is as Grandpa Leo says, "phantom pain does get better" (175).

Another good example of an allegory is the way Bauer ties the book together by alluding to the big white oak tree in Ripley Memorial Park, which Tree describes as having "serious bark." When he is in the park one day and thinking of it as a tree "with attitude," he stretches out his arms, tips his head, and freezes in imitation (3). A couple of pages later, Tree shares some of what his grandfather taught him about trees, how their roots can go as deep into the ground as their limbs go into the sky, and how the roots suck up food and energy much like the way Tree "slurps a milk shake through a straw" (5). The bark on a tree is comparable to the skin on a person, and in the plant world being a tree is being at the top—both literally and figuratively. The observation of Grandpa's that resonates the most with Tree is that "tallness is packed with great expectations" (5).

This leaves Tree feeling pretty good about himself, but then a dog runs up to the white oak, lifts his leg, and pees "on the noble gray bark." Tree sighs and realizes that being a tree isn't always easy (7). On page 41, Tree learns the unsettling news that trees "never stop growing." On page 57, when Sophie is again bullied by the same group of mean girls who first insulted her in the cafeteria, Tree is ashamed of himself that instead of thinking of some witty putdown, he just stands in the hall as if he has "grown roots." On page 96, Bauer shows the passing of time by describing the white oak standing "like a skeleton covered with snow." Near the end of the book, Tree is tired of winter and finds it hard to remember how full and lush the tree had been in the spring and then how its leaves turned wine-colored in the fall. He feels a little more hopeful after he finds an acorn and gives it a chance to grow by digging a hole with his boot and pushing the acorn into it and then covering it with snow and dirt.

A couple of months later spring has come, but so has the flood that devastates the town. Bauer uses the tree as a symbol of rebirth and new hope when five days after the flood, the giant oak begins to bud and birds come back to land in its branches. While the park's benches were upended and many trees had snapped in two or been uprooted, not one limb of the old oak is broken. Tree has a new appreciation for the serious root system that allowed the tree to hold "steady against the storm" (161).

A less optimistic image of trees is presented at Tree's home when he and his brothers have to pull off the wet wallboard and drag out the insulation so that "those rooms stood stark like a tree without leaves" (170). The final scene in the book takes place at the park, where the townspeople have gathered for a postflood ceremony of thankfulness and hope. The climax is to be the lighting of a large candle, but the wind is blowing so hard that Inez, the ministry intern from Ripley Presbyterian Church, can't get it to light. She says, "It's a metaphor, okay? We'll just be hopeful—no flame."

Sophie pushes Tree forward, telling him that he is bigger than those people who are trying to light the candle. She wants him to stand in front of the candle and stop the wind: "You can do it!" Tree resists, but Sophie pushes him forward anyway and so does his friend Sully. It works, and Tree guards the tiny flame until it gets "serious." Flashbulbs go off and people wave their flags. Tree's mom smiles proudly from one end of the crowd, while his dad smiles proudly from the other end, and his two brothers, Curtis and Larry, clap and shout as a tall boy stops "the wind so a candle of hope can burn bright" (182).

CHAPTER TEN

BEST FOOT FORWARD

J OAN BAUER PREFERS TO CALL *Best Foot Forward* a "companion" book rather than a "sequel" to *Rules of the Road* because when she wrote the first book about Jenna and Mrs. Gladstone she had no intention of continuing the story. As she told Jim Blasingame when he interviewed her for the *Journal of Adult and Adolescent Literacy,* she had already killed off one of her "absolute favorite characters" (Harry Bender), and she had tied up as many of the loose ends as was possible for a story dealing with such complex issues as family relationships that are affected by alcoholism and about the kind of greed that results in white-collar crimes. But then readers kept asking her to tell them more about Jenna, and as she talked with her editor and went back and re-read *Rules of the Road,* she realized that she had actually planted lots of seeds in the first book that could "grow another shoot to Jenna's story."

For one thing, Jenna is still in high school and has an exciting new job. She has also made some real progress in setting boundaries with her alcoholic father, and because of the recent company merger, Gladstone Shoes is about to change in more ways than any of the participants imagined. When she sat down to start writing *Best Foot Forward,* Bauer said it was like coming across some old friends she hadn't seen for years. As soon as they started conversing, it was as if they had said *goodbye* only yesterday.

One reason Bauer is attracted to the topic of shoes is that every person in the world intimately relates to their shoes. The manufacturing of shoes is a more complicated and technological process than the manufacturing of other clothing, and for the first time in the world's history ordinary people are wearing shoes that have already traveled halfway around the world.

Reading Bauer's two books on the topic interested me so much in the international aspects of the worldwide shoe marketing that I went to

Bauer prefers to think of *Best Food Forward* as a companion book to *Rules of the Road* rather than a sequel. When she wrote *Rules of the Road,* she had no intention of continuing the story and was, in fact, surprised when readers asked for more. She went back and discovered that, yes, there were still things to say. Photograph by A. P. Nilsen.

a big discount store and examined several of their best-selling shoes. As Bauer makes clear in the plot of *Best Foot Forward,* shoes are required by law to identify where they are made. I was surprised to discover that such American-looking and American-sounding names as NBA athletic sneakers, Sesame Street light-up shoes for kids, and Cherokee work boots for men were all "Made in China." I was also surprised to discover that the labels were very small and almost hidden underneath the tongues.

I appreciated finding this factual support for Bauer's fictional story, but I was even more pleased at the way Bauer succeeded in showing that the issue of where products are made is more complicated than simple prejudice in which people think that their own way of doing things is always superior. The problem introduces issues related to unfair competition and to the exploitation of people who are not protected by the kinds of labor and health laws that affect American workers. This is why Mrs. Gladstone's public statement about the company's bad practices is half-announcement and half-apology. She explains that Gladstone's has engaged in serious violations of the rights of workers in Thailand, including children between the ages of eleven and fourteen. They worked shifts lasting more than twelve hours and were exposed to health and safety risks, while not being given proper food or education.

MAIN CHARACTERS

Jenna is back from driving Mrs. Gladstone to Texas, and as she starts her junior year in high school she hopes for the first time ever that her teacher will assign an essay on "What I Did on My Summer Vacation" because she wants to write about Mrs. Gladstone's "all-out grit" and about how getting to know Harry Bender, even if only for a week, changed her life (17). Throughout *Best Foot Forward* Jenna takes on a caregiving role not only with Mrs. Gladstone, but with her grandmother, her sister, a crying girl at Al-Anon, and a new character named Tanner and his sister and little brother.

Mrs. Gladstone is a composite of some of the "tough" older women that Bauer has known, with a little bit of herself thrown in. What Bauer likes about Mrs. Gladstone in *Best Foot Forward* is that as she gets older, she is more willing to take chances in helping young people develop skills and attitudes that will make the world a better place.

Tanner Cobb is a cool-looking teenager with a good tan and short, curly hair. He has a scar that runs from his left eye clear down his face. He has served time in jail and has a probation officer. Tanner is a dynamic character who undergoes some real changes, but just as interesting as what happens to Tanner are the changes that other characters experience through their interactions with Tanner.

Elden Gladstone is now the general manager of Gladstone's Shoes. He has turned against all that his mother and father stood for when they built the Gladstone Shoe Company that he is inheriting. The sadness of this situation is the unfairness that Elden uses to fight his mother, but a positive aspect is that with Jenna's help Mrs. Gladstone does not give up.

Murray Castlebaum is the manager of the Gladstone store where Jenna works. When Jenna complains to him about Tanner, he good-naturedly makes a joke by telling her that when she came in looking for a job, she "also needed *work*." A surprised Jenna asks him if she was really that bad, and he tells her that he was impressed that she was brave enough to walk in and ask for a job, but it took her a while "to get her footing" (27). Then he chuckles at his own joke and tells her that what she has is *heart*.

Charlie Duran provides the light of hope at the end of the story when he arrives at the shoe store with his own revised work schedule (he's the youthful manager of Jenna's favorite doughnut shop) showing Jenna that they can go to a movie on Thursday, Saturday, or Monday, with a bonus if she chooses all three. When she asks what the bonus is, he gives her a kiss right there in front of everyone (175).

Jenna's grandmother ran a tailoring shop on Clark Street before she developed Alzheimer's. Jenna has a photograph of her bending over her Singer sewing machine surrounded by bright fabrics. Jenna fondly remembers how proud her grandmother was when, at the age of twelve, Jenna won the *Chicago Tribune* "Blood and Guts Award" for selling the most daily and Sunday subscriptions. After the celebration ceremony, her grandmother took her out to dinner at Wok World, Jenna's favorite Chinese restaurant, where she set Jenna's plaque in the middle of the table so everyone could see it right next to the soy sauce.

Jenna's sister, Faith, is a literary foil. She is so beautiful that she expects to become a high fashion model. The magazines she reads, her casual approach to school, the friends she has, and the things she says all serve as a contrast to highlight Jenna's hardworking dedication. Because Faith is a few years younger than Jenna, their mother thinks she is not bothered by the divorce, but Jenna knows better because every time Jenna gets off the phone with her dad or reports having seen him somewhere, Faith wants to know if he asked about her.

Yaley is Tanner's sister. Her main role in the story is to share information about Tanner as she does when she becomes Jenna's friend and tells her that Tanner isn't really bad, even though he got sent to jail for making the dumb move of stealing a judge's billfold. When Yaley asks Tanner why he didn't just ask a cop for his money, he protests that there was no way to know the man was a judge—he wasn't wearing a robe. Yaley is better at recognizing judges than Tanner is because she and their grandmother always go to court to support Tanner. Yaley, who is an artist, draws the faces of people in the courtroom and, consequently, has developed a keen sense of observation. One of her observations, which she shares with Jenna, is that although she does not know what happened to Tanner when he was in jail, something made him different, "like he doesn't care" (64).

Burt Odder is Tanner's probation officer. He is poorly dressed and has an unpleasant personality. One day when he comes in, Jenna sells him a pair of shoes and learns that on top of all his other unattractive characteristics, Mr. Odder's feet smell so bad that her eyes water.

Webster Cobb is Tanner's almost-five-year-old brother. He has asthma but is unusually smart, partly because Tanner taught him how to read and how to write his name.

SETTING

The Chicago setting is mostly backdrop, but it adds interest and makes the story specific, such as when Jenna drives home after she and Tanner have discovered that the executives of Gladstone's Shoes have been engaged in big-time fraud. Tanner, with his "street smarts," warns her to lock things up and to be extra careful. As she gets ready to leave work that night, she is glad her car has secure locks. She keeps glancing over her shoulder periodically while at the same time keeping her eyes on the road, because she knows that a person constantly looking in the rearview mirror is likely to get in a wreck. She muses that even though driver's ed teachers don't seem to know it, driving teaches people a lot about life.

She heads for Michigan Avenue and down what's called the Magnificent Mile. Off in the distance, she sees the old cream-colored Water Tower that looks like a medieval castle, and when she remembers it was one of the few things still standing after the Great Chicago Fire, she thinks about the way Mrs. Gladstone keeps standing even "when the fires of adversity blaze all around her" (160).

The shoe store and the crowded parking lot behind it are in the same part of town as Duran's Doughnuts and become part of the plot because a major difference from the year before is that Jenna used her summer earnings to buy a car—not exactly the dream car she wanted—but, as Jenna says, while others might talk about how light dances off a lake or how sunshine pours through kitchen windows, true beauty is "light beaming off the hood of a recently washed red car that is absolutely yours" (2). Later when Charlie Duran, the youthful manager of Duran's Doughnuts, drives into the parking lot and scratches the door of Jenna's bright red car, they get to know and like each other. Under ordinary circumstances, Jenna would have considered getting a scratch on her car a disaster, but in the context of the big events at Gladstone's Shoes it is a relatively minor misfortune, especially since Charlie goes to the trouble of buying touch-up paint and making the scratch almost disappear.

PLOT

Best Foot Forward begins where *Rules of the Road* ended: Jenna and Mrs. Gladstone are back in Chicago after their trip to Dallas, where Gladstone's formally merged with the Shoe Warehouse. Although Mrs. Gladstone is no longer president of the company, she is still on the board of directors and officially in charge of quality control, thanks at least in part to Jenna. Jenna sells shoes, but the more exciting part of the job is being Mrs. Gladstone's assistant.

Early in the book as Jenna drives away from her Al-Anon meeting, she recalls that Mr. Bouvier, her driver's ed teacher, often warned his students not to drive when they were emotional. He insisted that *only* people who are well adjusted and unemotional should be driving. He tried to model what he preached, but it would all go up in smoke whenever a student would forget to signal.

During the coming months Jenna has cause to remember Mr. Bouvier's advice because developments at Gladstone's Shoes keep her life at a high level of tension. Problems connected with the merger range from how employees should answer the telephone to worries about who will keep their jobs, whether salaries will be changed, and whether the writer behind the sales reports is fudging the data.

A few weeks after the merger, Elden brings a PowerPoint presentation to one of the suburban Chicago stores where he has invited various store managers to gather early on a Saturday morning. The managers, who in the conflict side with Mrs. Gladstone, let her know about the meeting so that she and Jenna can also attend. When they enter the room Elden freezes, but he soon recovers enough to launch into the presentation explaining that under the new plan each store will look exactly alike and the managers won't even have to plan their own displays or sales events. Jenna feels like they are all being sucked into an "extreme-makeover" show (102).

While the managers and the sales people, and even many of the customers, hate the decisions Elden makes regarding the appearance of the stores and the sales techniques, these prove to be only the tip of the iceberg. Underneath it all, Elden is laying the groundwork to have Gladstone's Shoes absorbed into the more profitable, but sleazy, Shoe Warehouse.

Jenna's suspicions are raised when she is wearing a new pair of Gladstone's highest quality Rollings Walker shoes and she gets a blister, which had never happened before. She asks a trusted shoe repairman what's wrong, and when he looks at the shoe he discovers several differences between the old Rollings Walker shoes and the new pair that is uncomfortable. The new shoe has synthetic soles instead of pure rubber, and parts of the uppers are from a man-made, instead of a natural, "leather." Since Mrs. Gladstone has been appointed by the new owner to be the director of quality control, she and Jenna ask Elden, who is now general manager, for an explanation of the differences. When no report is forthcoming, they launch a search-and-rescue mission with all the complications of an international spy story or a political cover-up.

A second strand in the plot of *Best Foot Forward* involves Tanner Cobb. He enters in chapter two when he sends his fourteen-year-old sister, Yaley, and his "four-and-three-eighths-year-old" (9) brother, Webster, into Gladstone's to create a distraction while he steals four pairs of shoes. As shoplifting goes, it wasn't a very good plan because by the time Tanner steals the shoes Jenna has made friends with Webster, who has written his name on a leaf for the tree that stands in the children's section. When Tanner runs out the door with the shoes, Yaley grabs Webster's hand and yanks him away from Jenna. Looking at the fleeing boy, Jenna asks Yaley if she knows him. Yaley says she doesn't know what Jenna is talking about. Murray, the store manager, informs Yaley that she cannot leave because she's now a witness to a crime.

By this time, Mrs. Gladstone has come from her office, and Webster has started crying and wheezing, trying to take a breath. Mrs. Gladstone recognizes Webster's asthma because Elden had it when he was a child. Yaley impatiently tells Webster to use his inhaler, while Mrs. Gladstone leans down and talks to him in a quiet voice and gets out the storybook *The Elves and the Shoemaker* hoping to calm him down. Everyone is surprised when the little boy stops crying and starts pointing to words he knows. When Mrs. Gladstone asks him who taught him to read, Webster answers "Tanner." Yaley shouts, "Shut up!" but it is too late and eventually everyone understands that Tanner was the boy who stole the shoes and that he is their brother.

About this time, Tanner is getting nervous and calls Yaley on her cell phone to see where she is. Mrs. Gladstone, who is escorting Yaley and Webster to her upstairs office, tells Yaley to tell Tanner to come back with the shoes. Soon after an upset Tanner arrives back at the store with the four boxes of shoes, his grandmother comes in. She is the children's guardian and appreciates that Mrs. Gladstone phoned her instead of the police.

The "wisdom" or "foolishness" of Mrs. Gladstone's decision is a question that Jenna, as well as readers, ponder throughout the rest of the book, especially when Mrs. Gladstone decides to accept Tanner's offer that he could work at the store to make up for what he has done. Murray expresses his opinion by warning Mrs. Gladstone that she has "a soft spot that could use some hardening" (29).

Jenna is especially resistant to Tanner. Partly, she's jealous because it appears that Mrs. Gladstone is giving Tanner the attention she had been giving Jenna. Also, Jenna is still smarting from all the second chances that she gave her alcoholic dad. At Al-Anon she has been training herself not to be an enabler and a "softie." When Mrs. Gladstone tells Jenna that she wants her to demonstrate good business sense and to take Tanner under her wing, Jenna insists she is "wingless." To emphasize her point, Jenna holds her arms flat against her sides, but Mrs. Gladstone ignores the gesture and says, "You soar more than you realize, dear." She tells Jenna that whatever she's doing, she should explain the steps to Tanner so that he can soak up the experience of how well Jenna does her job. Jenna concedes that when a request is wrapped in such a compliment, it's hard to say no (56).

Jenna is not at all sure she wants this job, but she guesses that it is a kind of promotion and so she stands tall and sucks in her stomach. As she and Tanner work more closely together she begins to appreciate his creativity and to forgive him for some of his rough edges, like the day she asked if he wanted to go for a pizza and he said, "Sure," and took off down the street. She had to shout out: "I meant together" (158). He is the one who first notices that the labels on the Rollings Walker shoes

don't feel right. And he knows enough about crimes and cover-ups to tell Jenna that they must let Mrs. Gladstone know what they have discovered as soon as possible. Although Jenna and Tanner do not get romantically involved, they do learn to like and respect one another.

THEMES

Because one of Bauer's beliefs is that adults and young people have more in common than today's culture assumes, she was happy to find that Mrs. Gladstone could still play a major role in the story. An incident illustrating how much Mrs. Gladstone means to Jenna occurs when Jenna gets home from work one night and her sister, Faith, is all excited about having seen a famous model. In her disappointment that Jenna isn't very impressed, Faith asks her if there isn't anyone Jenna admires and wants to be like. To Faith's amazement, Jenna responds by describing Mrs. Gladstone, a seventy-three-year-old woman nine inches shorter than Jenna and in need of a new hip (161).

Another theme that Bauer explores is the value of hard work. On a day that Tanner's parole officer comes in and humiliates him, Tanner loses his temper and uses some foul language. Afterwards he apologizes to Mrs. Gladstone for his language, but rather than just accepting his apology she says that she finds such talk "mostly tiresome and uncreative," but she does have her own favorite four-letter word. Everyone is surprised, and Jenna steps back when Mrs. Gladstone asks if he would like to hear it. "*Work!*" she snaps as she throws a mop to Tanner. And then she launches into a little sermon about the one thing she knows "to be true for rich and poor" (55). Honest labor has power in it, and she knows how to teach it and how to train people so that they can make a living. She tells Tanner that she is providing him with this opportunity, but she won't just hand it to him; he is going to have to earn it. A related belief is the idea that people need to be free to express their creativity and to feel respected and "in control." This is why Mrs. Gladstone takes a dim view of Elden deciding to centralize all the decision-making, down to the in-store displays and the advertising campaigns, for the 176 stores in the chain.

Another major theme revolves around how many facets there are to people's personalities and how difficult it is for people to make the kinds of changes that Tanner makes. But before readers will care about whether

Tanner is able to change his path, they have to know him well enough to feel an emotional attachment. Jenna gets an early glimpse into the positive side of Tanner's personality when she approaches a small man standing by a display of Oxfords but looking longingly over at the boots. When Jenna asks if she can help him, she also looks over to the boots and tells the man she's seen lots of people trying to decide if they should try on a pair. The man laughs at how impractical they are and then turns to Tanner, who is standing nearby, and asks if he would wear them. A grinning Tanner says, "Are you kidding? I'd sleep in 'em, they're so cool" (60). Of course Jenna makes the sale.

Another day Tanner is rushing into work—late as usual—where he finds everyone gathered around a package they describe as coming from "Mergers R Hell." It is a puffy foot costume printed with the company's "PUT YOUR BEST FOOT FORWARD" slogan. They are aghast at the idea that one of them is supposed to put on the tan tights and the puffy, flesh-colored costume and go out in public to hand out coupons advertising the big "Labor Day Blowout Sales Extravaganza." Jenna remembers the boundary-setting principles that she's learned at Al-Anon and says firmly that she's not wearing it. Murray thinks maybe he can get his nephew to do it, but then remembers that he has allergies and would soon be "spitting up phlegm" (85). Tanner says that in his neighborhood anyone wearing such a costume would get shot, but then Mrs. Gladstone announces that there will be a bonus "for whoever wears it." Tanner steps forward and asks what his bonus will be.

Mrs. Gladstone clears her throat and tells Tanner that the bonus would be a watch—which he "could sorely use," plus overtime pay. He quibbles over having to wear the tights but gives in when she says it's fine for him to wear his mirrored sunglasses. On the day of the sale, Tanner not only puts his *Best Foot Forward*, he waves and bows while handing out coupons and giving clever answers to kids' questions about such fellow hucksters as Ronald McDonald and Mickey Mouse. Other than telling one teenager that he was a foot fetish, he did himself and Gladstone's proud. He even managed to catch a shoplifter who was trying to take advantage of the crowds and all the hoopla.

But a few days after this happy turn of events, Tanner's parole officer, Burt Odder, comes in for his second visit. He demands to see where

Tanner works, and when he gets in the storage room, he says to Tanner, "Empty your pockets, Cobbie boy" (95). This kind of harassment goes on for a couple of minutes and then Odder turns Tanner's book bag upside down and out falls a pair of men's snakeskin boots.

Jenna is so shocked and angry at Tanner that she can't believe it when Mrs. Gladstone, who had been leaning on her cane and watching "in steely silence," says in a matter-of-fact way that she gave the boots to Tanner, which means no crime had been committed (96). Mr. Odder leaves and Mrs. Gladstone takes Tanner in her office to talk with him. Jenna has no idea what Mrs. Gladstone says to Tanner so she is shocked when Tanner comes out and asks Jenna what he should do next. She tells him that maybe he should go home. He forces a smile and tries to sweet-talk Jenna by telling her that her eyes look great, but she interrupts him with "*Don't*" (97).

When Jenna confronts Mrs. Gladstone about the way Tanner has "tricked" them, Mrs. Gladstone explains that she is giving Tanner a second chance because he did not come to work with Jenna's discipline, and that the "job has been crucial" (98). It is a few days before Tanner comes back to the store, and luckily when he arrives Jenna is trying to wait on four women at the same time. He walks in wearing a shirt and a tie. He smiles at Jenna and says that he has come to work.

"Well, good ... I guess," says Jenna as Tanner heads for the children's section, where he teaches a little girl how to write her name and hang her leaf on the tree. As more customers come in, Jenna grabs Tanner's arm and gives him a quick lesson in salesmanship, plus the warning that if he messes up she will kill him. Tanner heads toward the prettiest woman and gives her a big smile. When she holds out a blue evening shoe, he tells her the blue beads will look great with her eyes, and she melts into "a little pool right at his feet" (113).

Chapter 16 begins with Mrs. Gladstone having a conference with Tanner. When she asks him to describe his strengths, he's speechless. But when she incredulously asks how he could have walked this earth for sixteen years and not know a single thing that he is good at, he stumblingly answers that he was pretty good at shoplifting. As Mrs. Gladstone pursues this line by asking Tanner what he needed to know, he explains that he had to "read a situation," "know the patterns in a store," "move quickly," and "think of ways to hide the stuff" so as to get out the door. Then, as an afterthought, he adds that when it was a group job, someone had to make the plan and that was usually him. Tanner is amazed at how Mrs. Gladstone turns all of these qualities around to be positive attributes that he can use in business. She is partly amused and partly irritated about the fact that people put themselves into tiny little boxes. When she tries to get Tanner to think beyond his present circumstances, he says that he's "pretty good with the ladies." She agrees that this takes personality, "and *attitude*," he adds, which Mrs. Gladstone agrees he has plenty of (116). Readers see a less positive side of Tanner's attitude when after one of Mr. Odder's early visits Jenna tries to sympathize and he lashes out and asks her what she knows about it.

> "Nothing, I was just …"
> "What … trying to *help?* You want to rehabilitate me so you can put a badge on your arm, show you did your good deed for the day?" (54)

LITERARY TECHNIQUES

Bauer told an interviewer from Rhode Island College that she keeps an idea file where she jots down notes and drops in news clippings and interesting tidbits that she runs across when she gets ideas for characters that she would like to develop. In the early 1990s, she searched for facts about the shoe industry because she wanted to write a screenplay featuring a man like Harry Bender. Even though she never wrote the screenplay, many of the facts she put into both *Rules of the Road* and *Best Foot Forward* came right out of her idea file on shoes.

One of Bauer's best literary techniques is drawing original comparisons or metaphors out of her material. An especially succinct comparison is when the shoe repairman examines Jenna's new Rollings Walker shoe (the one that gives her a blister) and compares it to the old one that felt great. He confides that not everyone would be able to spot the differences immediately, but to his experienced eye, it's like the difference between "sirloin and Spam" (106).

Another effective metaphor is the idea of *harvesting the brand*. Mrs. Gladstone explains to Jenna that this is what Elden is doing with the

Rollings Walker shoe. Over the years, customers have grown to expect the very best from this line, and so even though the quality has been altered people will not recognize the difference until they have purchased one or maybe even two pairs. When the public recognizes the lesser quality, the company will discontinue the line. But by this time they will have made a big profit by saving more money on the manufacturing than they will discount on the final close-out prices.

In another example, one day while Jenna is driving to the Shady Oaks Nursing Home to visit her grandmother, she is having a hard time getting onto Lake Shore Drive, and it occurs to her that merging into traffic is a like two companies merging. Not everyone is thrilled about it, and like the man in the black Saab who tries to cut her off and the woman in the Jeep Cherokee who is offended when Jenna joins her lane, some of the people involved in the company merger are obnoxious (65).

And again, Bauer makes the most out of the names she creates for her characters. Part of the obnoxiousness of Tanner's parole officer, Burt Odder, is the disrespect he shows Tanner by calling him *Cobbie*. This is similar to the way that the villain in *Squashed* irritates Ellie by calling her *Missy*. When Mrs. Gladstone keeps Mr. Odder from punishing Tanner for having a pair of boots in his book bag, she explains to Jenna that she does not think justice could be served "through that reprehensible Odder person" (98).

When Jenna and Mrs. Gladstone walk into the meeting that Elden called at one of the western Chicago stores, the manager meets them at the back door and holds up a green shirt decorated with the emblem of the Shoe Warehouse and says, "I'm not wearing this, Madeline." She says she isn't either. By calling Mrs. Gladstone *Madeline,* the manager is emphasizing the strength of his resistance as well as the trust that he puts in Mrs. Gladstone. The idea is repeated a few lines later when another manager sits nearby and says to Mrs. Gladstone, "You're looking tougher than ever, Madeline" (101).

Inside the store, Jenna and Mrs. Gladstone see Elden busily shouting directions about setting up the screen and the projector, but when he senses their presence and turns to look at them, Jenna remembers something she had heard about snakes being able to sense prey even through grass or tall weeds. Jenna continues the snake theme by using such verbs as "slithering" to describe Elden's movements and calling him a "snake in the grass." The degree to which she dislikes him is shown by her reference to him as "Elden M. Gladstone, SI." The SI stands for "Shoe Insect" (70) and "General Manager in Charge of Always Doing the Wrong Thing" (25).

A happier kind of name play occurs as part of the denouement when Mrs. Gladstone enters the hospital for her hip replacement after she has done all she can to make things "right" for the company as well as for the children in Thailand who have been making Gladstone's shoes. Jenna drives Mrs. Gladstone to the hospital and stays with her. Through the pre-op procedures, which would be tiresome and annoying even under the best of circumstances, Mrs. Gladstone is sarcastic and rude. But then Jenna realizes that she is being "huffy" mainly to cover up the fact that she is afraid. After minor confrontations with a series of hospital workers, she is about to say something blustery to a nurse named Beatrice, but Beatrice beats her to it by confessing that they are behind and apologizing for the fact that Mrs. Gladstone has been waiting. Then she shares the secret of nurses, "It's always the doctors' fault" (177). This gets a laugh from Mrs. Gladstone, as well as from Jenna, who is amazed that one person is able to defuse the negative mood that had been in the room. Mrs. Gladstone lies back on her pillow and gives Jenna the sensible advice that it's better be part of the solution than part of the chaos.

When an attendant comes in with a gurney to take Mrs. Gladstone into surgery, he tells her that that her doctor is "as ready as I've ever seen him" (178). Mrs. Gladstone responds to his positive attitude by noticing that his name is Reginald. She tells him that she almost married a man named Reginald. He asks if her Reginald wasn't good enough for her. Mrs. Gladstone assures him that Reginald was fine, but just not as good as the man she got. But then she assures him that it's a first-rate name. It means "strong ruler."

As Reginald continues pushing the gurney into the hallway, Mrs. Gladstone smilingly tells him that she thinks the name fits him "like a good shoe." And as they move away, Jenna thinks of hugging Mrs. Gladstone but decides instead to just squeeze her hand. When Reginald tells Mrs. Gladstone that she is about to become "a woman of titanium" (titanium is what artificial hips are made from), Jenna proudly corrects him to say that Mrs. Gladstone already is such a woman (178).

CHAPTER ELEVEN

JOAN BAUER: STORYTELLER TO THE WORLD

I N OCTOBER OF 2006, when I sent an e-mail to Bauer to check on some little detail, I was surprised to get an answer from Croatia. Bauer was in Zadar at the invitation of the American State Department, which occasionally sends American writers or scholars on cultural exchange visits. She was visiting with teenagers, many of whom had read *Hope Was Here, Stand Tall,* and *Rules of the Road* as part of their English studies. I was heartened to learn that Bauer's books are being read internationally and that she is willing to serve as a personal envoy because as *New York Times* book reviewer (Charles Taylor, Nov. 17, 2002) observed:

> It's hard to imagine any ordinary young reader coming across a novel by Joan Bauer and not feeling at least a little bit better about the world. She reanimates that root desire we feel as fledgling readers that, at least within the pages of their book, authors be our friends.... There are certainly lessons being imparted in Bauer's novels: messages about valuing honesty, integrity, pride and dedication in your work, service to your community. The low-key miracle of her books is that those lessons come with the light, sure touch of a born entertainer.

Taylor went on to say that no author is better at portraying the American work ethic as it is practiced by young people. Bauer lovingly and respectfully portrays teenagers and adults with a passion for what they do and a willingness to work hard to improve their knowledge and their skills whether it is growing a giant pumpkin, writing a family history, taking photographs, selling shoes, or getting really good at playing pool. I agree with what I think Taylor is saying about Bauer's books providing a much needed balance to media images of easy wealth and fame and the old idea that in America the streets are paved with gold.

Croatian students could relate to the need for hope and honor in politics in *Hope Was Here,* and they understood the issues of war in *Stand Tall* because just ten years ago Croatia was at war. The students were all too familiar with experiences similar to the one Tree had in helping his grandfather both physically and emotionally after his leg was amputated because the injury he received during the Vietnam War never healed.

In Zadar, Bauer's visit was held in the American Corners section of the town library—a place where books about life in the United States are made available. Bauer was happy to see that her books were among those on the shelves. The library has an inspiring history. During the war, it had been bombed and because of the densely packed books on shelf-after-shelf the fire smoldered for twenty-eight days. While it was still burning, the library director, who helped to host Bauer's visit, called people asking for donations—books, a chair, or even a table. He was determined to show that the library would be rebuilt. His hard work and his demonstration of faith in people's willingness to help paid off and the library is now located in what used to be a Communist headquarters building. Walls and ceilings were torn out to let in natural light, and according to Bauer it is a beautiful place.

In January of 2007 she received a note from one of the sponsoring English teachers. She explained how they had tried to repeat the experience of Bauer's visit. One of the students volunteered to play the part of Mrs. Bauer and "was unbelievably good." She even succeeded in leading the students to create a character for a class story. Students had also written a bilingual news story (English and Croatian) about the event and put it on the school's Web site. Here are two excerpts:

> The meeting was much better than I expected. Actually, I thought it would be boring, that we'd sit and ask questions, and she'd just answer (of, course, with unavoidable silence because most of the students are ashamed of asking questions). But it wasn't boring. She told us about her life, all she'd been through before she became a writer, about her father who was an alcoholic, about a hard car accident she went through the day after she'd signed her first screenwriting contract. She told us about hope. About the hope that saved her, that led her, encouraged her, and made her not give up....

She showed us how by asking a few simple questions you can create characters and get a real novel.... For us students, this was more than just meeting a writer. She gave us the inspiration to always go after what we really want.... I learned a lot about writing and literature, but not as much as about life.

Because Bauer was coming from New York, the students had prepared for her visit by embarking on a project in which they envisioned "a perfect day in New York." They finished it after Bauer left and forwarded her their stories. Here are a few of the things different students wrote:

- In the moment I found myself above JFK, I could feel the vibe this town was sending me. It's the place where people don't find opportunities. They make them.
- After paying such a low price for food I was able to afford a visit to the Empire State Building. I didn't know, though, I was looking at a two-hour slow walk in a mile long line, but it was worth it!
- I saw George Clooney buying shoes in Fifth Avenue!
- After I ate my breakfast, I took my backpack and went to visit the well-known greenery of New York's Central Park. I had a great time there, people were very friendly and talkative. I was surprised when a couple that was just passing by stopped in front of me and introduced themselves!

Not all of Bauer's international e-mails are so fanciful and imaginative. One that she cherishes came from a thirteen-year-old boy in Israel who sent her a note after reading *Hope Was Here*. He wrote:

This letter is not a school task. I wrote it from my free will, so these are not the thoughts a teacher wants to hear. These are my true feelings....

With all the terror and fear here in Israel, that book is the only thing that gives me hope. It shows me how to be brave and not stay in my house, but to go out and live with hope no matter what.

Bauer has a soft spot in her international heart for *Squashed,* because it was her first book to be translated. She suspects that it was chosen early on by Korean publishers because vegetables are such an important part of the Korean diet. When she received the copy sent in the mail by her agent's secretary, the only thing she could "read" was the big orange pumpkin on the cover. She took it to a friend who had studied Korean. In a quick look, all he could figure out was that the blurb on the inside cover promised "a better story than Jack and the Beanstalk."

Bauer is not involved in the selection or marketing of her books in other countries. It is far too complicated and even her agent works through another agent who specializes in "foreign" marketing. As a Newbery Honor Book, *Hope Was Here* received lots of attention and so has been translated into German, Italian, Spanish, and Mandarin. Bauer's most popular translated book is *Thwonk,* which sells well to Italian, German, Portuguese, and Spanish speakers. And of course most of her books are distributed throughout the United Kingdom. When she reads them, she is surprised to see what has been changed. In *Hope Was Here,* the foods and the measurements were changed, while in *Rules of the Road,* the brand names for shoes were all different. *Backwater* is soon to come out in Indonesia. It might have been chosen because it is a cross-generational story and Indonesians traditionally honor older members of their extended families.

With the Italian version of *Hope Was Here,* even the title had been changed to *Letters to My Father* and the cover photo showed a peek of Hope's thong underwear. Bauer says that seeing her books in translation is sort of like seeing a friend who has undergone plastic surgery and come back with a new face. It takes a while to get accustomed. "I have my stories frozen in time," Bauer says. "A few times I've had to change the name of a character and it's hard for me to get used to the new identity." This happened with *Squashed.* Ellie's name in the first few drafts was Carolyn. When one of Bauer's friends convinced her that *Ellie* was a more "with-it" name, it took her about a year to stop calling her Carolyn.

Occasionally a translator will contact Bauer for information. This happened with the German translator of *Thwonk,* who sent an e-mail to ask whether the SAT tests that A. J. worried about were urine or blood tests. After Bauer straightened that out, the translator sent another note to ask what Twinkies were. Bauer consulted her brother-in-law who had lived in Germany for many years. Even he was puzzled as to how to explain Twinkies because in Germany there are bakeries on practically

The German version of *Thwonk*.

every corner so people always have fresh baked goods. He told her to describe them as "pre-packaged" and to say they were sort of like cheap éclairs. Bauer didn't want to use the word *cheap,* and so she said *tacky.* Back came another e-mail asking what *tacky* meant.

Bauer is careful with the details she uses in her books. For example with *Rules of the Road* she used MapQuest to figure out the route that Mrs. Gladstone and Jenna would take from Chicago to Dallas and even for Jenna's driving in Chicago she checked maps rather than relying on her own memories of growing up in Chicago. She wonders how such details are being changed to make the books more easily understandable to international audiences.

Some writers go around with little notebooks in their pockets or purses so that they can jot down ideas and clever lines that they happen to hear. Bauer does not do this, but she watches for such moments and tucks them away in her mind while waiting for someplace they might fit. For example, years ago when her sister moved to New Zealand and was getting used to all the changes of living in a different country, she called Bauer, laughing, and said she knew the worst was over because she had started flossing again. That is the kind of line that Bauer treasures, but since it's mostly adults who floss their teeth, she may never find a place to use it. Also, it probably won't translate very well, but she can't worry about translation problems since she figures "they get smoothed over somehow.... I just have to assume that the more intimate and the more honest I am, the more universal it will be."

Before going to Croatia to talk with readers, in 2002 Bauer was invited to spend a week at the American School in Shanghai, China, where, she was told, the students had read her books in English. She discovered that the student body was diverse—some were American, but many were from other Asian countries as well as Europe. What they all had in common was that they knew what it was like to move from place to place and so in the seminars and discussions they started by talking about Hope and Aunt Addie moving to Mulhoney, Wisconsin, and then worked their way around to talking about their own moves to Shanghai.

Luckily, Bauer's husband, Evan, had come with her and had brought his computer and his PowerPoint projector. As she worked with small groups to create stories, Evan would type their words into his computer and project them onto the ceiling. The stories the groups created were not about any one student's actual experiences; instead they were fictional composites. Bauer said that they used *Hope*'s story as a clothes hanger or even a coat rack, which they dressed up by putting on their own hats and their own jackets until it was layered enough to fit their individual feelings.

Some of the time while Bauer was working and eating lunch with the students and their teachers, her husband would go exploring and sampling the street foods; then he would take Joan back to enjoy his favorites. One of these was the soup dumplings, which although they look like a plain dumpling in the middle of a bowl of soup have a pleasant surprise. When you bite into them, you find a delicious mixture of pork and spices that you have to slurp up quickly lest it disappears into the soup or down your chin. The sound was part of the pleasure. Another memory

The Chinese cover of *Hope Was Here* shows a cross between an American restaurant and a Chinese tea shop.

that sticks in her mind is the beauty of the Shanghai museum and the items in it. It made her feel like she was in a new and different wing of the New York Metropolitan Museum.

She seems to have such good feelings related to her foreign visits that I asked her if she might write a book set in a foreign country. She said probably not because she would not know enough about a foreign culture to be able to work humor into the story, but she would like to create more characters from other countries like Yuri, the busboy turned waiter in *Hope Was Here,* and Lazar, the tango master from dance class in *Stand Tall.*

While her stories are basically serious, readers nevertheless find themselves smiling or even giggling. She says that she always starts with the serious parts of the stories and then only after she gets to know her characters really well can she imagine their flip conversations or the funny little mishaps that make people smile. Such incidents are so tied into a culture, that she doubts she could manage either a historical novel or a novel set in another country because she would not be able to predict where corners need rounding off or where she might lift up a rock to find the humor underneath. This is important to her because one of her goals for her future writing is to go deeper into humor, using it to make people take a fresh look at their circumstances.

She never makes fun of the really sad things in a story, such as G. T.'s cancer in *Hope Was Here* or the death of Ellie's mother in *Squashed,* but she builds a garden around the tragedy and plants little seeds that might bloom into humor for some, even if not for all, of her readers. One of Bauer's favorite memories is of a visit not to a foreign country but to a group of blind and handicapped high school students. When she does presentations, she prefers not to be stuck behind a podium or a desk and so she often walks out among the audience and gets close to people asking for their input. In this group a boy named Rodney who was severely crippled indicated that he wanted the microphone so he could say something. It took him a while to use his braced arms to push himself up from his chair and then to get a firm grasp on the mike. When at last he was in a position to speak, he said, "You might not have noticed but I'm handicapped." Then he gave his message: "Every day I need to laugh."

Bauer thinks often of Rodney and of the importance of his message. She wrote her first book, *Squashed,* when she was suffering both physically and emotionally. Just days after she signed her first contract to write a screenplay, she was in an automobile accident that was so serious it was as if Jean lost the best of her mother for two years. Bauer suffered spinal and nerve damage and knew that at least for the present she had to give up her dream of becoming a screenwriter because in that field there are tremendous time pressures and they are determined by a team of people, not an individual. When the neurosurgeon who operated on her told her that her particular kind of injury was very hard on creative people, she did not know whether to be grateful for his understanding or resentful in case he was predicting that she might never recover.

During her recovery she had to learn to focus by listening to tapes. "At first it doesn't seem like you're making progress," she says, "but eventually you see that you've really covered a lot of ground." She had to remember this and start all over after the September 11 disaster in New York City. The troubles that Tree and his family have in her 2002 *Stand Tall* grew out of her emotional response and gradual recovery from that event. She told the audience in Provo that she summed up her philosophy in just a couple of lines in *Stand Tall* that she worries are too easy to miss. When all the people who have been evicted from their homes by the flood are gathered in the school gymnasium, the mayor stands up and after welcoming and commiserating with the refugees, she says:

> It's going to be a long night, folks. Whatever you've learned about getting through hard times, I hope you'll share it with the people around you. (10)

Bauer has always been interested in traveling, even the kind of driving through nearby states that Jenna fantasizes about in *Rules of the Road* and then gets to experience when Mrs. Gladstone hires her to be her driver and assistant on the trip to Dallas. Bauer met her husband, Evan, in the lobby of a hotel in Puerto Rico when she went on vacation from her job selling advertisements. For their twentieth-fifth wedding anniversary, the two of them decided to go on a whale watch to Nova Scotia because Joan had always dreamed of seeing a whale beyond Sea World. On the first day, all they got to see was one dead seal. They drove up the coast for two hours—where there was rumored to be a man who always knew where the whales were. They hired him to take his sailboat out. The wind was so bad that some of the time the boat was more horizontal than vertical. They were strapped into their chairs, but still it was scary, and Joan remembers saying to Evan, "This is *soooo* not what I anticipated."

They finally had to give up and go back to connect with their original group and confess their failure. As their sorrow over being so unsuccessful gradually faded away, Bauer changed her thinking. She turned the experience into a metaphor. Now every time she starts a new book, she thinks of herself as embarking on a whale hunt. She's looking for something mysterious and huge, which she might not find. But even when the journey turns out to be frustrating, the experience will have enriched her life, as have many of her visits not only to foreign countries but to places in the United States, for example, when in the fall of 2002 she "brought Hope to Saginaw, Michigan."

Several newspaper clippings from *The Saginaw News* are reprinted on Bauer's Web site, http://www.joanbauer.com (consulted February 8, 2007), telling about Bauer visiting this central Michigan town on September 24, when she came at the climax of a months-long community reading of *Hope Was Here.* In the year and a half before Bauer's visit, traffic accidents had claimed the lives of seven students or recent graduates of the local Heritage High School. As a focus for the community's grieving, four women community school organizers for Saginaw Township schools came up with the idea of using *Hope Was Here* for a community read because while it is not "a heavy duty self-help book," it is a "good story with well-drawn characters learning to cope with life." These women delivered a few copies to key people in town, who as soon as they read the book climbed aboard and started promoting the idea. A pastor wrote an eight-page study guide for two adult groups at his church and another one for young readers. He said he wanted to help people make their discussions "life reviews" rather than "book reviews." He liked the way the book "allows people to come together on common ground." The guides were distributed far beyond his church and as of February 8, 2007, were still available on Bauer's website.

The owner of a bookstore supplied the group with paperback copies at cost (around $3.59), the Valley Lutheran High School provided each incoming freshman with a copy, and the director of the READ Association delivered copies to the Juvenile Detention Center. A high school junior who worked on the waitstaff at a retirement home read the book to eight sight-impaired residents while forty-eight others between the ages of seventy and ninety-nine read it on their own. The experience was so successful that the residents started a regular book club. The local beauty parlor kept copies on hand, and about half of the employees at a financial planning firm whose employees were between the ages of twenty-seven and fifty-two shared a copy in the lunchroom by using different colored stickies to mark their places.

In September, Bauer and her husband, Evan, and their daughter, Jean, traveled to Saginaw to talk with students at the high school as well as at the White Pine Middle School. The newspaper quoted Bauer as telling the high school students as she moved through their new, circular gymnasium:

> There is something about pain and loss that links you with other people. It hurts. I know it really hurts, but here we are. I don't know why bad things happen, but I know it takes courage to have hope beyond it. Hope is a miracle, a remarkable gift we

have. Hope, and with it, laughter. It always takes us a little into the future, and you are living that. What has happened to you is defining, significant, and profoundly important, and the sensitivity wrought because of it will carry you through all of your lives.

After the school presentations, Bauer signed autographs and visited at a public reception with people of all ages. Some who came from the retirement center willingly sat back and gave cuts in line to young readers who were stopping for autographs between school and soccer practice. After Bauer went home, the local restaurant still offered on its menu the "Keep Hoping" sandwich made from the recipe in the book; the local cable access Channel 98 inaugurated a new television show "Java with Jan" set in The Hope Café, and seven months after the idea first came up, *The Saginaw News* gave the event organizers its Critic's Choice Award for the "single most significant arts/cultural event of the year."

A couple of years later, three Florida towns (New Smyrna Beach, Edgewater, and Oak Hill) had Community-Read events modeled after the success of the Saginaw event. Bauer flew in for a May 6, 2004, celebration. One of the most exciting parts was being met at the airport by middle school students waving signs and carrying stuffed pelicans in honor of Hope's pelican named Edgar. They had a limousine and a police escort to the Smyrna Beach Middle School. Going through the red lights was something that Bauer assured the students they would never have been able to do in Brooklyn. At a dinner that night, two musicians performed a song about hope and a young woman in a wheelchair recited a poem she had written. Bauer was thrilled to see these community extensions of her book.

When Bauer begins a new book, she says that pretty soon she notices that the characters begin to sound like someone from the last book and so she has to tell them firmly to go back to their rooms: "This isn't your book; you've had your turn!" When she was telling me about the book she is working on right now, I asked her if the protagonist, who is a high school journalist, is sort of like Ivy Breedlove in *Backwater*. She looked a little startled and then said, "Definitely not." But then after thinking a while she added that yes, her protagonist shares some characteristics with Ivy. She is equally honest and determined to do a good job. And she's a good listener. Besides, Ivy was based on Bauer's daughter, Jean, who is now a Ph. D. student in American history at the University of Virginia in Charlottesville, and so it would be strange if there were not a few carry-overs from the young person that Bauer knows best.

Bauer's new protagonist is Hildy Biddle—a name that Bauer likes so much she says she won't let anyone change it. The theme of the book is fear mongering and how fear changes people and makes them do things they probably wouldn't do under ordinary circumstances. While the book is set in the United States, a foreign country does play a part because Hildy has a friend and mentor, an older woman who immigrated into the United States from Poland. She was a journalist in Poland during its take-over by the Soviet Union, and when clamps were put on the free press it was mostly women, who like Hildy's friend "flew under the radar" and ran the underground press. I'm eager to meet Bauer's two new protagonists and to see how they tell a story for our time.

Just as we were putting the finishing touches on this book, I received another e-mail from Bauer saying that the State Department will be sending her on a two-week visit to Kazakhstan in May–June 2007. She will be leading writing seminars and working with children in rural areas. The happiness and pride that I felt at hearing this news reminded me of the incident in *Hope Was Here,* when Hope takes pride in what G. T. says in his inaugural speech about politics not being about manipulating people for your own benefit but about "serving up your best." Hope identifies with G. T. because they are both in food service and she likes it that a short-order cook is the one "getting it right."

As someone working with young people and books, I identify with Joan Bauer, which is why I feel Hope's same kind of pride when I see Bauer "getting it right" by serving up honest stories to young and old living in places as different as Shanghai, China; Smyrna Beach, Florida; Zadar, Croatia; and rural and urban Kazakhstan. When I first taught children's literature at Eastern Michigan University, the more experienced teachers used to say that people will never feel like strangers in a country whose folktales they know. That was nearly forty years ago. Today, in what is variously called a *global village,* a *flat earth,* or in more pessimistic tones, *a world at risk,* I am glad that changing technologies and conditions are enabling teenagers and adults around the world to not only read their books, but also to communicate in person, with some of America's best authors, including Joan Bauer.

BIBLIOGRAPHY OF SOURCES

NOVELS BY JOAN BAUER

(Note: Various paperback editions are also available.)
Backwater. New York: G. P. Putnam's, 1999.
Best Foot Forward. New York: G. P. Putnam's, 2005.
Hope Was Here. New York: G. P. Putnam's, 2000.
Rules of the Road. New York: G. P. Putnam's, 1998.
Squashed. New York: Delacorte, 1992.
Stand Tall. New York: G. P. Putnam's, 2002.
Sticks. New York: Delacorte, 1996.
Thwonk. New York: Delacorte, 1995.

SHORT STORIES BY JOAN BAUER

"Blocked." In *Dreams and Visions,* edited by M. Jerry Weiss and Helen S. Weiss, 17–29. New York: Tom Doherty Associates, 2006.
"Children of War." In *911: The Book of Help,* edited by Michael Cart with Marc Aronson and Marianne Carus, 39–47. Chicago: Cricket Books, 2002.
"Clean Sweep." In *Shelf Life: Stories by the Book,* edited by Gary Paulsen, 151–64. New York: Simon & Schuster, 2003.
"Extra Virgin." In *Love & Sex: Ten Stories of Truth,* edited by Michael Cart, 1–17. New York: Simon & Schuster, 2001.
"Hardware." In *Necessary Noise: Stories about Our Families as They Really Are,* edited by Michael Cart, 3–21. New York: HarperCollins, 2003.
"A Letter from the Fringe." In *On the Fringe,* edited by Donald R. Gallo, 181–95. New York: Dial Books, 2001.
"Pancakes." In *Trapped: Cages of Mind and Body,* edited by Lois Duncan, 132–47. New York: Simon & Schuster, 1998.
"Smoke." In *Rush Hour: Sin,* edited by Michael Cart, 31–52. New York: Delacorte, 2004.

"Thin." In *What Are You Afraid Of? Stories about Phobias,* edited by Donald R. Gallo, 45–61. Cambridge, Mass.: Candlewick Press, 2006.

"The Truth about Sharks." In *From One Experience to Another: Award-Winning Authors Sharing Real-Life Experiences through Fiction,* edited by M. Jerry Weiss and Helen S. Weiss, 31–47. New York: Tom Doherty Associates, 1997.

ARTICLES BY JOAN BAUER

"Bearers of Light: The Caring Community of Young Adult Literature." *The ALAN Review* 33, no. 2 (2006): 29–33.

"Dear Bethany." In *Dear Author: Letters of Hope,* edited by Joan Kaywell, 22–31. New York: Philomel, 2007.

"Humor: Seriously." *The ALAN Review* 23, no. 2 (1996): 2–3.

"On Hooking Students with Humor." In *Literature for Today's Young Adults,* 6th ed., edited by Alleen Pace Nilsen and Kenneth L. Donelson, 199. New York: Addison Wesley Longman, 2001.

"On the Job." *Riverbank Review* (Winter 2002–2003): 29–31.

"Sticks: Between the Lines." *Book Links,* (July 1997): 9–12.

"Why I Read." In *Shelf Life: Stories by the Book,* edited by Gary Paulsen. New York: Simon & Schuster, 2003. Reprinted at http://www.joanbauer.com.

"Words." *Voices from the Middle* 7, no. 4 (2000): 45–46.

ARTICLES, BOOKS, AND WEB SITES ABOUT JOAN BAUER

The Alliance for the Study and Teaching of Adolescent Literature at Rhode Island. Interview with Joan Bauer. Reprinted at http://www.ric.edu/astal/authors/joanbauer.html.

Blasingame, James. Review of *Best Foot Forward* and "Interview with Joan Bauer." *Journal of Adolescent & Adult Literacy* 49, no. 3 (2005): 243–45.

Brown, Jean E. "Joan Bauer." In *Writers for Young Adults,* vol. 1, edited by Ted Hipple, 73–80.

Donelson, Kenneth L., and Alleen Pace Nilsen. "Literal Journeys, Figurative Quests." In *Literature for Today's Young Adults,* 7th ed., 137. New York: Pearson/Allyn and Bacon, 2005.

Hogan, Walter. *Humor in Young Adult Literature: A Time to Laugh.* Lanham, Md.: Scarecrow Press, 2005.

Joan Bauer Official Web site: http://www.joanbauer.com. Contains links to related Web sites, including The Children's Books UK Web site, The Authors 4 Teens Web site, American Library Association 2001 Newbery

Award Winners, the 2001 Christopher Award Winners, and a readers' companion guide to her first six novels prepared by Dr. Teri Lesesne and published by Penguin Putnam.

Koehler-Pentacoff, Elizabeth. "Interview with Joan Bauer." In *The ABC's of Writing for Children*. Sanger, Calif.: Quill Driver Books, 2003. Reprinted at http://www.joanbauer.com/ABC_Interview.html.

Nilsen, Alleen Pace, and Don L. F. Nilsen. "Humor That Works in YA Fiction." *Arizona English Bulletin* 48, no. 1 (2006): 11–16.

Taylor, Charles. "Children's Literature: You're a Big Boy Now." Review of *Stand Tall*. *The New York Times Review*, November 17, 2002. Reprinted at http://www.joanbauer.com/st-nyt-review.html.

Index

About the Author

ALLEEN PACE NILSEN is Professor of English and Director of English Education at Arizona State University in Tempe. She is founding editor of the *ALAN Review* (Assembly on Literature for Adolescents of NCTE) and co-author of the leading textbook on young adult literature, *Literature for Today's Young Adults*, 7th ed. She has written numerous articles about books for teenaged readers for such publications as *English Journal*, *School Library Journal*, and the *Journal of Adult and Adolescent Literature* (JAAL) of the International Reading Society.

DATE DUE

WITHDRAWN	
WITHDRAWN	
WITHDRAWN	

Karl Marx
Early Writings

KARL MARX

EARLY WRITINGS

TRANSLATED AND EDITED BY
T. B. BOTTOMORE

FOREWORD BY ERICH FROMM

McGRAW-HILL BOOK COMPANY
NEW YORK   TORONTO   LONDON

CONTENTS

FOREWORD

Few authors have had the fate of being misunderstood and distorted as Marx has been. Few authors, also, have been so often quoted and so little read. Yet we can see in the last few years a definite turn in this situation. After Marx had been looked upon as a devil by the antisocialist side, and as an idol —quoted and worshiped, but not understood—by the Soviet side, a new wave of interest and research in Marxist theory is sweeping Europe and America. Marx has truly been rediscovered, and one does not go too far in saying that we are witnessing the beginning of a renaissance of Marxist thought.

The effect of this renaissance is, first of all, to cease making a dead saint of Marx and to restore him to the position of a living thinker. Secondly, it tends to cease cutting Marx into two parts: the "young Marx," still an idealist and concerned with such concepts as the essence of man, and the "mature Marx," mainly or exclusively interested in economics, according to whom socialism (or communism) is defined as a system in which the means of production are in the hands of the state or the working class. It is true that Marx changed his terminology; thus, for instance, he stopped using the term "the essence of man"; but he did not fundamentally change the substance of his thought about man's nature. This holds specifically true for the concept of alienation, which is the key concept in the *Economic and Philosophical Manuscripts,* and which Marx retained until the end of his life. Nothing could demonstrate this better than comparing a sentence written by the young Marx with a paragraph from his last work, the third volume of *Capital.* In the *German Ideology,* Marx wrote: "Man's own deed becomes an alien power opposed to him, which enslaves him instead of being controlled by him." And "This crystallization of social activity, this consolidation of what we ourselves produce into an objective power above us, growing out of our control, thwarting our expectations, bringing to naught our calculations, is one of the chief factors in historical development up till now." At the end of *Capital*, volume III, Marx wrote:

The realm of freedom only begins, in fact, where that labour which is determined by need and external purposes, ceases; it is therefore, by its very nature, outside the sphere of material production proper. Just as the savage must wrestle with Nature in order to satisfy his wants, to maintain and reproduce his life, so also must civilized man, and he must do it in all forms of society and under any possible mode of production. With his development the realm of natural necessity expands, because his wants increase, but at the same time the forces of production, by which these wants are justified, also increase. Freedom in this field cannot consist of anything else but the fact that socialized mankind, the associated producers, regulate their interchange with Nature rationally, bring it under their common control, instead of being ruled by it as by some blind power, and accomplish their task with the least expenditure of energy and under such conditions as are proper and worthy for human beings. Nevertheless, this always remains a realm of necessity. Beyond it begins that development of human potentiality for its own sake, the true realm of freedom, which however, can only flourish upon that realm of necessity as its basis. The shortening of the working day is its fundamental prerequisite.

This paragraph represents the quintessence of Marx's thought: man can never transcend the realm of necessity, which is that of material production. But he can achieve an optimum of freedom even in this realm of necessity by the fact that "the associated producers regulate their interchange with Nature rationally, bring it under their common control, instead of being ruled by it as by some blind power. . . ." Here we find the same concept of alienation and de-alienation as in the early writings. In the following sentence Marx says that such a social order is the basis for the "development of human potentiality for its own sake, the true realm of freedom." Marx, at the end of his life, could not have expressed more clearly the goals and values which inspired him from the days of his youth, and thus confirmed the unity of his work against all later attempts at dividing and distorting it.

Marx was a humanist, for whom man's freedom, dignity, and activity were the basic premises of the "good society." As a humanist he believed in the unity of all men, and in man's capacity to find a new harmony with man and with nature. But Marx, while sharing the aims of Spinoza and Goethe, added a new dimension to humanism. He recognized that education alone will not transform man. He saw that man is to a large extent determined by his practice of life, and that if man wants to change he has to change the very circumstances which imprison him. In capitalism, so Marx thought, man is made to be a person who *has* much, who *uses* much, but who *is* little. Hence, in order to create the basis for the free development of man's potentialities, mankind must do away with a social-economic structure which by its very nature feeds man's greed and possessiveness. Socialization and planning are *means* to this end, but not an end in themselves. Socialism, if it is limited to the sphere of economics, is not humanism; it is not socialism.

These are the premises of those who participate in the renaissance of Marxism today. The representatives of this humanist socialism can be found in Great Britain, the United States, France, West Germany, Italy, Africa, India, Australia, Japan, and particularly the small socialist states: Yugoslavia, Poland, Czechoslovakia, and Hungary. It is an amazing fact that today there is more active Marx scholarship and study going on in the world than perhaps at any time since Marx's death.[1]

While we stress the differences between Marxist and non-

[1] Evidence of this renaissance is to be found in a symposium on socialist humanism, edited by Erich Fromm, to be published by Doubleday & Company, Inc.

Marxist humanists, we must realize that Marx's humanism is today part of a renaissance of humanism which is to be found among Catholics and Protestants as well as among nonreligious scientists and philosophers. This new humanism has arisen as a reaction to the double threat which menaces mankind today: the threat of nuclear war and the destruction of all life, or "at best" of civilization as we know it, and the threat of complete alienation in which man, in producing and serving things, transforms himself into a thing. Contemporary humanism, like Renaissance humanism, is an expression of protest against the danger of dehumanization. But it is more than a protest; it is the expression of faith in man's having the alternative to choose a full life instead of destruction, and in his capacity to make the right choice if only he is aware of the underlying forces inside himself and within society.

The works of Marx collected in this volume are among the most important of his humanist writings. Without understanding them one can hardly understand Marx's later writings, just as the earlier ones can hardly be understood without a knowledge of the later works.

A few comments on the three works published here may assist the reader in understanding them. The paper "On the Jewish Question" is one of the most brilliant of Marx's treatises, analysing the nature of bourgeois society and discussing the difference between political emancipation and human emancipation. It is one of the symptoms showing to what degree the falsification of Marx can go that some years ago a reputable publishing house in the United States published this work (in a bad and distorted translation) under the title "A World without Jews" (a title never thought of by Marx) and advertised the book with statements about Marx's being an anti-Semite and responsible for Hitler's and Stalin's anti-Semitism. Anyone familiar with Marx's views and personal life will realize the absurdity of this construction. He knows furthermore that Marx was a true internationalist who had no preference for any nation, and who was critical of all, never respecting the taboos of national feeling. While in this paper he said some harsh (and in my opinion not always correct) words about what he thought was the Jewish religion, he said equally harsh words about the British shopkeepers, the German philosophers, and the Russians. To designate Marx as an anti-Semite is nothing but cold-war propaganda; it is most fortunate that this propaganda will be counteracted by the excellent and honest translation offered in this collection.

In "The Critique of Hegel's Philosophy of Right" another widespread error is corrected: the error that Marx was against the "spiritual" and for the "material"; that his criticism of religion was motivated by this "materialism." The opposite is true. Marx saw in religion "the illusory happiness" of men, and in the abolition of religion a "demand for their real happiness." "The call to abandon their illusions," he wrote, "is a call to *abandon a condition which requires illusions.*" Marx's criticism of religion was not based on the idea that man should enjoy material satisfactions instead of spiritual ones. He maintained that religion failed in its function and gave man illusions, rather than enabling him "to pluck the living flower." "The criticism of religion disillusions man, so that he will think, act, and fashion his reality as a man who has lost his illusions and regained his reason; so that he will revolve about himself as his own true sun. Religion is only the illusory sun about which man revolves so long as he does not revolve about himself."

Marx's aim is the *dis*-illusioned, independent man, not the brainwashed object of manipulation. The man "who revolves about himself" is not a narcissistic or an egoistic man, but a free man who owes his existence to himself. This man is not only free *from* chains, but free *to be* himself, to be authentically related to his fellow man and to nature. Marx's free man is an *active* and *productive* man. Nowhere has Marx expressed this more beautifully than in his discussion of money in the third of the *Economic and Philosophical Manuscripts:*

"Let us assume *man* to be *man*, and his relation to the world to be a human one. Then love only can be exchanged for love, trust for trust, etc. If you wish to enjoy art you must be an artistically cultivated person; if you wish to influence other people you must be a person who really has a stimulating and encouraging effect upon others. Every one of your relations to man and to nature must be a *specific expression*, corresponding to the object of your will, of your *real individual* life. If you love without evoking love in return, i.e. if you are not able, by the *manifestation* of yourself as a loving person, to make yourself a *beloved person*, then your love is impotent and a misfortune."

Erich Fromm
May 1964

INTRODUCTION

In an earlier book [1] Dr. Rubel and I presented a selection of texts which was intended to show the nature of Marx's sociological thought and its relevance to modern sociology. Many of the texts, and especially those of the period 1843-5, were little known in the English-speaking countries.[2] Since then, Marx's early writings have been much discussed, but they are still not easily accessible in satisfactory English translations. In the present volume, therefore, I have provided translations of three of the most important of these early works: the two essays, " On the Jewish Question " and " Contribution to the Critique of Hegel's Philosophy of Right. Introduction," which were first published in the *Deutsch-Französische Jahrbücher* (1844); and the " Economic and Philosophical Manuscripts " (1844).[3]

The wider knowledge of Marx's early writings has played an important part, alongside the social and political changes in both Western and Eastern societies, in bringing about a reconsideration of his social theories. These writings have been interpreted in a number of different ways. In the first place, they have been regarded as expounding a moral doctrine which remained the basis of all Marx's intellectual and political activity even though it was less explicitly stated in his later writings.[4] This doctrine, which Marx calls

---

[1] T. B. BOTTOMORE and MAXIMILIEN RUBEL, *Karl Marx: Selected Writings in Sociology and Social Philosophy*, London, 1956, 2nd impression, 1961.

[2] Marx's early writings were first comprehensively discussed, in English, in H. P. ADAMS, *Karl Marx in his Earlier Writings*, London, 1940. This interesting book does not, however, contain many direct translations from the texts.

[3] Further notes on the texts and translations are given later in this Introduction. A part of my translation of the " Economic and Philosophical Manuscripts " has been published in ERICH FROMM, *Marx's Concept of Man*, New York, 1961.

[4] *See* the illuminating discussion in ERICH FROMM, op. cit. The " humanism " of the young Marx has provided much support for the intellectual opposition to bureaucratic and police rule in the Communist countries; for example

" humanism," formulates the ideal of a community of men who are able to develop freely, and in harmony with each other, all their personal qualities. Marx takes for granted the creed of the Enlightenment—the innate goodness of man, human perfectibility, the power of human reason [1]—but he expresses it in a new form which is influenced by the development of industrial capitalism and of the new science of political economy. Marx's ideal is the *productive* man, contrasted with the *acquisitive* man.[2] For this conception Marx is also indebted to Hegel, as he himself acknowledges: " The outstanding achievement of Hegel's *Phenomenology* . . . is, first, that Hegel grasps the nature of *labour*, and conceives of objective man . . . as the result of his *own labour*." [3] Moreover, Marx goes on to describe the actual condition of man in industrial society by the Hegelian term " alienation." Man is alienated in two senses: first, the vast majority of men (and perhaps all men) have lost control of the products of their own activity, which now confront them as inhuman ruling powers; secondly, in the process of work itself most men are not productive in the sense of exercising freely their natural powers, but are constrained to perform uninteresting and degrading tasks.[4] It should be clear, however, from a reading of these early texts that Marx is engaged in giving the concept of alienation a more empirical reference, by depicting a real situation of the worker in industrial society.[5]

---

in the writings of the East German philosopher Wolfgang Harich and of the Polish philosopher Leszek Kolakowski. *See* the latter's essays published in German under the title *Der Mensch ohne Alternative*, Munich, 1960.

[1] In *The Holy Family* Marx observes: " When one studies the materialist theories of the original goodness of man, the equality of intellectual endowment among men, the omnipotence of education, experience and habit, the influence of external circumstances upon man, the great importance of industry, the value of pleasure, etc. it requires no extraordinary insight to discover what necessarily connects them with communism and socialism."

[2] " Economic and Philosophical Manuscripts," pp. 127–9 below.

[3] Ibid., p. 202 below.

[4] Ibid., pp. 124–5 below.

[5] The close connexion between the ideas of Hegel and Marx concerning the self-creation of man through his own activity (cultural as well as material pro-

The empirical value of his observations upon productive work as an element in the mental health and happiness of the individual should be more apparent to us than it was to his contemporaries, although modern sociologists and psychologists have given surprisingly little attention to the subject.[1] In his later writings Marx describes the same situation of the industrial worker, and takes his stand upon the same moral doctrine, without using the term " alienation," which he had doubtless come to regard as unnecessarily metaphysical. It may also be that his confidence in the possibility of making industrial work inherently interesting and satisfying had diminished. In the third volume of *Capital* he writes: " The realm of freedom only begins, in fact, where that labour which is determined by need and external purposes, ceases; . . . [economic production] always remains a realm of necessity. Beyond it begins that development of human potentiality for its own sake, the true realm of freedom . . . " But he also suggests, in the same passage, that within the realm of production itself a certain degree of freedom might be established which would consist in the fact that " socialized

---

duction) and his self-estrangement through the reification of the products of his activity, only became fully apparent with the publication of Hegel's own early manuscripts, especially the *Jenenser Realphilosophie* I, Leipzig, 1932 and II, Leipzig, 1931, and of Marx's " Economic and Philosophical Manuscripts," Berlin, 1932. (For a brief account of Hegel's ideas in the *Realphilosophie, see* H. MARCUSE, *Reason and Revolution*, Part I, Chapter III.) But these manuscripts also help us to see the profound divergence between the two thinkers. Hegel begins, in his early writings, with the accounts of labour in modern capitalist society provided by the early economists and sociological historians (especially Adam Smith and Adam Ferguson) and then proceeds to develop, in his later philosophical system, the notion of labour as the abstract activity of a world spirit. Marx, on the contrary, begins with Hegel's mature philosophy and returns to the empirical accounts of industrial labour given by the economists. It should be added that Marx, as I have noted, incorporated in his conception of man ethical ideas derived from the eighteenth-century French materialists, and from other sources, which were quite foreign to Hegel's thought.

[1] There is an excellent brief discussion in I. MEYERSON, " Le travail, fonction psychologique," *Le travail, les métiers, l'emploi*, Paris, 1955. Georges Friedmann has examined the problem on several occasions, more particularly in the last two chapters of *The Anatomy of Work*, London, 1961; and Erich Fromm has also discussed it in the final chapter of *The Sane Society*, London, 1956.

mankind, the associated producers, regulate their interchange with nature rationally, bring it under their common control instead of being ruled by it as by some blind power, and accomplish their task with the least expenditure of energy and under such conditions as are proper and worthy for human beings "; and at another point, in the first volume of *Capital*, he observes that " the detail worker of today, the limited individual, the mere bearer of a particular social function, will be replaced by the fully developed individual, for whom the different social functions he performs are but so many alternative modes of activity." Whether he emphasizes more strongly the sphere of work, or that of leisure, Marx presents the same ideal conception of man as the fully developed individual who expresses his nature freely in his activity.

Marx's reflections upon alienation began, it is clear, in a more philosophical context. This is most evident in his discussion of religion as a form of alienation, in his use of the term " species-being " which he took from Feuerbach,[1] and in his formulation of the speculative question—which he does not answer—" How does it happen, we may ask, that *man alienates his labour?* How is this alienation founded in the nature of human development? "[2] The study of these early texts has also led, therefore, to a reconsideration of Marx's relation to Hegel. Marcuse[3] and Lukács[4] are among those who regard Marx as having always remained, in some sense, a Hegelian. They insist upon the historical character of Marx's thought, while denying that it constitutes a systematic philosophy of history. For both, it is a system of thought which arises out of, and is mainly concerned with, the social conditions of modern capitalism. Lukács says that " historical materialism, in its classical form, . . . is the *self-consciousness*

---

[1] *See* below, p. 13, note 2.
[2] " Economic and Philosophical Manuscripts," p. 133 below.
[3] H. MARCUSE, *Reason and Revolution*, New York, 1941.
[4] G. LUKÁCS, *Geschichte und Klassenbewusstsein*, Berlin, 1923. In this book Lukács anticipated in some respects a view of Marx's relation to Hegel which could later find support from the " Economic and Philosophical Manuscripts."

of capitalist society. . . . [It is] primarily a theory of bourgeois society and its economic structure." [1] Similarly, Marcuse conceives Marx's thought as a critical theory of capitalism, intimately connected with the situation and activity of the proletariat; " the correct theory is the consciousness of a practice which aims at changing the world." [2] Marx's theory has, therefore, the relativistic character of all historical thought, as Lukács is disposed to admit,[3] and as Marcuse attempts only in a cursory fashion to deny.[4] Marcuse emphasizes the historical and philosophical character of the theory, in contrast with positivistic sociology: " Social study was to be a science seeking social laws, the validity of which was to be analogous to that of physical laws. Social practice, especially the matter of changing the social system, was herewith throttled by the inexorable. Society was viewed as governed by rational laws that moved with a natural necessity. This position directly contradicted the view held by the dialectical social theory, that society is irrational precisely in that it is governed by natural laws. . . . The positivist repudiation of metaphysics was thus coupled with a repudiation of man's claim to alter and reorganize his social institutions in accordance with his rational will." [5]

A similar view—stressing the origins of Marx's thought in the social problems of capitalism—was advanced much earlier by Croce, who concluded that " historical materialism is not and cannot be a new philosophy of history or a new method; but it is properly this; a *mass of new data, of new experiences*, of which the historian becomes conscious. . . . The materialistic view of history arose out of the need to account for a definite social phenomenon [the French Revolution], not from an abstract inquiry into the factors of historical life."[6]

---

[1] Quoted from the French translation, *Histoire et conscience de classe*, Paris, 1960, pp. 263–4.

[2] MARCUSE, op. cit., p. 321.   [3] LUKÁCS, op. cit., p. 263.

[4] MARCUSE, op. cit., pp. 321–2.   [5] Ibid., pp. 343–4.

[6] BENEDETTO CROCE, *Historical Materialism and the Economics of Karl Marx*, London, 1913, p. 12 and pp. 16–17. The essay from which this quotation is taken was first published in 1896.

A more recent tendency in the discussion of Marx's early thought in relation to Hegel has been to emphasize the religious affinities of the concept of alienation. The attempt has been made, indeed, to portray Marx as essentially a religious thinker.[1] The argument is stated in the following way. Marx held strong moral views, but he was not a moral philosopher; his criticism of capitalist society and his moral vision of the future socialist society both resemble those of a religious thinker. Moreover, this religious conception of the world can be traced back, through Feuerbach, to Hegel—to the idea of man's self-realization as a divine being. This account of Marx's thought achieves two things: it depicts Marx once again as a thoroughgoing Hegelian, and by its emphasis upon one particular aspect of Hegel's thought it also portrays Marx as the creator of a religious myth in a secular form. It succeeds thereby in diminishing his stature as scientist, historian and political thinker.

Does this extreme view of the nature of Marx's thought find any support in his early writings? It is true that Marx reveals himself as a man of intense moral convictions, and as a fervent supporter of the socialist movement at a time when he had not worked out in detail his social theory. It is also true that he does not set forth a coherent moral philosophy. But these facts alone do not make him a religious thinker, nor dispose of the claim that he was above all a scientist. Marx expresses in a different language the moral principles of the Enlightenment, principles which he derived most immediately from Saint-Simon and Feuerbach, but which he later found confirmed by his reading of the economists, and especially of those, such as Schulz and Sismondi, who were early critics of capitalism. The formulations of his moral ideal have no undertones of religious feeling. Marx did not believe that men were, or would become, gods. In the " Economic and Philosophical Manuscripts," and still more in his later writings, he lays stress upon the *human* qualities and failings of

[1] R. C. TUCKER, *Philosophy and Myth in Karl Marx*, London, 1961.

men. On one occasion, at least, he declared expressly that the socialists do not regard the proletarians as gods, but simply as men who live under inhuman conditions and who are obliged to revolt against this inhumanity.[1] It is a reasonable conjecture that one ground for Marx's dissatisfaction with Feuerbach's philosophy was the excessive part which religious imagery and sentiment still played in it; and that his later distaste for Comte's positive philosophy was due in part to its culmination in a " religion of humanity," to its being, as he noted, " profoundly rooted in Catholic soil."

The cast of Marx's mind was fundamentally scientific. His whole life and work reveal not only a moral passion, but more strikingly a passion for empirical inquiry and factual knowledge. It is this scientific bent, and conversely his distaste for speculative philosophy,[2] which marks most clearly his divergence from Hegel's followers in Germany. In his early writings we see Marx proceeding from a critical examination of Hegelian philosophy to a direct study of the economic and political problems of modern society as they are represented in the works of the economists. He follows the course which he indicates in the " Critique of Hegel's Philosophy of Right "; " . . . the criticism of heaven is transformed into the criticism of earth, the criticism of religion into the criticism of law, and the criticism of theology into the criticism of politics." In the earliest of the texts translated here, " On the Jewish Question," Marx observes, in criticizing Bauer's presentation of the problem: " We do not turn secular questions into theological questions; we turn theological questions into secular ones. . . . The question of the relation between political emancipation and religion becomes for us a question of the relation between political emancipa-

---

[1] In *The Holy Family*, 1845.

[2] EDMUND WILSON, *To the Finland Station* (p. 192) quotes Marx's observation that " philosophy stands in the same relation to the study of the actual world as onanism to sexual love." Later in life Marx said to Paul Lafargue " I am not a Marxist "; a remark which I interpret as a protest against the tendency of the early Marxists (amplified by their successors) to transform his concepts and discoveries into a dogmatic philosophical system.

tion and human emancipation. We criticize the religious failings of the political state by criticizing the political state in its secular form, disregarding its religious failings." In the " Critique of Hegel's Philosophy of Right " Marx states more precisely, and in less philosophical language, the object which is to engage his attention: " the relation of industry, of the world of wealth in general, to the political world is a major problem of modern times." The " Economic and Philosophical Manuscripts," finally, show Marx grappling with contemporary economic problems. The completeness of his conversion to this field of study is shown not merely by his long analyses, in the Manuscripts, of wages, profit and rent, and of the conditions of the industrial workers, but also by his notebooks for the whole period 1844–53, which are filled with excerpts from, and commentaries upon, the works of the principal writers upon economic subjects in England, France and Germany.[1]

The reorientation of Marx's thought, after 1843, becomes much clearer if his early writings are seen, as they should be, as a stage in the development of his ideas, rather than as the expression of a distinctive doctrine which has to be brought in to correct our judgement of his later theories. In his early works Marx necessarily employs a philosophical form of expression, since he is engaged in criticizing a mode of thought which is itself philosophical; yet even here the most obvious feature is the transition from philosophical disputation about the nature of man, or of human social development as a whole, to the empirical study of modern economic and political problems. These works look forward to sociological studies of modern capitalism, not backwards to philosophical reflections upon human history. In *Capital*, Marx attempts to explain the origins and course of modern capitalism with the aid of what he considered a scientific theory of social evolution that is akin to the Darwinian theory of biological

---

[1] *See* MAXIMILIEN RUBEL, " Les cahiers de lecture de Karl Marx, 1840–1853," *International Review of Social History*, I (3) 1957. This article also contains some pertinent observations upon Marx's methods of scientific work.

evolution.[1] At the present day, when we are doubtful about
the scientific standing of any theory of evolution as a whole,
and especially about the value of the concept of social
evolution, we may find much to criticize in Marx's general
concepts. But it has still to be said in Marx's favour that
he made use of these concepts, in the manner of a scientist,
in a profound investigation of one type of society and of one
process of social change. Unlike Spencer, and some other
early sociologists, he did not propound far-fetched biological
analogies, nor attempt to depict the whole evolution of
human society on the basis of superficial historical data.

The presentation of Marx's thought by Marcuse and
Lukács raises a number of interesting problems which I can
only mention very briefly here.[2] Their views are based upon
two ideas. The first is that the natural world and the social
world are radically different objects, in such a sense that the
study of society calls for methods and concepts which are
quite different from those employed in the natural sciences.
The second is that the attempt to study society by the methods
of natural science has, in addition, undesirable practical consequences; for the description of society as it is, and the
subsumption of social phenomena under universal laws, encourage a conception of the social world as inalterable by
human will. As to the first of these ideas, it should be said
that it has been the source of a great variety of criticisms of
sociology as a " natural science of society," among which the
most substantial is still that which was expounded by Dilthey
in his *Einleitung in die Geisteswissenschaften* (1883). Marxism,
in the form Marcuse and Lukács preferred, is not, therefore, the most obvious alternative to a positivistic sociology.

---

[1] In the first volume of *Capital*, which he had wished to dedicate to Darwin,
Marx himself states the resemblance: " Darwin has aroused our interest in the
history of natural technology, i.e. in the formation of the organs of plants and
animals, as instruments of production for sustaining life. Does not the history
of the productive organs of man, of organs that are the material basis of all
social organization, deserve equal attention? "
[2] I shall discuss them in greater detail in a forthcoming volume of essays on
Marxism and sociology.

Moreover, as Lukács expounds Marx's method, it is difficult to see how it differs at all from that of Hegel, for the essential features which Lukács mentions [1]—the concepts of "historical process " and of " totality "—are due entirely to Hegel. As to the idea of the inalterability of the social world as depicted by a positive science, this could only be true (i) if sociology claimed to explain the whole social world, and (ii) if, in a psychological sense, the formulation of a social law did actually persuade men to continue acting as the law states that they do (or did) act.

At all events, there is little evidence in Marx's own writings (including the early writings) that he wished to make a radical distinction between the sciences of nature and of man, or that he regarded a positive science of man and society as being incompatible with the practical activity of changing society. On the contrary, like other nineteenth-century thinkers, but in an original manner, he saw a close connexion between humanism (socialism) and positivism (a science of society). As Arnold Toynbee later wrote: " It was the labour question . . . that revived the method of observation. Political Economy was transformed by the working classes." [2] The recent interest in Marx's moral doctrine arises, in great measure, from the deceptions of Marxist socialism. This is, however, a partial view if it neglects to observe that orthodox Marxism has equally abandoned Marx's science of society; and that the latter is Marx's essential contribution both to understanding society and to changing it.

*   *   *

Marx's essay " On the Jewish Question " was written during the autumn of 1843 and was published in the *Deutsch-Französische Jahrbücher* [3] early in 1844.[4]

[1] LUKÁCS, op. cit., pp. 17–45 " Qu'est-ce que le marxisme orthodoxe? "
[2] *The Industrial Revolution of the Eighteenth Century in England* (1908 ed.) p. 147.
[3] *Deutsch-Französische Jahrbücher*, edited by K. Marx and A. Ruge, Paris, 1844. Only one double issue of the journal was published, in February 1844.
[4] On pp. 182–214.

The essay entitled "Contribution to the Critique of
Hegel's Philosophy of Right. Introduction" was written
between the autumn of 1843 and January 1844, and was also
published in the *Deutsch-Französische Jahrbücher*.[1]

The title "Economic and Philosophical Manuscripts" has
been given to four manuscripts which Marx wrote in the
period from April to August 1844, and which are now in the
keeping of the International Institute of Social History,
Amsterdam. The manuscripts were first published in a full
and accurate version, prepared by D. Riazanov, by the Marx-
Engels Institute (now the Institute of Marxism-Leninism),
Moscow, in *Karl Marx, Friedrich Engels: Historisch-kritische
Gesamtausgabe*, Marx-Engels Verlag, Berlin, 1932; Abteilung
I, Band III. This edition will be referred to hereafter as the
MEGA. Each manuscript was separately paginated in
Roman numerals by Marx.

The first manuscript comprises nine double sheets (thirty-
six pages). Each page is divided by two vertical lines to form
three columns, which are headed respectively, "Wages of
Labour," "Profit of Capital," and "Rent of Land." These
constitute the first three sections of the published text. On
page XII of the manuscript, however, Marx began to write
on a different subject, ignoring the division of the pages into
three columns; this portion of the manuscript was given the
title "Alienated Labour" by the editors of the *MEGA*. The
manuscript breaks off on page XXVII.

The second manuscript comprises one double sheet (four
pages). The text begins in the middle of a sentence, and
this is evidently the concluding portion of a manuscript, the
rest of which has been lost.

The third manuscript comprises seventeen double sheets
(sixty-eight pages). Marx's pagination is faulty; page XXI
is followed by page XXIII, and page XXIV is followed by
page XXVI. The last twenty-three pages are blank. The
manuscript begins with two short sections which refer to

[1] On pp. 71–85.

a lost manuscript, and which the editors of the *MEGA* entitled " Private Property and Labour " and " Private Property and Communism " respectively. There follows a section which was given the title " Needs, Production and Division of Labour "; a critique of Hegel's philosophy, which the editors of the *MEGA* placed at the end of the published version in accordance with the indications given in the " Preface "; and the " Preface " itself (beginning on page XXXIX) which was clearly intended to introduce the whole work. On pages XLI–XLIII there is another independent section to which the editors of the *MEGA* gave the title " Money."

The fourth manuscript, comprising one double sheet (four pages), was found sewn into the third manuscript. It contains a résumé of the final chapter, on absolute knowledge, of Hegel's *Phenomenology of Spirit*, and it was published by the editors of the *MEGA* as an appendix to Abteilung I, Band III. Much of the text is used in the criticism of Hegel's philosophy in the third manuscript.

I have used the original publication for my translations of the two essays which Marx himself published in the *Deutsch-Französische Jahrbücher*. For the " Economic and Philosophical Manuscripts " I have used the *MEGA* edition, but have revised the text in a few places. I have not included here the fourth manuscript, since it adds nothing to the discussion of Hegel's philosophy in the third manuscript. I have shown Marx's pagination of the manuscripts by Roman numerals enclosed in square brackets.

Marx quotes extensively, particularly in the " Economic and Philosophical Manuscripts," from the works of English, French and German writers, but he sometimes omits or paraphrases a part of the text. I have restored the original texts of English quotations and have translated French and German quotations from the original texts. I have usually indicated the omissions and paraphrases, but where Marx merely summarizes a passage from another writer I have translated his own text and have referred in a footnote to the original source.

These early writings contain a number of philosophical terms derived from Hegel and Feuerbach; and those parts devoted to criticism of Hegel's philosophy employ many terms to which Hegel (and Marx) gave a technical meaning. In making my translation I have consulted the principal English translations of Hegel's writings, and I have been greatly helped by a recent study of Hegel by J. N. Findlay: *Hegel: A Re-Examination* (London, 1958). It is only necessary to mention here a few of the more common terms. I have translated *Wesen* as " being," " essence," or " life " according to the context; and *aufheben* as " annul " or " abolish " (negative sense) and " supersede " or " transcend " (positive sense). On the other hand I have translated both *Entäusserung* and *Entfremdung* as " alienation " (or occasionally " estrangement ") since Marx (unlike Hegel) does not make a systematic distinction between them; Marx distinguishes between *Entäusserung, Entfremdung* (alienation) and *Vergegenständlichung* (objectification).

I have indicated Marx's frequent emphases of certain words and phrases by the use of italics.

My notes to the translations are shown by the sign *Editor's note*, but I have inserted references to the source of quotations without distinguishing them in this way. My notes draw, in some cases, upon the references and critical notes appended to the *MEGA* edition.[1]

---

[1] Including the notes referring to the essays " On the Jewish Question " and " Contribution to the Critique of Hegel's Philosophy of Right. Introduction," both of which are reprinted in the *MEGA* edition, Abteilung I, Band I/1.

ON THE JEWISH QUESTION

1. Bruno Bauer, *Die Judenfrage* (The Jewish Question).

2. Bruno Bauer, " Die Fähigkeit der heutigen Juden und Christen, frei zu werden." (The Capacity of the present-day Jews and Christians to become free.)

1

BRUNO BAUER, *DIE JUDENFRAGE* [1]

THE German Jews seek emancipation. What kind of emancipation do they want? *Civic, political* emancipation.

Bruno Bauer replies to them: In Germany no one is politically emancipated. We ourselves are not free. How then could we liberate you? You Jews are *egoists* if you demand for yourselves, as Jews, a special emancipation. You should work, as Germans, for the political emancipation of Germany, and as men, for the emancipation of mankind. You should feel the particular kind of oppression and shame which you suffer, not as an exception to the rule but rather as a confirmation of the rule.

Or do the Jews want to be placed on a footing of equality with the *Christian subjects*? If they recognize the *Christian state* as legally established they also recognize the régime of general enslavement. Why should their particular yoke be irksome when they accept the general yoke? Why should the German be interested in the liberation of the Jew, if the Jew is not interested in the liberation of the German?

The *Christian* state recognizes nothing but *privileges*. The Jew himself, in this state, has the privilege of being a Jew. As a Jew he possesses rights which the Christians do not have. Why does he want rights which he does not have but which the Christians enjoy?

In demanding his emancipation from the Christian state he asks the Christian state to abandon its *religious* prejudice. But does he, the Jew, give up *his* religious prejudice? Has he then the right to insist that someone else should forswear his religion?

[1] Braunschweig, 1843.

The *Christian* state, *by its very nature*, is incapable of emancipating the Jew. But, adds Bauer, the Jew, by his very nature, cannot be emancipated. As long as the state remains Christian, and as long as the Jew remains a Jew, they are equally incapable, the one of conferring emancipation, the other of receiving it.

With respect to the Jews the Christian state can only adopt the attitude of a Christian state. That is, it can permit the Jew, as a matter of privilege, to isolate himself from its other subjects; but it must then allow the pressures of all the other spheres of society to bear upon the Jew, and all the more heavily since he is in *religious* opposition to the dominant religion. But the Jew likewise can only adopt a Jewish attitude, i.e. that of a foreigner, towards the state, since he opposes his illusory nationality to actual nationality, his illusory law to actual law. He considers it his right to separate himself from the rest of humanity; as a matter of principle he takes no part in the historical movement and looks to a future which has nothing in common with the future of mankind as a whole. He regards himself as a member of the Jewish people, and the Jewish people as the chosen people.

On what grounds, then, do you Jews demand emancipation? On account of your religion? But it is the mortal enemy of the state religion. As citizens? But there are no citizens in Germany. As men? But you are not men any more than are those to whom you appeal.

Bauer, after criticizing earlier approaches and solutions, formulates the question of Jewish emancipation in a new way. What, he asks, is the nature of the Jew who is to be emancipated, and the *nature* of the Christian state which is to emancipate him? He replies by a critique of the Jewish religion, analyses the religious opposition between Judaism and Christianity, explains the essence of the Christian state; and does all this with dash, clarity, wit and profundity, in a style which is as precise as it is pithy and vigorous.

How then does Bauer resolve the Jewish question? What is the result? To formulate a question is to resolve it. The critical study of the Jewish question is the answer to the Jewish question. Here it is in brief: we have to emancipate ourselves before we can emancipate others.

The most stubborn form of the opposition between Jew and Christian is the *religious* opposition. How is an opposition resolved? By making it impossible. And how is *religious* opposition made impossible? By abolishing *religion*. As soon as Jew and Christian come to see in their respective religions nothing more than *stages in the development of the human mind*—snake skins which have been cast off by *history*, and *man* as the snake who clothed himself in them— they will no longer find themselves in religious opposition, but in a purely critical, *scientific* and human relationship. *Science* will then constitute their unity. But scientific oppositions are resolved by science itself.

The *German* Jew, in particular, suffers from the general lack of political freedom and the pronounced Christianity of the state. But in Bauer's sense the Jewish question has a general significance, independent of the specifically German conditions. It is the question of the relations between religion and the state, of the *contradiction between religious prejudice and political emancipation*. Emancipation from religion is posited as a condition, both for the Jew who wants political emancipation, and for the state which should emancipate him and itself be emancipated.

"Very well, it may be said (and the Jew himself says it) but the Jew should not be emancipated because he is a Jew, because he has such an excellent and universal moral creed; the *Jew* should take second place to the citizen, and he will be a *citizen* although he is and desires to remain a Jew. In other words, he is and remains a *Jew*, even though he is a *citizen* and as such lives in a universal human condition; his restricted Jewish nature always finally triumphs over his human and political obligations. The bias persists even though it is overcome by general principles. But if it persists, it would be truer to say that it overcomes all the rest." " It is only in a sophistical and superficial sense that the Jew could remain a Jew in political life. Consequently, if he wanted to remain a Jew, this would mean that the superficial became the essential and thus triumphed. In other words, his life *in the state* would be only a semblance, or a momentary exception to the essential and normal." [1]

Let us see also how Bauer establishes the role of the state.

" France," he says, " has provided us recently,[2] in connexion with the Jewish question (and for that matter all other *political* questions), with the spectacle of a life which is free but which revokes its freedom by law and so declares it to be merely an appearance; and which, on the other hand, denies its free laws by its acts." [3]

" In France, universal liberty is not yet established by law, nor is the *Jewish question as yet resolved*, because legal liberty, i.e. the equality of all citizens, is restricted in actual life, which is still dominated and fragmented by religious privileges, and because the lack of liberty in actual life influences law in its turn and obliges it to sanction the division of citizens who are by nature free into oppressors and oppressed." [4]

When, therefore, would the Jewish question be resolved in France?

" The Jew would really have ceased to be Jewish, for example, if he did not allow his religious code to prevent his fulfilment of his duties towards the state and his fellow citizens; if he attended and took part in the public business of the Chamber of Deputies on the sabbath. It would be necessary, further, to abolish all *religious privilege*, including the monopoly of a privileged church. If, thereafter, some

---

[1] BAUER, " Die Fähigkeit der heutigen Juden und Christen, frei zu werden," *Einundzwanzig Bogen*, p. 57. Emphases added by Marx. [*Editor's note.*]
[2] Chamber of Deputies. Debate of 26th December, 1840.
[3] BAUER, *Die Judenfrage*, p. 64.
[4] Ibid., p. 65.

or many or *even the overwhelming majority felt obliged to fulfil
their religious duties*, such practices should be left *to them as an
absolutely* private matter." [1] " There is no longer any
religion when there is no longer a privileged religion. Take
away from religion its power to excommunicate and it will
no longer exist." [2] " Mr. Martin du Nord has seen, in the
suggestion to omit any mention of Sunday in the law, a
proposal to declare that Christianity has ceased to exist.
With equal right (and the right is well founded) the
declaration that the law of the sabbath is no longer binding
upon the Jew would amount to proclaiming the end of
Judaism." [3]

Thus Bauer demands, on the one hand, that the Jew
should renounce Judaism, and in general that man should
renounce religion, in order to be emancipated as a citizen.
On the other hand, he considers, and this follows logically,
that the political abolition of religion is the abolition of all
religion. The state which presupposes religion is not yet a
true or actual state. " Clearly, the religious idea gives some
assurances to the state. But to what state? *To what kind of
state?*" [4]

At this point we see that the Jewish question is considered
only from one aspect.

It was by no means sufficient to ask: who should emancipate? who should be emancipated? The critic should ask
a third question: *what kind of emancipation* is involved?
What are the essential conditions of the emancipation which
is demanded? The criticism of *political emancipation* itself
was only the final criticism of the Jewish question and its
genuine resolution into the " *general question of the age*."

Bauer, since he does not formulate the problem at this
level, falls into contradictions. He establishes conditions
which are not based upon the nature of *political* emancipation. He raises questions which are irrelevant to his

---

[1] Loc. cit. [2] BAUER, *Die Judenfrage*, p. 66.
[3] Ibid., p. 71. [4] Ibid., p. 97.

problem, and he resolves problems which leave his question
unanswered.   When Bauer says of the opponents of Jewish
emancipation that " Their error was simply to assume that
the Christian state was the only true one, and not to subject
it to the same criticism as Judaism," [1] we see his own error in
the fact that he subjects *only* the " Christian state," and not
the " state as such " to criticism, that he does not examine
the relation between political emancipation and human emancipation,
and that he, therefore, poses conditions which are only ex-
plicable by his lack of critical sense in confusing political
emancipation and universal human emancipation.   Bauer
asks the Jews: Have you, from your standpoint, the right to
demand *political emancipation*?   We ask the converse question: from the standpoint of *political* emancipation can the
Jew be required to abolish Judaism, or man be asked to
abolish religion?

The Jewish question presents itself differently according
to the state in which the Jew resides.   In Germany, where
there is no political state, no state as such, the Jewish
question is purely *theological*.   The Jew finds himself in
religious opposition to the state, which proclaims Christianity
as its foundation.   This state is a theologian *ex professo*.
Criticism here is criticism of theology; a double-edged
criticism, of Christian and of Jewish theology.   And so we
move always in the domain of theology, however *critically* we
may move therein.

In France, which is a *constitutional* state, the Jewish
question is a question of constitutionalism, of the incompleteness *of political emancipation*.   Since the *semblance* of a
state religion is maintained here, if only in the insignificant
and self-contradictory formula of a *religion of the majority*, the
relation of the Jews to the state also retains a semblance of
religious, theological opposition.

It is only in the free states of North America, or at least in
some of them, that the Jewish question loses its *theological*

[1] BAUER, *Die Judenfrage*, p. 3.

significance and becomes a truly *secular* question. Only where the state exists in its completely developed form can the relation of the Jew, and of the religious man in general, to the political state appear in a pure form, with its own characteristics. The criticism of this relation ceases to be theological criticism when the state ceases to maintain a *theological* attitude towards religion, that is, when it adopts the attitude of a state, i.e. a *political* attitude. Criticism then becomes *criticism of the political state*. And at this point, where the question ceases to be *theological*, Bauer's criticism ceases to be critical.

" There is not, in the United States, either a state religion or a religion declared to be that of a majority, or a pre-dominance of one religion over another. The state remains aloof from all religions." [1] There are even some states in North America in which " the constitution does not impose any religious belief or practice as a condition of political rights." [2] And yet, " no one in the United States believes that a man without religion can be an honest man." [3] And North America is pre-eminently the country of religiosity, as Beaumont,[4] Tocqueville [5] and the Englishman, Hamilton, [6] assure us in unison. However, the states of North America only serve as an example. The question is: what is the relation between *complete* political emancipation and religion? If we find in the country which has attained full political emancipation, that religion not only continues to *exist* but is *fresh* and *vigorous*, this is proof that the existence of religion is not at all opposed to the perfection of the state. But since the existence of religion is the existence of a defect,

---

[1] GUSTAVE DE BEAUMONT, *Marie ou l'esclavage aux États-Unis*, Bruxelles, 1835, 2 vols., II, p. 207. Marx refers to another edition, Paris, 1835. [*Editor's note.*]

[2] Ibid., p. 216. Beaumont actually refers to *all* the States of North America. [*Editor's note.*]

[3] Ibid., p. 217.   [4] G. DE BEAUMONT, op. cit.

[5] A. DE TOCQUEVILLE, *De la démocratie en Amérique.*

[6] THOMAS HAMILTON, *Men and Manners in North America*, Edinburgh, 1833, 2 vols. Marx quotes from the German translation, Mannheim, 1834. [*Editor's note.*]

the source of this defect must be sought in the *nature* of the state itself. Religion no longer appears as the basis, but as the *manifestation* of secular narrowness. That is why we explain the religious constraints upon the free citizens by the secular constraints upon them. We do not claim that they must transcend their religious narrowness in order to get rid of their secular limitations. We claim that they will transcend their religious narrowness once they have overcome their secular limitations. We do not turn secular questions into theological questions; we turn theological questions into secular ones. History has for long enough been resolved into superstition; but we now resolve superstition into history. The question of the *relation between political emancipation and religion* becomes for us a question of the *relation between political emancipation and human emancipation*. We criticize the religious failings of the political state by criticizing the political state in its *secular* form, disregarding its religious failings. We express in human terms the contradiction between the state and a *particular religion*, for example *Judaism*, by showing the contradiction between the state and particular *secular elements*, between the state and *religion in general* and between the state and its general *presuppositions*.

The *political* emancipation of the Jew or the Christian—of the *religious* man in general—is the *emancipation of* the state from Judaism, Christianity, and *religion* in general. The *state* emancipates itself from religion in its own particular way, in the mode which corresponds to its nature, by emancipating itself from the *state religion*; that is to say, by giving recognition to no religion and affirming itself purely and simply as a state. To be *politically* emancipated from religion is not to be finally and completely emancipated from religion, because political emancipation is not the final and absolute form of *human* emancipation.

The limits of political emancipation appear at once in the fact that the *state* can liberate itself from a constraint without man himself being *really* liberated; that a state may be a *free state* without man himself being a *free man*. Bauer himself tacitly admits this when he makes political emancipation depend upon the following condition—

" It would be necessary, moreover, to abolish all religious privileges, including the monopoly of a privileged church. If some people, or even the *immense majority, still felt obliged to fulfil their religious duties,* this practice should be left to them as a *completely private matter."* Thus the state may have emancipated itself from religion, even though the *immense majority* of people continue to be religious. And the immense majority do not cease to be religious by virtue of being religious *in private.*

The attitude of the state, especially the *free state,* towards religion is only the attitude towards religion of the individuals who compose the state. It follows that man frees himself from a constraint in a *political* way, through the state, when he transcends his limitations, in contradiction with himself, and in an *abstract, narrow* and partial way. Furthermore, by emancipating himself *politically,* man emancipates himself in a *devious way,* through an intermediary, however *necessary* this intermediary may be. Finally, even when he proclaims himself an atheist through the intermediary of the state, that is, when he declares the state to be an atheist, he is still engrossed in religion, because he only recognizes himself as an atheist in a roundabout way, through an intermediary. Religion is simply the recognition of man in a roundabout fashion; that is, through an intermediary. The state is the intermediary between man and human liberty. Just as Christ is the intermediary to whom man attributes all his own divinity and all his religious *bonds,* so the state is the intermediary to which man confides all his non-divinity and all his *human freedom.*

The *political* elevation of man above religion shares the weaknesses and merits of all such political measures. For example, the state as a state abolishes *private property* (i.e. man decrees by *political* means the *abolition* of private property) when it abolishes the *property qualification* for electors and representatives, as has been done in many of the North American States. Hamilton interprets this phenomenon quite correctly from the political standpoint: *The masses have gained a victory over property owners and financial wealth.* [1] Is not private property ideally abolished when the non-owner comes to legislate for the owner of property? The *property qualification* is the last *political* form in which private property is recognized.

But the political suppression of private property not only does not abolish private property; it actually presupposes its existence. The state abolishes, after its fashion, the distinctions established by *birth, social rank, education, occupation,* when it decrees that birth, social rank, education, occupation are *non-political* distinctions; when it proclaims, without regard to these distinctions, that every member of society is an *equal* partner in popular sovereignty, and treats all the elements which compose the real life of the nation from the standpoint of the state. But the state, none the less, allows private property, education, occupation, to *act* after *their* own fashion, namely as private property, education, occupation, and to manifest their *particular* nature. Far from abolishing these *effective* differences, it only exists so far as they are presupposed; it is conscious of being a *political state* and manifests its *universality* only in opposition to these elements. Hegel, therefore, defines the relation of the political state to religion quite correctly when he says: " In order for the state to come in to existence as the *self-knowing* ethical actuality of spirit, it is essential that it should be distinct from the forms of authority and of faith. But this distinction emerges only in so far as divisions occur within the ecclesiastical sphere itself. It is only in this way that the state, above the *particular* churches, has attained to the universality of thought—its formal principle—and is bringing

[1] HAMILTON, op. cit., I, pp. 288, 306, 309.

this universality into existence." [1] To be sure! Only in this manner, *above* the *particular* elements, can the state constitute itself as universality.

The perfected political state is, by its nature, the *species-life* [2] of man as *opposed* to his material life. All the presuppositions of this egoistic life continue to exist in *civil society outside* the political sphere, as qualities of civil society. Where the political state has attained to its full development, man leads, not only in thought, in consciousness, but in *reality*, in *life*, a double existence—celestial and terrestrial. He lives in the *political community*, where he regards himself as a *communal being*, and in *civil society* where he acts simply as a *private individual*, treats other men as means, degrades himself to the role of a mere means, and becomes the plaything of alien powers. The political state, in relation to civil society, is just as spiritual as is heaven in relation to earth. It stands in the same opposition to civil society, and overcomes it in the same manner as religion overcomes the narrowness of the profane world; i.e. it has always to acknowledge it again, re-establish it, and allow itself to be dominated by it. Man, in his *most intimate* reality, in civil society, is a profane being. Here, where he appears both to himself and to others as a real individual he is an *illusory* phenomenon. In the state,

---

[1] HEGEL, *Grundlinien der Philosophie des Rechts*, I[er] Aufgabe, 1821, p. 346. *See* the English translation by T. M. KNOX, *Hegel's Philosophy of Right*, Oxford, 1942, p. 173. [*Editor's note.*]

[2] The terms " species-life " (*Gattungsleben*) and " species-being " (*Gattungswesen*) are derived from Feuerbach. In the first chapter of *Das Wesen des Christentums* [*The Essence of Christianity*], Leipzig, 1841, Feuerbach discusses the nature of man, and argues that man is to be distinguished from animals not by " consciousness " as such, but by a particular kind of consciousness. Man is not only conscious of himself as an individual; he is also conscious of himself as a member of the human species, and so he apprehends a " human essence " which is the same in himself and in other men. According to Feuerbach this ability to conceive of " species " is the fundamental element in the human power of reasoning: " Science is the consciousness of species." Marx, while not departing from this meaning of the terms, employs them in other contexts; and he insists more strongly than Feuerbach that since this " species-consciousness " defines the nature of man, man is only living and acting authentically (i.e. in accordance with his nature) when he lives and acts deliberately as a " species-being," that is, as a *social* being. [*Editor's note.*]

on the contrary, where he is regarded as a species-being,[1] man is the imaginary member of an imaginary sovereignty, divested of his real, individual life, and infused with an unreal universality.

The conflict in which the individual, as the professor of a *particular* religion, finds himself involved with his own quality of citizenship and with other men as members of the community, may be resolved into the *secular* schism between the *political* state and *civil society*. For man as a *bourgeois* [2] " life in the state is only an appearance or a fleeting exception to the normal and essential." It is true that the *bourgeois*, like the Jew, participates in political life only in a sophistical way, just as the *citoyen* [3] is a Jew or a *bourgeois* only in a sophistical way. But this sophistry is not personal. It is the *sophistry of the political state* itself. The difference between the religious man and the citizen is the same as that between the shopkeeper and the citizen, between the day-labourer and the citizen, between the landed proprietor and the citizen, between the *living individual* and the *citizen*. The contradiction in which the religious man finds himself with the political man, is the same contradiction in which the *bourgeois* finds himself with the citizen, and the member of civil society with his *political lion's skin*.

This secular opposition, to which the Jewish question reduces itself—the relation between the political state and its presuppositions, whether the latter are material elements such as private property, etc., or spiritual elements such as culture or religion, the conflict between the *general interest* and *private interest*, the schism between the *political* state and *civil society*—these profane contradictions, Bauer leaves intact, while he directs his polemic against their *religious* expression. " It is precisely this basis—that is, the needs which assure the existence of *civil society* and *guarantee its necessity*—which ex-

---

[1] *See* previous note.
[2] I.e. as a member of civil society. [*Editor's note.*]
[3] I.e. the individual with political rights. [*Editor's note.*]

poses its existence to continual danger, maintains an element of uncertainty in civil society, produces this continually changing compound of wealth and poverty, of prosperity and distress, and above all generates change." [1] Compare the whole section entitled " Civil society," [2] which follows closely the distinctive features of Hegel's philosophy of right. Civil society, in its opposition to this political state, is recognized as necessary because the political state is recognized as necessary.

Political emancipation certainly represents a great progress. It is not, indeed, the final form of human emancipation, but it is the final form of human emancipation *within* the framework of the prevailing social order. It goes without saying that we are speaking here of real, practical emancipation.

Man emancipates himself *politically* from religion by expelling it from the sphere of public law to that of private law. Religion is no longer the spirit of the *state*, in which man behaves, albeit in a specific and limited way and in a particular sphere, as a species-being, in community with other men. It has become the spirit of *civil society*, of the sphere of egoism and of the *bellum omnium contra omnes*. It is no longer the essence of *community*, but the essence of *differentiation*. It has become what it was at the *beginning*, an expression of the fact that man is *separated* from the *community*, from himself and from other men. It is now only the abstract avowal of an individual folly, a private whim or caprice. The infinite fragmentation of religion in North America, for example, already gives it the *external* form of a strictly private affair. It has been relegated among the numerous private interests and exiled from the life of the community as such. But one should have no illusions about the scope of political emancipation. The division of man into the *public person* and the *private person*, the *displacement* of religion from the state to civil society—all this is not a

---

[1] BAUER, *Die Judenfrage*, p. 8.   [2] Ibid., pp. 8–9.

stage in political emancipation but its consummation. Thus
political emancipation does not abolish, and does not even
strive to abolish, man's *real* religiosity.

The *decomposition* of man into Jew and citizen, Protestant
and citizen, religious man and citizen, is not a deception
practised *against* the political system nor yet an evasion of
political emancipation. It is *political emancipation itself*, the
political mode of emancipation from religion. Certainly, in
periods when the political state as such comes violently to
birth in civil society, and when men strive to liberate themselves through political emancipation, the state can, and
must, proceed to *abolish and destroy religion*; but only in the
same way as it proceeds to abolish private property, by declaring a maximum, by confiscation, or by progressive taxation, or in the same way as it proceeds to abolish life, by the
guillotine. At those times when the state is most aware of
itself, political life seeks to stifle its own prerequisites—civil
society and its elements—and to establish itself as the genuine
and harmonious species-life of man. But it can only achieve
this end by setting itself in *violent* contradiction with its own
conditions of existence, by declaring a *permanent* revolution.
Thus the political drama ends necessarily with the restoration of religion, of private property, of all the elements of
civil society, just as war ends with the conclusion of peace.

In fact, the perfected Christian state is not the so-called
Christian state which acknowledges Christianity as its basis,
as the state religion, and thus adopts an exclusive attitude
towards other religions; it is, rather, the *atheistic* state, the
democratic state, the state which relegates religion among
the other elements of civil society. The state which is still
theological, which still professes officially the Christian
creed, and which has not yet dared to declare itself a *state*,
has not yet succeeded in expressing in a *human* and *secular*
form, in its political *reality*, the human basis of which
Christianity is the transcendental expression. The so-called
Christian state is simply a *non-state*; since it is not Christianity

as a religion, but only the *human core* of the Christian religion which can realize itself in truly human creations.

The so-called Christian state is the Christian negation of the state, but not at all the political realization of Christianity. The state which professes Christianity as a religion does not yet profess it in a political form, because it still has a religious attitude towards religion. In other words, such a state is not the *genuine realization* of the human basis of religion, because it still accepts the *unreal, imaginary* form of this human core. The so-called Christian state is an *imperfect* state, for which the Christian religion serves as the *supplement* and *sanctification* of its imperfection. Thus religion becomes necessarily one of its *means*; and so it is the *hypocritical* state. There is a great difference between saying: (i) that the *perfect* state, owing to a deficiency in the general *nature* of the state, counts religion as one of its *prerequisites*, or (ii) that the *imperfect* state, owing to a deficiency in its *particular existence* as an imperfect state, declares that religion is its *basis*. In the latter, religion becomes *imperfect politics*. In the former, the imperfection even of perfected *politics* is revealed in religion. The so-called Christian state needs the Christian religion in order to complete itself *as a state*. The democratic state, the real state, does not need religion for its political consummation. On the contrary, it can dispense with religion, because in this case the human core of religion is realized in a profane manner. The so-called Christian state, on the other hand, has a political attitude towards religion, and a religious attitude towards politics. It reduces political institutions and religion equally to mere appearances.

In order to make this contradiction clearer we shall examine Bauer's model of the Christian state, a model which is derived from his study of the German-Christian state.

" Quite recently," says Bauer, " in order to demonstrate the *impossibility* or the *non-existence* of a Christian state, those passages in the Bible have been frequently quoted with which the state *does not conform* and *cannot conform unless it wishes to dissolve itself entirely.*"

" But the question is not so easily settled.   What do these Biblical passages demand?   Supernatural renunciation, sub-mission to the authority of revelation, turning away from the state, the abolition of profane conditions.   But the Christian state proclaims and accomplishes all these things.   It has assimilated the *spirit of the Bible*, and if it does not reproduce it exactly in the terms which the Bible uses, that is simply because it expresses this spirit in political forms, in forms which are borrowed from the political system of this world but which, in the religious rebirth which they are obliged to undergo, are reduced to simple appearances.   Man turns away from the state and by this means realizes and completes the political institutions." [1]

Bauer continues by showing that the members of a Christian state no longer constitute a nation with a will of its own.   The nation has its true existence in the leader to whom it is subjected, but this leader is, by his origin and nature, alien to it since he has been imposed by God without the people having any part in the matter.   The laws of such a nation are not its own work, but are direct revelations. The supreme leader, in his relations with the real nation, the masses, requires privileged intermediaries; and the nation itself disintegrates into a multitude of distinct spheres which are formed and determined by chance, are differentiated from each other by their interests and their specific passions and prejudices, and acquire as a privilege the permission to isolate themselves from each other, etc.[2]

But Bauer himself says: " Politics, if it is to be nothing more than religion, should not be politics; any more than the scouring of pans, if it is treated as a religious matter, should be regarded as ordinary housekeeping." [3]   But in the German-Christian state religion is an " economic matter " just as " economic matters " are religion.   In the German-

---

[1] BAUER, *Die Judenfrage* p. 55.   [2] Ibid., p. 56.   [3] Ibid., p. 108.

Christian state the power of religion is the religion of power.

The separation of the " spirit of the Bible " from the " letter of the Bible " is an *irreligious* act. The state which expresses the Bible in the letter of politics, or in any letter other than that of the Holy Ghost, commits sacrilege, if not in the eyes of men at least in the eyes of its own religion. The state which acknowledges the Bible as its charter and Christianity as its supreme rule must be assessed according to the words of the Bible; for even the language of the Bible is sacred. Such a state, as well as the *human rubbish* upon which it is based, finds itself involved in a painful contradiction, which is insoluble from the standpoint of religious consciousness, when it is referred to those words of the Bible " with which it does not conform and *cannot conform unless it wishes to dissolve itself entirely.*" And why does it not wish to dissolve itself entirely? The state itself cannot answer either itself or others. In its own consciousness the official Christian state is an " ought" whose realization is impossible. It cannot affirm the *reality* of its own existence without lying to itself, and so it remains always in its own eyes an object of doubt, an uncertain and problematic object. Criticism is, therefore, entirely within its rights in forcing the state, which supports itself upon the Bible, into a total disorder of thought in which it no longer knows whether it is *illusion* or *reality*; and in which the infamy of its *profane* ends (for which religion serves as a cloak) enter into an insoluble conflict with the probity of its *religious* consciousness (for which religion appears as the goal of the world). Such a state can only escape its inner torment by becoming the *myrmidon* of the Catholic Church. In the face of this Church, which asserts that secular power is entirely subordinate to its commands, the state is powerless; powerless the secular power which claims to be the rule of the religious spirit.

What prevails in the so-called Christian state is not man but alienation. The only man who counts—the *King*—is

specifically differentiated from other men and is still a religious being associated directly with heaven and with God.
The relations which exist here are relations still based upon
faith. The religious spirit is still not really secularized.

But the religious spirit cannot be *really* secularized.   For
what is it but the *non-secular* form of a stage in the development of the human spirit?   The religious spirit can only be
realized if the stage of development of the human spirit
which it expresses in religious form, manifests and constitutes
itself in its *secular* form.   This is what happens in the *democratic* state.   The basis of this state is not Christianity but
the *human basis* of Christianity. Religion remains the ideal,
non-secular consciousness of its members, because it is the
ideal form of the *stage of human development* which has been
attained.

The members of the political state are religious because of
the dualism between individual life and species-life, between
the life of civil society and political life.   They are religious
in the sense that man treats political life, which is remote
from his own individual existence, as if it were his true life;
and in the sense that religion is here the spirit of civil society,
and expresses the separation and withdrawal of man from
man.   Political democracy is Christian in the sense that man,
not merely one man but every man, is there considered a
sovereign being, a supreme being; but it is uneducated, unsocial man, man just as he is in his fortuitous existence, man
as he has been corrupted, lost to himself, alienated, subjected
to the rule of inhuman conditions and elements, by the whole
organization of our society—in short man who is not yet a
real species-being.   Creations of fantasy, dreams, the postulates of Christianity, the sovereignty of man—but of man as
an alien being distinguished from the real man—all these
become, in democracy, the tangible and present reality,
secular maxims.

In the perfected democracy, the religious and theological
consciousness appears to itself all the more religious and

theological in that it is apparently without any political significance or terrestrial aims, is an affair of the heart withdrawn from the world, an expression of the limitations of reason, a product of arbitrariness and fantasy, a veritable life in the beyond. Christianity here attains the *practical* expression of its universal religious significance, because the most varied views are brought together in the form of Christianity, and still more because Christianity does not ask that anyone should profess Christianity, but simply that he should have some kind of religion (*see* Beaumont, op. cit.). The religious consciousness runs riot in a wealth of contradictions and diversity.

We have shown, therefore, that political emancipation from religion leaves religion in existence, although this is no longer a privileged religion. The contradiction in which the adherent of a particular religion finds himself in relation to his citizenship is only *one aspect* of the universal *secular contradiction between the political state and* civil society. The consummation of the Christian state is a state which acknowledges itself simply as a state and ignores the religion of its members. The emancipation of the state from religion is not the emancipation of the real man from religion.

We do not say to the Jews, therefore, as does Bauer: you cannot be emancipated politically without emancipating yourselves completely from Judaism. We say rather: it is because you can be emancipated politically, without renouncing Judaism completely and absolutely, that *political emancipation* itself is not *human* emancipation. If you want to be politically emancipated, without emancipating yourselves humanly, the inadequacy and the contradiction is not entirely in yourselves but in the *nature* and the *category* of political emancipation. If you are preoccupied with this category you share the general prejudice. Just as the state *evangelizes* when, although it is a state, it adopts a Christian attitude towards the Jews, the Jew *acts politically* when, though a Jew, he demands civil rights.

But if a man, though a Jew, can be emancipated politically and acquire civil rights, can he claim and acquire what are called the *rights of man*? Bauer *denies* it. " The question is whether the Jew as such, that is, the Jew who himself avows that he is constrained by his true nature to live eternally separate from men, is able to acquire and to concede to others the *universal rights of man*."

" The idea of the rights of man was only discovered in the Christian world, in the last century. It is not an innate idea; on the contrary, it is acquired in a struggle against the historical traditions in which man has been educated up to the present time. The rights of man are not, therefore, a gift of nature, nor a legacy from past history, but the reward of a struggle against the accident of birth and against the privileges which history has hitherto transmitted from generation to generation. They are the results of culture, and only he can possess them who has merited and earned them."

" But can the Jew really take possession of them? As long as he remains Jewish the limited nature which makes him a Jew must prevail over the human nature which should associate him, as a man, with other men; and it will isolate him from everyone who is not a Jew. He declares, by this separation, that the particular nature which makes him Jewish is his true and supreme nature, before which human nature has to efface itself."

" Similarly, the Christian as such cannot grant the rights of man." [1]

According to Bauer man has to sacrifice the " *privilege of faith* " in order to acquire the general rights of man. Let us consider for a moment the so-called rights of man; let us examine them in their most authentic form, that which they have among those who *discovered* them, the North Americans and the French! These rights of man are, in part, *political* rights, which can only be exercised if one is a member of a

[1] BAUER, *Die Judenfrage*, pp. 19–20.

community. Their content is *participation* in the *community* life, in the *political* life of the community, the life of the state. They fall in the category of *political liberty*, of *civil rights*, which as we have seen do not at all presuppose the consistent and positive abolition of religion; nor consequently, of Judaism. It remains to consider the other part, namely the *rights of man* as distinct from the *rights of the citizen*.

Among them is to be found the freedom of conscience, the right to practise a chosen religion. The *privilege of faith* is expressly recognized, either as a *right of man* or as a consequence of a right of man, namely liberty. *Declaration of the Rights of Man and of the Citizen*, 1791, Article 10: " No one is to be disturbed on account of his opinions, even religious opinions." There is guaranteed, as one of the rights of man, " the liberty of every man to practise the *religion* to which he adheres."

The *Declaration of the Rights of Man, etc.* 1793, enumerates among the rights of man (Article 7): " The liberty of religious observance." Moreover, it is even stated, with respect to the right to express ideas and opinions, to hold meetings, to practise a religion, that: " The necessity of enunciating these *rights* presupposes either the existence or the recent memory of despotism." Compare the Constitution of 1795, Section XII, Article 354.

Constitution of Pennsylvania, Article 9, § 3: " All men have received from nature the imprescriptible *right* to worship the Almighty according to the dictates of their conscience, and no one can be legally compelled to follow, establish or support against his will any religion or religious ministry. No human authority can, in any circumstances, intervene in a matter of conscience or control the forces of the soul."

Constitution of New Hampshire, Articles 5 and 6: " Among these natural rights some are by nature inalienable since nothing can replace them. The rights of conscience are among them." [1]

[1] BEAUMONT, op. cit., II, pp. 206–7.

The incompatibility between religion and the rights of
man is so little manifest in the concept of the rights of man
that the *right to be religious*, in one's own fashion, and to
practise one's own particular religion, is expressly included
among the rights of man.   The privilege of faith is a *universal right of man.*

A distinction is made between the rights of man and the
rights of the citizen.   Who is this *man* distinct from the
citizen?   No one but the *member of civil society.*   Why is the
member of civil society called " man," simply man, and why
are his rights called the " rights of man " ?   How is this fact
to be explained?   By the relation between the political state
and civil society, and by the nature of political emancipation.

Let us notice first of all that the so-called *rights of man*, as
distinct from the *rights of the citizen*, are simply the rights of a
member of civil society, that is, of egoistic man, of man separated
from other men and from the community.   The most radical
constitution, that of 1793, says: *Declaration of the Rights of
Man and of the Citizen:*   Article 2.   " These rights, etc. (the
natural and imprescriptible rights) are: *equality*, *liberty*,
security, *property.*

What constitutes liberty?

Article 6.   " Liberty is the power which man has to do
everything which does not harm the rights of others."

Liberty is, therefore, the right to do everything which does
not harm others.   The limits within which each individual
can act without harming others are determined by law, just
as the boundary between two fields is marked by a stake.   It
is a question of the liberty of man regarded as an isolated
monad, withdrawn into himself.   Why, according to Bauer,
is the Jew not fitted to acquire the rights of man?   " As long
as he remains Jewish the limited nature which makes him a
Jew must prevail over the human nature which should
associate him, as a man, with other men; and it will isolate
him from everyone who is not a Jew."   But liberty as a right
of man is not founded upon the relations between man and

man, but rather upon the separation of man from man.   It
is the right of such separation.   The right of the *circumscribed*
individual, withdrawn into himself.

The practical application of the right of liberty is the right
of private property.   What constitutes the right of private
property?

Article 16 (*Constitution* of 1793).   " The right of *property* is
that which belongs to every citizen of enjoying and disposing
as he will of his goods and revenues, of the fruits of his work
and industry."

The right of property is, therefore, the right to enjoy one's
fortune and to dispose of it as one will; without regard for
other men and independently of society.   It is the right of
self-interest.   This individual liberty, and its application,
form the basis of civil society.   It leads every man to see in
other men, not the *realization*, but rather the *limitation* of his
own liberty.   It declares above all the right " to enjoy and
to dispose of *as one will*, one's goods and revenues, the fruits of
one's work and industry."

There remain the other rights of man, equality and
security.

The term " equality " has here no political significance.
It is only the equal right to liberty as defined above; namely
that every man is equally regarded as a self-sufficient monad.
The Constitution of 1795 defines the concept of liberty in this
sense.

Article 5 (*Constitution* of 1795).   " Equality consists in the
fact that the law is the same for all, whether it protects or
punishes."

And security?

Article 8 (*Constitution* of 1793).   " Security consists in the
protection afforded by society to each of its members for the
preservation of his person, his rights, and his property."

Security is the supreme social concept of civil society; the
concept of the police.   The whole society exists only in order
to guarantee for each of its members the preservation of his

person, his rights and his property. It is in this sense that Hegel calls civil society " the state of need and of reason."

The concept of security is not enough to raise civil society above its egoism. Security is, rather, the *assurance* of its egoism.

None of the supposed rights of man, therefore, go beyond the egoistic man, man as he is, as a member of civil society; that is, an individual separated from the community, withdrawn into himself, wholly preoccupied with his private interest and acting in accordance with his private caprice. Man is far from being considered, in the rights of man, as a species-being; on the contrary, species-life itself—society— appears as a system which is external to the individual and as a limitation of his original independence. The only bond between men is natural necessity, need and private interest, the preservation of their property and their egoistic persons.

It is difficult enough to understand that a nation which has just begun to liberate itself, to tear down all the barriers between different sections of the people and to establish a political community, should solemnly proclaim (*Declaration* of 1791) the rights of the egoistic man, separated from his fellow men and from the community, and should renew this proclamation at a moment when only the most heroic devotion can save the nation (and is, therefore, urgently called for), and when the sacrifice of all the interests of civil society is in question and egoism should be punished as a crime. (*Declaration of the Rights of Man, etc.* 1793.) The matter becomes still more incomprehensible when we observe that the political liberators reduce citizenship, the *political community*, to a mere *means* for preserving these so-called rights of man; and consequently, that the citizen is declared to be the servant of egoistic " man," that the sphere in which man functions as a species-being is degraded to a level below the sphere where he functions as a partial being, and finally that it is man as a bourgeois and not man as a citizen who is considered the *true* and *authentic* man.

" The end of every *political association* is the *preservation* of the natural and imprescriptible rights of man." (*Declaration of the Rights of Man, etc.* 1791, Article 2.)   " Government is instituted in order to guarantee man's enjoyment of his natural and imprescriptible rights." (*Declaration, etc.* 1793, Article 1.)   Thus, even in the period of its youthful enthusiasm, which is raised to fever pitch by the force of circumstances, political life declares itself to be only a *means*, whose end is the life of civil society.   It is true that its revolutionary practice is in flagrant contradiction with its theory.   While, for instance, security is declared to be one of the rights of man, the violation of the privacy of correspondence is openly considered.   While the " unlimited freedom of the Press " (*Constitution* of 1793, Article 122), as a corollary of the right of individual liberty, is guaranteed, the freedom of the Press is completely destroyed, since " the freedom of the Press should not be permitted when it endangers public liberty." [1]   This amounts to saying: the right to liberty ceases to be a right as soon as it comes into conflict with *political* life, whereas in theory political life is no more than the guarantee of the rights of man—the rights of the individual man—and should, therefore, be suspended as soon as it comes into contradiction with its *end*, these rights of man.   But practice is only the exception, while theory is the rule.   Even if one decided to regard revolutionary practice as the correct expression of this relation, the problem would remain as to why it is that in the minds of political liberators the relation is inverted, so that the end appears as the means and the means as the end?   This optical illusion of their consciousness would always remain a problem, though a psychological and theoretical one.

But the problem is easily solved.

Political emancipation is at the same time the *dissolution* of the old society, upon which the sovereign power, the

[1] BUCHEZ et ROUX, " Robespierre jeune," *Histoire parlementaire de la Révolution française*, Tome XXVIII, p. 159.

alienated political life of the people, rests. Political revolution is a revolution of civil society. What was the nature of the old society? It can be characterized in one word: *feudalism*. The old civil society had a *directly political* character; that is, the elements of civil life such as property, the family, and types of occupation had been raised, in the form of lordship, caste and guilds, to elements of political life. They determined, in this form, the relation of the individual to the *state as a whole*; that is, his *political* situation, or in other words, his separation and exclusion from the other elements of society. For this organization of national life did not constitute property and labour as social elements; it rather succeeded in *separating* them from the body of the state, and made them *distinct* societies within society. Nevertheless, at least in the feudal sense, the vital functions and conditions of civil society remained political. They excluded the individual from the body of the state, and transformed the *particular* relation which existed between his corporation and the state into a general relation between the individual and social life, just as they transformed his specific civil activity and situation into a general activity and situation. As a result of this organization, the state as a whole and its consciousness, will and activity—the general political power—also necessarily appeared as the *private* affair of a ruler and his servants, separated from the people.

The political revolution which overthrew this power of the ruler, which made state affairs the affairs of the people, and the political state a matter of *general* concern, i.e. a real state, necessarily shattered everything—estates, corporations, guilds, privileges—which expressed the separation of the people from community life. The political revolution therefore *abolished* the *political character of civil society*. It dissolved civil society into its basic elements, on the one hand *individuals*, and on the other hand the *material and cultural elements* which formed the life experience and the civil situation of these individuals. It set free the political spirit which had, so to speak, been dissolved, fragmented and lost in the various culs-de-sac of feudal society; it reassembled these scattered fragments, liberated the political spirit from its connexion with civil life and made of it the community sphere, the *general* concern of the people, in principle independent of these particular elements of civil life. A *specific* activity and situation in life no longer had any but an individual significance. They no longer constituted the general relation between the individual and the state as a whole. Public affairs as such became the general affair of each individual, and political functions became general functions.

But the consummation of the idealism of the state was at the same time the consummation of the materialism of civil society. The bonds which had restrained the egoistic spirit of civil society were removed along with the political yoke. Political emancipation was at the same time an emancipation of civil society from politics and from even the *semblance* of a general content.

Feudal society was dissolved into its basic element, *man*; but into *egoistic* man who was its real foundation.

Man in this aspect, the member of civil society, is now the foundation and presupposition of the *political* state. He is recognized as such in the rights of man.

But the liberty of egoistic man, and the recognition of this liberty, is rather the recognition of the *frenzied* movement of the cultural and material elements which form the content of his life.

Thus man was not liberated from religion; he received religious liberty. He was not liberated from property; he received the liberty to own property. He was not liberated from the egoism of business; he received the liberty to engage in business.

The *formation of the political state*, and the dissolution of civil society into independent *individuals* whose relations are regulated by *law*, as the relations between men in the corporations and guilds were regulated by *privilege*, are accomplished by *one and the same act*. Man as a member of civil society— *non-political* man—necessarily appears as the *natural* man. The rights of man appear as natural rights because *conscious* activity is concentrated upon political *action*. *Egoistic* man is the *passive*, *given* result of the dissolution of society, an object of *direct apprehension* and consequently a *natural* object. The *political revolution* dissolves civil society into its elements without *revolutionizing* these elements themselves or subjecting them to criticism. This revolution regards civil society, the sphere of human needs, labour, private interests and civil law, as the *basis of its own existence*, as a self-subsistent *precondition*, and thus as its *natural basis*. Finally, man as a member of civil society is identified with *authentic man*, *man* as distinct from citizen, because he is man in his sensuous, individual and *immediate* existence, whereas *political* man is only abstract, artificial man, man as an *allegorical*, *moral* person. Thus man as he really is, is seen only in the form of *egoistic* man, and man in his *true* nature only in the form of the *abstract citizen*.

The abstract notion of political man is well formulated by Rousseau: " Whoever dares undertake to establish a people's institutions must feel himself capable of *changing*, as it were, *human nature* itself, of *transforming* each individual who, in isolation, is a complete but solitary whole, into a *part* of something greater than himself, from which in a sense, he derives his life and his being; [of changing man's nature in order to strengthen it;] of substituting a limited and moral existence for the physical and independent life [with which all of us are endowed by nature]. His task, in short, is to take from *a man his own powers*, and to give him in exchange alien powers which he can only employ with the help of other men." [1]

[1] J. J. ROUSSEAU, *Du contrat social*, Book II. Chapter VII, " The Legislator." Marx quoted this passage in French, and added the emphases; he omitted the portions enclosed in square brackets. [*Editor's note.*]

Every emancipation is a *restoration* of the human world and of human relationships to *man himself.*

Political emancipation is a reduction of man, on the one hand to a member of civil society, an *independent* and *egoistic* individual, and on the other hand, to a *citizen*, to a moral person.

Human emancipation will only be complete when the real, individual man has absorbed into himself the abstract citizen; when as an individual man, in his everyday life, in his work, and in his relationships, he has become a *species-being*; and when he has recognized and organized his own powers (*forces propres*) as *social* powers so that he no longer separates this social power from himself as *political* power.

BRUNO BAUER, "DIE FÄHIGKEIT DER HEUTIGEN JUDEN UND CHRISTEN, FREI ZU WERDEN."[1]

IT is in this form that Bauer studies the relation between the *Jewish and Christian religions*, and also their relation with modern criticism. This latter relation is their relation with " the capacity to become free."

He reaches this conclusion: " The Christian has only to raise himself one degree, to rise above his religion, in order to abolish religion in general," and thus to become free; but " the Jew, on the contrary, has to break not only with his Jewish nature, but also with the process towards the consummation of his religion, a process which has remained alien to him." [2]

Thus Bauer here transforms the question of Jewish emancipation into a purely religious question. The theological doubt about whether the Jew or the Christian has the better chance of attaining salvation is reproduced here in the more enlightened form: which of the two is more *capable of emancipation*? It is indeed no longer asked: which makes free—Judaism or Christianity? On the contrary, it is now asked: which makes free—the negation of Judaism or the negation of Christianity?

" If they wish to become free the Jews should not embrace Christianity as such, but Christianity in dissolution, religion in dissolution; that is to say, the Enlightment, criticism, and its outcome, a free humanity." [3]

It is still a matter, therefore, of the Jews professing some

---

[1] [The capacity of the present-day Jews and Christians to become free.] In *Einundzwanzig Bogen aus der Schweiz* (Ed. G. Herwegh), pp. 56–71.

[2] Loc. cit., p. 71.

[3] Ibid., p. 70.

kind of faith; no longer Christianity as such, but Christianity in dissolution.

Bauer asks the Jews to break with the essence of the Christian religion, but this demand does not follow, as he himself admits, from the development of the Jewish nature.

From the moment when Bauer, at the end of his *Judenfrage*, saw in Judaism only a crude religious criticism of Christianity, and, therefore, attributed to it only a religious significance, it was to be expected that he would transform the emancipation of the Jews into a philosophico-theological act.

Bauer regards the *ideal* and abstract essence of the Jew— his *religion*—as the *whole* of his nature. He, therefore, concludes rightly that " The Jew contributes nothing to mankind when he disregards his own limited law," when he renounces all his Judaism.[1]

The relation between Jews and Christians thus becomes the following: the only interest which the emancipation of the Jew presents for the Christian is a general human and *theoretical* interest. Judaism is a phenomenon which offends the religious eye of the Christian. As soon as the Christian's eye ceases to be religious the phenomenon ceases to offend it. The emancipation of the Jew is not in itself, therefore, a task which falls to the Christian to perform.

The Jew, on the other hand, if he wants to emancipate himself has to undertake, besides his own work, the work of the Christian—the " criticism of the gospels," of the " life of Jesus," etc.[2]

" It is for them to arrange matters; they will decide their own destiny. But history does not allow itself to be mocked." [3]

[1] Loc. cit., p. 65.

Marx alludes here to BRUNO BAUER, *Kritik der evangelischen Geschichte der Synoptiker*, Vols. I–II, Leipzig, 1841; Vol. III, Braunschweig, 1842, and DAVID FRIEDRICH STRAUSS, *Das Leben Jesu*, 2 vols. Tübingen, 1835–6. An English translation of Strauss' book by Marian Evans (George Eliot) was published in 1846 under the title *Life of Jesus Critically Examined*. [*Editor's note.*]

[3] BAUER, " Die Fähigkeit . . . etc.," p. 71.

We will attempt to escape from the theological formulation of the question. For us, the question concerning the capacity of the Jew for emancipation is transformed into another question: what specific *social* element is it necessary to overcome in order to abolish Judaism? For the capacity of the present-day Jew to emancipate himself expresses the relation of Judaism to the emancipation of the contemporary world. The relation results necessarily from the particular situation of Judaism in the present enslaved world.

Let us consider the real Jew: not the *sabbath Jew*, whom Bauer considers, but the *everyday Jew*.

Let us not seek the secret of the Jew in his religion, but let us seek the secret of the religion in the real Jew.

What is the profane basis of Judaism? *Practical* need, *self-interest*. What is the worldly cult of the Jew? *Huckstering*. What is his worldly god? *Money*.

Very well: then in emancipating itself from *huckstering* and *money*, and thus from real and practical Judaism, our age would emancipate itself.

An organization of society which would abolish the preconditions and thus the very possibility of huckstering, would make the Jew impossible. His religious consciousness would evaporate like some insipid vapour in the real, life-giving air of society. On the other hand, when the Jew recognizes his *practical* nature as invalid and endeavours to abolish it, he begins to deviate from his former path of development, works for general *human emancipation* and turns against the *supreme practical* expression of human self-estrangement.

We discern in Judaism, therefore, a universal *antisocial* element of the *present time*, whose historical development, zealously aided in its harmful aspects by the Jews, has now attained its culminating point, a point at which it must necessarily begin to disintegrate.

In the final analysis, the *emancipation of* the Jews is the emancipation of mankind from *Judaism*.

The Jew has already emancipated himself in a Jewish

fashion. " The Jew, who is merely tolerated in Vienna for example, determines the fate of the whole Empire by his financial power. The Jew, who may be entirely without rights in the smallest German state, decides the destiny of Europe. While the corporations and guilds exclude the Jew, or at least look on him with disfavour, the audacity of industry mocks the obstinacy of medieval institutions." [1]

This is not an isolated instance. The Jew has emancipated himself in a Jewish manner, not only by acquiring the power of money, but also because *money* had become, through him and also apart from him, a world power, while the practical Jewish spirit has become the practical spirit of the Christian nations. The Jews have emancipated themselves in so far as the Christians have become Jews.

Thus, for example, Captain Hamilton reports that the devout and politically free inhabitant of New England is a kind of Laocoon who makes not the least effort to escape from the serpents which are crushing him. *Mammon* is his idol which he adores not only with his lips but with the whole force of his body and mind. In his view the world is no more than a Stock Exchange, and he is convinced that he has no other destiny here below than to become richer than his neighbour. Trade has seized upon all his thoughts, and he has no other recreation than to exchange objects. When he travels he carries, so to speak, his goods and his counter on his back and talks only of interest and profit. If he loses sight of his own business for an instant it is only in order to pry into the business of his competitors. [2]

In North America, indeed, the effective domination of the Christian world by Judaism has come to be manifested in a common and unambiguous form; the *preaching of the Gospel* itself, Christian preaching, has become an article of commerce, and the bankrupt trader in the church behaves like the prosperous clergyman in business. " This man whom

---

[1] BAUER, *Die Judenfrage*, p. 14.
[2] HAMILTON, op. cit., I, p. 213. Marx paraphrases this passage. [*Editor's note.*]

you see at the head of a respectable congregation began as a
trader; his business having failed he has become a minister.
This other began as a priest, but as soon as he had accumulated some money he abandoned the priesthood for trade.
In the eyes of many people the religious ministry is a veritable
industrial career." [1]

According to Bauer, it is " a hypocritical situation when,
in theory, the Jew is deprived of political rights, while in
practice he wields tremendous power and exercises on a
wholesale scale the political influence which is denied him in
minor matters." [2]

The contradiction which exists between the effective
political power of the Jew and his political rights, is the
contradiction between politics and the power of money in
general.   Politics is in principle superior to the power of
money, but in practice it has become its bondsman.

Judaism has maintained itself *alongside* Christianity, not
only because it constituted the religious criticism of
Christianity and embodied the doubt concerning the religious origins of Christianity, but equally because the
practical Jewish spirit—Judaism or commerce [3]—has per-
petuated itself in Christian society and has even attained its
highest development there.   The Jew, who occupies a
distinctive place in civil society, only manifests in a distinctive
way the Judaism of civil society.

Judaism has been preserved, not in spite of history, but by
history.

It is from its own entrails that civil society ceaselessly
engenders the Jew.

What was, in itself, the basis of the Jewish religion?
Practical need, egoism.

The monotheism of the Jews is, therefore, in reality, a

---

[1] BEAUMONT, op. cit., II, p. 179.
[2] BAUER, *Die Judenfrage*, p. 14.
[3] The German word *Judentum* had, in the language of the time, the secondary meaning of " commerce," and in this and other passages Marx exploits the
two senses of the word.   [*Editor's note.*]

polytheism of the numerous needs of man, a polytheism which makes even the lavatory an object of divine regulation. *Practical need, egoism*, is the principle of *civil society*, and is revealed as such in its pure form as soon as civil society has fully engendered the political state. The god of *practical need and self-interest* is *money*.

Money is the jealous god of Israel, beside which no other god may exist. Money abases all the gods of mankind and changes them into commodities. Money is the universal and self-sufficient *value* of all things. It has, therefore, deprived the whole world, both the human world and nature, of their own proper value. Money is the alienated essence of man's work and existence; this essence dominates him and he worships it.

The god of the Jews has been secularized and has become the god of this world. The bill of exchange is the real god of the Jew. His god is only an illusory bill of exchange.

The mode of perceiving nature, under the rule of private property and money, is a real contempt for, and a practical degradation of, nature, which does indeed exist in the Jewish religion but only as a creature of the imagination.

It is in this sense that Thomas Münzer declares it intolerable "that every creature should be transformed into property—the fishes in the water, the birds of the air, the plants of the earth: the creature too should become free." [1]

That which is contained in an abstract form in the Jewish religion—contempt for theory, for art, for history, and for man as an end in himself—is the *real, conscious* standpoint and the virtue of the man of money. Even the species-relation itself, the relation between man and woman, becomes an object of commerce. Woman is bartered away.

[1] Quoted from Thomas Münzer's pamphlet against Luther, "Hochverrusachte Schutzrede und Antwort wider das geistlose, sanftlebende Fleisch zu Wittenberg, welches mit verkehrter Weise durch den Diebstahl der heiligen Schrift die erbärmliche Christenheit also ganz jämmerlich besudelt hat." (p. B. iii. 1524.)

The *chimerical* nationality of the Jew is the nationality of the trader, and above all of the financier.

The law, without basis or reason, of the Jew, is only the religious caricature of morality and right in general, without basis or reason; the purely *formal* rites with which the world of self-interest encircles itself.

Here again the supreme condition of man is his *legal* status, his relationship to laws which are valid for him, not because they are the laws of his own will and nature, but because they are dominant and any infraction of them will be *avenged*.

Jewish Jesuitism, the same practical Jesuitism which Bauer discovers in the Talmud, is the relationship of the world of self-interest to the laws which govern this world, laws which the world devotes its principal arts to circumventing.

Indeed, the operation of this world within its framework of laws is impossible without the continual supersession of law.

Judaism could not develop further as a *religion*, in a theoretical form, because the world view of practical need is, by its very nature, circumscribed, and the delineation of its characteristics soon completed.

The religion of practical need could not, by its very nature, find its consummation in theory, but only in *practice*, just because practice is its truth.

Judaism could not create a new world. It could only bring the new creations and conditions of the world within its own sphere of activity, because practical need, the spirit of which is self-interest, is always passive, cannot expand at will, but *finds* itself extended as a result of the continued development of society.

Judaism attains its apogee with the perfection of civil society; but civil society only reaches perfection in the *Christian* world. Only under the sway of Christianity, which *objectifies all* national, natural, moral and theoretical relationships, could civil society separate itself completely from the life of the state, sever all the species-bonds of man, establish egoism and selfish need in their place, and dissolve the human world into a world of atomistic, antagonistic individuals.

Christianity issued from Judaism. It has now been re-absorbed into Judaism.

From the beginning, the Christian was the theorizing Jew; consequently, the Jew is the practical Christian. And the practical Christian has become a Jew again.

It was only in appearance that Christianity overcame real Judaism. It was too *refined*, too spiritual to eliminate the crudeness of practical need except by raising it into the ethereal realm.

Christianity is the sublime thought of Judaism; Judaism is the vulgar practical application of Christianity. But this practical application could only become universal when Christianity as perfected religion had accomplished, in a *theoretical* fashion, the alienation of man from himself and from nature.

It was only then that Judaism could attain universal domination and could turn alienated man and alienated nature into *alienable*, saleable objects, in thrall to egoistic need and huckstering.

Objectification is the practice of alienation. Just as man, so long as he is engrossed in religion, can only objectify his essence by an *alien* and fantastic being; so under the sway of egoistic need, he can only affirm himself and produce objects in practice by subordinating his products and his own activity to the domination of an alien entity, and by attributing to them the significance of an alien entity, namely money.

In its perfected practice the spiritual egoism of Christianity necessarily becomes the material egoism of the Jew, celestial need is transmuted into terrestrial need, subjectivism into self-interest. The tenacity of the Jew is to be explained, not by his religion, but rather by the human basis of his religion —practical need and egoism.

It is because the essence of the Jew was universally realized and secularized in civil society, that civil society could not convince the Jew of the *unreality* of his *religious* essence, which is precisely the ideal representation of practical need.   It is not only, therefore, in the Pentateuch and the Talmud, but also in contemporary society, that we find the essence of the present-day Jew; not as an abstract essence, but as one which is supremely empirical, not only as a limitation of the Jew, but as the Jewish narrowness of society.

As soon as society succeeds in abolishing the *empirical* essence of Judaism—huckstering and its conditions—the Jew becomes *impossible*, because his consciousness no longer has an object. The subjective basis of Judaism—practical need—assumes a human form, and the conflict between the individual, sensuous existence of man and his species-existence, is abolished.

The *social* emancipation of the Jew is the *emancipation of society from Judaism.*

CONTRIBUTION TO THE CRITIQUE OF HEGEL'S PHILOSOPHY OF RIGHT

INTRODUCTION

CONTRIBUTION TO THE CRITIQUE OF HEGEL'S PHILOSOPHY OF RIGHT

INTRODUCTION

For Germany, the *criticism of religion* has been largely completed; and the criticism of religion is the premise of all criticism.

The *profane* existence of error is compromised once its *celestial oratio pro aris et focis* has been refuted. Man, who has found in the fantastic reality of heaven, where he sought a supernatural being, only his own reflection, will no longer be tempted to find only the *semblance* of himself—a non-human being—where he seeks and must seek his true reality.

The basis of irreligious criticism is this: *man makes religion*; religion does not make man. Religion is indeed man's self-consciousness and self-awareness so long as he has not found himself or has lost himself again. But *man* is not an abstract being, squatting outside the world. Man is *the human world*, the state, society. This state, this society, produce religion which is an *inverted world consciousness*, because they are an *inverted world*. Religion is the general theory of this world, its encyclopedic compendium, its logic in popular form, its spiritual *point d'honneur*, its enthusiasm, its moral sanction, its solemn complement, its general basis of consolation and justification. It is *the fantastic realization* of the human being inasmuch as the *human being* possesses no true reality. The struggle against religion is, therefore, indirectly a struggle against *that world* whose spiritual *aroma* is religion.

Religious suffering is at the same time an *expression* of real suffering and a *protest* against real suffering. Religion is the sigh of the oppressed creature, the sentiment of a heartless

43

world, and the soul of soulless conditions. It is the *opium* of the people.

The abolition of religion as the *illusory* happiness of men, is a demand for their *real* happiness. The call to abandon their illusions about their condition is a *call to abandon a condition which requires illusions.* The criticism of religion is, therefore, *the embryonic criticism of this vale of tears* of which religion is the *halo.*

Criticism has plucked the imaginary flowers from the chain, not in order that man shall bear the chain without caprice or consolation but so that he shall cast off the chain and pluck the living flower. The criticism of religion disillusions man so that he will think, act and fashion his reality as a man who has lost his illusions and regained his reason; so that he will revolve about himself as his own true sun. Religion is only the illusory sun about which man revolves so long as he does not revolve about himself.

It is the *task of history,* therefore, once the *other-world of truth* has vanished, to establish the *truth of this world.* The immediate *task of philosophy,* which is in the service of history, is to unmask human self-alienation in its *secular form* now that it has been unmasked in its *sacred form.* Thus the criticism of heaven is transformed into the criticism of earth, the *criticism of religion* into the *criticism of law,* and the *criticism of theology* into the *criticism of politics.*

The following exposition [1]—which is a contribution to this undertaking—does not deal directly with the original but with a copy, the German *philosophy* of the state and of right, for the simple reason that it deals with Germany.

If one were to begin with the *status quo* itself in Germany, even in the most appropriate way, i.e. negatively, the result

---

[1] Marx refers to his intention to publish a critical study of Hegel's *Philosophy of Right*, to which this essay was an introduction. One of Marx's preliminary manuscripts for such a study has been published entitled " Aus der Kritik der Hegelschen Rechtsphilosophie. Kritik des Hegelschen Staatsrechts." (*MEGA* I 1 1, pp. 403–553.) The "Economic and Philosophical Manuscripts" is another version of this study; *see* Marx's comment (p. 63 below). [*Editor's note.*]

would still be an *anachronism*. Even the negation of our political present is already a dusty fact in the historical lumber room of modern nations. I may negate powdered wigs, but I am still left with unpowdered wigs. If I negate the German situation of 1843 I have, according to French chronology, hardly reached the year 1789, and still less the vital centre of the present day.

German history, indeed, prides itself upon a development which no other nation had previously accomplished, or will ever imitate in the historical sphere. We have shared in the restorations of modern nations without ever sharing in their revolutions. We have been restored, first because other nations have dared to make revolutions, and secondly because other nations have suffered counter-revolutions; in the first case because our masters were afraid, and in the second case because they were not afraid. Led by our shepherds, we have only once kept company with liberty and that was on the *day of its internment*.

A school of thought, which justifies the infamy of today by that of yesterday, which regards every cry from the serf under the knout as a cry of rebellion once the knout has become time-honoured, ancestral and historical, a school for which history shows only its *a posteriori* as the God of Israel did for his servant Moses—the *Historical school of law* [1]—might be supposed to have invented German history, if it were not in fact itself an invention of German history. A Shylock, but a servile Shylock, it swears upon its bond, its historical, Christian-Germanic bond, for every pound of flesh cut from the heart of the people.

[1] The principal representative of the Historical school was F. K. von Savigny (1779–1861) who outlined its programme in his book *Vom Beruf unserer Zeit für Gesetzgebung und Rechtswissenschaft* (On the Vocation of our Age for Legislation and Jurisprudence), Heidelberg, 1814. Marx attended Savigny's lectures at the University of Berlin in 1836–7; but he was more attracted by the lectures of Eduard Gans (1798–1839), a liberal Hegelian influenced by Saint-Simon, who emphasized in his teaching and writings the part played by reason in the development of law, and who was Savigny's principal opponent in Berlin. [*Editor's note.*]

On the other hand, good-natured enthusiasts, German chauvinists by temperament and enlightened liberals by reflection, seek our history of liberty beyond our history, in the primeval Teutonic forests. But how does the history of our liberty differ from the history of the wild boar's liberty, if it is only to be found in the forests? And as the proverb has it: what is shouted into the forest, the forest echoes back. So peace upon the primeval Teutonic forests!

But *war* upon the state of affairs in Germany! By all means! This state of affairs is *beneath the level of history, beneath all criticism*; nevertheless it remains an object of criticism just as the criminal who is beneath humanity remains an object of the *executioner*. In its struggle against this state of affairs criticism is not a passion of the head, but the head of passion. It is not a lancet but a weapon. Its object is an *enemy* which it aims not to refute but to *destroy*. For the spirit of this state of affairs has already been refuted. It is not, in itself, an object worthy of our thought; it is an *existence* as contemptible as it is despised. Criticism itself has no need of any further elucidation of this object, for it has already understood it. Criticism is no longer an end in itself, but simply a means; *indignation* is its essential mode of feeling, and *denunciation* its principal task.

It is a matter of depicting the stifling pressure which the different social spheres exert upon each other, the universal but passive ill-humour, the complacent but self-deluding narrowness of spirit; all this incorporated in a system of government which lives by conserving this paltriness, and is itself *paltriness in government*.

What a spectacle! Society is infinitely divided into the most diverse races, which confront each other with their petty antipathies, bad conscience and coarse mediocrity; and which, precisely because of their ambiguous and mistrustful situation, are treated without exception, though in different ways, as merely tolerated existences by their masters. And they are forced to recognize and acknowledge this fact of being *dominated, governed* and *possessed*, as a *concession from heaven!* On the other side are the rulers themselves, whose greatness is in inverse proportion to their number.

The criticism which deals with this subject-matter is criticism in a hand-to-hand fight; and in such a fight it is of no interest to know whether the adversary is of the same rank, is noble or *interesting*—all that matters is to *strike* him. It is a question of denying the Germans an instant of illusion or resignation. The burden must be made still more irksome by awakening a consciousness of it, and shame must be made more shameful still by rendering it public. Every sphere of German society must be depicted as the *partie honteuse* of German society; and these petrified social conditions must be made to dance by singing their own melody to them. The nation must be taught to be *terrified* of itself, in order to give it *courage*. In this way an imperious need of the German nation will be satisfied, and the needs of nations are themselves the final causes of their satisfaction.

Even for the modern nations this struggle against the limited character of the German *status quo* does not lack interest; for the German *status quo* is the open *consummation of the ancien régime*, and the *ancien régime* is the *hidden defect of the modern state*. The struggle against the political present of the Germans is a struggle against the past of the modern nations, who are still continually importuned by the reminiscences of this past. It is instructive for the modern nations to see the *ancien régime*, which has played a *tragic* part in their history, play a *comic* part as a German ghost. The *ancien régime* had a *tragic* history, so long as it was the established power in the world while liberty was a personal fancy; in short, so long as it believed and had to believe in its own validity. So long as the *ancien régime*, as an existing world order, struggled against a new world which was just coming into existence, there was on its side a historical error but no personal error. Its decline was, therefore, tragic.

The present German régime, on the other hand, which is an anachronism, a flagrant contradiction of universally accepted axioms—the nullity of the *ancien régime* revealed to the whole world—only imagines that it believes in itself and asks the world to share its illusion.   If it believed in its own *nature* would it attempt to hide it beneath the *semblance* of an alien nature and look for its salvation in hypocrisy and sophistry?   The modern *ancien régime* is the comedian of a world order whose *real heroes* are dead.   History is thorough, and it goes through many stages when it conducts an ancient formation to its grave.   The last stage of a world-historical formation is comedy.   The Greek gods, already once mortally wounded in Aeschylus' tragedy *Prometheus Bound*, had to endure a second death, a comic death, in Lucian's dialogues.   Why should history proceed in this way?   So that mankind shall separate itself *gladly* from its past.   We claim this *joyful* historical destiny for the political powers of Germany.

But as soon as criticism concerns itself with modern social and political reality, and thus arrives at genuine human problems, it must either go outside the German *status quo* or approach its object indirectly.   For example, the relation of industry, of the world of wealth in general, to the political world is a major problem of modern times.   In what form does this problem begin to preoccupy the Germans?   In the form of *protective tariffs*, the *system of prohibition*, the *national economy*.   German chauvinism has passed from men to matter, so that one fine day our knights of cotton and heroes of iron found themselves metamorphosed into patriots.   The sovereignty of monopoly within the country has begun to be recognized since *sovereignty vis-à-vis foreign countries* was attributed to it.   In Germany, therefore, a beginning is made with what came as the conclusion in France and England.   The old, rotten order against which these nations revolt in their theories, and which they bear only as chains are borne, is hailed in Germany as the dawn of a glorious future which as yet hardly dares to move from a cunning [1] theory to a ruthless practice.   While in France and England the problem is put in the form: *political economy* or the *rule of society over wealth*; in Germany it is put in the form: *national economy* or the *rule of private property over nationality*.   Thus, in England and France it is a question of abolishing monopoly, which has developed to its final consequences; while in Germany it is a question of proceeding to the final consequences of monopoly.   There it is a question of the solution; here, only a question of the collision.   We can see very well from this example how modern problems are presented in Germany; the example shows that our history, like a raw recruit, has so far only had to do extra drill on old and hackneyed historical matters.

If the *whole* of German development were at the level of German *political* development, a German could have no greater part in contemporary problems than can a *Russian*. If the individual is not restricted by the limitations of his country, still less is the nation liberated by the liberation of one individual.   The fact that a Scythian was one of the Greek philosophers [2] did not enable the Scythians to advance a single step towards Greek culture.

Fortunately, we Germans are not Scythians.

Just as the nations of the ancient world lived their pre-history in the imagination, in mythology, so we Germans have lived our post-history in thought, in *philosophy*.   We are the *philosophical* contemporaries of the present day without being its *historical* contemporaries.   German philosophy is the *ideal prolongation* of German history.   When, therefore, we criticize, instead of the *oeuvres incomplètes* of our real history, the *oeuvres posthumes* of our ideal history—*philosophy*, our criticism stands at the centre of the problems of which the

---

[1] In German, *listigen*; Marx is punning upon the name of Friedrich List (1789–1846), the apostle of industrial capitalism in a nationalist and protectionist form, who published in 1840 his influential book, *Das nationale System der politischen Ökonomie*. [*Editor's note.*]

[2] Anacharsis. [*Editor's note.*]

present age says: *that is the question.* That which constitutes, for the advanced nations, a *practical* break with modern political conditions, is in Germany where these conditions do not yet exist, virtually a *critical* break with their philosophical reflection.

The German *philosophy of right and of the state* is the only German history which is *al pari* with the *official* modern times. The German nation is obliged, therefore, to connect its dream history with its present conditions, and to subject to criticism not only these existing conditions but also their abstract continuation. Its future cannot be restricted either to the direct negation of its real juridical and political circumstances, or to the direct realization of its ideal juridical and political circumstances. The direct negation of its real circumstances already exists in its ideal circumstances, while it has almost outlived the realization of its ideal circumstances in the contemplation of neighbouring nations. It is with good reason, therefore, that the *practical* political party in Germany demands the *negation of philosophy.* Its error does not consist in formulating this demand, but in limiting itself to a demand which it does not, and cannot, make effective. It supposes that it can achieve this negation by turning its back on philosophy, looking elsewhere, and murmuring a few trite and ill-humoured phrases. Because of its narrow outlook it does not take account of philosophy as part of *German* reality, and even regards philosophy as beneath the level of German practical life and its theories. You demand as a point of departure real germs of life, but you forget that the real germ of life of the German nation has so far sprouted only in its *cranium.* In short, *you cannot abolish philosophy without realizing it.*

The same error was committed, but in the opposite direction, by the *theoretical* party which originated in philosophy.

In the present struggle, this party saw *only* the *critical struggle of philosophy against the German world.* It did not consider that *previous philosophy* itself belongs to this world and is its complement, even if only an ideal complement. Critical as regards its counterpart, it was not self-critical. It took as its point of departure the *presuppositions* of philosophy; and either accepted the conclusions which philosophy had reached or else presented as direct philosophical demands and conclusions, demands and conclusions drawn from elsewhere. But these latter—assuming their legitimacy—can only be achieved by the *negation of previous philosophy*, that is, philosophy as philosophy. We shall provide later a more comprehensive account of this party. Its principal defect may be summarized as follows: *it believed that it could realize philosophy without abolishing it.*

The criticism of the *German philosophy of right and of the state* which was given its most logical, profound and complete expression by Hegel, is at once the critical analysis of the modern state and of the reality connected with it, and the definitive negation of all the past *forms of consciousness in German jurisprudence and politics*, whose most distinguished and most general expression, raised to the level of a *science*, is precisely the *speculative philosophy of right*. If it was only Germany which could produce the speculative philosophy of right—this extravagant and abstract thought about the modern state, the reality of which remains in the beyond (even if this beyond is only across the Rhine)—the *German* representative of the modern state, on the contrary, which leaves out of account the *real man* was itself only possible because, and to the extent that, the modern state itself leaves the *real man* out of account or only satisfies the *whole* man in an illusory way. In politics, the Germans have *thought* what other nations have *done*. Germany has been their *theoretical consciousness*. The abstraction and presumption of its philosophy was in step with the partial and stunted character of their reality. If, therefore, the *status quo* of the *German political system* expresses the *consummation of the ancien régime*, the thorn in the flesh of the modern state, the *status quo* of

German political science expresses the *imperfection of the modern state* itself, the degeneracy of its flesh.

As the determined adversary of the previous form of German political consciousness, the criticism of the speculative philosophy of right does not remain within its own sphere, but leads on to *tasks* which can only be solved by *means of practical activity*.

The question then arises: can Germany attain a practical activity *à la hauteur des principes*; that is to say, a revolution which will raise it not only to the *official level* of the modern nations, but to the *human level* which will be the immediate future of those nations.

It is clear that the arm of criticism cannot replace the criticism of arms. Material force can only be overthrown by material force; but theory itself becomes a material force when it has seized the masses. Theory is capable of seizing the masses when it demonstrates *ad hominem*, and it demonstrates *ad hominem* as soon as it becomes radical. To be radical is to grasp things by the root. But for man the root is man himself. What proves beyond doubt the radicalism of Germany theory, and thus its practical energy, is that it begins from the resolute *positive* abolition of religion. The criticism of religion ends with the doctrine that *man is the supreme being for man*. It ends, therefore, with the *categorical imperative to overthrow all those conditions* in which man is an abased, enslaved, abandoned, contemptible being—conditions which can hardly be better described than in the exclamation of a Frenchman on the occasion of a proposed tax upon dogs: "Wretched dogs! They want to treat you like men!"

Even from the historical standpoint theoretical emancipation has a specific practical importance for Germany. In fact Germany's *revolutionary* past is theoretical—it is the *Reformation*. In that period the revolution originated in the brain of a monk, today in the brain of the philosopher.

Luther, without question, overcame servitude through

devotion but only by substituting servitude through *conviction*. He shattered the faith in authority by restoring the authority of faith. He transformed the priests into laymen by turning laymen into priests. He liberated man from external religiosity by making religiosity the innermost essence of man. He liberated the body from its chains because he fettered the heart with chains.

But if Protestantism was not the solution it did at least pose the problem correctly. It was no longer a question, thereafter, of the layman's struggle against the priest outside himself, but of his struggle against his *own internal priest*, against his own *priestly nature*. And if the Protestant metamorphosis of German laymen into priests emancipated the lay popes— the *princes* together with their clergy, the privileged and the philistines—the philosophical metamorphosis of the priestly Germans into men will emancipate the *people*. But just as emancipation will not be confined to princes, so the *secularization* of property will not be limited to the *confiscation of church property*, which was practised especially by hypocritical Prussia. At that time, the Peasant War, the most radical event in German history, came to grief because of theology.

Today, when theology itself has come to grief, the most unfree phenomenon in German history—our *status quo*—will be shattered by philosophy. On the eve of the Reformation official Germany was the most abject servant of Rome. On the eve of its revolution Germany is the abject servant of those who are far inferior to Rome; of Prussia and Austria, of petty squires and philistines.

But a *radical* revolution in Germany seems to encounter a major difficulty.

Revolutions need a *passive* element, a *material* basis. Theory is only realized in a people so far as it fulfils the needs of the people. Will there correspond to the monstrous discrepancy between the demands of German thought and the answers of German reality a similar discrepancy between civil society and the state, and within civil society itself?

Will theoretical needs be directly practical needs? It is not enough that thought should seek to realize itself; reality must also strive towards thought.

But Germany has not passed through the intermediate stage of political emancipation at the same time as the modern nations. It has not yet attained in practice those stages which it has transcended in theory. How could Germany, in *salta mortale*, surmount not only its own barriers but also those of the modern nations, that is, those barriers which it must in reality experience and strive for as an emancipation from its own real barriers? A radical revolution can only be a revolution of radical needs, for which the conditions and breeding ground appear to be lacking.

But if Germany accompanied the development of the modern nations only through the abstract activity of thought, without taking an active part in the real struggles of this development, it has also experienced the *pains* of this development without sharing in its pleasures and partial satisfactions. The abstract activity on one side has its counterpart in the abstract suffering on the other. And one fine day Germany will find itself at the level of the European decadence, before ever having attained the level of European emancipation. It will be comparable to a fetishist who is sickening from the diseases of Christianity.

If the *German governments* are examined it will be found that the circumstances of the time, the situation of Germany, the outlook of German culture, and lastly their own fortunate instinct, all drive them to combine the *civilized deficiencies* of the *modern political world* (whose advantages we do not enjoy) with the *barbarous deficiencies* of the *ancien régime* (which we enjoy in full measure); so that Germany must participate more and more, if not in the reason at least in the unreason of those political systems which transcend its *status quo*. Is there, for example, any country in the whole world which shares with such naïveté as so-called constitutional Germany all the illusions of the constitutional régime without sharing its realities? And was it not, of necessity, a German government which had the idea of combining the torments of censorship with the torments of the French September laws [1] which presuppose the liberty of the Press? Just as the gods of all the nations were to be found in the Roman Pantheon, so there will be found in the Holy Roman German Empire all the *sins* of all the forms of State. That this eclecticism will attain an unprecedented degree is assured in particular by the *politico-aesthetic gourmandise* of a German king who proposes to play all the roles of royalty—feudal or bureaucratic, absolute or constitutional, autocratic or democratic—if not in the person of the people at least in his *own* person, and if not for the people, at least for *himself*. *Germany, as the deficiency of present-day politics constituted into a system*, will not be able to demolish the specific German barriers without demolishing the general barriers of present-day politics.

It is not *radical* revolution, *universal human* emancipation, which is a Utopian dream for Germany, but rather a partial, *merely* political revolution which leaves the pillars of the building standing. What is the basis of a partial, merely political revolution? Simply this: a *section of civil society* emancipates itself and attains universal domination; a determinate class undertakes, from its *particular situation*, a general emancipation of society. This class emancipates society as a whole, but only on condition that the whole of society is in the same situation as this class; for example, that it possesses or can easily acquire money or culture.

No class in civil society can play this part unless it can arouse, in itself and in the masses, a moment of enthusiasm in which it associates and mingles with society at large, identifies itself with it, and is felt and recognized as the *general representative* of this society. Its aims and interests must genuinely

---

[1] The laws of September 1835 which increased the financial guarantees required from the publishers of newspapers and introduced heavier penalties for " subversive " publications. [*Editor's note.*]

be the aims and interests of society itself, of which it becomes in reality the social head and heart. It is only in the name of general interests that a particular class can claim general supremacy. In order to attain this liberating position, and the political direction of all spheres of society, revolutionary energy and consciousness of its own power do not suffice. For a *popular revolution* and the *emancipation of a particular class* of civil society to coincide, for *one* class to represent the whole of society, another class must concentrate in itself all the evils of society, a particular class must embody and represent a general obstacle and limitation. A particular social sphere must be regarded as the *notorious crime* of the whole society, so that emancipation from this sphere appears as a general emancipation. For *one* class to be the liberating class *par excellence*, it is necessary that another class should be openly the oppressing class. The negative significance of the French nobility and clergy produced the positive significance of the bourgeoisie, the class which stood next to them and opposed them.

But in Germany every class lacks the logic, insight, courage and clarity which would make it a negative representative of society. Moreover, there is also lacking in every class the generosity of spirit which identifies itself, if only for a moment, with the popular mind; that genius which pushes material force to political power, that revolutionary daring which throws at its adversary the defiant phrase: *I am nothing and I should be everything*. The essence of German morality and honour, in classes as in individuals, is a *modest egoism* which displays, and allows others to display, its own narrowness. The relation between the different spheres of German society is, therefore, not dramatic, but epic. Each of these spheres begins to be aware of itself and to establish itself beside the others, not from the moment when it is oppressed, but from the moment that circumstances, without any action of its own, have created a new sphere which it can in turn oppress. Even the *moral sentiment of the German middle class* has no other basis than the consciousness of being the representative of the narrow and limited mediocrity of all the other classes.   It is not only the German kings, therefore, who ascend their thrones *mal à propos*.   Each sphere of civil society suffers a defeat before gaining the victory; it erects its own barrier before having destroyed the barrier which opposes it; it displays the narrowness of its views before having displayed their generosity, and thus every opportunity of playing an important role has passed before it properly existed, and each class, at the very moment when it begins its struggle against the class above it, remains involved in a struggle against the class beneath.   For this reason, the princes are in conflict with the monarch, the bureaucracy with the nobility, the bourgeoisie with all of them, while the proletariat is already beginning its struggle with the bourgeoisie.   The middle class hardly dares to conceive the idea of emancipation from its own point of view before the development of social conditions, and the progress of political theory, show that this point of view is already antiquated, or at least disputable.

In France it is enough to be something in order to desire to be everything.   In Germany no one has the right to be anything without first renouncing everything.   In France partial emancipation is a basis for complete emancipation. In Germany complet emancipation is a *conditio sine qua non* for any partial emancipation.   In France it is the reality, in Germany the impossibility, of a progressive emancipation which must give birth to complete liberty.   In France every class of the population is *politically idealistic* and considers itself first of all, not as a particular class, but as the representative of the general needs of society.   The role of liberator can, therefore, pass successively in a dramatic movement to different classes in the population, until it finally reaches the class which achieves social freedom; no longer assuming certain conditions external to man, which are none the less created by human society, but organizing all the conditions of human life on the basis of social freedom. In Germany, on the contrary, where practical life is as little intellectual as intellectual life is practical, no class of civil society feels the need for, or the ability to achieve, a general emancipation, until it is forced to it by its *immediate* situation, by *material* necessity and by its *fetters themselves*.

Where is there, then, a *real* possibility of emancipation in Germany?

This is our reply. A class must be formed which has *radical chains*, a class in civil society which is not a class of civil society, a class which is the dissolution of all classes, a sphere of society which has a universal character because its sufferings are universal, and which does not claim a *particular redress* because the wrong which is done to it is not a *particular wrong* but *wrong in general*. There must be formed a sphere of society which claims no *traditional* status but only a human status, a sphere which is not opposed to particular consequences but is totally opposed to the assumptions of the German political system; a sphere, finally, which cannot emancipate itself without emancipating itself from all the other spheres of society, without, therefore, emancipating all these other spheres, which is, in short, a *total loss* of humanity and which can only redeem itself by a *total redemption of humanity*. This dissolution of society, as a particular class, is the *proletariat*.

The proletariat is only beginning to form itself in Germany, as a result of the industrial movement. For what constitutes the proletariat is not *naturally existing* poverty, but poverty *artificially produced*, is not the mass of people mechanically oppressed by the weight of society, but the mass resulting from the *disintegration* of society and above all from the disintegration of the middle class. Needless to say, however, the numbers of the proletariat are also increased by the victims of natural poverty and of Christian-Germanic serfdom.

When the proletariat announces the *dissolution of the existing social order*, it only declares the *secret of its* own existence, for it *is* the *effective* dissolution of this order. When the proletariat demands the *negation of private property* it only lays down as a *principle for society* what society has already made a principle *for the proletariat*, and what the *latter* already involuntarily embodies as the negative result of society. Thus the proletarian has the same right, in relation to the new world which is coming into being, as the *German king* has in relation to the existing world when he calls the people *his* people or a horse *his* horse. In calling the people his private property the king simply declares that the owner of private property is king.

Just as philosophy finds its *material* weapons in the proletariat, so the proletariat finds its *intellectual* weapons in philosophy. And once the lightning of thought has penetrated deeply into this virgin soil of the people, the *Germans* will emancipate themselves and become *men*.

Let us sum up these results. The emancipation of Germany is only possible *in practice* if one adopts the point of view of that theory according to which man is the highest being for man. Germany will not be able to emancipate itself from the *Middle Ages* unless it emancipates itself at the same time from the *partial* victories over the Middle Ages. In Germany *no* type of enslavement can be abolished unless *all* enslavement is destroyed. Germany, which likes to get to the bottom of things, can only make a revolution which upsets *the whole order* of things. The *emancipation of Germany* will be an *emancipation of man*. *Philosophy* is the *head* of this emancipation and the *proletariat* is its *heart*. Philosophy can only be realized by the abolition of the proletariat, and the proletariat can only be abolished by the realization of philosophy.

ECONOMIC AND PHILOSOPHICAL
MANUSCRIPTS

PREFACE [1]

(from the Third Manuscript)

I HAVE already announced in the *Deutsch-Französische Jahrbücher* [2] a forthcoming critique of jurisprudence and political science in the form of a critique of the *Hegelian* philosophy of right. However, in preparing the work for publication it became apparent that a combination of the criticism directed solely against the speculative theory with the criticism of the various subjects would be quite unsuitable; it would hamper the development of the argument and make it more difficult to follow. Moreover, I could only have compressed such a wealth of diverse subjects into a *single* work by writing in an aphoristic style, and such an aphoristic presentation would have given the *impression* of arbitrary systematization. I shall, therefore, publish my critique of law, morals, politics, etc. in a number of independent brochures; and finally I shall endeavour, in a separate work, to present the interconnected whole, to show the relationships between the parts, and to provide a critique of the speculative treatment of this material. That is why, in the present work, the relationships of political economy with the state, law, morals, civil life, etc. are touched upon only to the extent that political economy itself expressly deals with these subjects.

It is hardly necessary to assure the reader who is familiar with political economy that my conclusions are the fruit of an entirely empirical analysis, based upon a careful critical study of political economy.

It goes without saying that in addition to the French and

---

[1] I have not included the few passages which Marx deleted in the manuscript. They add nothing of interest to the text. [*Editor's note.*]

[2] Marx refers to his essay " Zur Kritik der Hegelschen Rechtsphilosophie," which is translated in the present volume, pp. 43–59 above. [*Editor's note.*]

English socialists I have also used German socialist writings. But the *original* and important German works on this subject —apart from the writings of Weitling—are limited to the essays published by Hess in the *Einundzwanzig Bogen*,[1] and Engels' " Umrisse zur [2] Kritik des Nationalökonomie " in the *Deutsch-Französische Jahrbücher*.[3] In the latter publication I myself have indicated in a very general way the basic elements of the present work.[4]

The *positive*, humanistic and naturalistic criticism begins with Feuerbach. The less blatant Feuerbach's writings, the more certain, profound, extensive and lasting is their influence; they are the only writings since Hegel's *Phenomenology* and *Logic* which contain a real theoretical revolution.

Unlike the *critical theologians* of our time I have considered that a critical exposition of the *Hegelian dialectic* and general philosophy, which forms the final chapter of the present work, is absolutely essential, for the task has not yet been accomplished. This *lack of thoroughness* is not accidental, for the *critical* theologian remains a *theologian*. He must either begin from certain presuppositions of philosophy accepted as authoritative, or, if doubts have arisen in his mind concerning the philosophical presuppositions in the course of criticism and as a result of other people's discoveries, he abandons them in a cowardly and unjustified manner, *abstracts* from them, and shows both his servile dependence upon them and his resentment of this dependence in a negative, unconscious and sophistical way.

Looked at more closely, *theological criticism*, which was at the beginning of the movement a genuinely progressive factor, is seen to be, in the last analysis, no more than the

---

[1] *Einundzwanzig Bogen aus der Schweiz*, edited by Georg Herwegh. First part, Zürich and Winterthur, 1843. Marx refers to the articles by Hess: " Sozialismus und Kommunismus," pp. 79–91; " Die eine und ganze Freiheit," pp. 92–7; " Philosophie der Tat," pp. 309–31. [*Editor's note.*]

[2] This should read *zu einer*. [*Editor's note.*]

[3] *Deutsch-Französische Jahrbücher*, pp. 86–114.

[4] See note 1 on p. 44 above. [*Editor's note.*]

culmination and consequence of the old *philosophical,* and especially *Hegelian, transcendentalism* distorted into a *theological caricature.* I shall describe elsewhere, at greater length, this interesting act of historical justice, this Nemesis which now destines theology, ever the infected spot of philosophy, to portray in itself the negative dissolution of philosophy, i.e. the process of its decay.

FIRST MANUSCRIPT

WAGES OF LABOUR

[I] *Wages* are determined by the bitter struggle between capitalist and worker. The necessary victory of the capitalist. The capitalist can live longer without the worker than can the worker without the capitalist. Combination among capitalists is usual and effective, whereas combination among workers is proscribed and has painful consequences for them. Moreover, the landowner and capitalist can supplement their revenues with the profits of industry, while the worker has neither ground rent nor interest on capital to add to his industrial earnings. Hence, the intensity of competition among workers. Only for the workers, therefore, is the separation of capital, landed property and labour an inescapable, vital and harmful separation. Capital and landed property need not remain in this abstraction, as must the labour of the workers.

For the worker, therefore, the separation of capital, ground rent and labour is fatal.

The lowest and the only necessary rate of wages is that which provides for the subsistence of the worker during work and for a supplement adequate to raise a family so that the race of workers does not die out. According to Smith, the normal wage is the lowest which is compatible with common humanity [1] that is, with a bestial existence.

The demand for men necessarily regulates the production of men, as of every other commodity. If the supply greatly exceeds the demand, then a section of the workers declines into beggary or starvation. Thus, the existence of the worker is reduced to the same conditions as the existence of any other commodity. The worker has become a commodity and he is

---

[1] ADAM SMITH, *The Wealth of Nations* (2 vols. Everyman edition) I, p. 61. Marx quotes from the French translation: *Recherches sur la nature et les causes de la richesse des nations*; par Adam Smith. Traduction nouvelle, avec les notes et observations; par Germain Garnier. T. I–IV. Paris, 1802.

fortunate if he can find a buyer. And the demand, upon which the worker's life depends, is determined by the caprice of the wealthy and the capitalists. If the supply exceeds the demand, one of the elements entering into price—profit, ground rent, wages—will be paid below its *rate*; a part of the supply of these factors will then be withdrawn from this use and the market price will gravitate towards the natural price. But (1) where there is an extensive division of labour it is extremely difficult for the worker to direct his labour into other uses, and (2) because of his subordination to the capitalist, he is the first to suffer hardship.

The worker, therefore, loses most, and loses inevitably, from the gravitation of the market price to the natural price. At the same time, it is the ability of the capitalist to put his capital to other uses which either condemns the worker, who is limited to one employment of his labour, to starvation or forces him to accept every demand which the capitalist makes.

[II] The adventitious and sudden variations in market price affect ground rent less than those parts of the price which comprise profit and wages, but they affect profit less than wages. In most cases, for every wage which rises there is one which remains *stationary* and one which *falls*.

The worker does not necessarily gain when the capitalist gains, but he necessarily loses with him. Thus, the worker does not gain if the capitalist succeeds in maintaining the market price above the natural price by means of a manufacturing or commercial secret, a monopoly or the favourable situation of his property.

Further, *the prices of labour are much more stable than the prices of provisions.* They often vary inversely. In a dear year, wages fall, because of the decline in demand, but rise because of the increase in the price of provisions; so they balance. In any event, numbers of workers are without bread. In cheap years, wages rise because of increased demand, and fall because of the low prices of provisions; so they balance.[1]

[1] SMITH, I, pp. 76–7.

Another disadvantage of the worker: *The wage rates of different kinds of workers vary much more than do the profits in the different branches in which capital is employed.* In work, all the natural, spiritual and social differences of individual activity appear and are differently remunerated, while dead capital maintains an unvarying performance and is indifferent to *real* individual activity.

In general, it should be noted that where worker and capitalist both suffer, the worker suffers in his existence while the capitalist suffers in the profit on his dead mammon.

The worker has not only to struggle for his physical means of subsistence; he must also struggle to obtain work, i.e. for the possibility and the means to perform his activity. Let us take three conditions in which society may find itself, and consider the situation of the worker in each of them.[1]

1. If the wealth of society is diminishing, the worker suffers most, for although the working class cannot gain as much as the class of property owners in a prosperous state of society, *none suffers so cruelly from its decline as the working class*.[2]

[III] 2. Let us next take a society in which wealth is increasing. This situation is the only one favourable to the worker. In this case, there is competition among capitalists and the demand for workers exceeds the supply. But, *in the first place*, the raising of wages leads to *overwork* among the workers. The more they want to earn the more they must sacrifice their time and perform slave labour in which their freedom is totally alienated in the service of avarice. In so doing they shorten their lives. This shortening of the life span is a favourable circumstance for the working class as a whole, since it makes necessary an ever renewed supply of workers. This class must always sacrifice a part of itself, in order not to be uined as a whole.

---

[1] SMITH, I, pp. 61–5.   [2] Ibid., p. 230.

Furthermore, when is a society in a condition of increasing wealth? When the capital and revenues of a country are growing. But this is only possible (α) when much labour is accumulated, for capital is accumulated labour; when, therefore, more of the worker's product is taken from him, when his own labour becomes opposed to him as an alien possession, and when his means of existence and his activity are increasingly concentrated in the hands of the capitalist. (β) The accumulation of capital increases the division of labour, and the division of labour increases the number of workers; conversely, the increasing number of workers increases the division of labour, and the increasing division of labour increases the accumulation of capital. As a result of the division of labour on one hand, and the accumulation of capital on the other hand, the worker becomes even more completely dependent upon labour, and upon a particular, extremely one-sided, mechanical kind of labour. Just as he is reduced, therefore, both spiritually and physically to the condition of a machine, and from being a man becomes merely an abstract activity and a belly, so he becomes increasingly dependent upon all the fluctuations in market price, in the employment of capital, and in the caprices of the rich. Equally, the growth of the class of men who are [IV] entirely dependent upon work increases competition among the workers and lowers their price. In the factory system this situation of the workers reaches its climax.

(γ) In a society where prosperity is increasing, only the very wealthiest can live from the interest on money. All others must employ their capital in business or trade. As a result the competition among capitalists increases. The concentration of capital becomes greater, the large capitalists ruin the small ones, and some of the former capitalists sink into the working class which, as a result of this accession of numbers, suffers a further decline in wages and falls into still greater dependence upon the few great capitalists. Since, at the same time, the number of capitalists has diminished, the competition among them for workers hardly exists any longer, whereas the competition among workers, on account of the increase in their numbers, has become greater, more abnormal and more violent. Consequently, a part of the working class falls into a condition of beggary or starvation, with the same necessity as a section of the middle capitalists falls into the working class.

Thus, even in the state of society which is most favourable to the worker, the inevitable result for the worker is overwork and premature death, reduction to a machine, enslavement to capital which accumulates in menacing opposition to him, renewed competition, and beggary or starvation for a part of the workers.

[V] Rising wages awake in the worker the same desire for enrichment as in the capitalist, but he can only satisfy it by the sacrifice of his body and spirit. Rising wages presuppose, and also bring about, the accumulation of capital; thus they increasingly alienate the product of labour from the worker. Likewise, the division of labour makes him increasingly one-sided and dependent, and introduces competition not only from other men but also from machines. Since the worker has been reduced to a machine, the machine can compete with him. Finally, just as the accumulation of capital increases the amount of industry, and thus the number of workers, so as a result of this accumulation the same volume of industry produces a *greater quantity of products* which leads to overproduction and culminates either in putting a great part of the workers out of work or in reducing their wages to the most wretched minimum. Such are the consequences of a state of society which is most favourable to the worker, namely a state of increasing, developing wealth.

Eventually, however, this state of growth must reach its culmination. What is then the condition of the worker?

3. " In a country which had acquired that full complement of riches . . . both the wages of labour and the profits of stock would probably be very low . . . the competition for employment would necessarily be so great as to reduce the wages of labour to what was barely sufficient to keep up the number of labourers, and, the country being already fully peopled, that number could never be augmented." [1]   The excess would have to die.

Thus, in a declining state of society, increasing misery of the worker; in a progressive state, complicated misery; and in the final state, stationary misery.

[VI] Since, however, according to Smith a society is not happy in which the majority suffers, and since the wealthiest state of society leads to suffering for the majority, while the economic system (in general, a society of private interests) leads to this wealthiest state, it follows that social *misery* is the goal of the economy.

It should be noted in connexion with the relation between worker and capitalist that the capitalist is more than compensated for wage increases by the reduction of working time, and that wage increases and increases in the interest on capital affect the price of commodities in the manner of simple and compound interest.

Let us now adopt entirely the viewpoint of the economist and compare in his terms the theoretical and practical claims of the workers.

He tells us that originally, and in principle, the *whole product* of labour belongs to the worker. But he adds immediately that, in fact, the worker receives only the smallest and absolutely indispensable part of the product; just so much as is necessary for him to exist as a worker, not as a human being, and for him to engender the slave class of workers, not humanity.

The economist tells us that everything is bought with

[1] SMITH, I, p. 84.

labour, and that capital is only accumulated labour, but he adds immediately that the worker, far from being able to buy everything must sell himself and his human qualities.

While the ground rent of the idle landowner usually amounts to one-third of the produce of the land, and the profit of the busy capitalist amounts to double the rate of interest, the surplus which the worker earns in the most favourable case is so little that two of his four children are condemned to die of hunger.[1] [VII] Whereas according to the economists, it is through labour alone that man increases the value of natural products, and labour is man's active property; yet according to this same political economy the landowner and the capitalist, who as such are merely privileged and idle gods, are everywhere raised above the worker and prescribe laws for him.

According to the economists labour is the only unchanging price of things, yet nothing is more fortuitous nor subject to greater fluctuations than the price of labour.

Although the division of labour increases the productive power of labour and the wealth and refinement of society, it impoverishes the worker and makes him into a machine. Although labour promotes the accumulation of capital and thus the growing prosperity of society, it makes the worker increasingly dependent upon the capitalist, exposes him to greater competition, and drives him into the hectic course of overproduction followed by a corresponding slump.

Although, according to the economists, the interest of the worker is never opposed to the interest of society, society is always and necessarily opposed to the interest of the worker.

According to the economists the interest of the worker is never opposed to that of society (1) because the increase of wages is more than compensated by the reduction of working time, with the other consequences discussed earlier, and (2) because in relation to society the whole gross product is

[1] Smith, I, p. 60.

net product, and net product only has meaning for the private individual.

I maintain, however, that labour itself, not only in present conditions but universally in so far as its purpose is merely the increase of wealth, is harmful and deleterious, and that this conclusion follows from the economist's own argument, though he is unaware of it.

In theory, rent and profit are *deductions* which wages have to bear. In reality, however, wages are a deduction which land and capital allow to the worker, a concession made by the product of labour to the worker, to labour.

In the declining state of society, the worker suffers most. The particular severity of his hardship is due to his situation as a worker, but the hardship in general is due to the condition of society.

In the progressive state of society, however, the decline and impoverishment of the worker is the product of his own labour and of the wealth produced by him. Misery, therefore, emerges spontaneously out of the essence of present-day labour.

The most opulent state of society, which is an ideal, yet one which is gradually approached and which is at least the aim of political economy and of civil society, is a state of *stationary misery* for the workers.

It is self-evident that political economy treats the *proletarian*, i.e. one who lives, without capital or rent, simply from labour, and from one-sided, abstract labour, merely as a *worker*. It can, therefore, propound the thesis that he, like a horse, must receive just as much as will enable him to work. Political economy does not deal with him in his free time, as a human being, but leaves this aspect to the criminal law, doctors, religion, statistical tables, politics and the workhouse beadle.

Let us now rise above the level of political economy and

seek from the foregoing argument, which was presented almost in the words of the economists, answers to two questions—

1. What is the significance, in the development of mankind, of this reduction of the greater part of mankind to abstract labour?

2. What errors are committed by the advocates of piece-meal reform, who either want to raise wages and thereby improve the condition of the working class, or (like Proudhon) regard *equality* of wages as the aim of the social revolution?

In political economy *labour* appears only in the form of *acquisitive activity.*

[VIII] " It may be argued that those occupations which call for specific aptitudes or a longer training, have become, on the whole, more remunerative, while the wages for mechanical, uniform activity, which anyone can be taught quickly and easily, have fallen and must necessarily fall as a result of competition. And it is just *this* kind of labour which, in the present state of the organization of work, is the most common. If a worker in the first category now earns seven times as much, and one in the second category just as much as fifty years ago, then certainly the *average* earnings of the two together are now four times as much. But if, in a particular country, only one thousand people are occupied in the first category, and one million in the second, then 999,000 are no better off than fifty years earlier; and indeed they are *worse off* if the prices of the necessaries of life have risen. And yet it is with such superficial *average* calculations that one deceives, or tries to deceive, oneself about the condition of the most numerous class of the population. In addition, wage *rates* are only *one* element affecting the *incomes* of workers, for it is necessary to take into account also the guaranteed *duration* of work, and there can be no question of this in the anarchic system of free competition with its ever-recurring recessions and stagnation. Finally we must take into account the normal *hours of work* at the present time and in the past. For the English workers in the cotton industry these have risen to twelve to sixteen hours a day in the past twenty-five years, i.e. precisely since the introduction of labour-saving machinery, through the acquisitiveness of the entrepreneurs.

[IX] This increase in one country and in one branch of industry must, according to the well-recognized rights of unlimited exploitation of the poor by the rich, become more or less established elsewhere." [1]

" Even if it were as true, as it is in fact false, that the average incomes of *all* classes of society had increased, the disparity of incomes could still have increased, and thus the contrast between wealth and poverty could have appeared more clearly. For it is *because* total production increases, and in the same measure, that needs, desires and wants also increase, and *relative* poverty may grow while *absolute* poverty diminishes. The Samoyed is not poor with his blubber and rancid fish, because in *his* isolated society everyone has the same needs. But in a *developing* society, which in the course of a decade increases its total production in relation to the population by one-third, the worker who earns the same amount at the end of ten years has not remained as well off as he was, but has become more needy by a third." [2]

---

[1] WILHELM SCHULZ, *Die Bewegung der Produktion, Eine geschichtlich-statistiche Abhandlung.* Zürich and Winterthur, 1843, p. 65. Marx quotes this passage with minor omissions. [*Editor's note.*]

[2] Ibid., pp. 65–6. Marx himself used the same argument later in discussing the " increasing misery of the working class," even in the most favourable condition of society when wages are increasing: " An appreciable rise in wages presupposes a rapid growth of productive capital. Rapid growth of productive capital calls forth just as rapid a growth of wealth, of luxury, of social needs and social pleasures. Therefore, although the pleasures of the labourer have increased, the social gratification which they afford has fallen in comparison with the increased pleasures of the capitalist, which are inaccessible to the worker, in comparison with the stage of development of society in general. Our wants and pleasures have their origin in society; we therefore measure them in relation to society; we do not measure them in relation to the objects which serve for their gratification. Since they are of a social

But political economy conceives the worker only as a draught animal, as a beast whose needs are strictly limited to bodily needs.

"A nation which aims to develop its culture more freely can no longer remain the slave of its material needs, the bondsman of its body. It needs above all leisure *time* in which to produce and to enjoy culture. The progress of the organization of work creates this leisure. A single worker in the cotton industry now often produces, with the aid of new sources of power and improved machines, as much as 100, or even 250–350 workers produced formerly. There are similar achievements even if not on the same scale in all branches of production, as a necessary consequence of the fact that the forces of nature are more and more forced into collaboration [X] with human labour. If the amount of time and human effort which was needed at an earlier date, in order to satisfy a given sum of material needs, has been reduced by half, then the time available for cultural creation and enjoyment, without any diminution in material well-being, has increased by the same amount. . . . But the division of the spoils which we take from Father Time on his own ground is still determined by blind and inequitable chance. It has been calculated that in France, at the present level of production, an average of five hours' work daily from each person able to work would suffice to meet all the material needs of society . . . in spite of the saving of time through the improvements in machinery the duration of slave labour in factories has increased for a large number of people." [1]

"The transition from complex craftmanship presupposes that the work is divided into simple operations. But only *a part* of the uniform, repetitive operations is performed by

nature, they are of a relative nature." *Wage-Labour and Capital* (Lectures delivered to the German Workingmen's Club of Brussels in 1847, and first published as a series of leading articles in the *Neue Rheinische Zeitung* from 4th April, 1849). [*Editor's note.*]

[1] Op. cit., pp. 67–8. Quoted with minor omissions. [*Editor's note.*]

the machines, another part by men. Such continued, uniform work is, by its nature (and this is confirmed by investigation), harmful to the spirit no less than to the body; and when the use of machinery is *associated* with the division of labour among large numbers of men all the disadvantages of the latter make their appearance. These disadvantages are revealed, for example, by the high mortality of factory [XI] workers. . . . [1] The important distinction between how far men work *with* machines or *as* machines, has not received attention. . . . [2] "

" But in the future life of mankind, the mindless forces of nature at work in machinery will be our slaves and serfs." [3]

" In the English cotton spinning mills only 158,818 men are employed as against 196,818 women. For every 100 male workers in the Lancashire cotton mills there are 103 women workers, and in Scotland 209 women for every 100 men. In the English flax factories in Leeds there were 147 women for every 100 male workers; in Dundee and on the East coast of Scotland, 280 women for every 100 men. In the English silk factories . . . many women workers; in the wool factories, which require greater physical strength, there are more men . . . Likewise, in the North American cotton mills, in 1833, there were 38,927 women employed along with 18,593 men. Thus, the changes in the organization of work have brought a wider sphere of gainful activity for women . . . a more independent economic situation for married women . . . and closer social relationships between the sexes." [4]

" In the English cotton spinning mills operated by water and steam power, there were employed in 1835: 20,558 children between 8–12 years of age; 35,867 between 12–13; and 108,208 between 13–18 . . . It is true that the progress of

---

[1] This sentence comes from a footnote in the original. [*Editor's note.*]
[2] Ibid., p. 69.
[3] Ibid., p. 74.   [4] Ibid., pp. 71–2.

machinery, in so far as it removes all uniform operations more and more from human hands; tends towards a complete elimination [XII] of these evils. But there stands in the way of such rapid progress the fact that the capitalists can acquire the labour of the lower classes, even of children, very easily and cheaply, and use it *instead* of making use of machinery." [1]

" Lord Brougham's appeal to the workers: 'Become capitalists!' . . . the evil that millions of men are only able to gain a bare living by exhausting, physically injurious, and morally and spiritually crippling labour; that they must even consider themselves fortunate to have the misfortune to find *such* work." [2]

" In order to live, therefore, the non-owners are obliged to put themselves directly or indirectly in the service of the owners, i.e. to become their dependants." [3]

" Domestic servants—wages (*gages*); workers—wages (*salaires*); clerks—salaries or emoluments (*traitements ou émoluments*)." [4]

. . . " hire out one's labour," " lend one's labour at interest," " work in place of someone else."

. . . " hire out the materials of labour," " lend the materials of labour at interest," " make someone else work in one's place." [5]

[XIII] " This economic order condemns men to such abject occupations, to such desolate and bitter degradation, that by comparison savagery appears a royal condition." [6] " Prostitution of the non-owning class in every respect." [7] Ragpicker.

Ch. Loudon, in the work *Solution du problème de la population*,

---

[1] Op. cit., pp. 70–1.
[2] Ibid., p. 60.
[3] C. PECQUEUR, *Théorie nouvelle d'économie sociale et politique, ou études sur l'organisation des sociétés.* Paris 1842, p. 409.
[4] Ibid., pp. 409–10.
[5] Ibid., p. 411.
[6] Ibid., pp. 417–18.
[7] Ibid., pp. 421 *et seq.*

Paris 1842,[1] gives the number of prostitutes in England as 60–70,000. The number of women of " doubtful virtue " is about the same.[2]

" The average life of these unfortunate creatures on the streets, after they have entered the career of vice, is about six or seven years. So that in order to maintain the number of 60–70,000 prostitutes, there must be at least 8–9,000 women, in the three kingdoms, who adopt this infamous trade each year; that is, about twenty-four new victims every day, or an average of *one* every hour. Thus, if the same proportion holds throughout the world, there must constantly be one and a half million of these miserable beings." [3]

" . . . the numbers of the poor increase with their poverty, and it is in the most extreme state of want that human beings crowd in the greatest number to contend for the right to suffer. . . . In 1821, the population of Ireland was 6,801,827. In 1831, it had risen to 7,764,010; an increase of fourteen per cent in ten years. In Leinster, a province where there is least poverty, the population increased only by eight per cent, whereas in Connaught, the poorest province, the increase attained twenty-one per cent (*Extract from Reports on Ireland published in England*, Vienna 1840)." [4] Political economy considers labour abstractly as a thing. Labour is a commodity; if the price is high the demand is great, and if the price is low the supply is great. As with other commodities, the price of labour must diminish; it is partly the competition between capitalist and worker, partly the competition among workers themselves, which brings this about. " The working population, seller of labour, is necessarily

---

[1] CHARLES LOUDON, *Solution du problème de la population et de la subsistance, soumise à un médecin dans une série de lettres*, Paris, 1842.

[2] Ibid., p. 228. Loudon gives these figures for the " three kingdoms," i.e. for the United Kingdom, not for England alone. [*Editor's note.*]

[3] Ibid., p. 229.

[4] EUGÈNE BURET, *De la misère des classes laborieuses en Angleterre et en France*. T. I–II. Paris, 1840. I., pp. 36–7. The latter part of this quotation is from footnote 1 to p. 36. [*Editor's note.*]

reduced to the smallest part of the product. . . . Is the theory of labour as a commodity anything but a disguised theory of servitude? " [1]   " Why was labour regarded only as an exchange value? " [2]   The large factories prefer to buy the labour of women and children, because it is cheaper than that of men.   " The worker, *vis-à-vis* his employer is not at all in the situation of *someone who sells freely* . . . the capitalist is always free to employ labour, and the worker is always obliged to sell it.   The value of labour is completely destroyed, if it is not sold at every instant.   Labour can neither be accumulated nor saved, unlike genuine commodities. [XIV] Labour is life, and if life is not exchanged every day for food it soon suffers and perishes.   If the life of man is to be a commodity, then slavery must be acknowledged." [3] Thus, if labour is a commodity, it is a commodity of the most wretched kind.   But even according to economic principles, it is not a commodity, since it is not the *free product of a free market*.   The present economic system " reduces at the same time the price and the reward of labour, it perfects the worker and degrades the man." [4]   " Industry has become a war, and commerce a game." [5]

The cotton-spinning machines (in England) were equivalent to 84,000,000 handworkers.

Industry has been up to now in the situation of a war of conquest; " it has expended the lives of those who composed its army with the same indifference as the great conquerors. Its aim was the possession of wealth, not the happiness of mankind." [6]   " These interests [i.e. economic interests] if left entirely to themselves . . . must necessarily enter into conflict; they have no other arbiter but war, and the decisions of war assign defeat and death to one side and victory to the other . . . it is in the conflict of opposed forces that science looks for order and equilibrium: *perpetual war* is, in

[1] BURET, op. cit., p. 43.   [2] Ibid., p. 44.
[3] Ibid., pp. 49–50.   Emphasis added by Marx.   [*Editor's note.*]
[4] Ibid., pp. 52–3.   [5] Ibid., p. 62.   [6] Ibid., p. 20.

its view, the only way of obtaining peace; this war is called competition." [1]

" The industrial war, in order to produce results, requires very large armies which can be concentrated upon one point and sacrificed without restraint. The soldiers of this army support the burdens which are placed upon them neither from devotion nor from duty, but only to escape the hard fate of hunger. They have neither affection nor gratitude for their chiefs; the latter are not bound to their subordinates by any feeling of goodwill, and regard them not as men but as instruments of production which must yield as much as possible and cost as little as possible. These herds of workers, ever more crowded together, do not even have the assurance that they will always be employed. Industry, which has called them together, only allows them to live when it needs them; as soon as it can dispense with them, it abandons them without the slightest concern. Then the workers who have been dismissed are obliged to offer their bodies and their labour for whatever price is acceptable. The longer, more arduous and more wearisome the work which they are given, the less they are paid; one can see workers who work strenuously and without interruption for sixteen hours a day, and who barely manage to earn the right not to die." [2]

[XV] " We are convinced . . . and the conviction is shared [in England] by the commissioners appointed to investigate the conditions of the handloom weavers, that the large towns would lose their working population in a short time if they did not constantly receive from the neighbouring countryside, a regular influx of healthy individuals, of new blood." [3]

---

[1] BURET, op. cit., p. 23. Emphasis added by Marx. [*Editor's note.*]
[2] Ibid., pp. 68–9. Quoted with minor omissions. [*Editor's note.*]
[3] Ibid., p. 362.

PROFIT OF CAPITAL

[1] (1) *Capital*

1. What is the basis of capital, i.e. of private ownership of the products of other men's labour? " . . . Even supposing that capital is not simply the fruit of robbery . . . it still needs the help of legislation in order to sanctify inheritance. . . . "[1]

How does one become an owner of productive stock? How does one become the possessor of the products which are created by means of this stock?

Through *positive law*.[2]

What does one acquire with capital, with the inheritance of a great property, for example?

"But the person who either acquires, or succeeds to a great fortune, does not necessarily acquire or succeed to any political power. . . . The power which that possession immediately and directly conveys to him, is the power of purchasing; a certain command over all the labour, or over all the produce of labour, which is then in the market."[3]

Capital is thus the *power of command* over labour and its products. The capitalist possesses this power, not on account of his personal or human qualities, but as the *owner* of capital. His power is the *purchasing* power of his capital, which nothing can withstand.

We shall see later how the capitalist, by means of capital, exercises his power of command over labour, and further, how capital itself rules the capitalist.

What is capital?

"It is, as it were, a certain quantity of labour stocked and stored up . . . "[4]

Capital is *stored-up labour*.

---

[1] JEAN-BAPTISTE SAY, *Traité d'économie politique*, 3ème édition, T. I–II. Paris, 1817. I, p. 136, footnote 2.
[2] Ibid., II, p. 4.   [3] SMITH, I, pp. 26–7.   [4] Ibid., p. 295.

2. *Fonds*, or stock, is any accumulation of products of the land or of manufacture. Stock is only called *capital* when it yields its owner a revenue or profit.[1]

(2) *The Profit of Capital*

The *profit or gain of capital* is altogether different from the *wages of labour*. The difference is manifested in two ways: first, the profits of capital are regulated altogether by the value of the stock employed; although the labour of inspection and direction may be the same for different amounts of capital. Furthermore, in large factories this whole labour is entrusted to some principal clerk, whose remuneration is not related to the [II] capital of which he oversees the management. Although the labour of the owner is in this case reduced almost to nothing, he still expects profits in proportion to his capital.[2]

Why does the capitalist demand this proportion between profit and capital?

He would have no *interest* in employing the workers unless he expected from the sale of their work something more than is necessary to replace the stock advanced by him as wages; and he would have no *interest* in employing a large stock rather than a small one if his profit were not in proportion to the extent of his stock.[3]

The capitalist makes a profit, therefore, first on the wages and secondly on the raw materials which he advances.

What relation, then, does profit have to capital?

If it is difficult to determine the average wages of labour at a particular time and place, it is all the more difficult to determine the profit on capital. Variations in the price of commodities which the capitalist deals in, the good or bad fortune of his rivals and customers, a thousand other accidents to which his goods are liable in transit and in warehouses, all produce a daily, almost hourly, fluctuation in profits.[4] But though it may be impossible to determine,

---

[1] SMITH, I, p. 243. [2] Ibid., p. 43. [3] Ibid., p. 42. [4] Ibid., pp. 78–9.

with any precision, the average profits of capital, some notion may be formed of them from the *interest of money*. Wherever a great deal can be made by the use of money, a great deal will be given for the use of it; wherever little can be made, little will be given.[1] " The proportion which the usual market rate of interest ought to bear to the ordinary rate of clear profit, necessarily varies as profit rises or falls. Double interest is in Great Britain reckoned what the merchants call a good, moderate, reasonable profit, terms which . . . mean no more than a common and usual profit." [2]

The *lowest* rate of ordinary profit on capitals must always be *something more* than what is necessary to compensate the occasional losses to which every employment of capital is exposed. It is this surplus only which is the net or clear profit. The same holds for the lowest rate of interest.[3]

[III] The *highest rate* to which ordinary profits can rise is that which, in the price of the greater part of commodities, *eats up the whole of the rent of land* and reduces the wages of labour in the production and delivery of the commodity to the *lowest rate*, the bare subsistence of the labourer. The worker must always be fed in some way or other while he is engaged on the work; but the rent of land can disappear entirely. Example: the servants of the East India Company in Bengal.[4]

Besides all the advantages of limited competition which the capitalist is able to exploit in such a case, he can maintain the market price above the natural price by quite respectable means.

First, by *secrets in trade*, where the market is at a great distance from those who supply it; that is, by concealing a change in price, an increase above the natural level. The effect of this concealment is that other capitalists do not employ their capital in this sphere.

Next, by *secrets in manufacture*, which enable the capitalist to produce at lower cost, and to sell his goods at the same

[1] SMITH, I, p. 79. [2] Ibid., p. 87. [3] Ibid., p. 86. [4] Ibid., pp. 86–7.

price, or even at a lower price than his competitors, while making a higher profit. (Deceit by concealment is not immoral? Stock exchange dealings.) Furthermore, where production is confined to a particular locality (as in the case of choice wines) and the *effective demand* can never be satisfied. Finally, through monopolies granted to individuals or companies. Monopoly price is the highest that can be got.[1]

There are other fortuitous causes which can raise the profit on capital. The acquisition of new territory, or of new branches of trade, may sometimes raise the profit of stock even in a wealthy country, because part of the capital is withdrawn from the old branches of trade, competition is diminished, and the market is supplied with fewer goods, the prices of which then rise: those who deal in these goods can then afford to borrow at a higher rate of interest.[2]

As any commodity comes to be more manufactured, that part of the price which resolves itself into wages and profit comes to be greater in proportion to that which resolves itself into rent. In the progress of the manufacture of a commodity, not only do the number of the profits increase, but every subsequent profit is greater than the preceding one, because the capital from which [IV] it is derived must always be greater. The capital which employs the weavers, for example, must be greater than that which employs the spinners; because it not only replaces that capital with its profits, but pays, besides, the wages of the weavers; and the profits must always bear some proportion to the capital.[3]

Thus the increasing part which human labour, compared with raw material, plays in the manufactured product does not increase the wages of labour but increases partly the number of capitals and partly the size of every subsequent capital in relation to that which precedes it.

More will be said later about the profit which the capitalist derives from the division of labour.

He profits doubly, first from the division of labour, and

[1] SMITH, I, pp. 53-4.   [2] Ibid., p. 83.   [3] Ibid., p. 45.

secondly, above all, from the increasing share of human labour, as against raw material. The greater the human contribution to a commodity, the greater is the profit of dead capital.

In the same society the average rates of profit on capital are more nearly upon a level than are the wages of different kinds of labour.[1] In the different employments of capital, the ordinary rate of profit varies with the certainty or uncertainty of the return. " . . . the ordinary profit of stock, though it rises with the risk, does not always seem to rise in proportion to it." [2]

It goes without saying that the profits of capital also rise if the means of circulation become less expensive or more easily available (e.g. paper money).

(3) *The Rule of Capital over Labour and the Motives of the Capitalist*

" The consideration of his own private profit is the sole motive which determines the owner of any capital to employ it either in agriculture, in manufactures, or in some particular branch of the wholesale or retail trade. The different quantities of productive labour which it may put into motion, and the different values which it may add to the annual produce of the land and labour of the society, according as it is employed in one or other of those different ways, never enter into his thoughts." [3]

" The most useful employment of capital for the capitalist is that which, with the same degree of security, yields him the largest profit; but this employment is not always the most useful for society, . . . the most useful [for a nation] is that which . . . stimulates the productive power of its land and labour." [4]

" The plans and projects of the employers of stock regulate and direct all the most important operations of labour, and

---

[1] SMITH, I, p. 45.   [2] Ibid., pp. 99–100.   [3] Ibid., p. 335.
[4] SAY, op. cit., II., pp. 130–1. Marx paraphrases this passage. [*Editor's note.*]

profit is the end proposed by all those plans and projects. But the rate of profit does not, like rent and wages, rise with the prosperity and fall with the declension of the society. On the contrary, it is naturally low in rich and high in poor countries, and it is always highest in the countries which are going fastest to ruin. The interest of this third order, [those who live by profit. *Editor*] therefore, has not the same connexion with the general interest of the society as that of the other two. . . . The interest of the dealers, however, in any particular branch of trade or manufactures, is always in some respects different from, and even opposite to, that of the public. To widen the market and to narrow the competition, is always the interest of the dealers . . . an order of men whose interest is never exactly the same with that of the public, who have generally an interest to deceive and even to oppress the public. . . . " [1]

(4) *The Accumulation of Capitals and the Competition among Capitalists*

The *increase of capitals*, which raises wages, tends to lower profits, because of the *competition* among capitalists.[2]

If, for example, the capital which is necessary for the grocery trade of a particular town " is divided between two different grocers, their competition will tend to make both of them sell cheaper than if it were in the hands of one only; and if it were divided among twenty, their competition would be just so much the greater, and the chance of their combining together, in order to raise the price, just so much the less." [3]

Since we already know that monopoly prices are as high as possible, since the interest of the capitalists, even from the ordinary viewpoint of political economy, is in opposition to the interest of society, and since an increase in profits has an effect upon prices like that of compound interest, it follows that the only protection against the capitalists is *competition*,

[1] SMITH, op. cit., I, pp. 231-2.   [2] Ibid., p. 78.   [3] Ibid., p. 322.

which according to the evidence of political economy has the salutary effect of raising wages and reducing the prices of goods, to the advantage of the consuming public.

But competition is only possible if capitals multiply and are held in many hands. The formation of many capitals is only possible as a result of widespread accumulation, but widespread accumulation inevitably turns into accumulation by a few. Competition between capitals increases the concentration of capitals. Accumulation, which means, under the rule of private property, *concentration* of capital in a few hands, is a necessary consequence when capitals are left free to follow their natural course. It is through competition that the way is made clear for this natural tendency of capital.

We have seen that the profit of capital is proportionate to its size. Thus a large capital accumulates more rapidly, in proportion to its size, than does a small capital, quite apart from any deliberate competition.

[VIII] Accordingly the accumulation of large capital is much more rapid than that of smaller capital, even disregarding competition. But let us follow this process further.

With the increase of capitals, the profits of capitals diminish, as a result of competition. Thus the first to suffer is the small capitalist.

Further, the increase of capitals, and the existence of a large number of capitalists, presupposes a condition of increasing wealth in a country.

" In a country which had acquired its full complement of riches, . . . as the ordinary rate of clear profit would be very small, so the usual market rate of interest which could be afforded out of it would be so low as to render it impossible for any but the very wealthiest people to live upon the interest of their money. All people of small or middling fortunes would be obliged to superintend themselves the employment of their own stocks. It would be necessary that almost every man should be a man of business, or engage in some sort of trade." [1]

This is the situation most dear to the heart of political economy.

" The proportion between capital and revenue, therefore, seems everywhere to regulate the proportion between industry and idleness. Wherever capital predominates, industry prevails: wherever revenue, idleness." [2]

What about the employment of capital in this situation of increased competition?

" As the quantity of stock to be lent at interest increases, the interest, or the price which must be paid for the use of that stock, necessarily diminishes, not only from those general causes, which make the market price of things commonly diminish as their quantity increases, but from other causes which are peculiar to this particular case. As capitals increase in any country, the profits which can be made by employing them necessarily diminish. It becomes gradually more and more difficult to find within the country a profitable method of employing any new capital. There arises in consequence a competition between different capitals, the owner of one endeavouring to get possession of that employment which is occupied by another. But upon most occasions he can hope to jostle that other out of this employment by no other means but by dealing upon more reasonable terms. He must not only sell what he deals in somewhat cheaper, but in order to get it to sell, he must sometimes, too, buy it dearer. The demand for productive labour, by the increase of the funds which are destined for maintaining it, grows every day greater and greater. Labourers easily find employment, [IX] but the owners of capitals find it difficult to get labourers to employ. Their competition raises the wages of labour and sinks the profits of stock." [3]

Thus the small capitalist has the choice, either (1) to

---

[1] SMITH, I, p. 86.   [2] Ibid., p. 301.   [3] Ibid., p. 316.

consume his capital since he can no longer live upon the interest, and thus cease to be a capitalist, or (2) to set up in business himself, sell his goods cheaper and buy dearer than the wealthier capitalist, and pay higher wages, and thus ruin himself, since the market price is already low as a result of the intense competition which we have presupposed. If, on the other hand, the large capitalist wants to squeeze out the smaller capitalist, he has the same advantage over him as the capitalist has over the worker. The larger amount of his capital compensates him for the smaller profits, and he can support short-term losses until the smaller capitalist is ruined and he finds himself free of this competition. Thus he accumulates the profits of the small capitalist.

Furthermore: the large capitalist always buys more cheaply than the small capitalist, because he buys in larger quantities. Consequently, he can afford to sell more cheaply.

But if the fall in the rate of interest turns the medium capitalists from rentiers into businessmen, the increase in business capitals and the resulting lower rate of profit bring about, in turn, a fall in the rate of interest.

" But when the profits which can be made by the use of a capital are . . . diminished . . . the price which can be paid for the use of it, . . . must necessarily be diminished with them." [1]

" As riches, improvement, and population have increased, interest has declined," and consequently the profits of stock " . . . after these are diminished, stock may not only continue to increase, but to increase much faster than before. . . . A great stock, though with small profits, generally increases faster than a small stock with great profits. Money, says the proverb, makes money." [2]

If, therefore, this large capital is opposed by small capitals with small profits, as happens under the assumed conditions of intense competition, it completely crushes them. The inevitable consequence of this competition is a general

---

[1] SMITH, I, p. 316.   [2] Ibid., p. 83.

deterioration of goods, adulteration, shoddy production, universal contamination, as is found in large towns.

[X] Another important feature in the competition between large and small capitals is the relationship between *fixed capital* and *circulating capital*.

Circulating capital is capital " employed in raising, manufacturing or purchasing goods, and selling them again with a profit. The capital employed in this manner yields no revenue or profit to its employer, while it either remains in his possession or continues in the same shape. . . . His capital is continually going from him in one shape, and returning to him in another, and it is only by means of such circulation, or successive exchanges, that it can yield him any profit . . . " *Fixed capital* is capital " employed in the improvement of land, in the purchase of useful machines and instruments, or in such like things . . . "

" . . . every saving in the expense of supporting the fixed capital is an improvement of the net revenue [of the society]. The whole capital of the undertaker of every work is necessarily divided between his fixed and his circulating capital. While his whole capital remains the same, the smaller the one part, the greater must necessarily be the other. It is the circulating capital which furnishes the materials and wages of labour, and puts industry into motion. Every saving therefore, in the expense of maintaining the fixed capital, which does not diminish the productive powers of labour, must increase the fund which puts industry into motion, . . . " [1]

It will be seen at once that the relation between fixed and circulating capital is much more favourable in the case of the large capitalist than in that of the smaller capitalist. The additional fixed capital required by a great banker, compared with a very small one, is insignificant. Their fixed capital is limited to an office. The equipment of a large landowner does not increase in proportion to the size of his

[1] SMITH, I, p. 257.

estate.   Similarly, the credit which a large capitalist enjoys, in comparison with a smaller one, also represents a greater saving in fixed capital, namely in the amount of ready money which he must have available.   It is clear, finally, that where industrial labour has reached an advanced stage in which almost all manual labour has become factory labour, the entire capital of a small capitalist does not suffice to provide him even with the necessary fixed capital.   It is well known that large scale cultivation ordinarily provides employment only for a small number of hands.

In general a concentration and rationalization of fixed capital occurs with the accumulation of large amounts of capital, in comparison with the small capitalists.   The large capitalist introduces for himself some kind of organization of the instruments of labour.

" Similarly, in the sphere of industry, every factory is a comprehensive co-ordination of extensive material property with numerous and diversified intellectual abilities and technical skills, for the *common* purpose of production. . . . Where legislation maintains large landed property, the surplus of a growing population crowds into the workshops; and it is, therefore, the field of industry where the greater part of the proletarians are massed, as in Great Britain.   But where legislation allows the continuous partition of land, as in France, the number of small, debt-ridden proprietors increases, and they are thrust into the class of the needy and unsatisfied by the continuous subdivision of land.   If, finally, this subdivision and indebtedness reaches a high level, then the small proprietors are absorbed again by the great landowners, just as small industry is destroyed by large-scale industry.   Since, in this case, large landholdings are reconstituted, the propertyless workers who are no longer needed for the cultivation of the land are again driven into industry." [1]

" The nature of commodities of the same kind is changed

[1] SCHULZ, op. cit., pp. 58–9.

by the changes in the mode of production, and notably by the use of machinery. Simply by eliminating human labour, it has become possible to spin from a pound of cotton worth 3s. 8d., 350 hanks amounting to 167 English (or 36 German) miles in length, of a value of 25 guineas." [1]

" On average the prices of cotton goods in England have fallen by eleven-twelfths in the past forty-five years. According to Marshall's calculations the same quantity of products which cost sixteen shillings in 1814 can now be supplied for 1s. 10d. The greater cheapness of industrial products has increased internal consumption and the external market, and with this is connected the fact that in Britain the number of workers in the cotton industry has not only not diminished since the introduction of machinery, but has increased from forty thousand to one and a half million. [XII] As regards the earnings of industrial entrepreneurs and workers, the growing competition among factory owners has necessarily reduced their profits in relation to the quantity of products. Between 1820 and 1833 the gross profit of Manchester producers on a piece of calico fell from 4s. 1⅓d. to 1s. 9d. But in order to compensate this loss the scale of production has been greatly extended. The result is . . . that in some branches of the industry partial overproduction occurs; that there are frequent bankruptcies, which produce fluctuations of property *within* the class of the capitalists and lords of labour, and cast a proportion of those who are economically ruined into the proletariat; and that there are frequent and sudden increases or decreases in the demand for labour, the hardships of which are always bitterly experienced by the class of wage earners." [2]

" To hire out one's labour is to begin one's enslavement; to hire out the material of labour is to establish one's liberty. . . . Labour is man, but material contains nothing of man." [3]

<hr/>

[1] SCHULZ, op. cit., p. 62.　　　　[2] Ibid., p. 63.
[3] PECQUEUR, op. cit., pp. 411–12.

" The *material* element which can do nothing to create
wealth without the element of *labour*, receives the magical
power of being fruitful for them [property owners] as if they
themselves had contributed this indispensable element." [1]
" If we assume that the daily labour of a worker brings him
an average of 400 francs a year, and that this sum is enough
for an adult to live at subsistence level, then every property
owner who receives 2,000 francs in interest, tithes, rent, etc.
indirectly obliges five men to work for him; 100,000 francs
in interest represents the labour of 250 men, and 1,000,000
francs the labour of 2,500 individuals. [2] Consequently, 300
million (Louis Philippe) represents the labour of 750,000
workers.

" The owners of property have obtained from human
legislation the right to use and to abuse, i.e. to do as they
please with the materials of all labour . . . they are not in
the least obliged by law to provide work for the non-owners
as it is needed, or invariably; nor are they obliged to pay a
wage which is always adequate, etc." [3]

" Complete freedom as regards the nature, quantity,
quality, and occasion of production, and as regards the use
and consumption of wealth, the disposal of the materials of
labour. Everyone is free to exchange what he possesses as
he chooses, without regard to anything but his own self-
interest."

" Competition simply expresses voluntary exchange,
which itself is the logical consequence of the individual right
to use and abuse the instruments of production. These
three economic factors, which form a unity—the right to use
and abuse, free exchange, and arbitrary competition—have
the following consequences: everyone produces what he
will, how, when and where he will, produces well or ill, too
much or not enough, too soon or too late, too dear or too
cheap. No one knows whether he will be able to sell his
product, or how, when, where or to whom he will sell it;

[1] PECQUEUR, op. cit., p. 412.   [2] Ibid., pp. 412–13.   [3] Ibid., p. 413.

and the same applies to purchases. The producer does not know what are the needs and resources, the demand and supply. He sells when he likes or when he can, where he likes, to whom he likes and at the price he chooses. He buys in the same manner. In all this he is the plaything of chance, the slave of the law of the strongest, of the least pressed for time, of the richest . . . While there is great need at one point, there is surfeit and waste at another. While one producer sells much, or sells at high prices, and makes enormous profits, another sells nothing or sells at a loss . . . Supply knows nothing of the demand, and demand knows nothing of the supply. You produce on the strength of a taste or fashion which appears in the consuming public, but when you are ready to supply the goods, taste has already changed and has become attached to some other kind of product . . . the inevitable consequences, continual and widespread bankruptcies, frauds, sudden ruin and unexpected fortunes, commercial crises, unemployment, periodical surpluses or shortages, instability and swallowing up of wages and profits, massive lossses or waste of wealth, time and effort in the arena of desperate competition." [1]

Ricardo, in his book (rent of land): [2] The nations are only workshops. Man is a machine for consuming and producing, human life a capital. Economic laws rule the world blindly. For Ricardo men are nothing, the product is everything.[3] In Chapter 26 of the French translation [4] we read: " To an individual with a capital of £20,000, whose profits were £2,000 per annum, it would be a matter quite indifferent whether his capital would employ a

[1] PECQUEUR, op. cit., pp. 414–16.

[2] DAVID RICARDO, *Principles of Political Economy and Taxation*, London, 1816, Chapter II, " On Rent."

[3] These statements are not quoted from Ricardo but are Marx's own elaborations of J. B. Say's critical comments in Chapter 26 of the French edition of the book. *See* the following note. [*Editor's note.*]

[4] *Des principes de l'économie politique et de l'impôt* par David Ricardo, traduit de l'anglais par F. S. Constancio avec des notes explicatives et critiques par J. B. Say. 2ème édition. T. I–II. Paris, 1835, Ch. XXVI, " Du revenu brut et du revenu net."

hundred or a thousand men . . . is not the real interest of
the nation similar? Provided its net real income, its rents
and profits, be the same, it is of no importance whether the
nation consists of ten or of twelve millions of inhabitants." [1]
" In truth," says M. de Sismondi, " it remains only to desire
that the king, left alone in the island, should, by turning a
handle, get all the work of England performed by auto-
matons." [2]

" . . . the master who buys the labour of the worker at a
price so low that it barely suffices to meet the most
urgent needs, is responsible neither for the inadequacy of
wages nor for the excessive hours of work; he is also
subject to the law which he imposes. . . . it is not so
much from men as from the power of things that misery
comes." [3]

" The inhabitants of many different parts of Great Britain
have not capital sufficient to improve and cultivate all their
lands. The wool of the southern counties of Scotland is, a
great part of it, after a long land carriage through very bad
roads, manufactured in Yorkshire, for want of capital to
manufacture it at home. There are many little manufacturing towns in Great Britain, of which the inhabitants have
not capital sufficient to transport the produce of their own
industry to those distant markets where there is demand and
consumption for it. If there are any merchants among
them, [XIV] they are properly only the agents of wealthier
merchants who reside in some of the greater commercial
cities." [4] " The annual produce of the land and labour of
any nation can be increased in its value by no other means
but by increasing either the number of its productive labourers, or the productive powers of those labourers who

[1] RICARDO, op. cit. (Everyman edition), pp. 234-5. Marx quotes from
the French edition: see the previous note. [Editor's note.]
[2] J. C. L. SIMONDE DE SISMONDI, Nouveaux principes d'économie politique. T.
I-II. Paris, 1819. II, p. 331.
[3] BURET, op. cit., I, p. 82.
[4] SMITH, op. cit., I, pp. 326-7.

had before been employed." In either case, an increase of capital is almost always necessary.[1]

" As the accumulation of stock must, in the nature of things, be previous to the division of labour, so labour can be more and more subdivided in proportion only as stock is previously more and more accumulated. The quantity of materials which the same number of people can work up, increases in a great proportion as labour comes to be more and more subdivided; and as the operations of each workman are gradually reduced to a greater degree of simplicity, a variety of new machines come to be invented for facilitating and abridging these operations. As the division of labour advances, therefore, in order to give constant employment to an equal number of workmen, an equal stock of provisions, and a greater stock of materials and tools than what would have been necessary in a ruder state of things, must be accumulated beforehand. But the number of workmen in every branch of business generally increases with the division of labour in that branch, or rather it is the increase of their number which enables them to class and subdivide themselves in this manner." [2]

" As the accumulation of stock is previously necessary for carrying on this great improvement in the productive powers of labour, so that accumulation naturally leads to this improvement. The person who employs his stock in maintaining labour, necessarily wishes to employ it in such a manner as to produce as great a quantity of work as possible. He endeavours, therefore, both to make among his workmen the most proper distribution of employment, and to furnish them with the best machines which he can either invent or afford to purchase. His abilities in both these respects are generally in proportion to the extent of his stock, or to the number of people it can employ. The quantity of industry, therefore, not only increases in every country

[1] SMITH, op. cit., I, pp. 306–7.
[2] Ibid., pp. 241–2.

with the increase of the stock which employs it, but, in consequence of that increase, the same quantity of industry produces a much greater quantity of work." [1]   Hence *over-production*.

" Wider combinations of productive forces . . . in industry and trade through the combination of more numerous and diverse human and natural powers for enterprise on a larger scale.   Already here and there, closer interrelations among the principal branches of production.   Thus large manufacturers will seek to acquire large estates, in order to be able to obtain directly at least a part of the necessary raw material of their industry; or they will establish a trading organization in connexion with their industry, not only for the sale of their own products, but also for the purchase of other commodities and their resale to their workers.   In England, a number of factory owners control 10,000– 12,000 workers . . . , and such combinations of several branches of production under *one* directing mind, such small states or provinces within a state, are already not uncommon. Thus, the mine-owners near *Birmingham* recently took over the *whole* process of iron-smelting which was previously divided among several entrepreneurs and owners. [2] Finally, we see in the large joint-stock companies which have become so numerous, extensive combinations of the money resources of *many* shareholders with the scientific and technical knowledge of others who take on the management of the work.   Thereby, it is possible for the capitalists to utilize their savings in many branches of production, and indeed to spread them over agricultural, industrial and commercial production.   Thus their interests also become many-sided, [XVI] and the conflicts of interest between agriculture, industry and trade are moderated and fused.   But

---

[1] SMITH, op. cit., I, p. 242.
[2] This sentence is from a footnote in the original which refers to *Deutsche Vierteljahresschrift*, Stuttgart und Tübingen, 1838 (Erster Jahrgang) Heft 3, p. 47 *et seq.*   " Der bergmännische Distrikt zwischen Birmingham und Wolverhampton."   Von A. von Treskow.

these greater opportunities to employ capital fruitfully in the most varied ways must increase the conflict between the owning and non-owning classes."[1]

The monstrous profit which the landlord of dwelling houses gains from the poor. The greater the industrial misery, the higher is the rent.

Similarly with the interest obtained from the vices of the ruined proletarians. (Prostitution, drunkenness, the pawnbroker.) The accumulation of capitals increases, and the competition between them diminishes, when capital and landed property are united in the same hands and when capital is enabled by its size to combine different branches of production.

Indifference towards men. Smith's[2] twenty lottery tickets.[3]

Say's net and gross revenue.

---

[1] Schulz, op. cit., pp. 40–1.

[2] This appears as *Swift's* in the *MEGA* edition. [*Editor's note.*]

[3] Smith, op. cit., I, p. 94. " In a perfectly fair lottery, those who draw the prizes ought to gain all that is lost by those who draw the blanks. In a profession where twenty fail for one that succeeds, that one ought to gain all that should have been gained by the unsuccessful twenty." [*Editor's note.*]

RENT OF LAND

[I] The *right of landownership* has its source in robbery.[1] Landlords, like all other men, love to reap where they never sowed, and demand a rent even for the natural produce of the land.[2]

" The rent of land, it may be thought, is frequently no more than a reasonable profit or interest for the stock laid out by the landlord upon its improvement. This, no doubt, may be partly the case upon some occasions. . . . The landlord demands a rent even for unimproved land, and the supposed interest or profit upon the expense of improvement is generally an addition to this original rent. Those improvements, besides, are not always made by the stock of the landlord, but sometimes by that of the tenant. When the lease comes to be renewed, however, the landlord commonly demands the same augmentation of rent as if they had been all made by his own.

" He sometimes demands rent for what is altogether incapable of human improvement." [3]

Smith gives as an example of this latter case, kelp, a species of seaweed, which when burnt, yields an alkaline salt, useful for making glass, soap, etc. It grows in several parts of Great Britain, especially in Scotland, but only upon rocks which lie within the high water mark, which are covered by the sea twice a day, and of which the produce, therefore, was never augmented by human industry. The landlord of such a kelp shore, however, demands a rent for it just as much as for his corn fields. In the neighbourhood of the Islands of Shetland the sea is uncommonly abundant in fish. A large part of their inhabitants [II] live by fishing. But in

[1] Say, op. cit., I, p. 136, footnote 2.
[2] Smith, op. cit., I, p. 44.
[3] Ibid., p. 131.

order to profit by the produce of the sea they must have a habitation upon the neighbouring land.　The rent of the landlord is in proportion, not to what the farmer can make by the land, but to what he can make both by the land and by the sea.[1]

" This rent may be considered as the produce of those powers of nature, the use of which the landlord lends to the farmer.　It is greater or smaller according to the supposed extent of those powers, or in other words, according to the supposed natural or improved fertility of the land.　It is the work of nature which remains after deducting or compensating everything which can be regarded as the work of man." [2]

" The rent of land, therefore, considered as the price paid for the use of land, is naturally a monopoly price.　It is not at all proportioned to what the landlord may have laid out upon the improvement of the land, or to what he can afford to take; but to what the farmer can afford to give." [3]

" They [the proprietors of land] are the only one of the three orders whose revenue costs them neither labour nor care, but comes to them, as it were, of its own accord, and independent of any plan or project of their own." [4]

We have already learnt that the amount of rent depends upon the degree of *fertility* of the land.

Another factor in its determination is *situation*.

" The rent of land not only varies with its fertility, whatever be its produce, but with its situation, whatever be its fertility." [5]

" The produce of land, mines and fisheries, when their natural fertility is equal, is in proportion to the extent [III] and proper application of the capitals employed about them. When the capitals are equal and equally well applied, it is in proportion to their natural fertility." [6]

---

[1] SMITH, op. cit., I, p. 131.　　　　[2] Ibid., pp. 324–5.
[3] Ibid., p. 131.　　　　[4] Ibid., p. 230.
[5] Ibid., p. 133.　　　　[6] Ibid., p. 249.

These propositions of Smith are important, because they relate the rent of land, given equal costs of production and capital of equal size, to the greater or lesser fertility of the soil. Thus they show clearly the perversion of concepts in political economy, which transforms the fertility of the soil into an attribute of the landowner.

But let us now examine the rent of land as it is determined in real life.

The rent of land is established by the *struggle between tenant and landlord*. In all political economy we find that the hostile opposition of interests, struggle and warfare, are recognized as the basis of social organization.

Let us now see what are the relations between landlord and tenant.

" In adjusting the terms of the lease, the landlord endeavours to leave him no greater share of the produce than what is sufficient to keep up the stock from which he furnishes the seed, pays the labour, and purchases and maintains the cattle and other instruments of husbandry, together with the ordinary profits of farming stock in the neighbourhood. This is evidently the smallest share with which the tenant can content himself without being a loser, and the landlord seldom means to leave him any more. Whatever part of the produce, or, what is the same thing, whatever part of its price is over and above this share, he naturally endeavours to reserve himself as the rent of his land, which is evidently the highest the tenant can afford to pay in the actual circumstances of the land. [IV] . . . This portion . . . may still be considered as the natural rent of land, or the rent for which it is naturally meant that land should for the most part be let." [1]

" The landlords," observes Say, " operate a particular kind of monopoly against the tenants. The demand for their commodity, the land, can go on expanding indefinitely; but there is only a limited amount of their commodity . . .

[1] SMITH, op. cit., I, pp. 130–1.

The bargain struck between landlord and tenant is always as advantageous as possible to the former . . . Besides the advantage which the landlord derives from the nature of the case, he derives a further advantage from his position, which gives him a larger fortune and sometimes a greater credit and standing. But the first by itself is enough to ensure that he will always be able to profit from the favourable situation of the land. The opening of a canal, or a road; the increase of population and of the prosperity of a district, always raise the rent . . . Indeed the tenant himself may improve the land at his own expense, but he only enjoys the profit from this capital for the duration of his lease, on the expiry of which, since the capital cannot be removed, it remains with the landowner. Thereafter it is the latter who reaps the interest without having made the outlay, for there is now a proportionate increase in the rent." [1]

" Rent, considered as the price paid for the use of land, is naturally the highest which the tenant can afford to pay in the actual circumstances of the land." [2]

" The rent of an estate above ground commonly amounts to what is supposed to be a third of the gross produce; and it is generally a rent certain and independent of the occasional variations [V] in the crop." [3] Rent " is seldom less than a fourth, and frequently more than a third of the whole produce." [4]

Rent cannot be paid in the case of all commodities. For example, in many districts no rent is paid for building stone.

" Such parts only of the produce of land can commonly be brought to market of which the ordinary price is sufficient to replace the stock which must be employed in bringing them thither, together with its ordinary profits. If the ordinary price is more than this, the surplus part of it will naturally go to the rent of the land. If it is not more, though the

---

[1] SAY, op. cit., II, pp. 142–3. Marx quotes this passage with minor variations. [*Editor's note.*]

[2] SMITH, op. cit., I, p. 130.   [3] Ibid., p. 153.   [4] Ibid., p. 325.

commodity may be brought to market, it can afford no rent to the landlord. Whether the price is or is not more depends upon the demand." [1]

" Rent, it is to be observed, therefore, enters into the composition of the price of commodities in a different way from wages and profit. High or low wages and profit are the causes of high or low price; high or low rent is the effect of it." [2]

Among the *products* which always afford a *rent* is *food*.

" As men, like all other animals, naturally multiply in proportion to the means of their subsistence, food is always, more or less, in demand. It can always purchase or command a greater or smaller quantity of labour, and somebody can always be found who is willing to do something in order to obtain it. The quantity of labour, indeed, which it can purchase is not always equal to what it could maintain, if managed in the most economical manner, on account of the high wages which are sometimes given to labour. But it can always purchase such a quantity of labour as it can maintain, according to the rate at which that sort of labour is commonly maintained in the neighbourhood.

" But land, in almost any situation, produces a greater quantity of food than what is sufficient to maintain all the labour necessary for bringing it to market in the most liberal way in which that labour is ever maintained. The surplus, too, is always more than sufficient to replace the stock which employed that labour, together with its profits. Something, therefore, always remains for a rent to the landlord." [3]

" Food is in this manner not only the original source of rent, but every other part of the produce of land which afterwards affords rent derives that part of its value from the improvement of the powers of labour in producing food by means of the improvement and cultivation of land." [4]

" Human food seems to be the only produce of land which

[1] SMITH, op. cit., I, p. 132.   [2] Ibid., p. 132.
[3] Ibid., pp. 132-3.   [4] Ibid., p. 150.

always and necessarily affords a rent to the landlord." [1]
" Countries are populous not in proportion to the number of
people whom their produce can clothe and lodge, but in
proportion to that of those whom it can feed." [2]

" After food, clothing and lodging are the two great wants
of mankind." [3]　They usually afford a rent, but not necessarily and invariably.

[VIII] Let us now see how the landlord exploits everything which benefits society.

1. The rent of land increases with increasing population.[4]

2. We have already learnt from Say how the rent of
land increases with the building of railways, etc., and with
the improvement, security and multiplication of the means
of communication.

3. " . . . every improvement in the circumstances of
the society tends either directly or indirectly to raise the
real rent of land, to increase the real wealth of the landlord, his power of purchasing the labour, or the produce
of the labour of other people."

" The extension of improvement and cultivation tends
to raise it directly.　The landlord's share of the produce
necessarily increases with the increase of the produce."

" That rise in the real price of those parts of the rude
produce of land, . . . the rise in the price of cattle, for
example, tends too to raise the rent of land directly, and
in a still greater proportion.　The real value of the landlord's share, his real command of the labour of other
people, not only rises with the real value of the produce,
but the proportion of his share to the whole produce rises
with it.　That produce, after the rise in its real price,
requires no more labour to collect it than before.　A
smaller proportion of it will, therefore, be sufficient to
replace, with the ordinary profit, the stock which employs

---

[1] Smith, op. cit., I, p. 147.　　[2] Ibid., p. 149.
[3] Ibid., p. 147.　　　　　　　　　[4] Ibid., p. 146.

that labour. A greater proportion of it must, consequently, belong to the landlord." [1]

The greater demand for raw products, and, therefore, the rise in their value, may result in part from the increase of population and from the increase in their needs. But every new invention, every new application in manufacture of a hitherto unused or little-used raw material increases the rent of the land. Thus, for example, there was a tremendous rise in the rent of coal-mines with the advent of the railways, steamships, etc.

Besides this advantage which the landlord derives from manufacture, discoveries and labour, there is another which we shall see presently.

4. " All those improvements in the productive powers of labour, which tend directly to reduce the real price of manufactures, tend indirectly to raise the real rent of land. The landlord exchanges that part of his rude produce, which is over and above his own consumption, or what comes to the same thing, the price of that part of it, for manufactured produce. Whatever reduces the real price of the latter, raises that of the former. An equal quantity of the former becomes thereby equivalent to a greater quantity of the latter; and the landlord is enabled to purchase a greater quantity of the conveniencies, ornaments or luxuries, which he has occasion for." [2]

It is absurd to conclude, however, as Smith does, that since the landlord exploits everything which benefits society, [X] the interest of the landlord is always identical with that of society.[3] In the economic system under the domination of private property, the interest which an individual has in society is in exactly inverse proportion to the interest which society has in him—just as the interest of the moneylender in the spendthrift is by no means identical with the interest of the spendthrift.

[1] SMITH, op. cit., I, pp. 228-9.   [2] Ibid., p. 229.   [3] Ibid., p. 230.

We mention only in passing the landlord's obsession with monopoly directed against the landed property of foreign countries, from which the corn laws, for instance, derive. Equally, we pass over here, medieval serfdom, slavery in the colonies, and the miserable conditions of the rural population, the day-labourers, in Great Britain. Let us confine ourselves to the propositions of political economy itself.

1. The interest of the landlord in the well-being of society means, according to the principles of political economy, that he is interested in the growth of population and production, and the increase of needs, in short in the increase of wealth; and the increase of wealth is, according to our previous observations, identical with the increase of misery and enslavement. The developing relationship between rent and misery is an example of the landowner's interest in society, for with the increase in rent the ground rent (the interest on the land on which the house stands) also rises.

2. According to the economists themselves the interest of the landowner is bitterly opposed to the interest of the tenant, and hence to a large section of society.

[XI] 3. Since the landowner can demand more rent from the tenant the less the latter pays in wages, and since the tenant reduces wages more the more rent the landowner demands, the interest of the landowner is just as bitterly opposed to the interest of the agricultural labourers as is the interest of the manufacturer to that of his workers. It forces wages down to a minimum.

4. Since a real reduction in the price of manufactured goods increases the rent of land, the landowner has a direct interest in depressing the wages oᶠ industrial workers, in the growth of competition between capitalists, in over-production, in industrial misery.

5. Thus, the interest of the landowner, far from being identical with that of society, is bitterly opposed to the

interests of the tenants, the agricultural labourers, the industrial workers and the capitalists; and the interest of one landowner is not even identical with that of another, on account of competition, which we have now to consider.

In general, large landed property and small landed property stand in the same relation to each other as do large capital and small capital. There are, however, special circumstances which bring about directly the accumulation of large landed property and thereby the circumscription of small property.

[XII] 1. Nowhere does the number of workers and implements diminish so greatly in relation to the size of the funds employed as in the case of landed property. And nowhere does the possibility of many-sided exploitation, the saving of costs of production and the rational division of labour, increase proportionately more with the size of the funds employed. A plot of land may be as small as you like, but the implements required, plough, saw, etc., have a limit below which they cannot be reduced, while there is no limit to the reduction in the size of the plot.

2. Large landed property accumulates the interest which the tenant's capital has produced by improving the land and the soil. Small landed property has to use its own capital; and this particular profit disappears.

3. Whereas every improvement in society benefits the large estate, it harms the small estate since it makes necessary a larger supply of ready cash.

4. There are two further laws of this competition to consider—

(a) " . . . the rent of the cultivated land, of which the produce is human food, regulates the rent of the greater part of the other cultivated land." [1]

[1] SMITH, op. cit., I, p. 144.

In the last resort only the large estate can produce food such as cattle, etc.; it can, therefore, determine the rent of other land and reduce it to a minimum.

The small landowner who works on his own account stands, therefore, in the same relation to the large land-owner as does the artisan who possesses his *own* tools to the factory owner. The small estate has become merely a tool. [XVI] For the small landowner rent of land disappears entirely, and there remains at most the interest on his capital and the wages of his labour, since rent can be depressed to such an extent by competition that it becomes no more than the interest on capital which is not invested by the owner himself.

(β) Furthermore, we have already seen that given equal fertility and equally efficient exploitation of lands, mines and fisheries, the produce is proportionate to the amount of capital employed. Thus, the victory of the large landowner. Similarly, where equal amounts of capital are employed the produce is pro-portionate to fertility. Where capitals are equal the owner of the more fertile land triumphs.

(γ) " The most fertile coal-mine, too, regulates the price of coals at all the other mines in its neighbourhood. Both the proprietor and the undertaker of the work find, the one that he can get a greater rent, the other that he can get a greater profit by somewhat under-selling all their neighbours. Their neighbours are soon obliged to sell at the same price, though they cannot so well afford it, and though it always diminishes, and sometimes takes away altogether both their rent and their profit. Some works are abandoned altogether; others can afford no rent, and can be wrought only by the proprietor." [1] " After the discovery of the mines of Peru, the silver mines of Europe were, the greater part of them, abandoned . . . This was the case, too,

---

[1] SMITH, op. cit., I, pp. 152–3.

with the ancient mines of Peru, after the discovery of those of Potosi." [1] What Smith says here about the mines is more or less valid for landed property in general.

(δ) "The ordinary market price of land, it is to be observed, depends everywhere upon the ordinary market rate of interest . . . if the rent of land should fall short of the interest of money by a greater difference, nobody would buy land, which would soon reduce its ordinary price. On the contrary, if the advantages should much more than compensate the difference, everybody would buy land, which would soon raise its ordinary price." [2] It follows from this relation between rent of land and interest on money that rent must continue to decrease until finally only the wealthiest people can live on rent. Hence the competition between landowners who do not lease their land to tenants increases. Some of the landowners are ruined and there is further accumulation of large landed property.

[XVII] This competition has the further consequence that a large part of landed property falls into the hands of capitalists, who then become landed proprietors; while the smaller landowners, generally speaking, are already nothing but capitalists. Thus a part of large landed property becomes industrial property.

The final result is, therefore, the abolition of the distinction between capitalist and landowner, so that broadly speaking there remain only two classes in the population, the working class and the capitalist class. This disposal of landed property and transformation of the land into a commodity is the final ruin of the old aristocracy and the complete triumph of the aristocracy of money.

1. Romanticism sheds many sentimental tears over this event, but we shall not do so. Romanticism always confuses

---

[1] SMITH, op. cit., I, p. 154.   [2] Ibid., p. 320.

the infamy involved in this *disposal of land* with the wholly reasonable and, within the system of private property, necessary and desirable consequences of the *disposal of landed property*. In the first place, feudal landed property is already essentially land which has been disposed of, alienated from men and now confronting them in the shape of a few great lords.

Already in feudal landownership the ownership of the soil appears as an alien power ruling over men. The serf is the product of the land. In the same way, the heir, the first-born son, belongs to the land. It inherits him. The rule of private property begins with the ownership of land, which is its basis. But in feudal landownership the lord *appears* at least as king of the land. Likewise, there is the appearance of a more intimate connexion between the owner and the land than is the case in the possession of mere *wealth*. Landed property assumes an individual character with its lord, has its own status, is knightly or baronial with him, has its privileges, its jurisdiction, its political rights, etc. It appears as the inorganic body of its lord. Hence the adage, *nulle terre sans maître*, in which the joint growth of lordship and landed property is expressed. The rule of landed property does not, therefore, appear as the direct rule of capital. Its dependants stand to it more in the relation in which they stand to their fatherland. It is a narrow kind of nationality.

[XVIII] Feudal landed property gives its name to its lord, as a kingdom gives its name to a king. His family history, the history of his house, etc., all this makes the landed property individual to him, makes it formally belong to a house, to a person. Similarly, the workers on the estate are not in the condition of *day-labourers*, but are partly the property of the lord, as in the case of serfs, and partly stand to him in relations of respect, subordination and duty. His relation to them is therefore directly political and has even an *agreeable* side. Customs and character differ from one estate to another and seem to be in harmony with the type of land, whereas later only a man's pocket, not his own character or individuality, attracts him to an estate. Finally, the lord does not try to extract the maximum profit from his estate. He rather consumes what is there, and tranquilly leaves the care of producing it to the serfs and tenant farmers. That is the *aristocratic* condition of land-ownership which reflects a romantic *glory* upon its lords.

It is inevitable that this appearance should be abolished, that landed property, the *root* of private property, should be drawn completely into the movement of private property and *become a commodity*; that the rule of the property owner should appear as the naked rule of private property, of capital, dissociated from all political colouring; that the relation between property owner and worker should be confined to the economic relationship of exploiter and exploited; that all personal relationships between the property owner and his property should cease, and the latter become purely *material* wealth; that in place of the honourable marriage with the land there should be a marriage of interest, and the land as well as man himself be reduced to the level of an object of speculation. It is inevitable that the root of landed property, sordid self-interest, should also appear in a cynical form. It is inevitable that immovable monopoly should turn into mobile and restless monopoly—into competition; and that the idle enjoyment of the products of other people's blood and toil should turn into a bustling trade in the same commodity. Finally, it is inevitable that in this competition, landed property, in the form of capital, should manifest its domination over both the working class and the property owners themselves, who are being ruined or advanced by the laws governing the movement of capital. So the medieval adage, *nulle terre sans seigneur*, is replaced with a new adage, *l'argent n'a pas de maître*, which expresses the complete domination of living men by dead matter.

[XIX] 2. As regards the controversy over the division or non-division of landed property, the following is to be observed.

The *division of landed property* negates the *large-scale monopoly* of landed property, i.e abolishes it, but only by *generalizing* it. It does not abolish the basis of monopoly, private property. It attacks the existence, but not the real essence, of monopoly, and in consequence it falls victim to the laws of private property. For the division of landed property corresponds to the movement of competition in the industrial sphere. This division of the implements of production and separation of labour (which must be carefully distinguished from the division of labour: the work is not divided among many individuals, but the same work is carried out by each individual; it is a multiplication of the same kind of work) does not only bring economic disadvantages; like all competition it leads to further accumulation.

When the division of landed property takes place, therefore, the only alternatives are to return to an even more hateful form of monopoly, or to negate and abolish the division of landed property itself. This latter course is not, however, a return to feudal property, but the abolition of private property in land altogether. The first supersession of monopoly is always an extension and generalization of it. The supersession of monopoly which has attained its widest and most inclusive existence is its complete destruction. Association, applied to the land, has the advantage from an economic point of view of large-scale ownership, while at the same time it realizes the original tendency of the division of land, namely equality. Moreover, association restores the intimate relationships between man and the land in a rational way, instead of through serfdom, overlordship and a foolish mystique of property. The land ceases to be an object of sordid speculation, and through the freedom of work and enjoyment becomes once more man's real personal property. One great advantage of the division of landed property is that the property of the masses is destroyed in a different way from that of industry, and they are no longer willing to accept serfdom.

As for the large estates, their defenders have always sophistically identified the economic advantages of large-scale agricultural production with the existence of large landed property, as if these advantages would not reach their greatest extent, and bring social benefits for the first time, with the abolition of private property. Similarly, they have attacked the commercial spirit of the small landowners, as though the large estates did not contain this petty trading in germ, even in their feudal form—not to speak of the modern English form in which the feudalism of landlords, and the trading and industry of tenant farmers, are combined.

Just as large landed property can return the reproach of monopoly made from the standpoint of small landholdings, since the division of land is also based upon the monopoly of private property, so can the small holdings reject the reproach of having divided the land, for the division of land exists also in the case of large estates, but in an inflexible, crystallized form. Private property, indeed, is everywhere based upon division. Moreover, since the division of landed property leads again to large landed property as capital wealth, feudal property is bound to be divided, or at least to fall into the hands of capitalists, however it may twist and turn.

For large landed property, as in England, drives the greater part of the industrial population into poverty and reduces its own workers to utter misery. It thus creates and augments the power of its enemies, capital and industry, so far as it thrusts the poor and a whole sphere of activity into the other camp. It makes the majority of the country industrial, and thus the enemy of large landed property. Where industry has attained considerable power, as at present in England, it opposes foreign monopolies to that of large landed property and forces the latter into competition with foreign landed property. Under the rule of industry, landed property could only maintain its feudal dimensions with the help of a monopoly against foreign countries, in order to protect itself against the universal laws of trade which contradict its feudal nature. Once thrown into competition it must conform with the laws of competition like any other commodity which is subject to them. But it becomes thereby so fluctuating, growing and diminishing, passing from hand to hand, that no law can keep it any longer in a few predestined hands. [XXI] The direct consequence is its fragmentation in many hands, a prey to the power of industrial capital.

In the end, large landed property which has been kept in existence by force and has created alongside itself a formidable industry, leads more rapidly to crisis than does the division of landed property alongside which the power of industry remains in second place.

As we can see in England, large landed property has cast off its feudal character and has taken on an industrial character to the extent that it wants to make as much money as possible. It gives the owner the highest possible rent, and the tenant farmer the highest possible profit on his capital. Consequently the agricultural workers are soon reduced to the minimum level of subsistence, and the farmer class establishes the power of industry and capital within landed property. Through competition with foreign countries the rent of land ceases, in the main, to constitute an independent source of income. A large section of the landowners is obliged to take the place of the tenant farmers who sink in this way into the proletariat. On the other hand, many tenant farmers will acquire landed property, for the large landowners, who have abandoned themselves to the enjoyment of their comfortable revenues and are usually unfitted for large-scale agricultural management, have very often neither the capital nor the experience to exploit the land.

Consequently, a section of them is completely ruined. Ultimately, the wages which have already been reduced to a minimum must be further reduced, in the face of new competition; and that leads necessarily to revolution.

Landed property had to develop in both these ways, in order to experience in both of them its inevitable decline. So also industry had to ruin itself both in the form of monopoly and in the form of competition, in order to arrive at faith in man.

ALIENATED LABOUR

[XXII] WE have begun from the presuppositions of political economy. We have accepted its terminology and its laws. We presupposed private property; the separation of labour, capital and land, as also of wages, profit and rent; the division of labour; competition; the concept of exchange value, etc. From political economy itself, in its own words, we have shown that the worker sinks to the level of a commodity, and to a most miserable commodity; that the misery of the worker increases with the power and volume of his production; that the necessary result of competition is the accumulation of capital in a few hands, and thus a restoration of monopoly in a more terrible form; and finally that the distinction between capitalist and landlord, and between agricultural labourer and industrial worker, must disappear, and the whole of society divide into the two classes of property *owners* and *propertyless* workers.

Political economy begins with the fact of private property; it does not explain it. It conceives the *material* process of private property, as this occurs in reality, in general and abstract formulas which then serve it as laws. It does not *comprehend* these laws; that is, it does not show how they arise out of the nature of private property. Political economy provides no explanation of the basis for the distinction of labour from capital, of capital from land. When, for example, the relation of wages to profits is defined, this is explained in terms of the interests of capitalists; in other words, what should be explained is assumed. Similarly, competition is referred to at every point and is explained in terms of external conditions. Political economy tells us nothing about the extent to which these external and apparently accidental conditions are simply the expression of a necessary development. We have seen how exchange itself seems an accidental fact. The only motive forces which political economy recognizes are *avarice* and the *war between the avaricious, competition*.

Just because political economy fails to understand the interconnexions within this movement it was possible to oppose the doctrine of competition to that of monopoly, the doctrine of freedom of the crafts to that of the guilds, the doctrine of the division of landed property to that of the great estates; for competition, freedom of crafts, and the division of landed property were conceived only as accidental consequences brought about by will and force, rather than as necessary, inevitable and natural consequences of monopoly, the guild system and feudal property.

Thus we have now to grasp the real connexion between this whole system of alienation—private property, acquisitiveness, the separation of labour, capital and land, exchange and competition, value and the devaluation of man, monopoly and competition—and the system of *money*.

Let us not begin our explanation, as does the economist, from a legendary primordial condition. Such a primordial condition does not explain anything; it merely removes the question into a grey and nebulous distance. It asserts as a fact or event what it should deduce, namely, the necessary relation between two things; for example, between the division of labour and exchange. In the same way theology explains the origin of evil by the fall of man; that is, it asserts as a historical fact what it should explain.

We shall begin from a *contemporary* economic fact. The worker becomes poorer the more wealth he produces and the more his production increases in power and extent. The worker becomes an ever cheaper commodity the more goods he creates. The *devaluation* of the human world increases in direct relation with the *increase in value* of the world of things. Labour does not only create goods; it also produces itself and the worker as a *commodity*, and indeed in the same proportion as it produces goods.

This fact simply implies that the object produced by labour, its product, now stands opposed to it as an *alien being*, as a *power independent* of the producer. The product of labour is labour which has been embodied in an object and turned into a physical thing; this product is an *objectification* of labour. The performance of work is at the same time its objectification. The performance of work appears in the sphere of political economy as a *vitiation* of the worker, objectification as a *loss* and as *servitude to the object*, and appropriation as *alienation*.

So much does the performance of work appear as vitiation that the worker is vitiated to the point of starvation. So much does objectification appear as loss of the object that the worker is deprived of the most essential things not only of life but also of work. Labour itself becomes an object which he can acquire only by the greatest effort and with unpredictable interruptions. So much does the appropriation of the object appear as alienation that the more objects the worker produces the fewer he can possess and the more he falls under the domination of his product, of capital.

All these consequences follow from the fact that the worker is related to the *product of his labour* as to an *alien* object. For it is clear on this presupposition that the more the worker expends himself in work the more powerful becomes the world of objects which he creates in face of himself, the poorer he becomes in his inner life, and the less he belongs to himself. It is just the same as in religion. The more of himself man attributes to God the less he has left in himself. The worker puts his life into the object, and his life then belongs no longer to himself but to the object. The greater his activity, therefore, the less he possesses. What is embodied in the product of his labour is no longer his own. The greater this product is, therefore, the more he is diminished. The *alienation* of the worker in his product means not only that his labour becomes an object, assumes an *external* existence, but that it exists independently, *outside himself*, and alien to him, and that it stands opposed to him as an autonomous power.   The life which he has given to the object sets itself against him as an alien and hostile force.

[XXIII] Let us now examine more closely the pheno-menon of *objectification*; the worker's production and the *alienation* and *loss* of the object it produces, which is involved in it.   The worker can create nothing without *nature*, without the *sensuous external world*.   The latter is the material in which his labour is realized, in which it is active, out of which and through which it produces things.

But just as nature affords the *means of existence* of labour, in the sense that labour cannot *live* without objects upon which it can be exercised, so also it provides the *means of existence* in a narrower sense; namely the means of physical existence for the *worker* himself.   Thus, the more the worker *appro-priates* the external world of sensuous nature by his labour the more he deprives himself of *means of existence*, in two re-spects: first, that the sensuous external world becomes pro-gressively less an object belonging to his labour or a means of existence of his labour, and secondly, that it becomes pro-gressively less a means of existence in the direct sense, a means for the physical subsistence of the worker.

In both respects, therefore, the worker becomes a slave of the object; first, in that he receives an *object of work*, i.e. receives *work*, and secondly, in that he receives *means of sub-sistence*.   Thus the object enables him to exist, first as a *worker* and secondly, as a *physical subject*.   The culmination of this enslavement is that he can only maintain himself as a *physical subject* so far as he is a *worker*, and that it is only as a *physical subject* that he is a worker.

(The alienation of the worker in his object is expressed as follows in the laws of political economy: the more the worker produces the less he has to consume; the more value he creates the more worthless he becomes; the more refined his product the more crude and misshapen the worker; the more civilized the product the more barbarous the worker;

the more powerful the work the more feeble the worker; the more the work manifests intelligence the more the worker declines in intelligence and becomes a slave of nature.)

Political economy conceals the alienation in the nature of labour in so far as it does not examine the direct relationship between the worker (work) and production. Labour certainly produces marvels for the rich but it produces privation for the worker. It produces palaces, but hovels for the worker. It produces beauty, but deformity for the worker. It replaces labour by machinery, but it casts some of the workers back into a barbarous kind of work and turns the others into machines. It produces intelligence, but also stupidity and cretinism for the workers.

The direct relationship of labour to its products is the relationship of the worker to the objects of his production. The relationship of property owners to the objects of production and to production itself is merely a *consequence* of this first relationship and confirms it. We shall consider this second aspect later.

Thus, when we ask what is the important relationship of labour, we are concerned with the relationship of the *worker* to production.

So far we have considered the alienation of the worker only from one aspect; namely, *his relationship with the products of his labour.* However, alienation appears not merely in the result but also in the *process* of *production*, within *productive activity* itself. How could the worker stand in an alien relationship to the product of his activity if he did not alienate himself in the act of production itself? The product is indeed only the *résumé* of activity, of production. Consequently, if the product of labour is alienation, production itself must be active alienation—the alienation of activity and the activity of alienation. The alienation of the object of labour merely summarizes the alienation in the work activity itself.

What constitutes the alienation of labour? First, that the work is *external* to the worker, that it is not part of his nature;

and that, consequently, he does not fulfil himself in his work but denies himself, has a feeling of misery rather than well-being, does not develop freely his mental and physical energies but is physically exhausted and mentally debased. The worker, therefore, feels himself at home only during his leisure time, whereas at work he feels homeless. His work is not voluntary but imposed, *forced labour*. It is not the satisfaction of a need, but only a *means* for satisfying other needs. Its alien character is clearly shown by the fact that as soon as there is no physical or other compulsion it is avoided like the plague. External labour, labour in which man alienates himself, is a labour of self-sacrifice, of mortification. Finally, the external character of work for the worker is shown by the fact that it is not his own work but work for someone else, that in work he does not belong to himself but to another person.

Just as in religion the spontaneous activity of human fantasy, of the human brain and heart, reacts independently as an alien activity of gods or devils upon the individual, so the activity of the worker is not his own spontaneous activity. It is another's activity and a loss of his own spontaneity.

We arrive at the result that man (the worker) feels himself to be freely active only in his animal functions—eating, drinking and procreating, or at most also in his dwelling and in personal adornment—while in his human functions he is reduced to an animal. The animal becomes human and the human becomes animal.

Eating, drinking and procreating are of course also genuine human functions. But abstractly considered, apart from the environment of human activities, and turned into final and sole ends, they are animal functions.

We have now considered the act of alienation of practical human activity, labour, from two aspects: (1) the relationship of the worker to the *product of labour* as an alien object which dominates him. This relationship is at the same time the relationship to the sensuous external world, to natural objects, as an alien and hostile world; (2) the relationship of labour to the *act of production* within *labour*. This is the relationship of the worker to his own activity as something alien and not belonging to him, activity as suffering (passivity), strength as powerlessness, creation as emasculation, the *personal* physical and mental energy of the worker, his personal life (for what is life but activity?), as an activity which is directed against himself, independent of him and not belonging to him. This is *self-alienation* as against the above-mentioned alienation of the *thing*.

[XXIV] We have now to infer a third characteristic of *alienated labour* from the two we have considered.

Man is a species-being not only in the sense that he makes the community (his own as well as those of other things) his object both practically and theoretically, but also (and this is simply another expression for the same thing) in the sense that he treats himself as the present, living species, as a *universal* and consequently free being.[1]

Species-life, for man as for animals, has its physical basis in the fact that man (like animals) lives from inorganic nature, and since man is more universal than an animal so the range of inorganic nature from which he lives is more universal. Plants, animals, minerals, air, light, etc. constitute, from the theoretical aspect, a part of human consciousness as objects of natural science and art; they are man's spiritual inorganic nature, his intellectual means of life, which he must first prepare for enjoyment and perpetuation. So also, from the practical aspect, they form a part of human life and activity. In practice man lives only from these natural products, whether in the form of food, heating, clothing, housing, etc. The universality of man appears in practice in the universality which makes the whole of nature into his inorganic body: (1) as a direct means of life; and equally (2) as the material object and instrument of his life activity. Nature

---

[1] In this passage Marx reproduces Feuerbach's argument in *Das Wesen des Christentums*. *See* note 2 on p. 13 above. [*Editor's note*.]

is the inorganic body of man; that is to say nature, excluding the human body itself. To say that man *lives* from nature means that nature is his *body* with which he must remain in a continuous interchange in order not to die. The statement that the physical and mental life of man, and nature, are interdependent means simply that nature is interdependent with itself, for man is a part of nature.

Since alienated labour: (1) alienates nature from man; and (2) alienates man from himself, from his own active function, his life activity; so it alienates him from the species. It makes *species-life* into a means of individual life. In the first place it alienates species-life and individual life, and secondly, it turns the latter, as an abstraction, into the purpose of the former, also in its abstract and alienated form.

For labour, *life activity, productive life*, now appear to man only as *means* for the satisfaction of a need, the need to maintain his physical existence. Productive life is, however, species-life. It is life creating life. In the type of life activity resides the whole character of a species, its species-character; and free, conscious activity is the species-character of human beings. Life itself appears only as a *means of life*.

The animal is one with its life activity. It does not distinguish the activity from itself. It is *its activity*. But man makes his life activity itself an object of his will and consciousness. He has a conscious life activity. It is not a determination with which he is completely identified. Conscious life activity distinguishes man from the life activity of animals. Only for this reason is he a species-being. Or rather, he is only a self-conscious being, i.e. his own life is an object for him, because he is a species-being. Only for this reason is his activity free activity. Alienated labour reverses the relationship, in that man because he is a self-conscious being makes his life activity, his *being*, only a means for his *existence*.

The practical construction of an *objective world*, the

manipulation of inorganic nature, is the confirmation of man as a conscious species-being, i.e. a being who treats the species as his own being or himself as a species-being. Of course, animals also produce. They construct nests, dwellings, as in the case of bees, beavers, ants, etc. But they only produce what is strictly necessary for themselves or their young. They produce only in a single direction, while man produces universally. They produce only under the compulsion of direct physical needs, while man produces when he is free from physical need and only truly produces in freedom from such need. Animals produce only themselves, while man reproduces the whole of nature. The products of animal production belong directly to their physical bodies, while man is free in face of his product. Animals construct only in accordance with the standards and needs of the species to which they belong, while man knows how to produce in accordance with the standards of every species and knows how to apply the appropriate standard to the object. Thus man constructs also in accordance with the laws of beauty.

It is just in his work upon the objective world that man really proves himself as a *species-being*. This production is his active species-life. By means of it nature appears as *his* work and his reality. The object of labour is, therefore, the *objectification of man's species-life*; for he no longer reproduces himself merely intellectually, as in consciousness, but actively and in a real sense, and he sees his own reflection in a world which he has constructed. While, therefore, alienated labour takes away the object of production from man, it also takes away his *species-life*, his real objectivity as a species-being, and changes his advantage over animals into a disadvantage in so far as his inorganic body, nature, is taken from him.

Just as alienated labour transforms free and self-directed activity into a means, so it transforms the species-life of man into a means of physical existence.

Consciousness, which man has from his species, is transformed through alienation so that species-life becomes only a means for him. (3) Thus alienated labour turns the *species-life of man*, and also nature as his mental species-property, into an *alien* being and into a *means* for his *individual existence*. It alienates from man his own body, external nature, his mental life and his *human* life. (4) A direct consequence of the alienation of man from the product of his labour, from his life activity and from his species-life, is that *man* is *alienated* from other *men*. When man confronts himself he also confronts *other* men. What is true of man's relationship to his work, to the product of his work and to himself, is also true of his relationship to other men, to their labour and to the objects of their labour.

In general, the statement that man is alienated from his species-life means that each man is alienated from others, and that each of the others is likewise alienated from human life.

Human alienation, and above all the relation of man to himself, is first realized and expressed in the relationship between each man and other men. Thus in the relationship of alienated labour every man regards other men according to the standards and relationships in which he finds himself placed as a worker.

[XXV] We began with an economic fact, the alienation of the worker and his production. We have expressed this fact in conceptual terms as *alienated labour*, and in analysing the concept we have merely analysed an economic fact.

Let us now examine further how this concept of alienated labour must express and reveal itself in reality. If the product of labour is alien to me and confronts me as an alien power, to whom does it belong? If my own activity does not belong to me but is an alien, forced activity, to whom does it belong? To a being *other* than myself. And who is this being? The *gods*? It is apparent in the earliest stages of advanced production, e.g. temple building, etc. in Egypt, India, Mexico, and in the service rendered to gods, that the product belonged to the gods. But the gods alone were never the lords of labour. And no more was *nature*. What a contradiction it would be if the more man subjugates nature by his labour, and the more the marvels of the gods are rendered superfluous by the marvels of industry, the more he should abstain from his joy in producing and his enjoyment of the product for love of these powers.

The *alien* being to whom labour and the product of labour belong, to whose service labour is devoted, and to whose enjoyment the product of labour goes, can only be *man* himself. If the product of labour does not belong to the worker, but confronts him as an alien power, this can only be because it belongs to *a man other than the worker*. If his activity is a torment to him it must be a source of *enjoyment* and pleasure to another. Not the gods, nor nature, but only man himself can be this alien power over men.

Consider the earlier statement that the relation of man to himself is first *realized*, *objectified*, through his relation to other men. If he is related to the product of his labour, his objectified labour, as to an *alien*, hostile, powerful and independent object, he is related in such a way that another alien, hostile, powerful and independent man is the lord of this object. If he is related to his own activity as to unfree activity, then he is related to it as activity in the service, and under the domination, coercion and yoke, of another man.

Every self-alienation of man, from himself and from nature, appears in the relation which he postulates between other men and himself and nature. Thus religious self-alienation is necessarily exemplified in the relation between laity and priest, or, since it is here a question of the spiritual world, between the laity and a mediator. In the real world of practice this self-alienation can only be expressed in the real, practical relation of man to his fellow men. The medium through which alienation occurs is itself a *practical* one. Through alienated labour, therefore, man not only produces his relation to the object and to the process of production as to alien and hostile men; he also produces the relation of other men to his production and his product, and the relation between himself and other men. Just as he creates his own production as a vitiation, a punishment, and his own product as a loss, as a product which does not belong to him, so he creates the domination of the non-producer over production and its product. As he alienates his own activity, so he bestows upon the stranger an activity which is not his own.

We have so far considered this relation only from the side of the worker, and later on we shall consider it also from the side of the non-worker.

Thus, through alienated labour the worker creates the relation of another man, who does not work and is outside the work process, to this labour. The relation of the worker to work also produces the relation of the capitalist (or whatever one likes to call the lord of labour) to work. *Private property* is, therefore, the product, the necessary result, of *alienated labour*, of the external relation of the worker to nature and to himself.

Private property is thus derived from the analysis of the concept of *alienated labour*; that is, alienated man, alienated labour, alienated life, and estranged man.

We have, of course, derived the concept of *alienated labour* (*alienated life*) from political economy, from an analysis of the *movement of private property*. But the analysis of this concept shows that although private property appears to be the basis and cause of alienated labour, it is rather a consequence of the latter, just as the gods are *fundamentally* not the cause but the product of confusions of human reason. At a later stage, however, there is a reciprocal influence.

Only in the final stage of the development of private property is its secret revealed, namely, that it is on one hand the *product* of alienated labour, and on the other hand the *means* by which labour is alienated, *the realization of this alienation*.

This elucidation throws light upon several unresolved controversies—

1. Political economy begins with labour as the real soul of production and then goes on to attribute nothing to labour and everything to private property. Proudhon, faced by this contradiction, has decided in favour of labour against private property. We perceive, however, that this apparent contradiction is the contradiction of *alienated labour* with itself and that political economy has merely formulated the laws of alienated labour.

We also observe, therefore, that *wages* and *private property* are identical, for wages, like the product or object of labour, labour itself remunerated, are only a necessary consequence of the alienation of labour. In the wage system labour appears not as an end in itself but as the servant of wages. We shall develop this point later on and here only bring out some of the [XXVI] consequences.

An enforced *increase in wages* (disregarding the other difficulties, and especially that such an anomaly could only be maintained by force) would be nothing more than a *better remuneration of slaves*, and would not restore, either to the worker or to the work, their human significance and worth.

Even the *equality of incomes* which Proudhon demands would only change the relation of the present-day worker to his work into a relation of all men to work. Society would then be conceived as an abstract capitalist.

2. From the relation of alienated labour to private property it also follows that the emancipation of society from private property, from servitude, takes the political form of the *emancipation of the workers*; not in the sense that only the latter's emancipation is involved, but because this emancipation includes the emancipation of humanity as a whole. For all human servitude is involved in the relation of the worker to production, and all the types of

servitude are only modifications or consequences of this relation.

As we have discovered the concept of *private property* by an *analysis* of the concept of *alienated labour*, so with the aid of these two factors we can evolve all the *categories* of political economy, and in every category, e.g. trade, competition, capital, money, we shall discover only a particular and developed expression of these fundamental elements.

However, before considering this structure let us attempt to solve two problems.

1. To determine the general nature of *private property* as it has resulted from alienated labour, in its relation to *genuine human and social property.*

2. We have taken as a fact and analysed the *alienation of labour.* How does it happen, we may ask, that *man alienates his labour*? How is this alienation founded in the nature of human development? We have already done much to solve the problem in so far as we have *transformed* the question concerning the *origin of private property* into a question about the relation between *alienated labour* and the process of development of mankind. For in speaking of private property one believes oneself to be dealing with something external to mankind. But in speaking of labour one deals directly with mankind itself. This new formulation of the problem already contains its solution.

ad (1) *The general nature of private property and its relation to genuine human property.*

We have resolved alienated labour into two parts, which mutually determine each other, or rather, which constitute two different expressions of one and the same relation. *Appropriation* appears as *alienation* and *alienation* as *appropriation*, alienation as genuine acceptance in the community.

We have considered one aspect, *alienated* labour, in its bearing upon the *worker* himself, i.e. *the relation of alienated labour to itself.* And we have found as the necessary consequence of this relation the *property relation* of the *non-worker* to the *worker* and to labour. *Private property* as the material, summarized expression of alienated labour includes both relations; *the relation of the worker to labour, to the product of his labour and to the non-worker,* and the relation of the *non-worker* to *the worker and to the product of the latter's labour.*

We have already seen that in relation to the worker, who *appropriates* nature by his labour, appropriation appears as alienation, self-activity as activity for another and of another, living as the sacrifice of life, and production of the object as loss of the object to an alien power, an alien man. Let us now consider the relation of this *alien* man to the worker, to labour, and to the object of labour.

It should be noted first that everything which appears to the worker as an *activity of alienation*, appears to the non-worker as a *condition of alienation*. Secondly, the *real, practical* attitude (as a state of mind) of the worker in production and to the product appears to the non-worker who confronts him as a *theoretical* attitude.

[XXVII] Thirdly, the non-worker does everything against the worker which the latter does against himself, but he does not do against himself what he does against the worker.

Let us examine these three relationships more closely.[1]

----

[1] The manuscript breaks off unfinished at this point. [*Editor's note.*]

SECOND MANUSCRIPT

THE RELATIONSHIP OF PRIVATE
PROPERTY

[XL] . . . forms the interest on his capital. The worker is the subjective manifestation of the fact that capital is man wholly lost to himself, just as capital is the objective manifestation of the fact that labour is man lost to himself. However, the *worker* has the misfortune to be a *living* capital, a capital with *needs*, which forfeits its interest and consequently its livelihood during every moment that it is not at work. As capital, the *value* of the worker varies according to supply and demand, and his *physical existence*, his *life*, was and is considered as a supply of goods, similar to any other goods. The worker produces capital and capital produces him. Thus he produces himself, and man as a *worker*, as a *commodity*, is the product of the whole process. Man is simply a *worker*, and as a worker his human qualities only exist for the sake of capital which is *alien* to him. Since labour and capital are alien to each other, and thus related only in an external and accidental manner, this alien character must *appear* in reality. As soon as it occurs to capital—either necessarily or voluntarily—not to exist any longer for the worker, he no longer exists for himself; he has *no* work, *no* wage, and since he exists only as a *worker* and not as a *human being*, he may as well let himself starve, be buried, etc. The worker is only a worker when he exists as capital *for himself*, and he only exists as capital when *capital* is there *for him*. The existence of capital is *his* existence, his life, since it determines the content of his life independently of him. Political economy thus does not recognize the unoccupied worker, the working man so far as he is outside this work relationship. Swindlers, thieves, beggars, the unemployed, the starving, poverty-stricken and criminal working man, are figures which do not exist for political economy, but only for other eyes; for doctors, judges, grave-diggers, beadles, etc. They are ghostly figures outside the domain of political economy. The needs of the worker are thus reduced to the need to maintain him *during work*, so that the race of workers does not die out. Consequently, wages have exactly the same significance as the *maintenance* of any other productive instrument, and as the *consumption of capital* in general so that it can reproduce itself with interest. They are like the oil which is applied to a wheel to keep it running. Wages thus form part of the necessary *costs* of capital and of the capitalist, and they must not exceed this necessary amount. Thus it was quite logical for the English factory lords, before the Amendment Bill of 1834, to deduct from the wages which they themselves paid, the public alms which workers received from the poor-law taxes, i.e. to treat public alms as an integral part of total wages.

Production does not only produce man as a *commodity*, the *human commodity*, man in the form of a *commodity*; in conformity with this situation it produces him as a *mentally* and *physically* dehumanized being. . . . Immorality, miscarriage, helotism of workers and capitalists. . . . Its product is the *self-conscious* and *self-acting commodity*. . . . The *human* commodity. . . . It is a great step forward by Ricardo, Mill, *et al.*, as against Smith and Say, to declare the *existence of* human beings—the greater or lesser human productivity of the commodity—as *indifferent* or indeed harmful. The true end of production is not the number of workers a given capital maintains, but the amount of interest it earns, the total annual saving. It was likewise a great and logical advance in recent [XLI] English political economy that, while establishing *labour* as the only principle of political economy, it clearly distinguished the inverse relation between wages and interest on capital, and observed that as a rule the capitalist could *only* increase his gains by the depression of wages and vice versa. The *normal* relation is seen to be not the defrauding of the consumer, but the mutual cheating of capitalist and worker. The relation of private property includes within itself, in a latent state, the relation of private property as labour, the relation of private property as capital, and the mutual influence of these two. On the one hand, there is the production of human activity as *labour*, that is, as an activity which is alien to itself, to man and to nature, and thus alien to consciousness and to the realization of human life; the abstract existence of man as a mere *working man*, who, therefore, plunges every day from his fulfilled nothingness into absolute nothingness, into social, and thus real, non-existence. On the other hand, there is the production of objects of human labour as *capital*, in which every natural and social characteristic of the object is *dissolved*, in which private property has lost its natural and social quality (and has thereby lost all political and social disguise and no longer even *appears* to be connected with human relationships), and in which the *same* capital remains the *same* in the most varied natural and social conditions, which have no relevance to its *real* content. This contradiction, at its highest point, is necessarily the summit and the point of decline of the whole relation.

It is, therefore, another great achievement of recent English political economy to have defined ground rent as the difference between the returns on the worst and the best cultivated land, to have demolished the romantic illusions of the landowner—his alleged social importance and the identity of his interests with those of society at large (a view which Adam Smith held even after the Physiocrats)—and to have anticipated and prepared the development in reality, which will transform the landowner into an ordinary, prosaic capitalist and thereby simplify the contradiction, bring it to a head and prepare its solution. *Land* as *land*, *ground rent* as *ground rent*, have lost their distinctive status and have become dumb *capital* and *interest*, or rather, capital and interest which only talk money.

The *distinction* between capital and land, profit and ground rent, and the distinction of both from wages, *industry*, *agriculture*, *immovable* and *movable* private property, is a *historical* distinction, not one inscribed in the nature of things. It is a *fixed* stage in the formation and development of the antithesis between capital and labour.   In industry, etc., as opposed to immovable landed property, only the mode of origin and the antithesis to agriculture through which industry has developed, is expressed.   As a *particular* kind of labour, as a more *significant, important* and *comprehensive* distinction, it exists only so long as industry (town life) is established *in opposition to* landed property (aristocratic feudal life) and still bears the characteristics of this contradiction in itself in the form of monopolies, crafts, guilds, corporations, etc.   In such a situation, labour still appears to have a *social* meaning, still has the significance of *genuine* communal life, and has not yet progressed to *neutrality* in relation to its content, to full self-sufficient being, i.e. to abstraction from all other existence and thus to *liberated* capital.

[LXII] But the necessary *development* of labour is liberated *industry*, constituted for itself alone, and *liberated capital*.   The power of industry over its opponent is shown by the rise of *agriculture* as a real industry, whereas formerly most of the work was left to the soil itself and to the *slave* of the soil through whom the land cultivated itself.   With the transformation of the slave into a *free* worker, i.e. into a *hireling*, the landowner himself is transformed into a lord of industry, a capitalist.

This transformation takes place at first through the medium of the tenant farmer.   But the tenant is the representative, the revealed *secret*, of the landowner.   Only through him does the landowner have an *economic* existence, existence as a property owner; for the ground rent of his land only exists as a result of the competition between tenants. Thus the landowner *has* already become to a large extent, in the person of the tenant farmer, a *common* capitalist. And this must be fulfilled in reality; the capitalist directing agriculture (the tenant) must become a landowner, or vice versa. The *industrial trade* of the tenant is that of the landowner, for the existence of the former establishes that of the latter.

Recollecting their contrasting origins and descent the landowner recognizes the capitalist as his insubordinate, liberated and enriched slave of yesterday, and sees himself as a *capitalist* who is threatened by him. The capitalist sees the landowner as the idle, cruel and egoistical lord of yesterday; he knows that as a capitalist he injures the landowner, and yet that industry is responsible for the latter's present social significance, for his possessions and pleasures. He regards the landowner as the antithesis of *free* enterprise and of *free* capital which is independent of every natural limitation. This opposition is extremely bitter and each side expresses the truth about the other. It is only necessary to read the attacks upon immovable property by representatives of movable property, and vice versa, in order to obtain a clear picture of their respective worthlessness. The landowner emphasizes the noble lineage of his property, feudal souvenirs, reminiscences, the poetry of remembrance, his open-hearted character, his political importance, etc., and when he talks in economic terms asserts that agriculture *alone* is productive. At the same time he portrays his opponent as a sly, bargaining, deceitful, mercenary, rebellious, heartless and soulless individual, an extortionate, pimping, servile, smooth, flattering, desiccated rogue, without honour, principles, poetry or anything else, who is alienated from the community which he freely trades away, and who breeds, nourishes and cherishes competition and along with it poverty, crime and the dissolution of all social bonds. (*See* among others the Physiocrat, Bergasse, whom Camille Desmoulins scourged in his journal *Révolutions de France et de*

Brabant; *see also* von Vincke, Lancizolle, Haller, Leo,[1] Kosegarten and Sismondi.) [2]

Movable property, for its part, points to the miracle of modern industry and development. It is the child, the legitimate, native-born son, of the modern age. It pities its opponent as a simpleton, *ignorant* of his own nature (and this is entirely true) who wishes to replace moral capital and free labour by crude, immoral coercion and serfdom. It depicts him as a Don Quixote who, beneath the appearance of *directness, decency,* the *general interest* and stability, conceals his incapacity for development, greedy self-indulgence, selfishness, sectional interest and evil intention. It exposes him as a cunning *monopolist*; it pours cold water upon his reminiscences, his poetry and his romanticism, by a historical and satirical recital of the baseness, cruelty, degradation, prostitution, infamy, anarchy and revolt, of which the romantic castles were the workshops.

It (movable property) claims to have won political freedom for the people, to have removed the chains which bound civil society, to have linked together different worlds, to have established commerce which promotes friendship between peoples, to have created a pure morality and an agreeable culture. It has given the people, in place of their crude wants, civilized needs and the means of satisfying them. But the landowner—this idle speculator

---

[1] *See* the pompous Old-Hegelian theologian Funke who, according to Herr Leo, related with tears in his eyes how a slave had refused, when serfdom was abolished, to cease being a *noble possession*. *See also* JUSTUS MÖSER's *Patriotische Phantasien*, which are distinguished by the fact that they never for a moment abandon the ingenuous, petty-bourgeois, "home-made," ordinary, limited horizon of the philistine, and yet remain pure fantasy. It is this contradiction which has made them so attractive to the German mind.

[2] Here, and in his footnote, Marx refers especially to the following writings: CAMILLE DESMOULINS, *Révolutions de France et de Brabant*. Second trimestre contenant mars, avril, mai. Paris, l'an Ier. No. 16, p. 139 *et seq.*; No. 23, p. 425 *et seq.*; No. 26, p. 580 *et seq.* G. L. W. FUNKE, *Die aus der unbeschränkten Teilbarkeit des Grundeigentums hervorgehenden Nachteile*, Hamburg and Gotha 1829, quoted by HEINRICH LEO, *Studien und Skizzen zu einer Naturlehre des Staats*. 1 Abt. Halle 1833. JUSTUS MÖSER, *Patriotische Phantasien*. Berlin 1775-8. J. C. L. SIMONDE DE SISMONDI, op. cit. [*Editor's note.*]

in grain—raises the price of the people's basic necessities of life and thereby forces the capitalist to raise wages without being able to increase productivity, thus hindering and ultimately arresting the growth of national income and the accumulation of capital upon which depends the creation of work for the people and of wealth for the country. He brings about a general decline, and parasitically exploits *all* the advantages of modern civilization without making the least contribution to it, and without abandoning any of his feudal prejudices. Finally, let him—for whom cultivation and the land itself exist only as a heaven-sent source of money—regard the *tenant farmer* and say whether he himself is not a *straightforward, fantastic, cunning* scoundrel, who in his heart and in reality has long been captivated by *free* industry and by the *delights* of trade, however much he may resist them and prattle about historical reminiscences or moral and political aims. Everything which he can really bring forward in justification is true only of the *cultivator of the land* (the capitalist and the labourers) of whom the landowner is rather the *enemy*; thus he testifies against himself. *Without* capital, landed property is lifeless and worthless matter. It is indeed the civilized victory of movable property to have discovered and created human labour as the source of wealth, in place of the lifeless thing. (*See* Paul Louis Courier, Saint-Simon, Ganilh, Ricardo, Mill, MacCulloch, Destutt de Tracy, and Michel Chevalier.)

From the *real* course of development (to be inserted here) there follows the necessary victory of the capitalist, i.e. of developed private property, over undeveloped, immature private property, the landowner. In general, movement must triumph over immobility, overt self-conscious baseness over concealed, unconscious baseness, *avarice* over *self-indulgence*, the avowedly restless and able self-interest of *enlightenment* over the local, worldly-wise, simple, idle and fantastic *self-interest of superstition*, and *money* over the other forms of private property.

The states which have a presentiment of the danger represented by fully developed free industry, pure morality, and trade which promotes the amity of peoples, attempt, but quite in vain, to arrest the capitalization of landed property.

Landed property, as distinct from capital, is private property, capital, which is still afflicted by local and political prejudices; it is capital which has not yet emerged from its involvement with the world, *undeveloped* capital. In the course of its *formation on a world scale* it must achieve its abstract, i.e. *pure* expression.

The relations of private property are capital, labour and their interconnexions.

The movements through which these elements have to go are—

First—*unmediated* and *mediated unity of the two.* Capital and labour are at first still united; later indeed separated and alienated, but reciprocally developing and promoting each other as *positive* conditions.

Opposition between the two—they mutually exclude each other; the worker recognizes the capitalist as his own non-existence and vice versa; each seeks to rob the other of his existence.

Opposition of each *to* itself. Capital = accumulated labour = labour. As such it divides into *capital itself* and *interest*; the latter divides into *interest* and *profit*. Complete sacrifice of the capitalist. He sinks into the working class, just as the worker—but only exceptionally—becomes a capitalist. Labour as a moment of capital, its *costs.* Thus wages a sacrifice of capital.

Labour divides into *labour itself* and *wages of labour.* The worker himself a capital, a commodity.

Clash of reciprocal contradictions.[1]

---

[1] The second manuscript ends here. [*Editor's note.*]

THIRD MANUSCRIPT

PRIVATE PROPERTY AND LABOUR

[I] *ad* page XXXVI. The subjective essence of *private* property, private property as activity for itself, as *subject*, as *person*, is labour. It is evident, therefore, that only the political economy which recognized labour as its principle (Adam Smith) and which no longer regarded private property as merely a *condition* external to man, can be considered as both a product of the real *dynamism* and *development* of private property,[1] a product of modern *industry*, and a force which has accelerated and extolled the dynamism and development of industry and has made it a power in the domain of *consciousness*.

Thus, from the viewpoint of this enlightened political economy which has discovered the *subjective* essence of wealth within the framework of private property, the partisans of the monetary system and the mercantilist system, who consider private property as a *purely objective* being for man, are *fetishists* and *Catholics*. Engels is right, therefore, in calling Adam Smith the *Luther of political economy*. Just as Luther recognized religion and *faith* as the essence of the real *world*, and for that reason took up a position against Catholic paganism; just as he annulled *external* religiosity while making religiosity the *inner* essence of man; just as he negated the distinction between priest and layman because he transferred the priest into the heart of the layman; so wealth external to man and independent of him (and thus only to be acquired and conserved from outside) is annulled. That is to say, its *external* and *mindless objectivity* is annulled by the fact that private property is incorporated in man himself, and man himself is recognized as its essence. But as a result, man himself is brought into the sphere of private property,

[1] It is the independent movement of private property become conscious of itself; modern industry as Self.

just as, with Luther, he is brought into the sphere of religion. Under the guise of recognizing man, political economy, whose principle is labour, carries to its logical conclusion the denial of man. Man himself is no longer in a condition of external tension with the external substance of private property; he has himself become the tension-ridden being of private property. What was previously a phenomenon of *being external to oneself*, a real external manifestation of man, has now become the act of objectification, of alienation. This political economy seems at first, therefore, to recognize man with his independence, his personal activity, etc. It incorporates private property in the very essence of man, and it is no longer, therefore, conditioned by the local or national *characteristics of private property* regarded as existing outside itself. It manifests a cosmopolitan, universal activity which is destructive of every limit and every bond, and substitutes itself as the *only* policy, the *only* universality, the *only* limit and the *only* bond. But in its further development it is obliged to discard this hypocrisy and to show itself in all its cynicism. It does this, without any regard for the apparent contradictions to which its doctrine leads, by showing in a more one-sided fashion, and thus with greater logic and clarity, that *labour* is the sole *essence of wealth*, and by demonstrating that this doctrine, in contrast with the original conception, has consequences which are *inimical to man*. Finally, it gives the death-blow to *ground rent*; that last individual and natural form of private property and source of wealth existing independently of the movement of labour, which was the expression of feudal property but has become entirely its economic expression and is no longer able to put up any resistance to political economy. (The Ricardo School.) Not only does the *cynicism* of political economy increase from Smith, through Say, to Ricardo, Mill, *et al.* inasmuch as for the latter the consequence of *industry* appeared more and more developed and contradictory; from a positive point of view they become more alienated, and more consciously alienated, from man, in comparison with their predecessors. This is *only* because their science develops with greater logic and truth. Since they make private property in its active form the subject, and since at the same time they make man as a non-being into a being, the contradiction in reality corresponds entirely with the contradictory essence which they have accepted as a principle. The divided [II] *reality* of *industry* is far from refuting, but instead confirms, its *self-divided* principle. Its principle is in fact the principle of this division.

The physiocratic doctrine of Quesnay forms the transition from the mercantilist system to Adam Smith. *Physiocracy* is in a direct sense the *economic* decomposition of feudal property, but for this reason it is equally directly the *economic transformation*, the re-establishment, of this same feudal property; with the difference that its language is no longer feudal but economic. All wealth is reduced to *land* and *cultivation* (agriculture). Land is not yet *capital* but is still a particular mode of existence of capital, whose value is claimed to reside in, and derive from, its natural particularity; but land is none the less a natural and universal *element*, whereas the mercantilist system regarded only precious metals as wealth. The object of wealth, its matter, has, therefore, been given the greatest universality within natural limits—inasmuch as it is also, as nature, directly objective wealth. And it is only by labour, by agriculture, that land exists for man. Consequently, the subjective essence of wealth is already transferred to labour. But at the same time agriculture is the *only productive labour*. Labour is, therefore, not yet taken in its universality and its abstract form; it is still bound to a particular *element of nature as its matter*, and is only recognized in a particular *mode of existence determined by nature*. Labour is still only a *determinate, particular* alienation of man, and its product is also conceived as a determinate part of wealth due more to nature than to labour itself. Land is still regarded here as something which exists naturally and independently of man, and not yet as capital, i.e. as a factor of labour. On the contrary, labour appears to be a factor of *nature*. But since the fetishism of the old external wealth, existing only as an object, has been reduced to a very simple natural element, and since its essence has been partially, and in a certain way, recognized in its subjective existence, the necessary advance has been made in recognizing the *universal nature* of wealth and in raising *labour* in its absolute form, i.e. in abstraction, to the *principle*. It is demonstrated against the Physiocrats that from the economic point of view (i.e. from the only valid point of view) agriculture does not differ from any other industry; and that it is not, therefore, a specific kind of labour, bound to a particular element, or a particular manifestation of labour, but *labour in general* which is the *essence* of wealth.

Physiocracy denies *specific*, external, purely objective wealth, in declaring that labour is its essence. For the Physiocrats, however, labour is in the first place only the *subjective essence* of landed property. (They begin from that kind of property which appears historically as the predominant recognized type.) They merely turn landed property into alienated man. They annul its feudal character by declaring that *industry* (agriculture) is its *essence*; but they reject the industrial world and accept the feudal system by declaring that *agriculture* is the only industry.

It is evident that when the *subjective essence*—industry in opposition to landed property, industry forming itself as industry—is grasped, this essence includes within itself the opposition. For just as industry incorporates the superseded landed property, its subjective essence incorporates the subjective essence of the latter.

Landed property is the first form of private property, and industry first appears historically in simple opposition to it, as a particular form of private property (or rather, as the liberated slave of landed property); this sequence is repeated in the scientific study of the *subjective* essence of private property, and labour appears at first only as *agricultural labour* but later establishes itself as *labour in general.*

[III] All wealth has become *industrial wealth,* the *wealth* of labour, and *industry* is realized labour; just as the *factory system* is the realized essence of *industry* (i.e. of labour), and as *industrial capital* is the realized objective form of private property. Thus we see that it is only at this stage that private property can consolidate its rule over man and become, in its most general form, a world-historical power.

PRIVATE PROPERTY AND COMMUNISM

ad page XXXIX. But the antithesis between *propertylessness* and *property* is still an indeterminate antithesis, which is not conceived in its *active reference* to its intrinsic relations, not yet conceived as a contradiction, so long as it is not understood as an antithesis between *labour* and *capital*. Even without the advanced development of private property, e.g. in ancient Rome, in Turkey, etc. this antithesis may be expressed in a primitive form. In this form it does not yet *appear* as established by private property itself. But labour, the subjective essence of private property as the exclusion of property, and capital, objective labour as the exclusion of labour, constitute *private property* as the developed relation of the contradiction and thus a dynamic relation which drives towards its resolution.

ad ibidem. The supersession of self-estrangement follows the same course as self-estrangement. *Private property* is first considered only from its objective aspect, but with labour conceived as its essence. Its mode of existence is, therefore, *capital* which it is necessary to abolish " as such " (Proudhon). Or else the *specific form* of labour (labour which is brought to a common level, subdivided, and thus unfree) is regarded as the source of the *nocivity* of private property and of its existence alienated from man. Fourier, in accord with the Physiocrats, regards *agricultural labour* as being at least the exemplary kind of labour. Saint-Simon asserts on the contrary that *industrial labour* as such is the essence of labour, and consequently he desires the *exclusive* rule of the industrialists and an amelioration of the condition of the workers. Finally, *communism* is the positive expression of the abolition of private property, and in the first place of universal private property. In taking this relation in its *universal aspect* communism is, in its first form, only the generalization and fulfilment of the relation. As such it appears in a double form; the domination of material property looms so large that it aims to destroy everything which is incapable of being possessed by everyone as private property. It wishes to eliminate talent, etc. by *force*. Immediate physical possession seems to it the unique goal of life and existence. The role of *worker* is not abolished, but is extended to all men. The relation of private property remains the relation of the community to the world of things. Finally, this tendency to oppose general private property to private property is expressed in an animal form; *marriage* (which is incontestably a form of *exclusive private property*) is contrasted with the community of women, in which women become communal and common property. One may say that this idea of the *community of women* is the *open secret* of this entirely crude and unreflective communism. Just as women are to pass from marriage to universal prostitution, so the whole world of wealth (i.e. the objective being of man) is to pass from the relation of exclusive marriage with the private owner to the relation of universal prostitution with the community. This communism, which negates the *personality* of man in every sphere, is only the logical expression of private property, which is this negation. Universal *envy* setting itself up as a power is only a camouflaged form of cupidity which re-establishes itself and satisfies itself in a different way. The thoughts of every individual private property are *at least* directed against any *wealthier* private property, in the form of envy and the desire to reduce everything to a common level; so that this envy and levelling in fact constitute the essence of competition. Crude communism is only the culmination of such envy and levelling-down on the basis of a *preconceived* minimum. How little this abolition of private property represents a genuine appropriation is shown by the abstract negation of the whole world of culture and civilization, and the regression to the *unnatural* [IV] simplicity of the poor and wantless individual who has not only not surpassed private property but has not yet even attained to it.

The community is only a community of *work* and of *equality of wages* paid out by the communal capital, by the *community* as universal capitalist. The two sides of the relation are raised to a *supposed* universality; *labour* as a condition in which everyone is placed, and *capital* as the acknowledged universality and power of the community.

In the relationship with *woman*, as the prey and the handmaid of communal lust, is expressed the infinite degradation in which man exists for himself; for the secret of this relationship finds its *unequivocal*, incontestable, *open* and revealed expression in the relation of man to woman and in the way in which the *direct* and *natural* species-relationship is conceived. The immediate, natural and necessary relation of human being to human being is also the *relation* of *man* to *woman*. In this *natural* species-relationship man's relation to nature is directly his relation to man, and his relation to man is directly his relation to nature, to his own *natural* function. Thus, in this relation is *sensuously revealed*, reduced to an observable *fact*, the extent to which human nature has become nature for man and to which nature has become human nature for him. From this relationship man's whole level of development can be assessed. It follows from the character of this relationship how far *man* has become, and has understood himself as, a *species-being*, a *human being*. The relation of man to woman is the *most natural* relation of human being to human being. It indicates, therefore, how far man's *natural* behaviour has become *human*, and how far his *human* essence has become a *natural* essence for him, how far his *human nature* has become *nature* for him. It also shows how far man's needs have become *human* needs, and consequently how far the other person, as a person, has become one of his needs, and to what extent he is in his individual existence at the same time a social being. The first positive annulment of private property, crude communism, is, therefore, only a *phenomenal form* of the infamy of private property representing itself as positive community.

2. Communism (*a*) still political in nature, democratic or despotic; (*b*) with the abolition of the state, yet still incomplete and influenced by private property, that is, by the alienation of man. In both forms communism is already aware of being the reintegration of man, his return to himself, the supersession of man's self-alienation. But since it has not yet grasped the positive nature of private property, or the *human* nature of needs, it is still captured and contaminated by private property. It has well understood the concept, but not the essence.

3. *Communism* is the *positive* abolition of *private property*, of *human self-alienation*, and thus the real *appropriation* of *human* nature through and for man. It is, therefore, the return of man himself as a *social*, i.e. really human, being, a complete and conscious return which assimilates all the wealth of previous development. Communism as a fully developed naturalism is humanism and as a fully developed humanism is naturalism. It is the *definitive* resolution of the antagonism between man and nature, and between man and man. It is the true solution of the conflict between existence and essence, between objectification and self-affirmation, between freedom and necessity, between individual and species. It is the solution of the riddle of history and knows itself to be this solution.

[V] Thus the whole historical development, both the *real* genesis of communism (the birth of its empirical existence) and its thinking consciousness, is its comprehended and conscious process of becoming; whereas the other, still undeveloped, communism seeks in certain historical forms opposed to private property a *historical* justification founded upon what already exists, and to this end tears out of their context isolated elements of this development (Cabet [1] and

---

[1] ETIENNE CABET (1788–1856); author of *Voyage en Icarie* (1840) and founder of a Utopian Community, Icaria, in Illinois. [*Editor's note.*]

Villegardelle are pre-eminent among those who ride this hobby-horse) and asserts them as proofs of its historical pedigree. In doing so, it makes clear that by far the greater part of this development contradicts its own assertions, and that if it has ever existed its past existence refutes its pretension to *essential being*.

It is easy to understand the necessity which leads the whole revolutionary movement to find its empirical, as well its as theoretical, basis in the development of *private property*, and more precisely of the economic system.

This material, directly *perceptible* private property is the material and sensuous expression of *alienated human* life. Its movement—production and consumption—is the *sensuous* manifestation of the movement of all previous production, i.e. the realization or reality of man. Religion, the family, the state, law, morality, science, art, etc. are only *particular* forms of production and come under its general law. The positive supersession of *private property*, as the appropriation of *human* life, is, therefore, the positive supersession of all alienation, and the return of man from religion, the family, the state, etc. to his *human*, i.e. social life. Religious alienation as such occurs only in the sphere of *consciousness*, in the inner life of man, but economic alienation is that of *real life* and its supersession, therefore, affects both aspects. Of course, the development in different nations has a different beginning according to whether the actual and *established* life of the people is more in the realm of mind or more in the external world, is a real or ideal life. Communism begins where atheism begins (Owen), but atheism is at the outset still far from being *communism*; indeed it is still for the most part an abstraction.[1]

---

[1] Marx inserted a note here which referred back to his discussion of " crude communism ": " Prostitution is only a *specific* expression of the *universal* prostitution of the worker, and since prostitution is a relationship which includes both the one who is prostituted and the one who prostitutes (and the latter is much more base), so the capitalist, etc. comes within this category." [*Editor's note.*]

Thus the philanthropy of atheism is at first only an abstract *philosophical* philanthropy, whereas that of communism is at once *real* and oriented towards *action*.

We have seen how, on the assumption that private property has been positively superseded, man produces man, himself and then other men; how the object which is the direct activity of his personality is at the same time his existence for other men and their existence for him. Similarly, the material of labour and man himself as a subject are the starting-point as well as the result of this movement (and because there must be this starting-point private property is a historical necessity). Therefore, the *social* character is the universal character of the whole movement; *as* society itself produces *man* as *man*, so it is *produced* by him. Activity and mind are social in their content as well as in their *origin*; they are *social* activity and social mind. The *human* significance of nature only exists for *social* man, because only in this case is nature a *bond* with other *men*, the basis of his existence for others and of their existence for him. Only then is nature the *basis* of his own *human* experience and a vital element of human reality. The *natural* existence of man has here become his *human* existence and nature itself has become human for him. Thus *society* is the accomplished union of man with nature, the veritable resurrection of nature, the realized naturalism of man and the realized humanism of nature.

[VI] Social activity and social mind by no means exist *only* in the form of activity or mind which is directly communal. Nevertheless, communal activity and mind, i.e. activity and mind which express and confirm themselves directly in a *real association* with other men, occur everywhere where this direct expression of sociability arises from the content of the activity or corresponds to the nature of mind. Even when I carry out *scientific* work, etc., an activity which I can seldom conduct in direct association with other men, I perform a *social*, because *human*, act. It is not only the material of my activity—such as the language itself which the thinker uses—which is given to me as a social product. My *own existence* is a social activity. For this reason, what I myself produce I produce for society, and with the consciousness of acting as a social being.

My universal consciousness is only the *theoretical* form of that whose *living* form is the real community, the social entity, although at the present day this universal consciousness is an abstraction from real life and is opposed to it as an enemy. That is why the *activity* of my universal consciousness as such is my *theoretical* existence as a social being.

It is above all necessary to avoid postulating " society " once again as an abstraction confronting the individual. The individual *is* the *social being*. The manifestation of his life—even when it does not appear directly in the form of a communal manifestation, accomplished in association with other men—is, therefore, a manifestation and affirmation of *social life*. Individual human life and species-life are not different things, even though the mode of existence of individual life is necessarily either a more *specific* or a more *general* mode of species-life, or that of species-life a *specific* or more *general* mode of individual life.

In his *species-consciousness* man confirms his real *social life*, and reproduces his real existence in thought; while conversely, species-life confirms itself in species-consciousness and exists for itself in its universality as a thinking being. Though man is a unique individual—and it is just his particularity which makes him an individual, a really *individual* communal being—he is equally the *whole*, the ideal whole, the subjective existence of society as thought and experienced. He exists in reality as the representation and the real mind of social existence, and as the sum of human manifestations of life.

Thought and being are indeed *distinct* but they also form a unity. *Death* seems to be a harsh victory of the species over the individual and to contradict their unity; but the particular individual is only a *determinate species-being* and as such he is mortal.

4. Just as *private property* is only the sensuous expression of the fact that man is at the same time an *objective* fact for himself and becomes an alien and non-human object for himself; just as his manifestation of life is also his alienation of life and his self-realization a loss of reality, the emergence of an *alien* reality; so the positive supersession of private property, i.e. the *sensuous* appropriation of the human essence and of human life, of objective man and of human *creations*, by and for man, should not be taken only in the sense of *immediate*, exclusive *enjoyment*, or only in the sense of *possession* or *having*. Man appropriates his manifold being in an all-inclusive way, and thus as a whole man. All his *human* relations to the world—seeing, hearing, smelling, tasting, touching, thinking, observing, feeling, desiring, acting, loving—in short, all the organs of his individuality, like the organs which are directly communal in form, [VII] are in their objective action (their *action in relation to the object*) the appropriation of this object, the appropriation of human reality. The way in which they react to the object is the confirmation of *human reality*.[1] It is human effectiveness and human *suffering*, for suffering humanly considered is an enjoyment of the self for man.

Private property has made us so stupid and partial that an object is only *ours* when we have it, when it exists for us as capital or when it is directly eaten, drunk, worn, inhabited, etc., in short, *utilized* in some way. But private property itself only conceives these various forms of possession as *means of life*, and the life for which they serve as means is the *life* of *private property*—labour and creation of capital.

Thus *all* the physical and intellectual senses have been replaced by the simple alienation of *all* these senses; the

---

[1] It is, therefore, just as varied as the determinations of human nature and activities are diverse.

sense of *having*. The human being had to be reduced to this absolute poverty in order to be able to give birth to all his inner wealth. (On the category of *having* see Hess in *Einundzwanzig Bogen*.) [1]

The supersession of private property is, therefore, the complete *emancipation* of all the human qualities and senses. It is such an emancipation because these qualities and senses have become *human*, from the subjective as well as the objective point of view. The eye has become a *human* eye when its *object* has become a *human*, social object, created by man and destined for him. The senses have, therefore, become directly theoreticians in practice. They relate themselves to the thing for the sake of the thing, but the thing itself is an *objective human* relation to itself and to man, and vice versa.[2] Need and enjoyment have thus lost their *egoistic* character and nature has lost its mere *utility* by the fact that its utilization has become *human* utilization.

Similarly, the senses and minds of other men have become my *own* appropriation. Thus besides these direct organs, *social* organs are constituted, in the form of society; for example, activity in direct association with others has become an organ for the manifestation of life and a mode of appropriation of *human* life.

It is evident that the human eye appreciates things in a different way from the crude, non-human eye, the human *ear* differently from the crude ear. As we have seen, it is only when the object becomes a *human* object, or objective *humanity*, that man does not become lost in it. This is only possible when man himself becomes a *social* object; when he himself becomes a social being and society becomes a being for him in this object.

On the one hand, it is only when objective reality everywhere becomes for man in society the reality of human

---

[1] *Einundzwanzig Bogen aus der Schweiz*, op. cit., p. 329.
[2] In practice I can only relate myself in a human way to a thing when the thing is related in a human way to man.

faculties, human reality, and thus the reality of his own faculties, that all *objects* become for him the *objectification of himself.* The objects then confirm and realize his individuality, they are *his own* objects, i.e. man himself becomes the object. *The manner in which these objects* become his own depends upon the *nature of the object* and the nature of the corresponding faculty; for it is precisely the *determinate character* of this relation which constitutes the specific *real* mode of affirmation. The object is not the same for the *eye* as for the *ear,* for the ear as for the eye. The *distinctive character* of each faculty is precisely its *characteristic* essence and thus also the characteristic mode of its objectification, of its *objectively real,* living *being.* It is therefore not only in thought, [VIII] but through *all* the senses that man is affirmed in the objective world.

Let us next consider the subjective aspect. Man's musical sense is only awakened by music. The most beautiful music has no meaning for the non-musical ear, is not an object for it, because my object can only be the confirmation of one of my own faculties. It can only be so for me in so far as my faculty exists for itself as a subjective capacity, because the meaning of an object for me extends only as far as the sense extends (only makes sense for an appropriate sense). For this reason, the *senses* of social man are *different* from those of non-social man. It is only through the objectively deployed wealth of the human being that the wealth of subjective *human* sensibility (a musical ear, an eye which is sensitive to the beauty of form, in short, senses which are capable of human satisfaction and which confirm themselves as human faculties) is cultivated or created. For it is not only the five senses, but also the so-called spiritual senses, the practical senses (desiring, loving, etc.), in brief, human sensibility and the human character of the senses, which can only come into being through the existence of *its* object, through humanized nature. The cultivation of the five senses is the work of all previous history. Sense which is subservient to crude needs has only a restricted meaning. For a starving man the human form of food does not exist, but only its abstract character as food. It could just as well exist in the most crude form, and it is impossible to say in what way this feeding-activity would differ from that of animals. The needy man, burdened with cares, has no appreciation of the most beautiful spectacle. The dealer in minerals sees only their commercial value, not their beauty or their particular characteristics; he has no mineralogical sense. Thus, the objectification of the human essence, both theoretically and practically, is necessary in order to *humanize* man's senses, and also to create the *human senses* corresponding to all the wealth of human and natural being.

Just as society at its beginnings finds, through the development of *private property* with its wealth and poverty (both intellectual and material), the materials necessary for this *cultural development*, so the fully constituted society produces man in all the plenitude of his being, the wealthy man endowed with all the senses, as an enduring reality. It is only in a social context that subjectivism and objectivism, spiritualism and materialism, activity and passivity, cease to be antinomies and thus cease to exist as such antinomies. The resolution of the *theoretical* contradictions is possible *only* through practical means, only through the *practical* energy of man. Their resolution is not by any means, therefore, only a problem of knowledge, but is a *real* problem of life which philosophy was unable to solve precisely because it saw there a purely theoretical problem.

It can be seen that the history of *industry* and industry as it *objectively* exists is an *open* book of the *human faculties*, and a human *psychology* which can be sensuously apprehended. This history has not so far been conceived in relation to human *nature*, but only from a superficial utilitarian point of view, since in the condition of alienation it was only possible to conceive real human faculties and *human* species-action in the form of general human existence, as religion, or as history in its abstract, general aspect as politics, art and literature, etc. *Everyday material industry* (which can be conceived as part of that general development; or equally, the general development can be conceived as a specific part of industry since all human activity up to the present has been labour, i.e. industry, self-alienated activity) shows us, in the form of *sensuous useful objects*, in an alienated form, the *essential human faculties* transformed into objects. No psychology for which this book, i.e. the most tangible and accessible part of history, remains closed, can become a *real* science with a genuine content. What is to be thought of a science which stays aloof from this enormous field of human labour, and which does not feel its own inadequacy even though this great wealth of human activity means nothing to it except perhaps what can be expressed in the single phrase— " need," " common need "?

The *natural sciences* have developed a tremendous activity and have assembled an ever-growing mass of data. But philosophy has remained alien to these sciences just as they have remained alien to philosophy. Their momentary *rapprochement* was only a *fantastic* illusion. There was a desire for union but the power to effect it was lacking. Historiography itself only takes natural science into account incidentally, regarding it as a factor making for enlightenment, for practical utility and for particular great discoveries. But natural science has penetrated all the more *practically* into human life through industry. It has transformed human life and prepared the emancipation of humanity, even though its immediate effect was to accentuate the dehumanization of man. *Industry* is the actual historical relationship of nature, and thus of natural science, to man. If industry is conceived as the *exoteric* manifestation of the essential human *faculties*, the *human* essence of nature and the *natural* essence of man can also be understood. Natural science will then abandon its abstract materialist, or rather idealist, orientation, and will become the basis of a *human* science, just as it has already become—though in an alienated form—the basis of actual human life. One basis for life and another for science is *a priori* a falsehood. Nature, as it develops in human history, in the act of genesis of human society, is the *actual* nature of man; thus nature, as it develops through industry, though in an *alienated* form, is truly *anthropological* nature.

Sense experience (*see* Feuerbach) must be the basis of all science. Science is only genuine science when it proceeds from sense experience, in the two forms of *sense perception* and *sensuous* need; i.e. only when it proceeds from nature. The whole of history is a preparation for " man " to become an object of *sense* perception, and for the development of human needs (the needs of man as such). History itself is a *real* part of *natural history*, of the development of nature into man. Natural science will one day incorporate the science of man, just as the science of man will incorporate natural science; there will be a *single* science.

Man is the direct object of natural science, because directly *perceptible nature* is for man directly human sense experience (an identical expression) in the form of the *other person* who is directly presented to him in a sensuous way. His own sense experience only exists as human sense experience for himself through the *other person*. But *nature* is the direct object of the *science of man*. The first object for man—man himself—is nature, sense experience; and the particular sensuous human faculties, which can only find objective realization in *natural* objects, can only attain self-knowledge in the science of natural being. The element of thought itself, the element of the living manifestation of thought, language, is sensuous in character. The *social* reality of nature and *human* natural science, or the *natural science of man*, are identical expressions.

It will be seen from this how, in place of the *wealth* and *poverty* of political economy, we have the *wealthy* man and the plenitude of *human* need. The wealthy man is at the same

time one who *needs* a complex of human manifestations of
life, and whose own self-realization exists as an inner
necessity, a *need*. Not only the wealth but also the *poverty* of
man acquires, in a socialist perspective, a *human* and thus a
social meaning. Poverty is the passive bond which leads
man to experience a need for the greatest wealth, the *other*
person. The sway of the objective entity within me, the
sensuous eruption of my life-activity, is the passion which
here becomes the *activity* of my being.

A being does not regard himself as independent unless he
is his own master, and he is only his own master when he
owes his existence to himself. A man who lives by the
favour of another considers himself a dependent being. But
I live completely by another person's favour when I owe to
him not only the continuance of my life but also *its creation*;
when he is its *source*. My life has necessarily such a cause
outside itself if it is not my own creation. The idea of
creation is thus one which it is difficult to eliminate from
popular consciousness. This consciousness is *unable to conceive* that nature and man exist on their own account, because such an existence contradicts all the tangible facts of
practical life.

The idea of the creation of the *earth* has received a severe
blow from the science of geogeny, i.e. from the science which
portrays the formation and development of the earth as a
process of spontaneous generation. *Generatio aequivoca* (spontaneous generation) is the only practical refutation of the
theory of creation.

But it is easy indeed to say to the particular individual
what Aristotle said: You are engendered by your father and
mother, and consequently it is the coitus of two human
beings, a human species-act, which has produced the human
being. You see, therefore, that even in a physical sense man
owes his existence to man. Consequently, it is not enough
to keep in view only one of the two aspects, the *infinite* progression, and to ask further: who engendered my father and

my grandfather? You must also keep in mind the *circular movement* which is perceptible in that progression, according to which man, in the act of generation reproduces himself; thus *man* always remains the subject. But you will reply: I grant you this circular movement, but you must in turn concede the progression, which leads ever further to the point where I ask; who created the first man and nature as a whole? I can only reply: your question is itself a product of abstraction. Ask yourself how you arrive at that question. Ask yourself whether your question does not arise from a point of view to which I cannot reply because it is a perverted one. Ask yourself whether that progression exists as such for rational thought. If you ask a question about the creation of nature and man you abstract from nature and man. You suppose them *non-existent* and you want me to demonstrate that they *exist*. I reply: give up your abstraction and at the same time you abandon your question. Or else, if you want to maintain your abstraction, be consistent, and if you think of man and nature as non-existent, [XI] think of yourself too as non-existent, for you are also man and nature. Do not think, do not ask me any questions, for as soon as you think and ask questions your abstraction from the existence of nature and man becomes meaningless. Or are you such an egoist that you conceive everything as non-existent and yet want to exist yourself?

You may reply: I do not want to conceive the nothingness of nature, etc.; I only ask you about the act of its creation, just as I ask the anatomist about the formation of bones, etc.

Since, however, for socialist man, the *whole of what is called world history* is nothing but the creation of man by human labour, and the emergence of nature for man, he, therefore, has the evident and irrefutable proof of his *self-creation*, of his own *origins*. Once the essence of man and of nature, man as a natural being and nature as a human reality, has become evident in practical life, in sense experience, the quest for an *alien* being, a being above man and nature (a quest which is an avowal of the unreality of man and nature) becomes impossible in practice. *Atheism*, as a denial of this unreality, is no longer meaningful, for atheism is a *negation of God* and seeks to assert by this negation the *existence of man.* Socialism no longer requires such a roundabout method; it begins from the *theoretical* and *practical sense perception* of man and nature as essential beings. It is positive human *self-consciousness*, no longer a self-consciousness attained through the negation of religion; just as the *real life* of man is positive and no longer attained through the negation of private property, through *communism.* Communism is the phase of negation of the negation and is, consequently, for the next stage of historical development, a real and necessary factor in the emancipation and rehabilitation of man. Communism is the necessary form and the dynamic principle of the immediate future, but communism is not itself the goal of human development—the form of human society.

NEEDS, PRODUCTION, AND DIVISION OF LABOUR

[XIV] (7) We have seen the importance which must be attributed, in a socialist perspective, to the *wealth* of human needs, and consequently also to a *new mode of production* and to a new *object* of production.   A new manifestation of *human* powers and a new enrichment of the human being.   Within the system of private property it has the opposite meaning. Every man speculates upon creating a *new* need in another in order to force him to a new sacrifice, to place him in a new dependence, and to entice him into a new kind of pleasure and thereby into economic ruin.   Everyone tries to establish over others an alien power in order to find there the satisfaction of his own egoistic need.   With the increasing mass of objects, therefore, the realm of alien entities to which man is subjected also increases.   Every new product is a new *potentiality* of mutual deceit and robbery.   Man becomes increasingly poor as a man; he has increasing need of *money* in order to take possession of the hostile being.   The power of his *money* diminishes directly with the growth of the quantity of production, i.e. his need increases with the increasing *power* of money.   The need for money is, therefore, the real need created by the modern economic system, and the only need which it creates.   The *quantity* of money becomes increasingly its only important quality.   Just as it reduces every entity to an abstraction, so it reduces itself in its own development to a *quantitative* entity.   Excess and immoderation become its true standard.   This is shown subjectively, partly in the fact that the expansion of production and of needs becomes an *ingenious* and always *calculating* subservience to inhuman, depraved, unnatural and *imaginary* appetites. Private property does not know how to change crude need into *human* need; its *idealism* is *fantasy*, *caprice* and *fancy*.

No eunuch flatters his tyrant more shamefully or seeks by more infamous means to stimulate his jaded appetite, in order to gain some favour, than does the eunuch of industry, the entrepreneur, in order to acquire a few silver coins or to charm the gold from the purse of his dearly beloved neighbour. (Every product is a bait by means of which the individual tries to entice the essence of the other person, his money. Every real or potential need is a weakness which will draw the bird into the lime. Universal exploitation of human communal life. Just as every imperfection of man is a bond with heaven, a point from which his heart is accessible to the priest, so every want is an opportunity for approaching one's neighbour, in simulated friendship, and saying, " Dear friend, I will give you what you need, but you know the *conditio sine qua non*. You know what ink you must use in signing yourself over to me. I shall swindle you while providing your enjoyment.") The entrepreneur accedes to the most depraved fancies of his neighbour, plays the role of pander between him and his needs, awakens unhealthy appetites in him, and watches for every weakness so that later on he may claim the remuneration for this labour of love.

This alienation is shown in part by the fact that the refinement of needs and of the means to satisfy them produces as its counterpart a bestial savagery, a complete, primitive and abstract simplicity of needs; or rather, that it simply reproduces itself in its opposite sense. For the worker even the need for fresh air ceases to be a need. Man returns to the cave dwelling again, but it is now poisoned by the pestilential breath of civilization. The worker has only a *precarious* right to inhabit it, for it has become an alien dwelling which may suddenly not be available, or from which he may be evicted if he [XV] does not pay the rent. He has to *pay* for this mortuary. The dwelling full of light which Aeschylus' Prometheus indicates as one of the great gifts by which he has changed savages into men, ceases to exist for the worker. Light, air, and the simplest *animal* cleanliness cease to be human needs. *Filth*, this corruption and putre-faction which runs in the *sewers* of civilization (this is to be taken literally) becomes the *element in which man lives*. Total and *unnatural* neglect, putrefied nature, becomes the *element in which he lives*. None of his senses exist any longer, either in a human form, or even in a non-human, animal form. The crudest *methods* (and *instruments*) of human labour re-appear; thus the *treadmill* of the Roman slaves has become the mode of production and mode of existence of many English workers. It is not enough that man should lose his human needs; even animal needs disappear. The Irish no longer have any need but that of *eating—eating potatoes*, and then only the worst kind, *mildewed potatoes*. But France and England already possess in every industrial town a *little* Ireland. Savages and animals have at least the need for hunting, exercise and companionship. But the simplifica-tion of machinery and of work is used to make workers out of those who are just growing up, who are still immature, *children*, while the worker himself has become a child de-prived of all care. Machinery is adapted to the weakness of the human being, in order to turn the weak human being into a machine.

The fact that the growth of needs and of the means to satisfy them results in a lack of needs and of means is de-monstrated in several ways by the economist (and by the capitalist; in fact, it is always empirical businessmen we refer to when we speak of economists, who are their *scientific* self-revelation and existence). First, by reducing the needs of the worker to the miserable necessities required for the maintenance of his physical existence, and by reducing his activity to the most abstract mechanical movements, the economist asserts that man has no needs, for activity or en-joyment, beyond that; and yet he declares that this kind of life is a *human* way of life. Secondly, by reckoning as the general standard of life (general because it is applicable to the mass of men) the *most impoverished* life conceivable, he turns the worker into a being who has neither senses nor needs, just as he turns his activity into a pure abstraction from all activity.   Thus all working-class *luxury* seems to him blameworthy, and everything which goes beyond the most abstract need (whether it be a passive enjoyment or a manifestation of personal activity) is regarded as a *luxury*. Political economy, the science of *wealth*, is, therefore, at the same time, the science of renunciation, of privation and of saving, which actually succeeds in depriving man of fresh *air* and of physical *activity*.   This science of a marvellous industry is at the same time the science of *asceticism*.   Its true ideal is the *ascetic* but *usurious* miser and the *ascetic* but *productive* slave.   Its moral ideal is the *worker* who takes a part of his wages to the savings bank.   It has even found a servile art to embody this favourite idea, which has been produced in a sentimental manner on the stage.   Thus, despite its worldly and pleasure-seeking appearance, it is a truly moral science, and the most moral of all sciences.   Its principal thesis is the renunciation of life and of human needs.   The less you eat, drink, buy books, go to the theatre or to balls, or to the public house, and the less you think, love, theorize, sing, paint, fence, etc. the more you will be able to save and the *greater* will become your treasure which neither moth nor rust will corrupt—your *capital*.   The less you *are*, the less you express your life, the more you *have*, the greater is your *alienated* life and the greater is the saving of your alienated being.   Everything [XVI] which the economist takes from you in the way of life and humanity, he restores to you in the form of *money* and *wealth*.   And everything which you are unable to do, your money can do for you; it can eat, drink, go to the ball and to the theatre. It can acquire art, learning, historical treasures, political power;   and it can travel.   It *can* appropriate all these things for you, can purchase everything;   it is the true *opulence*.   But although it can do all this, it only *desires* to create itself, and to buy itself, for everything else is subservient to it. When one owns the master, one also owns the servant, and one has no need of the master's servant. Thus all passions and activities must be submerged in *avarice*. The worker must have just what is necessary for him to want to live, and he must want to live only in order to have this.

It is true that some controversy has arisen in the field of political economy. Some economists (Lauderdale, Malthus, *et al.*) advocate luxury and condemn saving, while others (Ricardo, Say, *et al.*) advocate saving and condemn luxury. But the former admit that they desire luxury in order to create *work*, i.e. absolute saving, while the latter admit that they advocate saving in order to create *wealth*, i.e. luxury. The former have the *romantic* notion that avarice alone should not determine the consumption of the rich, and they contradict their own laws when they represent *prodigality* as being a direct means of enrichment; their opponents then demonstrate in detail and with great earnestness that prodigality diminishes rather than augments my *possessions*. The second group are hypocritical in not admitting that it is caprice and fancy which determine production. They forget the " refined needs," and that without consumption there would be no production. They forget that through competition production must become ever more universal and luxurious, that it is use which determines the value of a thing, and that use is determined by fashion. They want production to be limited to " useful things," but they forget that the production of too many useful things results in too many *useless* people. Both sides forget that prodigality and thrift, luxury and abstinence, wealth and poverty are equivalent.

You must not only be abstemious in the satisfaction of your direct senses, such as eating, etc., but also in your participation in general interests, your sympathy, trust, etc. if you wish to be economical and to avoid being ruined by illusions.

Everything which you own must be made *venal*, i.e. useful. Suppose I ask the economist: am I acting in accordance with economic laws if I earn money by the sale of my body, by prostituting it to another person's lust (in France, the factory workers call the prostitution of their wives and daughters the *n*th hour of work, which is literally true); or if I sell my friends to the Moroccans (and the direct sale of men occurs in all civilized countries in the form of the trade in conscripts)? He will reply: you are not acting contrary to my laws, but you must take into account what Cousin Morality and Cousin Religion have to say. My *economic* morality and religion have no objection to make, but . . . But then whom should we believe, the economist or the moralist? The morality of political economy is *gain*, work, thrift and sobriety—yet political economy promises to satisfy my needs. The political economy of morality is the riches of a good conscience, of virtue, etc., but how can I be virtuous if I am not alive and how can I have a good conscience if I am not aware of anything? The nature of alienation implies that each sphere applies a different and contradictory norm, that morality does not apply the same norm as political economy, etc., because each of them is a particular alienation of man; [XVII] each is concentrated upon a specific area of alienated activity and is itself alienated from the other.

Thus M. Michel Chevalier reproaches Ricardo with leaving morals out of account. But Ricardo lets political economy speak its own language; he is not to blame if this language is not that of morals. M. Chevalier ignores political economy in so far as he concerns himself with morals, but he really and necessarily ignores morals when he is concerned with political economy; for the bearing of political economy upon morals is either arbitrary and accidental and thus lacking any scientific basis or character, is a mere *sham*, or else it is *essential* and can then only be a relation between economic laws and morals. If there is no such relation, can Ricardo be held responsible? Moreover, the antithesis between morals and political economy is itself only *apparent*; there is an antithesis and equally no antithesis. Political economy expresses, *in its own fashion*, the moral laws.

The absence of needs, as the principle of political economy, is shown in the most *striking* way in its *theory of population*. There are *too many* men. The very existence of man is a pure luxury, and if the worker is " *moral* " he will be *economical* in procreation. (Mill proposes that public commendation should be given to those who show themselves abstemious in sexual relations, and public condemnation to those who sin against the sterility of marriage. Is this not the moral doctrine of asceticism?) The production of men appears as a public misfortune.

The significance which production has in relation to the wealthy is *revealed* in the significance which it has for the poor. At the top its manifestation is always refined, concealed, ambiguous, an appearance; at the bottom it is rough, straightforward, candid, a reality. The *crude* need of the worker is a much greater source of profit than the *refined* need of the wealthy. The cellar dwellings in London bring their landlords more than do the palaces; i.e. they constitute *greater wealth* so far as the landlord is concerned and thus, in economic terms, greater *social* wealth.

Just as industry speculates upon the refinement of needs so also it speculates upon their *crudeness*, and upon their artificially produced crudeness whose spirit, therefore, is *self-stupefaction*, the *illusory* satisfaction of needs, a civilization *within* the crude barbarism of need. The English gin-shops are, therefore, symbolic representations of private property. Their *luxury* reveals the real relation of industrial luxury and wealth to man. They are, therefore, rightly the only Sunday enjoyment of the people, treated mildly at least by the English police.

We have already seen how the economist establishes the

unity of labour and capital in various ways: (1) capital is *accumulated* labour; (2) the purpose of capital within production—partly the reproduction of capital with profit, partly capital as raw material (material of labour), partly capital as itself a *working instrument* (the machine is fixed capital which is identical with labour)—is *productive work*; (3) the worker is capital; (4) wages form part of the costs of capital; (5) for the worker, labour is the reproduction of his life-capital; (6) for the capitalist, labour is a factor in the activity of his capital.

Finally (7) the economist postulates the original unity of capital and labour as the unity of capitalist and worker. This is the original paradisaical condition. How these two factors, [XIX] as two persons, spring at each other's throats is for the economist a *ortuitous* occurrence, which, therefore, requires only to be explained by external circumstances (*see* Mill).

The nations which are still dazzled by the sensuous glitter of precious metals and who thus remain fetishists of metallic money are not yet fully developed money nations. Contrast between France and England. The extent to which the solution of a theoretical problem is a task of practice, and is accomplished through practice, and the extent to which correct practice is the condition of a true and positive theory is shown, for example, in the case of *fetishism*. The sense perception of a fetishist differs from that of a Greek because his sensuous existence is different. The abstract hostility between sense and spirit is inevitable so long as the human sense for nature, or the human meaning of nature, and consequently the *natural* sense of *man*, has not been produced through man's own labour.

Equality is nothing but the German "Ich=Ich" translated into the French, i.e. political, form. Equality as the *basis* of communism is a *political* foundation; and it is the same as when the German bases communism upon the fact that he conceives man as *universal self-consciousness*. Of course, the transcendence of alienation always proceeds from the form of alienation which is the *dominant* power; in Germany, *self-consciousness*; in France, *equality*, because politics; in England, the real, material, self-sufficient, *practical* need. Proudhon should be appreciated and criticized from this point of view.

If we now characterize *communism* itself (for as negation of the negation, as the appropriation of human existence which mediates itself with itself through the negation of private property,. it is not the *true*, self-originating position, but rather one which begins from private property) . . . [1] the alienation of human life remains and a much greater alienation remains the more one is conscious of it as such) can only be accomplished by the establishment of communism.   In order to supersede the *idea* of private property communist *ideas* are sufficient, but *genuine* communist activity is necessary in order to supersede *real* private property.   History will produce it, and the development which we already recognize in thought as self-transcending will in reality involve a severe and protracted process.   We must consider it an advance, however, that we have previously acquired an awareness of the limited nature and the goal of the historical development and can see beyond it.

When communist *artisans* form associations, teaching and propaganda are their first aims.   But their association itself creates a new need—the need for society—and what appeared to be a means has become an end.   The most striking results of this practical development are to be seen when French socialist workers meet together.   Smoking, eating and drinking are no longer simply means of bringing people together.   Society, association, entertainment which also has society as its aim, is sufficient for them; the brotherhood of man is no empty phrase but a reality, and the nobility of man shines forth upon us from their toil-worn bodies.

---

[1] A part of the page is torn away here, and there follow fragments of six lines which are insufficient to reconstruct the passage.   [*Editor's note.*]

[XX] When political economy asserts that supply and demand always balance each other, it forgets at once its own contention (the theory of population) that the supply of *men* always exceeds the demand, and consequently, that the disproportion between supply and demand is most strikingly expressed in the essential end of production—the existence of man.

The extent to which money, which has the appearance of a means, is the real power and the unique *end*, and in general the extent to which *the* means which gives me being and possession of the alien objective being, is an *end in itself*, can be seen from the fact that landed property, where land is the source of life, and *horse* and *sword*, where these are the *real means of life*, are also recognized as the real political powers. In the middle ages an estate becomes emancipated when it has the right to carry the sword. Among nomadic peoples it is the *horse* which makes me a free man and a member of the community.

We said above that man is regressing to the *cave dwelling*, but in an alienated, malignant form. The savage in his cave (a natural element which is freely offered for his use and protection) does not feel himself a stranger; on the contrary he feels as much at home as a *fish* in water. But the cellar dwelling of the poor man is a hostile dwelling, " an alien, constricting power which only surrenders itself to him in exchange for blood and sweat." He cannot regard it as his home, as a place where he might at last say, " here I am at home." Instead, he finds himself in *another person's* house, the house of a *stranger* who lies in wait for him every day and evicts him if he does not pay the rent. He is also aware of the contrast between his own dwelling and a human dwelling such as exists in *that other world*, the heaven of wealth.

Alienation is apparent not only in the fact that *my* means of life belong to *someone else*, that *my* desires are the unattainable possession of *someone else*, but that everything is *something different* from itself, that my activity is *something else*, and finally (and this is also the case for the capitalist) that *an inhuman power* rules over everything. There is a kind of wealth which is inactive, prodigal and devoted to pleasure, the beneficiary of which *behaves* as an *ephemeral*, aimlessly active individual who regards the slave labour of others, human *blood and sweat*, as the prey of his cupidity, and who sees mankind and himself as a sacrificial and superfluous being. Thus he acquires a contempt for mankind, expressed in the form of arrogance and the squandering of resources which would support a hundred human lives, and also in the form of the infamous illusion that his unbridled extravagance and endless unproductive consumption is a condition for the *labour* and *subsistence* of others. He regards the realization of the *essential powers* of man only as the realization of his own disorderly life, his whims and his capricious, bizarre ideas. Such wealth, however, which sees wealth merely as a means, as something to be consumed, and which is, therefore, both master and slave, generous and mean, capricious, presumptuous, conceited, refined, cultured and witty, has not yet discovered *wealth* as a wholly *alien power* but sees in it its own power and enjoyment rather than wealth . . . final aim.[1]

. . . [XXI] and the glittering illusion about the nature of wealth produced by its dazzling sensuous appearance, is confronted by the *hard-working, sober, economical, prosaic* industrialist who is enlightened about the nature of wealth and who, while increasing the scope of the other's self-indulgence and flattering him by his products (for his products are just so many base compliments to the spendthrift's appetites) knows how to appropriate to himself, in the only *useful* way, the other's declining power. Although, therefore, industrial wealth appears at first to be the product of prodigal, fantastic wealth, it nevertheless dispossesses the

---

[1] The bottom of the page is torn and several lines of the text are missing. [*Editor's note.*]

latter in an active way by its own development. The fall in the *rate of interest* is a necessary consequence of industrial development. Thus the resources of the spendthrift rentier dwindle *in proportion to* the increase in the means and occasions of enjoyment. He is obliged either to consume his capital and thus ruin himself, or to become an industrial capitalist himself . . . On the other hand, there is a constant increase in the *rent of land* in the course of industrial development, but as we have already seen there must come a time when landed property, like every other form of property, falls into the category of capital which reproduces itself through profit—and this is a result of the same industrial development. Thus the spendthrift landowner must either squander his capital and ruin himself, or become the tenant farmer of his own estate—an agricultural industrialist.

The decline in the rate of interest (which Proudhon regards as the abolition of capital and as a tendency towards the socialization of capital) is thus rather a direct symptom of the complete victory of working capital over spendthrift wealth, i.e. the transformation of all private property into industrial capital. It is the complete victory of private property over all its *apparently* human qualities, and the total subjection of the property owner to the essence of private property—*labour*. Of course, the industrial capitalist also has his pleasures. He does not by any means return to an unnatural simplicity in his needs, but his enjoyment is only a secondary matter; it is recreation subordinated to production and thus a *calculated, economic* enjoyment, for he charges his pleasures as an expense of capital and what he squanders must not be more than can be replaced with profit by the reproduction of capital. Thus enjoyment is subordinated to capital and the pleasure-loving individual is subordinated to the capital-accumulating individual, whereas formerly the contrary was the case. The decline in the rate of interest is, therefore, only a symptom of the abolition of capital in so far as it is a symptom of its increasing domination and increasing alienation which hastens its own abolition. In general, this is the only way in which that which exists affirms its opposite.

The dispute between economists over luxury and saving is, therefore, only a dispute between the political economy which has become clearly aware of the nature of wealth and that political economy which is still burdened with romantic, anti-industrial memories. Neither side, however, knows how to express the subject of the dispute in simple terms, or is able, therefore, to settle the issue.

Further, the *rent of land*, *qua* rent of land, has been abolished; for against the argument of the Physiocrats that the landowner is the only genuine producer, modern political economy demonstrates rather that the landowner as such is the only completely unproductive rentier. Agriculture is the affair of the capitalist, who employs his capital in it when he can expect a normal rate of profit. The assertion of the Physiocrats that landed property as the only productive property should alone pay taxes, and consequently should alone sanction them and participate in state affairs, is transformed into the contrary conviction that the taxes upon the rent of land are the only taxes upon an unproductive revenue and thus the only ones which are not detrimental to the national output. It is evident that from this point of view no political privileges for the landowners follow from their situation as the principal taxpayers.

Everything which Proudhon conceives as a movement of labour against capital is only the movement of labour in the form of capital, of *industrial capital* against that which is not consumed *as* capital, i.e. industrially. And this movement goes upon its triumphant way, the way of the victory of industrial capital. It will be seen that only when labour is conceived as the essence of private property can the real characteristics of the economic movement itself be analysed.

Society, as it appears to the economist, is *civil* society, in which each individual is a totality of needs and only exists for another person, as the other exists for him, in so far as each becomes a means for the other. The economist (like politics in its *rights of man*) reduces everything to man, i.e. to the individual, whom he deprives of all characteristics in order to classify him as a capitalist or a worker.

The *division of labour* is the economic expression of the *social character of labour* within alienation. Or, since *labour* is only an expression of human activity within alienation, of life activity as alienation of life, the *division of labour* is nothing but the *alienated* establishment of human activity as a *real species-activity* or *the activity of man as a species-being*.

The economists are very confused and self-contradictory about the nature of the *division of labour* (which of course has to be regarded as a principal motive force in the production of wealth once labour is recognized as the *essence of private property*), i.e. about the *alienated form of human activity as species-activity*.

Adam Smith: " The division of labour . . . is not originally the effect of any human wisdom. . . . It is the necessary, though very slow and gradual consequence of the propensity to truck, barter and exchange one thing for another. [Whether this propensity be one of those original principles of human nature . . .] or whether, as seems more probable, it be the necessary consequence of the faculties of reason and of speech [it belongs not to our present subject to inquire]. It is common to all men, and to be found in no other race of animals . . . [In almost every other race of animals the individual] when it is grown up to maturity is entirely independent. . . . But man has almost constant occasion for the help of his brethren, and it is in vain for him to expect it from their benevolence only. He will be more likely to prevail if he can interest their self-love in his favour, and show them that it is for their own advantage to do for him what he requires of them. . . . We address ourselves not to their humanity but to their self-love, and never talk to them of our own necessities but of their advantages." [1]

"As it is by treaty, by barter, and by purchase that we obtain from one another the greater part of those mutual good offices that we stand in need of, so it is this same trucking disposition which originally gives occasion to the division of labour. In a tribe of hunters or shepherds a particular person makes bows and arrows, for example, with more readiness and dexterity than any other. He frequently exchanges them for cattle or for venison with his companions; and he finds at last that he can in this manner get more cattle and venison than if he himself went to the field to catch them. From a regard to his own interest, therefore, the making of bows and arrows grows to be his chief business. . . ." [2]

"The difference of natural talents in different men . . . is not . . . so much the cause as the effect of the division of labour. . . . Without the disposition to truck, barter and exchange, every man must have procured to himself every necessary and conveniency of life which he wanted. All must have had . . . the same work to do, and there could have been no such difference of employment as could alone give occasion to any great difference of talents." [3]

"As it is this disposition which forms that difference of talents . . . among men, so it is this same disposition which renders that difference useful. Many tribes of animals . . . of the same species derive from nature a much more remarkable distinction of genius than what, antecedent to custom and education, appears to take place among men. By nature a philosopher is not in genius and in disposition half so different from a street-porter, as a mastiff is from a greyhound, or a greyhound from a spaniel, or this last from a shepherd's dog. Those different tribes of animals, however, though all of the same species, are of scarce any use to

---

[1] Adam Smith, op. cit., I, pp. 12–13. I have indicated the parts of this quotation which Marx paraphrased by square brackets. [Editor's note.]

[2] Ibid., pp. 13–14.   [3] Ibid., p. 14.

one another.   The strength of the mastiff [XXXVI] is not, in the least, supported either by the swiftness of the grey-hound, or . . . The effects of those different geniuses and talents, for want of the power or disposition to barter and exchange, cannot be brought into a common stock, and do not in the least contribute to the better accommodation and conveniency of the species.   Each animal is still obliged to support and defend itself, separately and independently, and derives no sort of advantage from that variety of talents with which nature has distinguished its fellows.   Among men, on the contrary, the most dissimilar geniuses are of use to one another; the different produces of their respective talents, by the general disposition to truck, barter and exchange, being brought, as it were, into a common stock, where every man may purchase whatever part of the produce of other men's talents he has occasion for." [1]

" As it is the power of exchanging that gives occasion to the division of labour, so the extent of this division must always be limited by the extent of that power, or, in other words, by the extent of the market.   When the market is very small, no person can have any encouragement to dedicate himself entirely to one employment, for want of the power to exchange all that surplus part of the produce of his own labour, which is over and above his own consumption, for such parts of the produce of other men's labour as he has occasion for." [2]

In an advanced state of society: " Every man thus lives by exchanging, or becomes in some measure a merchant, and the society itself grows to be what is properly a commercial society." [3]   (*See* Destutt de Tracy: [4] " Society is a series of reciprocal exchanges; commerce contains the whole essence of society.")   The accumulation of capital increases with the division of labour and vice-versa.—Thus far Adam Smith.

---

[1] SMITH, op cit., I, pp. 14–15.   [2] Ibid., p. 15.   [3] Ibid., p. 20.
[4] DESTUTT DE TRACEY, *Eléments d'idéologie. Traité de la volonté et de ses effets.* 2 ème édition.   Paris, 1818, pp. 131, 143.

" . . . if every family . . . produced all that it consumed society could keep going although no exchange of any kind took place . . . in our advanced state of society, exchange, though *not fundamental*, is indispensable." [1] " The division of labour is a skilful employment of man's powers; it increases society's production—its power and its pleasures —but it diminishes the ability of every person taken individually." [2] Production cannot take place without exchange.—Thus J. B. Say.

" The powers inherent in man are his intelligence and his physical capacity for work. Those which arise from the condition of society consist of the capacity to divide and to distribute among different people the tasks necessary for procuring the means of subsistence [and of increasing their well-being]; and the capacity to exchange the services and products which constitute these means. . . . [The motive which impels a man to give his services to another is self-interest; he requires a return for the services rendered. The right of exclusive private property is indispensable to the establishment of exchange among men. . . . Exchange and division of labour mutually condition each other.] " [3] —Thus Skarbek.

Mill presents developed exchange—*trade*—as a *consequence* of the *division of labour*: " . . . the agency of man can be traced to very simple elements. He can, in fact, do nothing more than produce motion. He can move things towards one another, and he can separate them from one another [XXXVII]: the properties of matter perform all the rest. . . . In the employment of labour and machinery, it is often found that the effects can be increased by skilful

---

[1] JEAN-BAPTISTE SAY, op. cit., I, p. 300. Emphasis added by Marx. [*Editor's note.*]

[2] Ibid., pp. 76–7.

[3] F. SKARBEK, *Théorie des richesses sociales, suivie d'une bibliographie de l'économie politique.* Paris 1829. Tomes I–II; I, p. 25. The final section enclosed in square brackets is a paraphase of statements taken from various chapters of Skarbek's book. [*Editor's note.*]

distribution, by separating all those operations which have any tendency to impede one another, by bringing together all those operations which can be made in any way to aid one another. As men in general cannot perform many different operations with the same quickness and dexterity with which they can by practice learn to perform a few, it is always an advantage to limit as much as possible the number of operations imposed upon each. For dividing labour, and distributing the powers of men and machinery, to the greatest advantage, it is in most cases necessary to operate upon a large scale; in other words, to produce the commodities in great masses. It is this advantage which gives existence to the great manufactories; a few of which, placed in the most convenient situations, sometimes supply not one country, but many countries, with as much as they desire of the commodity produced." [1]—Thus Mill.

The whole of modern political economy is agreed, however, upon the fact that division of labour and abundance of production, division of labour and accumulation of capital, are mutually determining; and also that liberated and autonomous private property alone can produce the most effective and extensive division of labour.

Adam Smith's argument may be summarized as follows: The division of labour confers upon labour an unlimited capacity to produce. It arises from the *propensity to exchange and barter*, a specifically human propensity which is probably not fortuitous but determined by the use of reason and speech. The motive of those who engage in exchange is not humanity but *egoism*. The diversity of human talents is more the effect than the cause of the division of labour, i.e. of exchange. Furthermore, it is only the latter which makes this diversity useful. The particular qualities of the different tribes within an animal species are by nature more

---

[1] JAMES MILL, *Elements of Political Economy*, London, 1821, pp. 5–9. Marx quotes from the French translation by J. T. Parisot (Paris 1823). [*Editor's note.*]

pronounced than the differences between the aptitudes and
activities of human beings.   But since animals are not able
to exchange, the diversity of qualities in animals of the same
species but of different tribes is of no benefit to any individual
animal.   Animals   are   unable   to   combine   the   various
qualities of their species, or to contribute to the *common* advantage and comfort of the species.   It is otherwise with *men*,
whose most diverse talents and forms of activity are useful to
each other, *because* they can bring their *different* products
together in a common stock, from which each man can buy.
As the division of labour arises from the propensity to *exchange*, so it develops and is limited by the *extent of exchange*,
by the *extent of the market*.   In developed conditions every
man is a *merchant* and society is a *commercial association*.   Say
regards *exchange* as fortuitous and not fundamental.   Society
could exist without it.   It becomes indispensable in an
advanced state of society.   Yet *production* cannot take place
without it.   The division of labour is a *convenient* and *useful*
means, a skilful deployment of human powers for social
wealth, but it diminishes *the capacity of each person* taken *individually*.   The last remark is an advance on the part of Say.
   Skarbek distinguishes the *individual innate* powers of man,
intelligence and physical capacity for work, from the powers
derived from society—*exchange and division of labour* which
mutually determine each other.   But the necessary pre-
condition of exchange is private property.   Skarbek here
expresses objectively what Smith, Say, Ricardo, *et al.* say
when they designate *egoism* and *self-interest* as the basis of
exchange, and *commercial haggling* as the *essential* and *adequate*
form of exchange.
   Mill represents *trade* as the consequence of the *division of
labour*.   For him, human activity is reduced to mechanical
motion.   The division of labour and the use of machinery
promote abundance of production.   Each individual must
be given the smallest possible range of operations.   The
division of labour and the use of machinery, for their part,

require the mass production of wealth, i.e. of products. This is the reason for large-scale manufacture.

[XXXVIII] The consideration of *division of labour* and *exchange* is of the greatest interest, since they are the *perceptible, alienated* expression of human *activity* and *capacities* as the activity and capacities *proper to a species*.

To state that *private property* is the basis of the *division of labour* and *exchange* is simply to assert that *labour* is the essence of private property; an assertion which the economist cannot prove and which we wish to prove for him.   It is precisely in the fact that the *division of labour* and *exchange* are manifestations of private property that we find the proof, first that *human* life needed *private property* for its realization, and secondly, that it now requires the supersession of private property.

The *division of labour* and *exchange* are the two phenomena which lead the economist to vaunt the social character of his science, while in the same breath he unconsciously expresses the contradictory nature of his science—the establishment of society through unsocial, particular interests.

The factors we have to consider are as follows: the *propensity to exchange*—whose basis is egoism—is regarded as the cause or the reciprocal effect of the division of labour.   Say considers exchange as being not *fundamental* to the nature of society. Wealth and production are explained by the division of labour and exchange.   The impoverishment and denaturing of individual activity through the division of labour are admitted.   Exchange and division of labour are recognized as the sources of the *great diversity of human talents*, a diversity which in turn becomes useful as a result of exchange.   Skarbek distinguishes two parts in man's productive powers: (1) those which are individual and innate, his intelligence and his specific aptitudes or abilities; (2) those which are *derived* not from the real individual, but from society—the division of labour and exchange.   Further, the division of labour is limited by the *market*.   Human labour is simple *mechanical motion*; the major part is done by the material properties of the objects. The smallest possible number of operations must be allocated to each individual. Fission of labour and concentration of capital; the nullity of individual production and the mass production of wealth. Meaning of free private property in the division of labour.

MONEY

[XLI] I_F man's *feelings*, passions, etc. are not merely anthropological characteristics in the narrower sense, but are true *ontological* affirmations of being (nature), and if they are only really affirmed in so far as their *object* exists as an object of sense, then it is evident—

1. that their mode of affirmation is not one and unchanging, but rather that the diverse modes of affirmation constitute the distinctive character of their existence, of their life. The manner in which the object exists for them is the distinctive mode of their *gratification*;

2. where the sensuous affirmation is a direct annulment of the object in its independent form (as in drinking, eating, working up of the object, etc.) this is the affirmation of the object;

3. in so far as man, and hence also his feelings, etc. are *human*, the affirmation of the object by another person is also his own gratification;

4. only through developed industry, i.e. through the mediation of private property, does the ontological essence of human passions, in its totality and its humanity, come into being; the science of man itself is a product of man's self-formation through practical activity;

5. the meaning of private property—released from its alienation—is the *existence of essential objects* for man, as objects of enjoyment and activity.

Money, since it has the *property* of purchasing everything, of appropriating objects to itself, is, therefore, the *object par excellence*. The universal character of this *property* corresponds to the omnipotence of money, which is regarded as an omnipotent being . . . money is the *pander* between

need and object, between human life and the means of subsistence. But *that which* mediates *my* life mediates also the
existence of other men for me. It is for me the *other* person.

> " What, man! confound it, hands and feet
> And head and backside, all are yours!
> And what we take while life is sweet,
> Is that to be declared not ours?
> Six stallions, say, I can afford,
> Is not their strength my property?
> I tear along, a sporting lord,
> As if their legs belonged to me."
>
> (Goethe, *Faust*—Mephistopheles) [1]

Shakespeare in *Timon of Athens*—

> " Gold? yellow, glittering, precious gold?   No, gods,
> I am no idle votarist: roots, you clear heavens!
> Thus much of this will make black, white; foul, fair;
> Wrong, right; base, noble; old, young; coward, valiant.
> . . . Why this
> Will lug your priests and servants from your sides;
> Pluck stout men's pillows from below their heads:
> This yellow slave
> Will knit and break religions; bless th'accurst;
> Make the hoar leprosy ador'd; place thieves,
> And give them title, knee, and approbation,
> With senators on the bench: this is it
> That makes the wappen'd widow wed again;
> She whom the spital-house and ulcerous sores
> Would cast the gorge at, this embalms and spices
> To th'April day again.   Come, damned earth,
> Thou common whore of mankind, that putt'st odds
> Among the rout of nations, I will make thee
> Do thy right nature." [2]

And later on—

> " O thou sweet king-killer, and dear divorce
> 'Twixt natural son and sire!   Thou bright defiler
> Of Hymen's purest bed!   Thou valiant Mars!
> Thou ever young, fresh, loved and delicate wooer,
> Whose blush doth thaw the consecrated snow

---

[1] GOETHE, *Faust*. Part I, Scene 4.   This passage is taken from the translation by Philip Wayne; Penguin Books, 1949.   [*Editor's note.*]

[2] SHAKESPEARE, *Timon of Athens*. Act IV, Scene 3.   Marx quotes from
the Schlegel-Tieck translation.   [*Editor's note.*]

That lies on Dian's lap! thou visible god,
That solder'st close impossibilities,
And mak'st them kiss! that speak'st with every tongue,
[XLII] To every purpose!   O thou touch of hearts!
Think, thy slave man rebels; and by thy virtue
Set them into confounding odds, that beasts
May have the world in empire! " [1]

Shakespeare portrays admirably the nature of *money*.   To understand him, let us begin by expounding the passage from Goethe.

That which exists for me through the medium of *money*, that which I can pay for (i.e. which money can buy), that *I am*, the possessor of the money.   My own power is as great as the power of money.   The properties of money are my own (the possessor's) properties and faculties.   What I *am* and *can do* is, therefore, not at all determined by my individuality.   I *am* ugly, but I can buy the most beautiful woman for myself.   Consequently, I am not *ugly*, for the effect of ugliness, its power to repel, is annulled by money. As an individual I am *lame*, but money provides me with twenty-four legs.   Therefore, I am not lame.   I am a detestable, dishonourable, unscrupulous and stupid man, but money is honoured and so also is its possessor.   Money is the highest good, and so its possessor is good.   Besides, money saves me the trouble of being dishonest; therefore, I am presumed honest.   I am *stupid*, but since money is *the real mind* of all things, how should its possessor be stupid? Moreover, he can buy talented people for himself, and is not he who has power over the talented more talented than they? I who can have, through the power of money, *everything* for which the human heart longs, do I not possess all human abilities?   Does not my money, therefore, transform all my incapacities into their opposites.

If *money* is the bond which binds me to *human* life, and society to me, and which links me with nature and man, is it not the bond of all *bonds*?   Is it not, therefore, also the

[1] Loc. cit.

universal agent of separation? It is the real means of both *separation* and *union*, the galvano-*chemical* power of society.

Shakespeare emphasizes particularly two properties of money: (1) it is the visible deity, the transformation of all human and natural qualities into their opposites, the universal confusion and inversion of things; it brings incompatibles into fraternity; (2) it is the universal whore, the universal pander between men and nations.

The power to confuse and invert all human and natural qualities, to bring about fraternization of incompatibles, the *divine* power of money, resides in its *character* as the alienated and self-alienating species-life of man. It is the alienated *power* of *humanity*.

What I as a *man* am unable to do, and thus what all my individual faculties are unable to do, is made possible for me by *money*. Money, therefore, turns each of these faculties into something which it is not, into its *opposite*.

If I long for a meal, or wish to take the mail coach because I am not strong enough to go on foot, money provides the meal and the mail coach; i.e. it transforms my desires from representations into *realities*, from imaginary being into *real being*. In mediating thus money is a *genuinely creative* power.

Demand also exists for the individual who has no money, but his demand is a mere creature of the imagination which has no effect, no existence for me, for a third party, for . . .,[1] (XLIII) and which thus remains *unreal* and *without object*. The difference between effective demand, supported by money, and ineffective demand, based upon my need, my passion, my desire, etc. is the difference between *being* and *thought*, between the merely inner representation and the representation which exists outside myself as a *real object*.

If I have no money for travel I have no *need*—no real and self-realizing need—for travel. If I have a *vocation* for study but no money for it, then I have *no* vocation, i.e. no *effective*, genuine vocation. Conversely, if I really have *no* vocation

---

[1] Marx omitted a word here in the manuscript. [*Editor's note.*]

for study, but have money and the urge for it, then I have an *effective* vocation. *Money* is the external, universal means and power (not derived from man as man nor from human society as society) to change *representation* into *reality* and *reality* into *mere representation*. It transforms *real human and natural faculties* into mere abstract representations, i.e. *imperfections* and tormenting chimeras; and on the other hand, it transforms *real imperfections and fancies*, faculties which are really impotent and which exist only in the individual's imagination, into *real faculties and powers*. In this respect, therefore, money is the general inversion of *individualities*, turning them into their opposites and associating contradictory qualities with their qualities.

Money, then, appears as a *disruptive* power for the individual and for the social bonds, which claim to be self-subsistent *entities*. It changes fidelity into infidelity, love into hate, hate into love, virtue into vice, vice into virtue, servant into master, stupidity into intelligence and intelligence into stupidity.

Since money, as the existing and active concept of value, confounds and exchanges everything, it is the universal *confusion and transposition* of all things, the inverted world, the confusion and transposition of all natural and human qualities.

He who can purchase bravery is brave, though a coward. Money is not exchanged for a particular quality, a particular thing, or a specific human faculty, but for the whole objective world of man and nature. Thus, from the standpoint of its possessor, it exchanges every quality and object for every other, even though they are contradictory. It is the fraternization of incompatibles; it forces contraries to embrace.

Let us assume *man* to be *man*, and his relation to the world to be a human one. Then love can only be exchanged for love, trust for trust, etc. If you wish to enjoy art you must be an artistically cultivated person; if you wish to influence

other people you must be a person who really has a stimulating and encouraging effect upon others.   Every one of your
relations to man and to nature must be a *specific expression*,
corresponding to the object of your will, of your *real individual* life.   If you love without evoking love in return, i.e.
if you are not able, by the *manifestation* of yourself as a loving
person, to make yourself a *beloved person*, then your love is
impotent and a misfortune.

CRITIQUE OF HEGEL'S DIALECTIC AND
GENERAL PHILOSOPHY

THIS is perhaps an appropriate point at which to explain and substantiate what has been said, and to make some general comments upon Hegel's dialectic, especially as it is expounded in the *Phenomenology* and *Logic*, and upon its relation to the modern critical movement.

Modern German criticism was so much concerned with the past, and was so hampered by its involvement with its subject-matter, that it had a wholly uncritical attitude to the methods of criticism and completely ignored the partly formal, but in fact *essential* question—how do we now stand with regard to the Hegelian *dialectic*? This ignorance of the relationship of modern criticism to Hegel's general philosophy and his dialectic in particular was so great that critics such as Strauss and Bruno Bauer (the former in all his writings; the latter in his *Synoptiker*,[1] where, in opposition to Strauss, he substitutes the " self-consciousness " of abstract man for the substance of " abstract nature," and even in *Das entdeckte Christentum* [2]) were, at least implicity, ensnared in Hegelian logic. Thus, for instance, in *Das entdeckte Christentum* it is argued: " As if self-consciousness in positing the world, that which is different, did not produce itself in producing its object; for it then annuls the difference between itself and what it has produced, since it exists only in this creation and movement, has its purpose only in this movement, etc." [3] Or again: " They (the French

---

[1] BRUNO BAUER, *Kritik der evangelischen Geschichte des Johannes*, Bremen, 1840; *Kritik der evangelischen Geschichte der Synoptiker*, II Band, Leipzig, 1841; III Band, Braunschweig, 1842.

[2] Ibid., *Das entdeckte Christentum. Eine Erinnerung an das achtzehnte Jahrhundert und ein Beitrag zur Krisis des neunzehnten*, Zürich and Winterthur, 1843.

[3] Ibid., p. 113. Marx paraphrases the end of this passage. [*Editor's note.*]

materialists) could not see that the movement of the universe has only become real and unified in itself in so far as it is the movement of self-consciousness." [1] These expressions not only do not differ from the Hegelian conception, but reproduce it textually.

[XLII] How little these writers, in undertaking their criticism (Bauer in his *Synoptiker*), were aware of their relation to Hegel's dialectic, and how little such an awareness emerged from the criticism, is demonstrated by Bauer in his *Gute Sache der Freiheit* [2] when, instead of replying to the indiscreet question put by Gruppe, " And now what is to be done with logic?", he transmits it to future critics.

Now that Feuerbach, in his " Thesen " in the *Anecdotis* [3] and in greater detail in his *Philosophie der Zukunft*,[4] has demolished the inner principle of the old dialectic and philosophy, the " Critical School," which was unable to do this itself but has seen it accomplished, has proclaimed itself the pure, decisive, absolute, and finally enlightened criticism, and in its spiritual pride has reduced the whole historical movement to the relation existing between itself and the rest of the world, which comes into the category of " the mass." It has reduced all dogmatic antitheses to the single dogmatic antithesis between its own cleverness and the stupidity of the world, between the critical Christ and mankind—" the rabble." [5]   At every moment of the day it has demonstrated its own excellence *vis-à-vis* the stupidity of the mass, and it has finally announced the critical *last judgement* by proclaim-

---

[1] Op. cit., p. 114.

[2] BRUNO BAUER, *Die gute Sache der Freiheit und meine eigene Angelegenheit*, Zürich and Winterthur, 1842, p. 193.   Bauer's reference is to Marheinecke, not Gruppe.   [*Editor's note*.]

[3] ARNOLD RUGE (Ed.), *Anekdota zur neuesten deutschen Philosophie und Publizistik*, Zürich and Winterthur, 1843, Band II, p. 62 *et seq.*   " Vorläufige Thesen zur Reformation der Philosophie " von Ludwig Feuerbach.

[4] LUDWIG FEUERBACH, *Grundsätze der Philosophie der Zukunft*, Zürich and Witherthur, 1843.

[5] *See*, for example, *Allgemeine Literatur-Zeitung Monatsschrift*, edited by Bruno Bauer, Band I–II.   Charlottenburg, 1844; no. 1, p. 1 *et seq.*, no. 5, p. 23 *et seq.*, no. 8, p. 18 *et seq.*   [*Editor's note*.]

ing that the day is at hand when the whole of fallen mankind will assemble before it and will be divided up into groups each of which will be handed its *testimonium paupertatis* (certificate of poverty).[1] The Critical School has made public its superiority to all human feelings and to the world, above which it sits enthroned in sublime solitude, content to utter occasionally from its sarcastic lips the laughter of the Olympian gods. After all these entertaining antics of idealism (of Young Hegelianism) which is expiring in the form of criticism, the Critical School has not even now intimated that it was necessary to discuss critically its own source, the dialectic of Hegel; nor has it given any indication of its relation with the dialectic of Feuerbach. This is a procedure totally lacking in critical sense.

Feuerbach is the only person who has a *serious* and *critical* relation to Hegel's dialectic, who has made real discoveries in this field, and above all, who has vanquished the old philosophy. The magnitude of Feuerbach's achievement and the unassuming simplicity with which he presents his work to the world are in striking contrast with the behaviour of others.

Feuerbach's great achievement is—

1. to have shown that philosophy is nothing more than religion brought into thought and developed by thought, and that it is equally to be condemned as another form and mode of existence of human alienation;

2. to have founded *genuine materialism* and *positive science* by making the social relationship of " man to man " the basic principle of his theory;

3. to have opposed to the negation of the negation which claims to be the absolute positive, a self-subsistent principle positively founded on itself.

Feuerbach explains Hegel's dialectic, and at the same time justifies taking the positive phenomenon, that which is

---

[1] *Allgemeine Literatur-Zeitung Monatsschrift*, no. 5, p. 15.

perceptible and indubitable, as the starting-point, in the following way.

Hegel begins from the alienation of substance (logically, from the infinite, the abstract universal) from the absolute and fixed abstraction; i.e. in ordinary language, from religion and theology. Secondly, he supersedes the infinite, and posits the real, the perceptible, the finite, and the particular. (Philosophy, supersession of religion and theology.) Thirdly, he then supersedes the positive and re-establishes the abstraction, the infinite. (Re-establishment of religion and theology.)

Thus Feuerbach conceives the negation of the negation as being *only* a contradiction within philosophy itself, which affirms theology (transcendence, etc.) after having superseded it, and thus affirms it in opposition to philosophy.

For the positing or self-affirmation and self-confirmation which is implied in the negation of the negation is regarded as a positing which is still uncertain, burdened with its contrary, doubtful of itself and thus incomplete, not demonstrated by its own existence, and implicit. [XIII] The positing which is perceptually indubitable and grounded upon itself is directly opposed to it.

In conceiving the negation of the negation, from the aspect of the positive relation inherent in it, as the only true positive, and from the aspect of the negative relation inherent in it, as the only true act and the self-confirming act of all being, Hegel has merely discovered an *abstract*, *logical* and *speculative* expression of the historical process, which is not yet the *real* history of man as a given subject, but only the history of the *act of creation*, of the *genesis of man*.

We shall explain both the abstract form of this process and the difference between the process as conceived by Hegel and by modern criticism, by Feuerbach in *Das Wesen des Christentums*; or rather, the critical form of this process which is still so uncritical in Hegel.

Let us examine Hegel's system. It is necessary to begin

with the *Phenomenology*,[1] because it is there that Hegel's philosophy was born and that its secret is to be found.

Phenomenology

A. *Self-consciousness*

I. *Consciousness.* (α) Certainty in sense experience, or the " this " and meaning. (β) Perception, or the thing with its properties, and illusion. (γ) Power and understanding, phenomena and the supersensible world.

II. *Self-consciousness.* The truth of certainty of oneself. (*a*) Independence and dependence of self-consciousness, domination and servitude. (*b*) Freedom of self-consciousness. Stoicism, scepticism, the unhappy consciousness.

III. *Reason.* Certainty and truth of reason. (*a*) Observational reason: observation of nature and of self-consciousness. (*b*) Self-realization of the rational self-consciousness. Pleasure and necessity. The law of the heart and the frenzy of vanity. Virtue and the way of the world. (*c*) Individuality which is real in and for itself. Legislative reason. Reason which tests laws.

B. *Spirit*

I. True spirit; customary morality.

II. Self-alienated spirit; culture.

III. Spirit certain of itself; morality.

C. *Religion*

Natural religion, the religion of art, revealed religion.

D. *Absolute knowledge* [2]

Hegel's *Encyclopaedia* [3] begins with logic, with *pure speculative thought*, and ends with *absolute knowledge*, the self-conscious

---

[1] G. W. F. HEGEL, *System der Wissenschaft, Erster Teil: Die Phänomenologie des Geistes*, Bamberg and Würzburg, 1807.

[2] These are the chapter and section headings of Hegel's *Phenomenology of Spirit.* [*Editor's note.*]

[3] G. W. F. HEGEL, *Encyclopädie der philosophischen Wissenschaften im Grundrisse*.

and self-conceiving philosophical or absolute mind, i.e. the superhuman, abstract mind. The whole of the *Encyclopaedia* is nothing but the extended being of the philosophical mind, its self-objectification; and the philosophical mind is nothing but the alienated world-mind thinking within the bounds of its self-alienation, i.e. conceiving itself in an abstract manner. *Logic* is the *money* of the mind, the speculative *thought-value* of man and of nature, their essence indifferent to any real determinate character and thus unreal; *thought* which is *alienated* and abstract and ignores real nature and man. *The external character of this abstract thought . . . nature* as it exists for this abstract thought. Nature is external to it, loss of itself, and is only conceived as something external, as abstract thought, but alienated abstract thought. Finally, spirit, this thought which returns to its own origin and which, as anthropological, phenomenological, psychological, customary, artistic-religious spirit, is not valid for itself until it discovers itself and relates itself to itself as absolute knowledge in the absolute (i.e. abstract) spirit, and so receives its conscious and fitting existence. For its real mode of existence is *abstraction*.

Hegel commits a double error. The first appears most clearly in the *Phenomenology*, the birthplace of his philosophy. When Hegel conceives wealth, the power of the state, etc. as entities alienated from the human being, he conceives them only in their thought form. They are entities of thought and thus simply an alienation of *pure* (i.e. abstract) philosophical thought. The whole movement, therefore, ends in absolute knowledge. It is precisely abstract thought from which these objects are alienated, and which they confront with their presumptuous reality. The *philosopher*, himself an abstract form of alienated man, sets himself up as the *measure* of the alienated world. The whole *history of alienation*, and of the retraction of alienation, is, therefore, only the *history of the production* of abstract thought, i.e. of absolute, logical, speculative thought. *Estrangement*, which thus forms the real interest of this alienation and of the supersession of this alienation, is the opposition of *in itself* and *for itself*, of *consciousness* and *self-consciousness*, of *object* and *subject*, i.e. the opposition in thought itself between abstract thought and sensible reality or real sensuous existence. All other contradictions and movements are merely the *appearance*, the *cloak*, the *exoteric* form of these two opposites which are alone important and which constitute the *significance* of the other, profane contradictions. It is not the fact that the human being *objectifies* himself *inhumanly*, in opposition to himself, but that he *objectifies* himself by *distinction* from and in *opposition* to abstract thought, which constitutes alienation as it exists and as it has to be transcended.

[XVIII] The appropriation of man's objectified and alienated faculties is thus, in the first place, only an *appropriation* which occurs in *consciousness*, in *pure thought*, i.e. in abstraction. It is the appropriation of these objects as *thoughts* and as *movements of thought*. For this reason, despite its thoroughly negative and critical appearance, and despite the genuine criticism which it contains and which often anticipates later developments, there is already implicit in the *Phenomenology*, as a germ, as a potentiality and a secret, the uncritical positivism and uncritical idealism of Hegel's later works—the philosophical dissolution and restoration of the existing empirical world.   *Secondly*, the vindication of the objective world for man (for example, the recognition that *sense* perception is not *abstract* sense perception but *human* sense perception, that religion, wealth, etc. are only the alienated reality of *human* objectification, of *human* faculties put to work, and are, therefore, a *way* to genuine *human* reality), this appropriation, or the insight into this process, appears in Hegel as the recognition of *sensuousness, religion,* state power, etc. as *mental* phenomena, for *mind* alone is the *true* essence of man, and the true form of mind is thinking mind, the logical, speculative mind. The *human character* of nature, of historically produced nature, of man's products, is shown by their being *products* of abstract mind, and thus phases of *mind, entities of thought.* The *Phenomenology* is a concealed, unclear and mystifying criticism, but in so far as it grasps the *alienation* of man (even though man appears only as mind) *all* the elements of criticism are contained in it, and are often *presented* and *worked out* in a manner which goes far beyond Hegel's own point of view. The sections devoted to the " unhappy consciousness," the " honest consciousness," the struggle between the " noble " and the " base " consciousness, etc., etc. contain the *critical* elements (though still in an alienated form) of whole areas such as religion, the state, civil life, etc. Just as the *entity,* the *object,* appears as an entity of thought, so also the *subject* is always *consciousness* or *self-consciousness*; or rather, the object appears only as *abstract* consciousness and man as *self-consciousness.* Thus the distinctive forms of alienation which are manifested are only different forms of consciousness and self-consciousness. Since abstract consciousness (the form in which the object is conceived) is in *itself* merely a distinctive moment of self-consciousness, the outcome of the movement is the identity of self-consciousness and consciousness—absolute knowledge— the movement of abstract thought not directed outwards but proceeding within itself; i.e. the dialectic of pure thought is the result.

[XXIII] The outstanding achievement of Hegel's *Phenomenology*—the dialectic of negativity as the moving and creating principle—is, first, that Hegel grasps the self-creation of man as a process, objectification as loss of the object, as alienation and transcendence of this alienation, and that he, therefore, grasps the nature of *labour,* and conceives objective man (true, because real man) as the result of his *own labour.* The *real,* active orientation of man to himself as a species-being, or the affirmation of himself as a real species-being (i.e. as a human being) is only possible so far as he really brings forth all his *species-powers* (which is only possible through the co-operative endeavours of mankind and as an outcome of history) and treats these powers as objects, which can only be done at first in the form of alienation.

We shall next show in detail Hegel's one-sidedness and limitations, as revealed in the final chapter of the *Phenomenology*, on absolute knowledge; a chapter which contains the concentrated spirit of the *Phenomenology*, its relation to the dialectic, and also Hegel's *consciousness* of both and of their interrelations.

For the present, let us make these preliminary observations: Hegel's standpoint is that of modern political economy. He conceives *labour* as the *essence*, the self-confirming essence of man; he observes only the positive side of labour, not its negative side. Labour is *man's coming to be for himself* within *alienation*, or as an *alienated* man. Labour as Hegel understands and recognizes it is *abstract mental* labour. Thus, that which above all constitutes the *essence* of philosophy, the *alienation of man knowing himself*, or *alienated* science *thinking* itself, Hegel grasps as its essence. Consequently, he is able to bring together the separate elements of earlier philosophy and to present his own as the philosophy. What other philosophers did, that is, to conceive separate elements of nature and of human life as phases of self-consciousness and indeed of abstract self-consciousness, Hegel *knows* by *doing* philosophy; therefore, his science is absolute.

Let us now turn to our subject.

Absolute knowledge. The final chapter of the " Phenomenology."

The main point is that the *object of consciousness* is nothing else but *self-consciousness*, that the object is only *objectified* self-consciousness, self-consciousness as an object. (Positing man = self-consciousness.)

It is necessary, therefore, to surmount the *object of consciousness*. *Objectivity* as such is regarded as an alienated human relationship which does not correspond with the *essence of man*, self-consciousness. The reappropriation of the objective essence of man, which was produced as something alien and determined by alienation, signifies the super-session not only of *alienation* but also of *objectivity*; that is, man is regarded as a *non-objective, spiritual* being.

The process of *overcoming the object of consciousness* is described by Hegel as follows: The *object* does not reveal itself only as *returning* into the Self (according to Hegel that is a *one-sided* conception of the movement, considering only one aspect). Man is equated with self. The Self, however, is only man conceived *abstractly* and produced by abstraction. Man is self-referring. His eye, his ear, etc. are *self-referring*; every one of his faculties has this quality of *self*-reference. But it is entirely false to say on that account, " *Self-consciousness* has eyes, ears, faculties." Self-consciousness is rather a quality of human nature, of the human eye, etc.; human nature is not a quality of [XXIV] *self-consciousness*.

The Self, abstracted and determined for itself, is man as an *abstract egoist,* purely abstract *egoism* raised to the level of thought. (We shall return to this point later.)

For Hegel, *human life, man,* is equivalent to *self-consciousness.* All alienation of human life is, therefore, *nothing* but *alienation of self-consciousness.* The alienation of self-consciousness is not regarded as the *expression,* reflected in knowledge and thought, of the *real* alienation of human life. Instead, *actual* alienation, that which appears real, is in its *innermost* hidden nature (which philosophy first discloses) only the *phenomenal being* of the alienation of real human life, of *self-consciousness.* The science which comprehends this is therefore called *Phenomenology.* All reappropriation of alienated objective life appears, therefore, as an incorporation in self-consciousness. The person who takes possession of his being is only the self-consciousness which takes possession of objective being; the return of the object into the Self is, therefore, the reappropriation of the object.

Expressed in a *more comprehensive way* the *supersession of the object of consciousness* means: (1) that the object as such presents itself to consciousness as something disappearing;

(2) that it is the alienation of self-consciousness which establishes " thinghood ";   (3) that this alienation has *positive* as well as *negative* significance;   (4) that it has this significance not only *for us* or in itself, but also *for self-consciousness itself*;   (5) that for *self-consciousness* the negative of the object, its self-supersession, has *positive* significance, or self-consciousness *knows* thereby the nullity of the object in that self-consciousness alienates itself, for in this alienation it establishes *itself* as object or, for the sake of the indivisible unity of *being-for-itself*, establishes the object as itself; (6) that, on the other hand, this other " moment " is equally present, that self-consciousness has superseded and reabsorbed this alienation and objectivity, and is thus *at home* in its other being as such;   (7) that this is the movement of consciousness, and consciousness is, therefore, the totality of its " moments ";   (8) that similarly, consciousness must have related itself to the object in all its determinations, and have conceived it in terms of each of them.   This totality of determinations makes the object *intrinsically* a *spiritual being*, and it becomes truly so for consciousness by the apprehension of every one of these determinations as the Self, or by what was called earlier the *spiritual* attitude towards them.

ad (1) That the object as such presents itself to consciousness as something disappearing is the above-mentioned *return of the object into the Self*.

ad (2) *The alienation of self-consciousness* establishes " thinghood." Because man equals self-consciousness, his alienated objective being or " *thinghood* " is equivalent to *alienated self-consciousness*, and " thinghood " is established by this alienation.   (" Thinghood " is that which is *an object for him*, and an object for him is really only that which is an essential object, consequently his *objective* essence.   And since it is not the *real man*, nor *nature*—man being *human nature*—who becomes as such a subject, but only an abstraction of man, self-consciousness, " thinghood " can only be *alienated self-consciousness*.)   It is quite understandable that a living, natural being endowed with objective (i.e. material) faculties should have *real natural objects* of its being, and equally that its self-alienation should be the establishment of a *real*, objective world, but in the form of *externality*, as a world which does not belong to, and dominates, its being. There is nothing incomprehensible or mysterious about this. The converse, rather, would be mysterious. But it is equally clear that a self-consciousness, i.e. its alienation, can only establish " *thinghood*," i.e. only an abstract thing, a thing created by abstraction and not a real thing. It is [XXVI] clear, moreover, that " thinghood " is totally lacking in *independence*, in *being*, *vis-à-vis* self-consciousness; it is a mere *construct* established by self-consciousness. And what is established is not self-confirming; it is the confirmation of the act of establishing, which for an instant, but only for an instant, fixes its energy as a product and *apparently* confers upon it the role of an independent, real being.

When real, corporeal *man*, with his feet firmly planted on the solid ground, inhaling and exhaling all the powers of nature, *posits* his real objective faculties, as a result of his alienation, as alien objects, the *positing* is not the subject of this act but the subjectivity of *objective* faculties whose action must also, therefore, be *objective*. An objective being acts objectively, and it would not act objectively if objectivity were not part of its essential being. It creates and establishes *only objects*, *because* it is established by objects, and because it is fundamentally *natural*. In the act of establishing it does not descend from its " pure activity " to the *creation of objects*; its *objective* product simply confirms its *objective* activity, its activity as an objective, natural being.

We see here how consistent naturalism or humanism is distinguished from both idealism and materialism, and at the same time constitutes their unifying truth. We see also that only naturalism is able to comprehend the process of world history.

Man is directly a *natural being*. As a natural being, and as a living natural being he is, on the one hand, endowed with *natural powers* and *faculties*, which exist in him as tendencies and abilities, as *drives*. On the other hand, as a natural, embodied, sentient, objective being he is a *suffering*, conditioned and limited being, like animals and plants. The *objects* of his drives exist outside himself as *objects* independent of him, yet they are *objects* of his *needs*, essential *objects* which are indispensable to the exercise and confirmation of his faculties. The fact that man is an *embodied*, living, real, sentient, objective being with natural powers, means that he has *real, sensuous objects* as the objects of his being, or that he can only express his being in real, sensuous objects. *To be* objective, natural, sentient and at the same time to have object, nature and sense outside oneself, or to be oneself object, nature and sense for a third person, is the same thing. *Hunger* is a natural *need*; it requires, therefore, a *nature* outside itself, an *object* outside itself, in order to be satisfied and stilled. Hunger is the objective need of a body for an *object* which exists outside itself and which is essential for its integration and the expression of its nature. The sun is an *object*, a necessary and life-assuring object, for the plant, just as the plant is an object for the sun, an *expression* of the sun's life-giving power and *objective* essential powers.

A being which does not have its nature outside itself is not a *natural* being and does not share in the being of nature. A being which has no object outside itself is not an objective being. A being which is not itself an object for a third being has no being for its *object*, i.e. it is not objectively related and its being is not objective.

[XXVII] A non-objective being is a *non-being*. Suppose a being which neither is an object itself nor has an object. In the first place, such a being would be the *only* being; no other being would exist outside itself and it would be solitary and alone. For as soon as there exist objects outside myself, as soon as I am not *alone*, I am *another*, *another reality* from the object outside me. For this third object I am thus an *other reality* than itself, i.e. *its object*.   To suppose a being which is not the object of another being would be to suppose that *no* objective being exists.   As soon as I have an object, this object has me for its object.   But a *non-objective* being is an unreal, non-sensuous, merely conceived being; i.e. a merely imagined being, an abstraction.   To be *sensuous*, i.e. real, is to be an object of sense or *sensuous* object, and thus to have sensuous objects outside oneself, objects of one's sensations. To be sentient is to *suffer* (to experience).

Man as an objective sentient being is a *suffering* being, and since he feels his suffering, a *passionate* being.   Passion is man's faculties striving to attain their object.

But man is not merely a natural being; he is a *human* natural being.   He is a being for himself, and, therefore, a *species-being*; and as such he has to express and authenticate himself in being as well as in thought.   Consequently, *human* objects are not natural objects as they present themselves directly, nor is *human sense*, as it is immediately and objectively *given*, *human* sensibility and human objectivity. Neither objective nature nor subjective nature is directly presented in a form adequate to the *human* being.   And as everything natural must have its *origin* so *man* has his process of genesis, *history*, which is for him, however, a conscious process and thus one which is consciously self-transcending. (We shall return to this point later.)

Thirdly, since this establishment of " thinghood " is itself only an appearance, an act which contradicts the nature of pure activity, it has to be annulled again and " thinghood " has to be denied.

ad 3, 4, 5, 6. (3) This alienation of consciousness has not only a negative but also a positive significance, and (4) it has this positive significance not only *for us* or in itself, but for consciousness itself.   (5) For *consciousness* the negation of the object, or its annulling of itself by that means, has positive significance; it *knows* the nullity of the object by the fact that it alienates *itself*, for in this alienation it *knows* itself as the object or, for the sake of the indivisible unit of *being-for self*, knows the object as itself. (6) On the other hand, this other " moment " is equally present, but consciousness has superseded and reabsorbed this alienation and objectivity and is thus *at home in its other being as such.*

We have already seen that the appropriation of alienated objective being, or the supersession of objectivity in the form of *alienation* (which has to develop from indifferent otherness to real antagonistic alienation), signifies for Hegel also, or primarily, the supersession of *objectivity*, since it is not the determinate character of the object but its *objective* character which is the scandal of alienation for self-consciousness. The object is therefore negative, self-annulling, a *nullity*. This nullity of the object has a positive significance because it *knows* this nullity, objective being, as its *self-alienation*, and knows that this nullity exists only through its self-alienation. . . .

The way in which consciousness is, and in which something is for it, is *knowing*. Knowing is its only act. Thus something comes to exist for consciousness so far as it *knows* this *something*. Knowing is its only objective relation. It knows, then, the nullity of the object (i.e. knows the non-existence of the distinction between itself and the object, the non-existence of the object for it) because it knows the object as its *self-alienation*. That is to say, it knows itself (knows knowing as an object), because the object is only the *semblance* of an object, a deception, which is intrinsically nothing but knowing itself which has confronted itself with itself, has established in face of itself a *nullity*, a " something " which has *no* objective existence outside the knowing itself. Knowing knows that in relating itself to an object it is only *outside* itself, alienates itself, and that *it* only *appears* to itself as an object; or in other words, that that which appears to it as an object is only itself.

On the other hand, Hegel says, this other " moment " is present at the same time; namely, that consciousness has

equally superseded and reabsorbed this alienation and objectivity, and consequently is *at home in its other being as such.*

In this discussion all the illusions of speculation are
assembled.

First, consciousness—self-consciousness—is *at home in its
other being as such.* It is, therefore—if we abstract from
Hegel's abstraction and substitute the self-consciousness of
man for self-consciousness—*at home in its other being as such.*
This implies, first, that consciousness (knowing as knowing,
thinking as thinking) claims to be directly the *other* of itself,
the sensuous world, reality, life; it is thought over-reaching
itself in thought (Feuerbach). This aspect is contained in it,
in so far as consciousness as mere consciousness is offended
not by the alienated objectivity but by *objectivity as such.*

Secondly, it implies that self-conscious man, in so far as he
has recognized and superseded the spiritual world (or the
universal spiritual mode of existence of his world) then confirms it again in this alienated form and presents it as his
true existence; he re-establishes it and claims to *be at home in
his other being.* Thus, for example, after superseding religion, when he has recognized religion as a product of self-
alienation, he then finds a confirmation of himself in *religion
as religion.* *This is* the root of Hegel's *false* positivism, or of
his merely *apparent* criticism; what Feuerbach calls the
positing, negation and re-establishment of religion or theology, but which has to be conceived in a more general way.
Thus reason is at home in unreason as such. Man, who has
recognized that he leads an alienated life in law, politics, etc.
leads his true human life in this alienated life as such. Self-
affirmation, in contradiction with itself, with the knowledge
and the nature of the object, is thus the true *knowledge* and
life.

There can no longer be any question about Hegel's com-
promise with religion, the state, etc., for this falsehood is the
falsehood of his whole argument.

[XXIX] If I *know* religion as *alienated* human self-consciousness what I know in it as religion is not my self-consciousness but my alienated self-consciousness confirmed in it. Thus my own self, and the self-consciousness which is its essence, is not confirmed in *religion* but in the *abolition* and *supersession* of religion.

In Hegel, therefore, the negation of the negation is not the confirmation of true being by the negation of illusory being. It is the confirmation of illusory being, or of self-alienating being in its denial; or the denial of this illusory being as an objective being existing outside man and independently of him, and its transformation into a subject.

The act of *supersession* plays a strange part in which *denial* and preservation, denial and affirmation, are linked together. Thus, for example, in Hegel's *Philosophy of Right*, *private right* superseded equals *morality*, morality superseded equals *the family*, the family superseded equals *civil society*, civil society superseded equals the *state*, and the state superseded equals *world history*. But in *actuality* private right, morality, the family, civil society, the state, etc. remain; only they have become " moments," modes of existence of man, which have no validity in isolation but which mutually dissolve and engender one another. *They are " moments " of the movement.*

In their actual existence this *mobile* nature is concealed. It is first revealed in thought, in philosophy; consequently, my true religious existence is my existence in the *philosophy of religion*, my true political existence is my existence in the *philosophy of right*, my true natural existence is my existence in the *philosophy of nature*, my true artistic existence is my existence in the *philosophy of art*, and my true human existence is my existence in *philosophy*. In the same way, the true existence of religion, the state, nature and art, is the *philosophy* of religion, of the state, of nature, and of art. But if the philosophy of religion is the only true existence of religion I am only truly religious as a *philosopher of religion*, and I deny *actual* religious sentiment and the actual *religious* man. At the same time, however, I *confirm* them, partly in my own existence or in the alien existence with which I confront them (for this *is* only their philosophical expression), and partly in their own original form, since they are for me the merely *apparent* other being, allegories, the lineaments of their own true existence (i.e. of my *philosophical* existence) concealed by sensuous draperies.

In the same way, *quality* superseded equals *quantity*, quantity superseded equals *measure*, measure superseded equals *being*, being superseded equals *phenomenal being*, phenomenal being superseded equals *actuality*, actuality superseded equals the *concept*, the concept superseded equals *objectivity*, objectivity superseded equals the *absolute idea*, the absolute idea superseded equals *nature*, nature superseded equals *subjective* spirit, subjective spirit superseded equals *ethical* objective spirit, *ethical* spirit superseded equals *art*, art superseded equals *religion*, and religion superseded equals *absolute knowledge*.

On the other hand, this supersession is supersession of an entity of thought; thus, private property *as thought* is superseded in the *thought* of morality. And since thought imagines itself to be, without mediation, the other aspect of itself, namely *sensuous reality*, and takes its own action for *real, sensuous action*, this supersession in thought, which leaves its object in existence in the real world, believes itself to have really overcome it. On the other hand, since the object has now become for it a " moment " of thought, it is regarded in its real existence as a confirmation of thought, of self-consciousness, of abstraction.

[XXX] From the one aspect the existent which Hegel *supersedes* in philosophy is not therefore the *actual* religion, state or nature, but religion itself as an object of knowledge, i.e. *dogmatics*; and similarly with *jurisprudence, political science* and *natural science*. From this aspect, therefore, he stands in opposition both to the actual being and to the direct, non-philosophical science (or the non-philosophical *concepts*) of this being. Thus he contradicts the conventional conceptions.

From the other aspect, the religious man, etc. can find in Hegel his ultimate confirmation.

We have now to consider the *positive* moments of Hegel's dialectic, within the condition of alienation.

(*a*) *Supersession* as an objective movement which *reabsorbs* alienation into itself. This is the insight, expressed within alienation, into the *appropriation* of the objective being through the supersession of its alienation. It is the alienated insight into the *real objectification* of man, into the real appropriation of his objective being by the destruction of the *alienated* character of the objective world, by the annulment of its alienated mode of existence. In the same way, atheism as the annulment of God is the emergence of theoretical humanism, and communism as the annulment of private property is the vindication of real human life as man's property. The latter is also the emergence of practical humanism, for atheism is humanism mediated to itself by the annulment of religion, while communism is humanism mediated to itself by the annulment of private property. It is only by the supersession of this mediation (which is, however, a necessary pre-condition) that the self-originating *positive* humanism can appear.

But atheism and communism are not flight or abstraction from, nor loss of, the objective world which men have created by the objectification of their faculties. They are not an impoverished return to unnatural, primitive simplicity. They are rather the first real emergence, the genuine actualization, of man's nature as something real.

Thus Hegel, in so far as he sees the *positive* significance of the self-referring negation (though in an alienated mode) conceives man's self-estrangement, alienation of being, loss of objectivity and reality, as self-discovery, change of nature, objectification and realization. In short, Hegel conceives labour as man's *act of self-creation* (though in abstract terms);

he grasps man's relation to himself as an alien being and the emergence of *species-consciousness* and *species-life* as the demonstration of his alien being.

(*b*) But in Hegel, apart from, or rather as a consequence of, the inversion we have already described, this act of genesis appears, in the first place, as one which is merely *formal*, because it is abstract, and because human nature itself is treated as merely *abstract, thinking nature*, as self-consciousness.

Secondly, because the conception is *formal* and *abstract* the annulment of alienation becomes a confirmation of alienation. For Hegel, this movement of *self-creation* and *self-objectification* in the form of *self-estrangement* is the *absolute* and hence final *expression of human life*, which has its end in itself, is at peace with itself and at one with its own nature.

This movement, in its abstract [XXXI] form as dialectic, is regarded therefore as *truly human life*, and since it is nevertheless an abstraction, an alienation of human life, it is regarded as a *divine process* and thus as the divine process of mankind; it is a process which man's abstract, pure, absolute being, as distinguished from himself, traverses.

Thirdly, this process must have a bearer, a subject; but the subject first emerges as a result. This result, the subject knowing itself as absolute self-consciousness, is therefore *God, absolute spirit, the self-knowing and self-manifesting idea*. Real man and real nature become mere predicates, symbols of this concealed unreal man and unreal nature. Subject and predicate have, therefore, an inverted relation to each other; a *mystical subject-object*, or a *subjectivity reaching beyond the object*, the *absolute subject* as a process of self-alienation and of return from alienation into itself, and at the same time of reabsorption of this alienation, the *subject* as this process; pure, *unceasing* revolving within itself.

First, the formal and abstract conception of man's act of self-creation or self-objectification.

Since Hegel equates man with self-consciousness, the

alienated object, the alienated real being of man, is simply *consciousness*, merely the thought of alienation, its abstract and hence vacuous and unreal expression, the *negation*. The annulment of alienation is also, therefore, merely an abstract and vacuous annulment of this empty abstraction, the *negation of the negation*. The replete, living, sensuous, concrete activity of self-objectification is, therefore, reduced to a mere abstraction, *absolute negativity*, an abstraction which is then crystallized as such and is conceived as an independent activity, as activity itself.   Since this so-called negativity is merely the *abstract, vacuous* form of that real living act, its content can only be a *formal* content produced by abstraction from all content. They are, therefore, general, abstract *forms of abstraction* which refer to any content and are thus neutral towards, and valid for, any content; forms of thought, logical forms which are detached from *real* spirit and *real* nature.   (We shall expound later the *logical* content of absolute negativity.)

Hegel's positive achievement in his speculative logic is to show that the *determinate concepts*, the universal *fixed thought-forms*, in their independence from nature and spirit, are a necessary result of the general alienation of human nature and also of human thought; and to depict them as a whole as moments in the process of abstraction.   For example, being superseded is essence, essence superseded is concept, the concept superseded is . . . the absolute idea.   But what is the absolute idea?   It must supersede itself if it does not want to traverse the whole process of abstraction again from the beginning and to rest content with being a totality of abstractions or a self-comprehending abstraction.   But the self-comprehending abstraction knows itself to be nothing; it must abandon itself, the abstraction, and so arrives at an entity which is its exact opposite, *nature*.   The whole *Logic* is therefore, a demonstration that abstract thought is nothing for itself, that the absolute idea is nothing for itself, that only *nature* is something.

[XXXII] The absolute idea, the *abstract* idea which " *regarded* from the aspect of its unity with itself, is *intuition* " (Hegel's *Encyclopaedia*, 3rd ed., p. 222), and which " in its own absolute truth *resolves* to let the moment of its particularity or of initial determination and other-being, the *immediate idea*, as its reflection, *emerge freely from itself as nature* " (ibid.) ; this whole idea which behaves in such a strange and fanciful way and which has given the Hegelians such terrible headaches is throughout nothing but *abstraction*, i.e. the abstract thinker. It is abstraction which, made wise by experience and enlightened about its own truth, resolves under various (false and still abstract) conditions to *abandon* itself, and to establish its other being, the particular, the determinate, in place of its self-absorption, non-being, universality and indeterminateness; and which resolves to let nature, which it concealed within itself only as an abstraction, as an entity of thought, *emerge freely from itself.* That is, it decides to forsake abstraction and to observe nature *free* from abstraction. The abstract idea, which without mediation becomes *intuition*, is nothing but abstract thought which abandons itself and decides for *intuition*. This whole transition from logic to the philosophy of nature is simply the transition from *abstracting* to *intuiting*, a transition which is extremely difficult for the abstract thinker to acomplish and which he therefore describes in such strange terms. The *mystical feeling* which drives the philosopher from abstract thinking to intuition is *ennui*, the longing for a content.

(Man alienated from himself is also the thinker alienated from his *being*, i.e. from his natural and human life. His thoughts are consequently spirits existing outside nature and man. In his *Logic* Hegel has imprisoned all these spirits together, and has conceived each of them first as negation, i.e. as *alienation of human* thought, and secondly as negation of the negation, i.e. as the supersession of this alienation and as the real expression of human thought. But since this negation of the negation is itself still confined within the alienation, it is in part a restoration of these fixed spiritual forms in their alienation, in part an immobilization in the final act, the act of self-reference, as the true being of these spiritual forms.[1]   Further, in so far as this abstraction conceives itself, and experiences an increasing weariness of itself, there appears in Hegel an abandonment of abstract thought which moves solely in the sphere of thought, devoid of eyes, ears, teeth, everything, and a resolve to recognize *nature* as being and to go over to intuition.)

[XXXIII] But *nature* too, taken abstractly, for itself, and rigidly separated from man, is *nothing* for man.   It goes without saying that the abstract thinker who has committed himself to intuition, intuits nature abstractly.   As nature lay enclosed in the thinker in a form which was obscure and mysterious even to himself, as absolute idea, as an entity of thought, so in truth, when he let it emerge from himself it was still only *abstract nature*, nature as an *entity of thought*, but now with the significance that it is the other-being of thought, is real, intuited nature, distinguished from abstract thought. Or, to speak in human language, the abstract thinker discovers from intuiting nature that the entities which he thought to create out of nothing, out of pure abstraction, to create in the divine dialectic as the pure products of thought endlessly shuttling back and forth in itself and never regarding external reality, are simply *abstractions* from *natural characteristics*.   The whole of nature, therefore, reiterates to him the logical abstractions, but in a sensuous, external form.   He *analyses* nature and these abstractions again.

---

[1] That is, Hegel substitutes the act of abstraction revolving within itself, for these fixed abstractions.   In so doing, he has first of all the merit of having indicated the source of all these inappropriate concepts which originally belonged to different philosophies, and of having brought them together and established the comprehensive range of abstractions, instead of some particular abstraction, as the object of criticism.   We shall see later why Hegel separates thought from the *subject*.   It is already clear, however, that if man is not human the expression of his nature cannot be human, and consequently thought itself could not be conceived as an expression of man's nature, as the expression of a human and natural subject, with eyes, ears, etc. living in society, in the world, and in nature.

His intuition of nature is, therefore, simply the act of confirmation of his abstraction from the intuition of nature; his conscious re-enactment of the process of generating his abstraction. Thus, for example, Time equals Negativity which refers to itself (loc. cit., p. 238). In the natural form, superseded Movement as Matter corresponds to superseded Becoming as Being. In the *natural* form Light is *Reflection-in-itself*. Body as *Moon* and *Comet* is the natural form of the antithesis which, according to the *Logic*, is on the one hand the *positive grounded upon itself*, and on the other hand, the *negative grounded upon itself*. The Earth is the *natural* form of the logical *ground*, as the negative unity of the antithesis, etc.

Nature as nature, i.e. so far as it is sensuously distinguished from that secret sense concealed within it, nature separated and distinguished from these abstractions is *nothing* (a *nullity demonstrating its nullity*), is *devoid of sense*, or has only the sense of an external thing which has been superseded.

" In the finite-*teleological* view is to be found the correct premise that nature does not contain within itself the absolute purpose " (loc. cit., p. 225). Its purpose is the confirmation of abstraction. " Nature has shown itself to be the idea in the *form* of *other-being*. Since the idea is in this form the negative of itself, or *external to itself*, nature is not just relatively external *vis-à-vis* this idea, but *externality* constitutes the form in which it exists as nature " (loc. cit., p. 227).

Externality should not be understood here as the *self-externalizing world of sense*, open to the light and to man's senses. It has to be taken here in the sense of alienation, as error, a defect, that which ought not to be. For that which is true is still the idea. Nature is merely the form of its other-being. And since abstract thought is *being*, that which is external to it is by its nature a merely *external thing*. The abstract thinker recognizes at the same time that *sensuousness, externality* in contrast to thought which shuttles back and forth *within itself*, is the essence of nature. But at the same time he expresses this antithesis is such a way that this *externality* of nature, and its *contrast* with thought, appears as a deficiency, and that nature distinguished from abstraction appears as a deficient being. [XXXIV] A being which is deficient, not simply for me or in my eyes, but in itself, has something outside itself which it lacks. That is to say, its being is something other than itself. For the abstract thinker, nature must therefore supersede itself, because it is already posited by him as a potentially *superseded* being.

" *For us*, spirit has *nature as its premise*, being the *truth* of nature and thereby its *absolute primus*. In this truth nature has *vanished*, and spirit has surrendered itself as the idea which has attained being-for-itself, whose *object*, as well as the *subject*, is the *concept*. This identity is *absolute negativity*, for whereas in nature the concept has its perfect external objectivity, here its alienation has been superseded and the concept has become identical with itself. It is this identity only so far as it is a return from nature " (loc. cit., p. 392).

" *Revelation*, as the *abstract* idea, is unmediated transition to, the *coming-to-be* of, nature; as the revelation of the spirit, which is free, it is the *establishment* of nature as *its own* world, an establishment which, as reflection, is simultaneously the *presupposition* of the world as independently existing nature. Revelation in conception is the creation of nature as spirit's own being, in which it acquires the *affirmation* and *truth* of its freedom." " *The absolute is spirit*; this is the highest definition of the absolute."

AUTHORS AND WORKS CITED BY MARX

AESCHYLUS (525–456 B.C.)

ANACHARSIS (sixth century B.C.). Scythian philosopher; sometimes mentioned as one of the Seven Sages of Greece.

ARISTOTLE (384–322 B.C.)

BAUER, BRUNO (1809–82)
Kritik der evangelischen Geschichte der Synoptiker, Vols. I–II (1841), III (1842).
Die gute Sache der Freiheit und meine eigene Angelegenheit (1842).
" Die Fähigkeit der heutigen Juden und Christen, frei zu werden," in *Einundzwanzig Bogen aus der Schweiz*, ed. Georg Herwegh (1843).
Die Judenfrage (1843).
Das entdeckte Christentum (1843).
(ed.) *Allgemeine Literatur-Zeitung Monatsschrift*, Vols. I–II (1844).

BEAUMONT, GUSTAVE DE LA BONNINIÈRE DE (1802–66)
Marie, ou l'esclavage aux États-Unis (1835).

BERGASSE, NICOLAS (1750–1832). French publicist; member of the National Assembly.

BUCHEZ, P. J. B. (1796–1865) and ROUX-LAVERGNE, P. C. (1802–94)
Histoire parlementaire de la Révolution française, Vol. 28 (1836).

BURET, ANTOINE-EUGÈNE (1810–42)
De la misère des classes laborieuses en Angleterre et en France (1840).

CABET, ETIENNE (1788–1856)

CHEVALIER, MICHEL (1806–79). French economist.

COURIER DE MÉRÉ, P. L. (1772–1825). French publicist.

DESMOULINS, CAMILLE (1760–94)
Révolutions de France et de Brabant (Weekly journal, 1789–91).

DESTUTT DE TRACY, A. L. C. (1754–1836)
Eléments d'idéologie. Traité de la volonté et de ses effets (2ème édition, 1818).

ENGELS, FRIEDRICH (1820–95)
" Umrisse zu einer Kritik der Nationalökonomie " in *Deutsch-Französische Jahrbücher* (1843).

FEUERBACH, LUDWIG (1804–72)
Das Wesen des Christentums (1841).
" Vorläufige Thesen zur Reformation der Philosophie," in

221

Anekdota zur neuesten deutschen Philosophie und Publizistik, ed. A. Ruge (1843).

Grundsätze der Philosophie der Zukunft (1843).

FOURIER, CHARLES (1772–1837)

FUNKE, G. L. W.
Die aus der unbeschränkten Teilbarkeit des Grundeigentums hervorgehenden Nachteile (1839).

GANILH, CHARLES (1759–1836).   French economist and politician.

GOETHE, J. W. VON (1749–1832)
Faust.

HALLER, K. L. VON (1768–1854).   German official and publicist.

HAMILTON, THOMAS (1789–1842)
Men and Manners in America (1833).

HEGEL, G. W. F. (1770–1831)
Die Phänomenologie des Geistes (1807).
Wissenschaft der Logik (1812–16).
Encyklopädie der philosophischen Wissenschaften im Grundrisse (1817).
Grundlinien der Philosophie des Rechts (1821).

HERWEGH, GEORG (1817–75).   German poet.
(ed.) *Einundzwanzig Bogen aus der Schweiz* (1843).

HESS, MOSES (1812–75)
" Sozialismus und Kommunismus," " Die eine und ganze Freiheit," and " Philosophie der Tat " in *Einundzwanzig Bogen aus der Schweiz* (1843).

KOSEGARTEN, WILHELM (1792–1868).   German publicist.

LANCIZOLLE, K. W. VON DELEUZE DE (1796–1871).   German historian of law.

LAUDERDALE, J. M., Earl of (1759–1839).   Economist.

LEO, HEINRICH (1799–1878)
Studien und Skizzen zu einer Naturlehre des Staates (1833).

LOUDON, CHARLES (1801–44).   Scottish medical writer.
Solution du problème de la population et de la subsistance, soumise à un médicin dans une série de lettres (1842).

LUTHER, MARTIN (1483–1546)

McCULLOCH, J. R. (1789–1864).   Economist.

MALTHUS, T. R. (1766–1834)

MILL, JAMES (1773–1836)
Elements of Political Economy (1821).

MÖSER, JUSTUS (1720–94)
Patriotische Phantasien (1775–78).

MÜNZER, THOMAS (*c.* 1490–1525)
Hochverursachte Schutzrede und Antwort . . . (1524).

OWEN, ROBERT (1771–1858)
PECQUEUR, CONSTANTIN (1801–87)
   Théorie nouvelle d'économie sociale et politique, ou études sur l'organisation des sociétés (1842).
PROUDHON, PIERRE-JOSEPH (1809–65)
QUESNAY, FRANÇOIS (1694–1774)
RICARDO, DAVID (1772–1823)
   Principles of Political Economy and Taxation (1816). French edition, with notes and criticisms by J. B. Say (2ème édition, 1835).
ROUSSEAU, JEAN-JACQUES (1712–78)
   Du contrat social, ou principes du droit politique (1762).
RUGE, ARNOLD (1802–80)
   (ed.) *Anekdota zur neuesten deutschen Philosophie und Publizistik* (1843).
   With Marx (ed.) *Deutsch-Französische Jahrbücher* (1844).
SAINT-SIMON, CLAUDE-HENRI, COMTE DE (1760–1825)
SAY, JEAN-BAPTISTE (1767–1832)
   Traité d'économie politique (3ème édition, 1817).
SCHULZ, WILHELM (1797–1860)
   Die Bewegung der Produktion. Eine geschichtlich-statistische Abhandlung (1843).
SHAKESPEARE, W. (1564–1616)
   Timon of Athens.
SISMONDI, J. C. L. SIMONDE DE (1773–1842)
   Nouveaux principes d'économie politique (1819).
SKARBEK, FRYDERYK (1792–1866)
   Théorie des richesses sociales, suivie d'une bibliographie de l'économie politique (1829).
SMITH, ADAM (1723–90)
   An Inquiry into the Nature and Causes of the Wealth of Nations (1776). French translation, with notes by G. Garnier (1802).
STRAUSS, DAVID FRIEDRICH (1808–74)
   Das Leben Jesu (1835–36).
TOCQUEVILLE, A. C. H. CLÉREL DE (1805–59)
   De la démocratie en Amérique (1835).
VILLEGARDELLE, FRANÇOIS (1810–56). French publicist; Fourierist; author of *Accord des intérêts dans l'association* (1844).
VINCKE, F. L. W. VON (1774–1844). German official and writer on public administration.
WEITLING, WILHELM (1808–71)

INDEX

Catalog

If you are interested in a list of fine Paperback
books, covering a wide range of subjects
and interests, send your name and address,
requesting your free catalog, to:

McGraw-Hill Paperbacks
330 West 42nd Street
New York, New York 10036